SUGARTIME

THE SWEET AND STICKY LIFE OF COUNTRY MUSIC LEGEND CHARLIE "SUGARTIME" PHILLIPS

Louise,

Thank you so much for helping me save a piece of country music history!

Love,
CP

Copyright © 2016 by Cy Cushenberry

All rights reserved. No part of this publication may be reproduced, stored in a retrieval system, or transmitted, in any form or by any means, electronic, mechanical, photocopying, recording, or otherwise, without proper permission of the publisher or author with the exception of brief quotations in scholarly works, educational manuscripts and papers, media reviews and brief mentions including television, radio, newspapers, magazines, and blogs.

Hardcover ISBN: 978-1-63490-517-6
Paperback ISBN: 978-1-63490-516-9

"Sugartime" by Charlie Phillips and Odis Echols Copyright © 1956, 1957 by MPL Communications Inc. Copyright Renewed Used by Permission All Rights Reserved

To obtain additional permissions, write www.charliesugartimephillips.com.

All photographs from the private collection of Charlie Phillips unless otherwise noted.

Cover design by Todd Engel http://www.toddengel-engelcreative.com/
Contents set in Times New Roman 12 point
Cover Photo from the personal collection of Charlie Phillips- 1962 Promo Photo

Book Title created by Therese Kelley

Library of Congress Cataloguing in Publication Data
Cushenberry, Cy
Sugartime- The Sweet and Sticky Life of Country Music Legend Charlie "Sugartime" Phillips by Cy Cushenberry
Library of Congress Control Number 2015921352

Published by Sugarberry Publications in conjunction with Booklocker

Printed on acid-free paper.

SUGARTIME

THE SWEET AND STICKY LIFE OF COUNTRY MUSIC LEGEND CHARLIE "SUGARTIME" PHILLIPS

Cy Cushenberry

SUGARBERRY PUBLICATIONS

This book is dedicated to Therese Kelley and Mike McMillen
for their love, dedication and support

And to
Gloria Cushenberry, a woman who after every battle in life,
Is the first to raise the flag
And rally the troops to victory

And of course to
Charlie Phillips

Acknowledgements

After three years and hundreds of contacts, I felt it was necessary to compile a list of the many people who helped make this book a success. If it takes a village to raise a child, it took a whole lot of people to create this book. Without each and every person's contribution listed in this section, this book would have never become a reality.

Very special thanks-

It never dawned on me when I began interviewing people, at some point, I would be required to transcribe hundreds of hours of digital and cassette tapes. It would be an impossible task for a guy who types as slowly as I do. **Katie Schettler** then entered my life. Katie, I will never be able to thank you enough for your dedication to Charlie's book. How you listened to hundreds of hours of tapes and was actually able to transliterate the many voices and conversations, I'll never know. You're the best.

My friend **Calder Gabroy** is the man who knows how to get things done. I contacted Calder at the beginning of this project and asked if he could get me in touch with an obscure former musician. He never even asked me why, he simply stated, "I'm on it!" Thank you Calder for all of your help and support. You stuck with me through this whole project and I'm so grateful.

Very special thanks to **E. A. Allonah Rubin** and **Marisa Madge Cutlip** for providing an unbelievable amount of hours, editing what I deem grammar. Ladies, without your persevering assistance this book would be riddled with errors. To my reader's chagrin, much of this book is written in Texas-speak and has little correlation with what some might label "proper English." Ms. Ruben and Ms. Cutlip sorted through the gobbledygook, probably cringing as they reorganized the subject matter and semantics throughout its entirety. You gals are tops in my book.

My journey began in Clovis, New Mexico where the knowledgeable **Kenneth Broad** gave me a tour of the location where all of the magic began- the original Norman Petty Studio. Ken, you have given so much of your life to the preservation of Norman and Vi Petty's existence. I'm sure you and **Shirley** were wonderful friends to the Petty's during their lives, but y'all have been remarkable friends since their passing. No one has so selflessly given their time and energy recording and preserving their lives more than you guys. Because of your efforts, history has been saved. The world and I thank you.

Very special thanks to Louisiana attorney, **Kent Gill**. Kent was the guitar player for the legendary David Houston. His interview produced numerous solutions regarding the *Grand Ole Opry* days, as Kent was present during many of the band's off-times. This book began running longer than planned and I wasn't able to include some of the fascinating stories Kent and other band members experienced, but he deserves much thanks nonetheless.

This manuscript would have been filled with incorrect dates and misinformation had it not been for the assistance of one of the most knowledgeable Buddy Holly and Norman Petty historians in the world. **John Ingman**, you have been an absolute blessing helping me enhance this overwhelming project. Thank you for creating an outstanding booklet for Charlie's Bear Family CD. Without your aid, I'm afraid so much detailed information about Charlie Phillips, Norman and Vi Petty, Buddy Holly and the Crickets, and so many other notable people would be lost. You contribute to projects like this and never ask for anything in return. In case no one has ever thanked you, well then, thanks. The world of music owes you a debt of gratitude!

To the owner of Rollercoaster Records, **John Beecher**, I thank you so much for taking time out of your busy schedule for this project. I could have never retrieved many of the promo photos of Charlie and the McGuire Sisters without your assistance. John is another person who cringed when he saw a couple of unedited chapters from this book, probably spending hours correcting my grammar, at least in his head. I always joke you Brits are all facts and no fluff. Your help and advice is greatly appreciated.

I fell in love with the current owners of the *Louisiana Hayride*, **Maggie and Alton Warwick**. Your Shreveport southern hospitality helped launch this project. Your knowledge of country music and your connections were so priceless to me. Thank you for all you do, as country music and I wouldn't be the same without you.

Frank Blanas, you authored probably one of the finest books ever written on Norman Petty and Buddy Holly! ***The King of Clovis*** is fantastic. Thank you for answering questions in my dozens of emails. You are a true scholar my friend.

Jon Sisco created one of Charlie Phillips' sunniest albums, the *Full Circle* album. Jon, you are a fine musician and your contributions to this project were invaluable. Your knowledge of obscure country music is almost unparalleled. Thank you.

I would like to especially thank **Jimmy Schell, Tiny Lynn and Lash** for telling me stories about Charlie's early days. These stories have never been told until now and without you, they would have been lost forever. Charlie could have never asked for better friends.

She may have been the muse for two of rock 'n' roll's greatest hits, but **Peggy Sue Gerron** was much more than that to me. Peggy, thank you for taking time out of your hard working schedule to inform me about the early days at the Norman Petty Studio and your former associations with Buddy Holly, J.I. (Jerry) Allison and Charlie Phillips. I could listen to your stories for hours and I'm so proud to have spoken with you.

Thank you to the employees of the **Country Music Hall of Fame**, the **Ryman Auditorium** and the ***Grand Ole Opry***. Your assistance was instrumental in learning about Charlie's history within your organizations. I got a true feel for what it must have been like in the early country music days in Nashville.

I interviewed so many country music and rock 'n' roll celebrities either over the phone, in person or through emails- in addition to many other knowledgeable people who contributed in some way to this project. I decided not to single out particular people, giving favor to one over another. Each person listed here either purposefully or inadvertently gave information, support or even a financial contribution and I thank you all. Many folks on this list are written about in this book and whether living or dead, contributed in some fashion. I've simply listed each person in alphabetical order, not in order of perceived importance. With any project of this size, it's entirely possible someone might be unintentionally left out and if so, I humbly beg forgiveness. Thank you all!

45 & Uppers Dance Hall (Amarillo, TX) • *Accent West Magazine* • Adams, Jana • Aldrich, Dawna • Allee, David • Allison, (Jerry) J.I. • Amarillo College • *Amarillo Globe- News* • Amarillo Public Library • Amarillo Senior Citizens Center • *American Music Magazine* • Anglin, Russell • Ashmead, Victoria • Bane, Jason and Rose • Bear Family Records • Beasley, Cherry • Beauchamp, Wayne • Beecher, John • Bell, Stuart (Publicist to Paul McCartney) • Bella Bird Photography • Bieber, Darlene • *Billboard Magazine* • Black, Kimberly • Blanas, Frank • Boyd, Nancy • Brigman, Carroll • Broad, Kenneth and Shirley • Bronnenberg, Joshua • Buddy Holly Center • Burgess, Frances • Burke Steve • Burke-Guckert, Susen • Caldwell, Barbara • Campbell, Norma • Cantrell, Don • Carlson, Paul H. • Cash, Roseanne • Casso, Carlos • Cedar Chiropractic Clinic (Flagstaff, AZ) • Chandler, Chip • Cherwin, Natalie • City Printing Inc. (Clovis, NM) • Cliff, Earl and Gladys • Clovis Chamber of Commerce • *Clovis News-Journal* • Clovis Public Library • Coldiron, Todd • Colorado College Albert Seay Library of Music and Art • Cook, Brandan • Country Music Hall of Fame • Cox, Mike • Cruz, Adam and Robbin • Cundiff, Andy Chase • Cushenberry, Gloria • Cutlip, Marisa Madge • Czechchowski, Ted • Darnell, Millie • Davis, Carl and Gail • Denison, Lehman (Tiny Lynn) • Dickens, Little Jimmy • Doherty, Ray and Danny • Donahue, Holly and Rusty • Dossett, Bernard • Dowdy, Glen and Margaret • Durango Ladies •

Eason, Roanna • Edwards, Scott • Engel, Todd • Ezziddine, David • Fiola, Connie Phillips • Folsom, Donna • Fong-Torres, Ben • Fox, Mike • Freyer, Molly • Fuller, Kristy and Mike • Funderburk, Janet • Gabroy, Calder • Gerron, Peggy Sue • Gentry, Robert • Gibson, Susan • Gill, Kent • Graham, Gloria and Les • the *Grand Ole Opry* • Guajardo, Israel • Guerrero, Antonio • Hacker, Bobby • Haggard, Merle • Hal Leonard Corporation • Hatch Show Print • Hatch Show Print's Haley Gallery • Hatfield, Lynn • Hauser, Cellany • HBO (Home Box Office) • Hethcox, Myrna • Hodges-Winkler, Bette • Hogue, David • Hoy, Angela • Hughes, Joe • Hwang, Eunyoung • Ingman, John • Irby, Linda Phillips • Iwai, Kristen • Jácome, David • Jefferson, Macie •Jenkins, Donita K • Joe, Jason • Johnson, Kay and Loudilla • Jones, George • Jones, Keith • Kantrowitz, Dani • KDI Photography (Flagstaff, AZ) • Kelley, Therese • Keltner, Gina • Kirby, Leigh • LaCroix, Ron • Lamphere, Al • Langrell, Rob • LaRue, Carroll "Lash" • Leahy, Mike • Lee, Brenda • Leverette, Robert • Lewis, Jerry Lee • Lewis, Ruby "Lady Cool Breeze" • the *Louisiana Hayride* • LSU Library • *Lubbock Avalanche-Journal* • Mack, Bill • Martel, Marty • Mauldin, Joe B • McAlavy, Don • McClish, Dennis and Dianne • McCune, Sue • McElreath, Amber and Jimmy • McGuire, Phyllis • McMillen, Mike • Melton, Barbara and Jim • *Miami Daily* News • Michaels, Theresa • Miller, Louise • Nashville Area Chamber of Commerce • Neillrae Music • Nelson, Willie • Newman, Jimmy C • *New Mexico Magazine* • Norman & Vi Petty Rock & Roll Museum • Norman Petty Studio • O'Donnell, Sharon • O'Hair, Kristi Loden • Oxford University Press • Paquette, Janice • Parker, Mary-Louise • *People Magazine* • Peoples, Curtis • Penninger, Doris and Travis • Petterson, Ron • Petty, Norman • Petty, Vi • Phillips, Carthon • Phillips, Charlie • Pikes Peak Library District • Pitt, Deven and Kristin • Pitt, Pam • Pletcher, Kris • Pochop, Jana • Pope, Jim • Price, Ray • Pride, Charley • Rael, David and Gloria • Rich, Steve (Lewis) • Ristau, Aaron • Robinson, Jo • Rodger, Peter • Rollercoaster Records • Rubin, Allonah E.A. • Rumple, Frances • Ryman Auditorium • Sands, Tommy • Schell, Jimmy • Schettler, Katie • Schultz, Vince • Seim, Hunter • Sherraden, Jim • Shields, Andrea • Short, Wendell • Shreveport Chamber of Commerce • Shreveport Memorial Library • Shreveport Tourist Bureau • Sisco, Jon • Smith-Ritter, Tommy • Sorelle, Charles and Helen • Spence, Carla • Staples, Brian • *State Line Tribune* • Steagall, Red (Rusty) •

Stevens, Daryll • Stewart, Marty • Stubbon, DJ • Stull, Billy • *Teen Magazine* • Texas Country Music Hall of Fame • Texas Panhandle Heritage Foundation • Texas Tech University Southwest Collections/Special Collections Library • Thurlow, Gary • Tucker, Matt • Tucker, Tommy • Tucker, Willie • *TV Guide* • University of Texas Libraries • Voisin, Sam • Warwick, Alton and Maggie • Weaver-Bennett, Betsy • *Welcome Partner* • Western Swing Music Hall of Fame • White, Danny • White, Guin and Jo Ed • Whitfield, Liz • Williams, Stephanie • Wood, Dan and Susan • Woodburn, Alicia and David • Woodburn, Caroline • Woodburn, Livia (Polly) • Young, Jimmy

CONTENTS

Prologue xv
Chapter 1 - On the Road to Texas 1
Chapter 2 - Welcome to Farwell, Texas - A Tumor is Born 7
Chapter 3 - Rising from the Dust 23
Chapter 4 - Petty Days- The Clovis Music Scene 35
Chapter 5 - My Buddy- Holly 53
Chapter 6 - Sugar in the Morning 71
Chapter 7 - Talk About Pop's Music 105
Chapter 8 - The Grand Ole' Louisiana Heydays 115
Chapter 9 - Jolly Cholly and the Radio Biz 133
Chapter 10 - Amarillo in the Evening 151
Chapter 11 - The Music Man 201
Chapter 12 - Sugartimers at Suppertime An All-Star Troupe 237
Chapter 13 - Finale 289
Bibliography 309
Index 346

Prologue

I had known Charlie Phillips mildly for many years and I spoke to him only when we ran into one another. I had no idea he was even a musician as he rarely spoke with me regarding his personal life- just chitchat and small talk. One day while meeting with some mutual peers, Charlie left the festivity. A friend of mine asked me how I knew the great Charlie Phillips. I explained I had been acquainted with him for years. My friend then began telling me about the song "Sugartime" and some of Charlie's exploits over his long career. I had no idea, as Charlie had always been so humble and would never be seen tooting his own horn, so to speak.

The next time I sat down with Charlie, I asked him questions unmercifully, and he graciously answered anything I asked him. As I listened, I became enamored with his stories and his fascinating life. I distinctly remember asking, "Charlie is there a book I could buy and read about your life?" "I want to know everything," I said as I awaited his reply. He explained to me that a guy from Europe had once worked on the story of his life, but it's possible the guy was simply a Buddy Holly souvenir collector. The guy had rummaged through much of Charlie's extensive collection of photographs and paraphernalia he had painstakingly collected throughout his 60-plus year career, and pocketed anything he thought valuable.

It took months for me to build up the courage to ask Charlie if *I* could be the man to tell the story of his life. Always the frugal one, Charlie replied, "Sure, you can write the story just as long as I don't have to spend any money out of pocket." I chuckled a bit and told him he wouldn't need to pay a dime.

The plan was simple. I was going to gather all of the information on Charlie's life, put together a few decent chapters, and pay to have a few hundred books self-published. Then I would move on with my life. How wrong I was in thinking two long careers from such an accomplished musician and radio personality could be crammed into a few short months of life. The can of worms opened quickly when I visited the once, musically vibrant town of Clovis, New Mexico. I spoke to the curator of the Norman Petty Studio, Kenneth Broad, who cordially gave me full access to and a private tour of the original legendary Norman Petty domain.

During my tour with Ken, he asked me if I wanted to listen to something cool. "Of course," I said as Ken expertly slid some reel-to-reel tapes onto the once state-of-the-art music recorder. It was one of the first cuts of "Sugartime" with Charlie singing loud and proud. When it was over, I nodded and thanked him. He then asked me if I heard the background instruments and singing. I hadn't. Ken then told me that the cut he had just played was Charlie Phillips being backed-up by Buddy Holly and a Cricket or two, among others. "Well, I never," was all I could input.

I honestly had no idea Charlie had any association with the late, great Buddy Holly. I sat in Norman's not-so-comfortable chair and stared blankly at Ken and the equipment behind him. I didn't know what to say, after all, *I* was Charlie's biographer and I should have known *that* small tidbit of information before I ever stepped into the studio. But I didn't.

After leaving my grand tour and bidding Ken adieu, I quietly loaded my recording equipment and cameras into my truck. I picked up my cell phone and dialed Charlie, who was at home in Amarillo, Texas. I explained to Charlie I was at the Norman Petty Studio and had completed a journey down memory lane with Ken Broad. Then I quietly asked him, "Charlie, was Buddy Holly and the Crickets on one of your first cuts of 'Sugartime?'" "Oh yes," he timidly explained. Then I asked, "Listen, Charlie, you do know I'm writing your biography, right?" "Yes," he said questionably. "Listen Charlie, if Buddy Holly and the Crickets were on your first record, or Elvis and the Beatles dropped by for lunch- well, you really need to tell me about it." Since that phone conversation, Charlie opened up and began filling me in on any and all pertinent information regarding his compelling life.

Thinking I was only going to spend around six months on this project, I started having unquestionable doubts the more information I dug up and the more people I interviewed. I remember saying "holy moly" to myself when I had compiled around 1000 pages of notes and hadn't even begun to touch the surface of his two long careers. With Buddy Holly and the Crickets on Charlie's "big break" song which landed him a record deal with Coral Records out of New York, to discovering Glen Campbell's involvement on several of Charlie's records with Warner Bros. (Reprise) Records, to following Charlie's appearances on television and radio shows like the *Grand Ole Opry*, Red Foley's *Ozark Jubilee* and the *Louisiana Hayride*, I quickly realized my little six-month undertaking was going to turn into monstrous project. And it did.

As days and weeks passed, more and more people became involved with the writing process and most importantly, the recounting of Charlie's life. I began discovering so many stories told by both country music celebrities and folks who witnessed events as they occurred- many have never been written about until now. Chronicling Charlie's life story became an obsession when I learned that he, at 80 years old, and many of the guys he knew and played with over the years were either dead, getting too old to remember details or were too sick to speak with me regarding past events. I knew when I eventually called to speak with Glen Campbell and was told they could put him on the phone, but he wouldn't have a clue who I was or wouldn't remember anything about Charlie, I was running out of time.

Less than two years after beginning this project, I stopped counting the deaths of musicians who merely passed after my initial and only interview with them. George Jones, Ray Price, Little Jimmy Dickens, Jimmy Young, Joe B. Mauldin, and Jimmy C. Newman all passed away within a seemingly short time of each other and Glen Campbell was stricken with Alzheimer's disease. With the death of each and every soul, a fire burned hot under my hindquarters forcing me to chronicle and complete this biography with expediency. After all, if I didn't tell this story, much of the information would be forever lost.

Shortly before finishing this book, tragedy struck. I began experiencing chest pains and recurring heart palpitations. Without going into too many details, my heart had enough and let me know it in a rather abrupt way. Already two years into my planned six-month project and six months behind schedule, I had to take a breather and write in my spare time. Often tragedy strikes us at the most inopportune times, but we grind forward, and we get the job done. The book you are about to read was written with utmost respect and love.

Please remember when reading through Charlie's life story, *most* everything in this book is the truth, *or* the truth as a particular individual recalled it. Since many of these stories have never been written about, it was difficult as an author to crosscheck my facts as I simply had few references to check my facts with. With that being said, use your judgment and take some of the stories to heart and others with a grain of salt.

Many of the "old farts" I interviewed- their words, not mine- truly enjoyed telling me their accounts of Charlie and the music industry. Whether or not their accounts are wholly accurate, at least they told a whopper of a good story and isn't that, after all, what makes Texas so great? To this day, I don't know what really happened at the Alamo. In fact, historians still debate it today. I just know the Texans were outgunned and outmanned and struggled, sacrificed and fought like heck in an attempt to defeat Santa Anna and his troops. "Remember the Alamo!" would be the battle cry when Sam Houston and his troops later confronted and defeated Santa Anna at the Battle of San Jacinto.

"Remember Charlie!" will be this book's motto. Any man who can continuously play country, rockabilly and western swing music to adoring fans for over six decades while simultaneously: recording hundreds of songs, being a number one radio personality, performing on television and radio, playing thousands of live gigs, writing a number one tune and dozens of other songs, winning a Gold Record, becoming a real estate investor, being loved and admired by countless fans... well, that guy deserves to be remembered. It's my hope you enjoy reading the story of Charlie's life as much as I've enjoyed writing it. Without further sendoff, I give you a big Texas YeeHaw and Howdy!

"Sugartime" is one of the most beloved songs in history. These are the lyrics made famous by the McGuire Sisters. You can sing along if you'd like:

Well, sugar in the morning
Sugar in the evening
Sugar at suppertime
Be my little sugar
And love me all the time

Honey in the morning
Honey in the evening
Honey at suppertime
So be my little honey
And love me all the time

Put your arms around me
And swear by stars above
You'll be mine forever
In a heaven of love

Sugar in the morning
Sugar in the evening
Sugar at suppertime
Be my little sugar
And love me all the time

Now Sugartime
Is anytime

That you're near
'Cause you're so dear
So don't you roam
Just be my honeycomb
And live in a heaven of love

Sugar in the morning
Sugar in the evening
Sugar at suppertime
Be my little sugar
And love me all the time

Be my little sugar
And love me (love me)
All (all), all the time

"Sugartime" by Charlie Phillips and Odis Echols Copyright © 1956, 1957 by MPL Communications Inc. Copyright Renewed Used by Permission All Rights Reserved

Ladies and gentlemen, this is the story of a good ole' Texas farm boy who fought poverty and accomplished a lifelong career in the bustling world of country music.

Ponder for a minute, if you will, and pretend you were asked to name some stars from the early days of country music- you might say, Bob Wills, Hank Williams, or Dolly Parton. Or maybe you remember Loretta Lynn and her heartwarming story as a coal miners' daughter. Yep, we laughed when Minnie Pearl disembarked onstage donning her new hat with the price tag still dangling from the rim. *Hee Haw* and the *Grand Ole Opry* provided us with countless hours of music, entertainment and laughs. Heck, how often do we see Willie Nelson in the news for something or another? Well, one thing's for sure, we followed our country music stars, their lives and the music they sang.

Let me tell you the story about a country music icon whose songs you've heard, even though you probably don't know his name. Believe it or not, this guy has been playing country music just about every week for 60 years now. Heck, he even wrote a country song that traveled up to No. 1 on the pop music charts for a few weeks, earning him an esteemed Gold Record. He played numerous times on the *Louisiana Hayride*, the *Grand Ole Opry*, the *Big "D" Jamboree* and Red Foley's *Ozark Jubilee*. He's received honors like Mr. DJ, USA, is inducted into the Western Swing Music Hall of Fame and is inaugurated into the Texas Panhandle Association of Broadcasters Hall of Fame.

Ladies and gentlemen, this is the real story of Charlie "Sugartime" Phillips.

Chapter 1
On the Road to Texas

If there's one thing you can count on in West Texas, it's the wind, and this day in 1934 was no different from any other. The hot sun bore down from the Texas sky, baking both the people and the crops on this windy, dusty July afternoon. The ever-present singing of locusts could be heard for miles as they broadcast their mating sounds from high atop the sparse elm trees. It was business as usual at the old Donaldson place situated on a small plot of land positioned 5 miles southeast of Farwell, Texas. Two sharecroppers operated the farm- Frank Phillips, a man who labored in the dusty cotton fields and his wife, Katherine Luella Phillips, lovingly known as "Ma Kate," who toiled with her household chores. Well, there was *one* exception on this day. Ma Kate was about to have her fifth child and unlike her other four children who'd been born at home by a midwife, this child would unknowingly and surprisingly be born in a hospital.

Farm life was different in those days. After the American Civil War and the end of slavery, it was common in the South for families to live and work together on farms. Those who could afford to buy a few acres of land would, and those who could not afford land of their own, became sharecroppers. Now, for you non-southerners, sharecropping was pretty much a method of farming where the landowner allowed a family to manage his land to live, farm and raise kids and in return at the end of a growing season, the crop would be harvested and sold. Truth be told, when the crop *did* finally sell and it was time to divvy up the profits for the year, the landowner usually took one-third to one-half of the profits and left just enough money for the tenant family to stay and do it all again next year. Sounds pretty fair, supposin' you were the landowner.

Most folks spent much of their energy focusing on basic survival. Only the brave and hardy could survive in the South during the late 1800's and early 1900's. Crossing the plains and learning to grow crops in a dusty, dry wilderness were challenges faced by almost every poor southerner in those days.

Now, Thad and Mary Massongill were no strangers to work. Parents to Katherine Luella, they worked their days running a successful sawmill, gristmill (a mill for grinding grain) and cotton gin near the small town of Pencil Bluff, Arkansas just up the road from Mt. Ida, Arkansas. Pencil Bluff is pretty much situated smack-dab in the middle of the Ouachita National Forest and just a few short miles from Lake Ouachita. Running a sawmill in the early 1900's was no easy task. Montgomery County, Arkansas was filled with trees like blackjack oak, white oak and shortleaf pine and lumber became an increasing necessity as towns and businesses were popping up across our great nation. When felled trees were delivered to the mill, Thad and his men would load the logs onto a carriage and onto the tracks, ready to be sawn into lumber.

Just to let you know some of the basics and without going into too much technical jargon, the mill cutting was run with an ingenious set of flat belts and friction wheels as the casing between the saw blade and the drive pulley allowed control and movement of the heavy logs. Whoever was operating and overseeing the cuttin' of the logs would maneuver a lever, which would move an ole' black tire back and forth eventually guiding the logs through the saw blade. After cutting the initial slab from a log, boards would be sliced by running the log over the saw and then bringing it back again. It was possible back in those days to make as many as 300 boards in a given day which would be used to build houses, businesses and what-not or even to be temporarily stored at lumberyards.

As one can visualize, with that many logs havin' been sawed each day, a lot of sawdust is kicked up. Hundreds of pounds of dust would be piled outside of the mill and spread around on the ground oftentimes mounded up in dunes higher than a building. Every now and then a farmer might retrieve some sawdust to spread around his animal pens, but more often than not, the sawdust would just accumulate. The men working these sawmills often covered their mouths with cut-up pieces of fabric tied behind their necks maybe like a kerchief, but do what you will, you're still going to breathe a lot of dust into your chest. Thad Massongill was no exception, and after years of breathing dust into his lungs, began developing congestive respiratory problems leading to a severe case of asthma and a hacking cough lasting throughout his whole life.

Somewhere around this time, young Katherine Luella met a handsome local boy by the name of Albert Frank Phillips and they began courtin'. No one remembers if Frank worked at one of the mills or the cotton gin, but no matter, he and Katherine met and fell in love. With that being said, it wouldn't be a stretch to say the Massongills were no fans of Frank Phillips and didn't think too kindly of him dating their lovely daughter, Kate. You see, Frank and his brother, Bartley, were known locally as moonshiners and had been apprehended for stealing a sack of sugar, a necessary ingredient for making whiskey or moonshine, which the boys had been conjuring up to make some money. One small run-in with the law was all Thad needed to mistrust the boy.

Well, sometimes folks just can't get along! No, we're not talking about Frank or Katherine or the Massongills. We're talking about Germany and Austria-Hungary against the rest of the world, thus spawning The Great War. President Woodrow Wilson declared war on Germany on April 6, 1917, and every able-bodied young man waited until his country called him for duty or they volunteered to go fight.

Within a year or so, Frank Phillips was notified by the draft board and he willfully reported for service, leaving behind his future in-laws and his sweet gal, Katherine. After basic training, Frank was deployed onto a battleship headed for Europe. His battleship was en route across the Atlantic Ocean when, as fate would have it, the Central Powers surrendered to The Allies and Frank returned back home without seeing a lick of combat. Hindsight always being twenty-twenty, it was probably a good thing Frank never saw any fighting. He was destined to raise several kids who would be fated for success and would later prove their importance to the United States of America.

Although becoming wealthy by any standard in those days, taking his doctor's advice and with his lungs still intact, Thad sold the mills and the cotton gin, packed up his family and moved to the great state of Texas. They arrived in Baylor County in the early half of the 1900's. There in a small town located west of Seymour called Vera, Texas, they took up farming and ranching. Thad decided to set up shop and become a cotton farmer. The clear Texas air agreed with him and seemed to keep his asthma at bay, thus most everything seemed to be going well with the Massongill family.

After returning home from his battleship after World War I, Frank Phillips, who reluctantly but temporarily stayed behind in Pencil Bluff, began missing his lovely belle. The woman he treasured above all others was gone and it seemed the hole in his heart would not be filled. Out of adoration, he packed up his belongings and embarked on the long journey to Texas. The Massongills forgave Frank's former indiscretions and within weeks he was reunited with his lovely Katherine. They were quickly married.

Frank worked alongside Thad and year after year they produced their crops. Living was good, well, as good as it could be in those days. Frank and Katherine began having offspring. The first of their children was a boy they named Carthon, born in 1920.

Carthon was a go-getter sort of boy. Little did anyone know at the time, but Carthon would live well into his 90's! When World War II began, Carthon would leave his college studies at Texas Technical College (later Texas Tech University) in Lubbock, Texas and volunteer for the Army Air Corps. Young Mr. Phillips became a pilot and flew planes throughout the duration of the Second World War and made a career out of the Air Corps. That lucky son-of-a-gun became a highly decorated Colonel and not only lived through WWII, but also lived to speak about his service in the Korean War and the Vietnam War. We're getting a little too far ahead of ourselves though.

The following year in 1921, Frank and Katherine had a daughter they named Mary Elaine. Elaine was a spunky young lady with looks to match her sweet personality. Also born during this time was Albert Frank Jr., who the family nicknamed "Bunk," for short. The extended Massongill and Phillips family was growing and Thad and Frank soon became role models of their Vera, Texas community.

After the First World War, economic conditions improved in the United States, but little did most folks know, a dark cloud was billowing over the horizon, which would send turmoil throughout the United States. On October 29, 1929, a day known as Black Tuesday, the U.S. stock market crashed causing millions of Americans to lose their jobs. It is said that cotton crop prices in rural areas fell from around 80-cents a pound to 10-cents a pound! Thad Massongill and Frank Phillips were virtually bankrupted overnight, leaving their families in crisis.

For those of you old enough to remember, there was a television comedy broadcast on CBS in the 1960's called *The Beverly Hillbillies*. The series was about some simple country folks who strike oil on their land and become millionaires overnight. Wanting to see his family have a better life, the patriarch of the family, Jed Clampett, moves his family from Bug Tussle to Beverly Hills and into a mansion. If you're familiar with this series, think of the exact opposite.

Thad Massongill and his son-in-law were completely broke, forcing them to load their whole family into an automobile. They desperately needed to find work for themselves to support their growing families. After moving from farm to farm, opportunity knocked and Thad Massongill uprooted his extended family and moved to Farwell, Texas some 200 miles away. Desperate times often call for desperate measures, but there's one thing that's certain, one never gave up in those days.

Chapter 2
Welcome to Farwell, Texas - A Tumor is Born

With three kids and $30 to their name, the whole clan arrived in Farwell, Texas. Thad and the family moved onto the old Donaldson place, named after the landlord who owned the farmland and the modest house. Some folks use the term railroad-house, and others say shotgun-house to describe the type of home the Massongill and Phillips family moved into. Unlike homes of today, these dwellings were built with one room connecting to the next much like railroad cars. If you wanted to go into the kitchen, sometimes you'd have to travel through someone's bedroom. A large front porch ran across the entire front of the house. There was no electricity, simply oil lamps for light. A tin vessel served as the family bathtub, which was usually kept outside.

Outback, was an old outhouse strangely located on the southwest corner of the home. Now, that's odd because if you remember, West Texas is known for its wind and, by the way, the wind is almost always blowing from the southwest. If you've ever driven through that part of the world, you'll notice most of the trees are pointing to the northeast as a result of wind abuse. So with the outhouse located on the southwest corner, a pleasant aroma might sweep through the house on certain days.

Coal was the primary source of heat in the winter, but often too expensive for poor folks like the Phillips family. If one couldn't afford coal, other materials could be burned- even cow chips, the dried excrement from livestock containing just enough grass to keep a fire going in desperate times.

Wood posts and barbed wire surrounded this modest working farm. Dirt roads led to the property where the main house, chicken coop, as well as pens for the horses, were located. There was a water-well on the property located near the windmill. If you needed to bathe or cook, someone had to take a bucket out to the well, pump water into it, and haul it back to the house. God forbid you'd better hope the well wasn't frozen in the wintertime. There was even an underground storm shelter, which wasn't used much for storms, but more for keeping jarred and pickled foods. Though humble, the house had everything one needed to raise a family. And that's just what they did. In 1927, another son and the Phillips' fourth child, Glenn, was born into the Phillips clan.

Farwell itself might not have seemed like much by today's standards, but back in those days it was a nice small-town community offering many of the basics of life. It was a hardworking conservative community situated in what some might now consider the "Bible Belt." As luck might have it, the great state of Texas was in need of a new three- million dollar capitol building to be situated in Austin, TX. The State eventually struck a deal with a couple of Chicago Yankee brothers, John and Charles Farwell, along with some British investors, to trade three-million acres of land for three-million dollars used to build the capitol building. Texas eventually got its fancy new Capitol building, and the Farwell brothers obtained more land than just about anyone had ever seen at the time.

Thus, the small Texas town was born and named after the Farwell Brothers, the original owners of the XIT Ranch, and is located right on the border of New Mexico and Texas. Farwell is about 95 miles from Amarillo, Texas, which is to the northeast and about 10 miles to Clovis, New Mexico, which lies directly to the west. If you walk down Main Street in Farwell and cross the railroad tracks, you'd be in the small town of Texico, New Mexico. The township of Farwell is situated in Parmer County and has close associations with the famed XIT Ranch, which used to stretch across twelve counties.

Katherine, now endowed with the name, Ma Kate, had not been feeling well for several months. She had been vomiting and was getting stomach cramps something fierce. She had gained a bit of weight and could feel something growing in her abdomen. She feared the worst and began stating the obvious, "she had a tumor." When she could take no more, she traveled across the state line with Mary Massongill and family to the closest hospital located just a few miles away in Clovis. To her dismay, the tumor growing inside of her was no tumor at all; it was her fifth child who was in desperate need to escape her body. On that blistering July the 2nd day in 1934, Charles Don Phillips was born. Baby Charlie came into the world and was quickly nicknamed "Tumor" by his other siblings.

This fateful decision and quick trip to the hospital would later come back to haunt Charlie Phillips over the years. Although he spent the first 48 hours of his life in New Mexico and the next 80 plus years in Texas, Charlie would never be considered an actual Texan by many of his country music peers. Several awards and Hall of Fame inductions would not be granted over the years simply because he was not *born* on Texas soil. Like the old saying goes, "I wasn't born in Texas, but I got here as quick as I could!" certainly applies to this circumstance. "I've NEVER lived anywhere but Texas, and I wouldn't have it any other way!" Charlie adamantly insists decades later.

Only fourteen years old at the time, the now retired Lt. Colonel Carthon Phillips recalls the day Charlie was brought home from the hospital stating, "Charlie was the youngest of our whole pack and I was runnin' the cultivator behind our two mules layin' the crop out in front of the house where we lived. Well, I was watchin' them comin' back and bringin' him down, so I pulled my team closer to the house so I could get a closer look at my new brother. I didn't stop 'cause Dad was pretty strict about getting' the plowin' done. I can't remember, but I think I was finishing up that field of cotton – or maybe it was corn- I don't know. And, so I was lookin' at Charlie, and we were carryin' on at the house there and dad said, 'Well,

Carthon, now you've seen him. Get back on that cultivator there and finish that up before dark.' I'll never forget that." By the time Carthon finally reached college age, he couldn't wait to graduate high school so he could, "get out from behind those danged-ole mules and cultivator and get an education." He eventually did both.

Charlie was, of course, the baby in the family and his brothers and sister coddled him until he was half-grown at least. Other than being called Tumor, one other nickname his siblings had given him was Chick. He cried a little bit at night and sounded like a chicken, or so the other siblings thought. Years later, Charlie sported a new nickname, Scrooge, but we're getting ahead of ourselves again.

This part of Texas did not have irrigation at this time and growing crops was always a gamble of nature. Dry-land farming was the primary method of growing crops, and if it didn't rain, you could starve. Anyone who's ever grown up on a farm knows that every able-bodied person is required to pull his or her weight. So when Charlie became old enough to walk, he was given his first job-gathering eggs from the chicken coop. For you city folks who think eggs come from the supermarket, well, they don't. They come out of a chicken's hindquarters, and someone's got to go collect them. This was one of Charlie's many jobs on the farm for years to come.

Talk about some good ole' home-cookin'. Ma Kate was one of the best cooks that ever lived, 'course everyone says that about their mom. Grandma Mary Massongill was another great cook who had learned to make good food out of just about anything when she lived in Arkansas and gladly trained in Ma Kate. Ma Kate could cook some of the best fried-chicken around. Fruits and vegetables were often pickled and canned in those days. In fact, one farm delicacy was canned tomatoes. The secret ingredient you ask? A spoonful of sugar was poured atop of the tomatoes and the juice just before biting into their delicious goodness.

Now if you're a vegetarian, or one of those vegan folks, or you're just plain squeamish, it'd be best if you just skip the next few paragraphs. No really, we won't mind, just skip down a few paragraphs.

There we go. For the rest of you folks, the Phillips family and all of their neighbors raised their own hogs. As the hot summer weather subsided, and colder fall weather began creeping in, a very important festivity would take place on the farm called "hog-killin's." As you can already surmise, there were no refrigerators back then, so it was always better to wait until it was cold, and the colder, the better, before slaughtering a hog.

Mr. Cassidy was a neighbor of the Phillips' and was a butcher by trade. After folks from neighboring farms chose the best two or three hogs from their stock, Mr. Cassidy would slaughter them and hang them up in his smokehouse. You have to realize this was an all-day affair for several neighborhood-farming families. The pig carcasses would be hung up, as full-size pots would be brought in to boil off the fat, making chitlins, created from the small fatty parts of the pig.

Some folks even called this festivity a "pig killin' party" because everyone except the pig had a good time. You've got to remember there was no television at the time and for entertainment, folks would bring playing cards or dominoes and maybe play a game of 42. Of course, Mr. Cassidy always had a pint or two of his medicinal remedy to ward off the cold, you see. To top it all off, Mr. Cassidy was, according to himself, a world famous Son-of-a-Gun maker. For the laymen, this is when you take the worst part of the pig, and you make a stew or chili-like stew out of it.

Veggie lovers, you better skip down a little further as we're not quite done yet. Yep, there you go, just a few more paragraphs. Thanks. It's always better to be politically correct these days, don't you think? The Son-of-a-Gun stew mainly consisted of all the meat entrails most wasteful folks would throw away: like the guts, the tongue, the heart, the liver and the tail. To fashion the stew into an edible meal, all sorts of peppers and spices were thrown into the concoction. Mr. Cassidy even separated the stew into three different varieties: The Papa Bear, which was so hot it might put hair on your chest; the Mama Bear, which was spicy yet tolerable; and the Baby Bear, which was the mildest and didn't have much kick to it. No matter which type of stew you ordered, you were sure to fill your belly with some of the tastiest stew man ever created.

While the adults played their games into the wee hours of the night, it was up to the youngsters to create their own entertainment. There were about a dozen or so community kids, and they'd usually segregate themselves by age. By this time, Charlie and a few of his neighbor friends were at that rambunctious age of doing what boys do best, which is getting into trouble.

Now, boys will be boys and this particular afternoon, Charlie and three of his friends proved just that. This specific incident can only be akin to an episode of the *Little Rascals*. All boys are curious, but this day Charlie, Ted Magnus, Phillip Cassidy and Jerry Don Utsman, all being around ten years of age, bit off a little more than they could chew.

The back of the Cassidy place had an old well out in the pasture, which had long been forgotten. It had some sort of cover over it, and the boys had always been curious what was underneath it. They knew there was a hole there, but they wondered how deep. They guessed the hole was probably 150- 200 feet deep. Now, they had been told to stay away from it, but their curiosity got the best of them, as they wanted to see what was at the bottom of this old well. One of the boys had a brilliant idea and said, "I'll tell you what we do. Let's pour some gasoline down this hole and we'll let enough of it get on the bottom. Then… we'll drop a match down, and it'll stay lit so we can see whatever's down there so deep."

So the boys walked to the barn and borrowed a couple of gallons or so of gasoline. Being as smart as they were, they knew to pour the liquid into the center of the hole where it would drop directly to the bottom. They thought they were brilliant because they didn't get any gas on the side of the hole. Yup, they were too smart for that. After the container of gasoline doused the opening, the boys all gathered in a circle around the gaping hole and someone said,

"Ok, it's time." So one of the boys struck a match and dropped it down there, with all four peering intently at the bottom, of course. "Ker Whoom!!" A big spray of shotgun-flames disbursed up into the air!

Since all four boys were standing over the blast, the heat and flames scorched their hair, eyebrows and skin on their faces. Blisters immediately popped from their skin. Phillip Cassidy didn't have any eyebrows left on his face! Charlie still claims this incident was "the most stupid thing I've ever done." Now, no one was seriously hurt, but what do boys do when they implement a plan so stupid and don't want others to know what they did? They lie. But, unfortunately in this case, the four keen and penetrating minds couldn't think of a lie good enough to hide their battle scars. They all got their butts whooped when they arrived back home. Keep in mind there weren't any "timeouts" in those days.

Even the oldest and wisest of the bunch, Carthon, pulled a death-defying shenanigan as a youngster. He and his cousin, Oscar Finch, cleverly nicknamed Foskar Orange, decided they'd make a giant yo-yo out of two latched coaster wagon wheels using a rope as the string. Their new toy was so big and they maneuvered the oversized yo-yo up the ladder of a thirty-foot windmill. They decided they'd drop it from the top creating a fun new game with the world's largest yo-yo. Thank God Frank Phillips chanced upon the two crazy boys. Just a little knowledge of gravity would have sent the holder of the yo-yo string plummeting thirty feet to the hard Texas dirt below. "I guess I owe my dad my life," Carthon said, "because I was gonna hold that string." There were more ways to get into trouble growing up on a farm and ranch!

With Carthon being the oldest boy and Charlie being the youngest, a special brotherly bond was formed as Carthon always looked out for his younger sibling. "Charlie was always my favorite brother," he explains as he describes Charlie being kicked around by his other two brothers, Bunk and Glenn. "I tried to put a stop to it," he laughs, "I just wasn't there enough." Well, brotherly love.

Always trying to create a good time, the youngsters would sometimes create their own rodeos and try and ride the dairy cows roaming on the property. Jerry Don Utsman always seemed afraid of everything, so the boys would often try and talk him into doing something he didn't want to do. They ganged up on him one day stating he was "gonna hafta" ride one of the cows. Sometimes the cows would buck and sometimes they wouldn't. They talked Jerry Don into getting on one of those calves and sure as heck, the steer kicked him straight up in the air and he fell face-first into a pile of cow manure.

Now, huntin' rabbits was another pastime. There were so many jackrabbits back in those days you might trip over one if you didn't watch where you were going. These critters were truly a menace and if left unchecked, would eat up a crop. Offering ample cover for the rabbits, plenty of prairie grass was present in West Texas before irrigation came along, so it gave the boys something to hunt in their spare time. As a matter of fact, just a few years before Charlie's time, the jackrabbit population began to soar, and some say it was a godsend. After the onslaught of the Great Depression, it's speculated many folks would have starved to death had it not been for the large population of jackrabbits and cottontails.

Around the time of Charlie's birth, a momentous catastrophe struck the Texas Panhandle as well as its adjoining states. The Dust Bowl of 1935 sent a devastating shockwave through the farmlands of the South. Newspapers at the time coined the phrase "Black Sunday" describing the black rolling blizzards of dirt, which swept through the country- killing innocent folks and burying properties. Farwell, Texas was greatly affected by the dust storms. Many years after the origin of the dust bowl, communities were still being swept by high winds and heavy amounts of dust.

Sweet milk, now called whole milk, was served at almost every meal. One of the primary chores was milkin' the cows. There were many times as a young boy, Charlie would take a bucket out into the middle of the cow lot with the West Texas gales blowin' something fierce. He almost couldn't see across the dirt roads, as he'd stumble down the path and set the bucket under the cow and begin milkin' her. Grime and cow manure would be blowin' everywhere and yes, even into the fresh milk. Milk would simply be poured through a cheese strainer to sift out the impurities. "It's amazing in this day and time people worry about disease. If kids were raised on a farm like I was- well, I guess they'd get such an immune system…" Charlie recounts while also stating, "Well, my God! How are you still alive, people often ask? I think that's the reason people raised on a farm, lots of times, have longevity."

The cows still needed to be milked in the morning and at night, as they were an important aspect of the working farm's crop. Of course, it was never pasteurized or homogenized, as it was drunk in its natural form. Milk was sold for drinking, but just as importantly, the sweet liquid could be churned into butter. Ma Kate, or any other able-bodied person, would let the milk sit for a spell and allow the cream to rise to the top. Once fermented enough, you'd skim the cream off. The leftovers would be poured into a wooden butter churn, and you'd begin to churn the liquid, and churn and churn until the top portion of the milk turned to solid butter.

Any folks who've ever churned butter before knows it's a tedious and muscle-building exercise but is worth it in the end, because the treat-of-all-treats is created- BUTTERMILK! This is why some folks say real buttermilk is better for you- because all the fat's taken out. But it might also be the exercise achieved from hours of churning. Charlie vividly remembers, "I've done hundreds and hundreds of hours churnin'- hundreds of hours. I should look like the Hulk, as many hours as I did crankin' that darned ole' separator, which, the early ones didn't have electric motors. You had to turn 'em by hand."

Carthon, the eldest of the Phillips boys, had a couple of show pigs that were given to him by his father. He cared for and nurtured those pigs, but arrived home one day to find the pigs had gone missing. He looked up and down the farm trying to locate his sows, but couldn't find hide-nor-hair of them. It turns out his dad, Frank, had traded his two pigs for a young Thistle Tail mare (Slang for a long-tailed "mutt" horse aptly named because the common Thistle weed often became entwined in its tail). Of course Carthon named the horse Thistletail and cared for and rode her until he went off to college. "God I loved that ole' mare," Carthon reminisces. The killin' and tradin' of animals was common for farm folks.

It can be said that little Charlie Phillips was also an animal lover from the get-go. Frank and Ma Kate joked he'd name all of the animals on the farm and make pets out of them! Horses, pigs, cows, goats, chickens, it didn't matter; Charlie would make them his favorite. One of his first pets was a goat named Gracie. Gracie was about as domesticated as any goat could be. She foller'd Charlie most everywhere he went around that farm. One morning at breakfast, the family looked out of their window to find Gracie had climbed on top of their brand-spanking new 1941 Black Ford automobile so she could get a better look inside the house. She wanted Charlie to come out and play! Scratches appeared all over the fender and hood of that new car. Well, needless to say, that was the end of Gracie's stay at the Phillips home as she was traded to a neighboring farm simply for scuffing the paint off of the new vehicle.

William "Willie" Dannhelm and his wife were the Phillips' first farmhands and although just employees, really became a part of the extended family. They enjoyed Charlie so much they even named one of their children after him years later. Knowing Charlie's love of animals, Willie brought home a small dog and gave it to young Charlie as a gift. Midgie was a mixed-breed white and brown spotted dog with medium length shaggy hair. An early photo of Midgie shows her riding on the back of Charlie's tricycle like a circus performer. Charlie fell in love with Midgie. She perhaps started his lifelong love of dogs.

Every boy during this time deserved a good horse and Charlie had one of the best. The Calloway family lived on a neighboring farm in proximity to the Phillips family. Mr. Calloway was a Commissioner for Parmer County and highly regarded in the local community. His son owned a beautifully trained horse named Paint, who was as smart as a whip and could perform a variety of tricks as well as respond to a few commands. Tragedy struck Mr. Calloway's son on a cloudy Texas day as lightning struck his boy while riding on their tractor, killing him instantly. As one can imagine, the death shook the small community, but no one was more devastated than Mr. Calloway and his family. The loss of his son prompted him to sell their beloved Paint in order to perhaps alleviate the memory of his son's association with the fine horse. Frank Phillips bought Paint from Mr. Calloway and gave him to Charlie, who provided the horse with a loving home for many years to come.

Paint proved to have a penchant for mischief as he demonstrated a very special talent for a horse- he could open doors! Who could count the times Ma Kate would be in her kitchen shelling peas or cooking dinner and Paint would quietly slip up behind her and give her the surprise of her life? She would often turn around to see Paint standing in the middle of her kitchen. Paint never liked to stay penned, so many a time he'd open up the gate and wander around the farm. As mischievous as Paint was, he also proved to be a great companion and often took Charlie into town for school or leisure. Townsfolk reminisce seeing Charlie tie Paint up to a post outside the schoolhouse.

Although maze, corn, grain sorghum, cotton and Sudan grass seeds were the staple of the Phillips farm, Charlie began his first business venture breeding and selling English border collies. Many years later as a hobby, he was the first to bring the Australian Silky Terrier to the Texas Panhandle. For a young whippersnapper, the dog breeding business turned into quite a lucrative income producer. The revenue from his dog occupation allowed Charlie some light luxuries possibly other children his age couldn't afford. As a young man, not yet a teenager, Charlie purchased his first guitar for $10 at a pawnshop on a trip to Muleshoe, Texas. Charlie remembers the very worn F-hole guitar seemed to have a neck like a two-by-four and required a pair of pliers to thread the strings. "I never learned to play that danged ole' guitar very well," he'd say.

Saturday was a special day for the Phillips clan as it meant the family could "go into town!" as many folks might say. The majestic growing town of Farwell had all of the amenities a small community could ask for. The Parmer County courthouse was situated in Farwell and served as the county seat. The town sported a post office, churches, barbershops, a lumberyard, the Santa Fe Railroad depot, grocery and variety stores, a coal yard, lumberyard, a bank, and a movie house. Like many towns of its day, most local shops and businesses were located right on Main Street, which crossed over the railroad tracks and continued as the main street into Texico, New Mexico. Texico even had a three-story hotel fittingly named the Texico Hotel housing a post office and a drugstore with a big marble soda fountain.

Saturday was the most important day for town folk and farm folk alike because the business owners of Farwell would hold The Merchants Drawing in the afternoon. As each person entered one of the many town businesses, tickets were handed out where one would tear off the stub and place the other half in a container. A drawing would be held for cash or often store merchandise sometime later in the day. The pot might get up to around $50, but boy that was a lot of money in those days. The town would explode with kids running up and down the wooden planked and newly formed concrete sidewalks and streets.

As a special treat, the Phillips children were often purchased a pop with flavors like Ni-Hi flavored soda and Crown Cola, which cost a whole nickel. Little Charlie's favorite beverage was Nu Grape soda, which he thought tasted just like real grape juice. Haircuts were administered by Bob Kiker, who was a local barber, and although he was a professional, the boys often thought their haircuts looked like a bowl had been placed on their head and cut around. Charlie could always be seen around town with a big straw hat creased down the middle, like Hopalong Cassidy, who was his fictional childhood hero. He donned a pair of cutoff shorts, always hand-me-downs from his older brothers and was usually barefooted. He'd frequently head into all of the stores, but as a youngster, he never had money to buy nothin'.

Occasionally, maybe once a month, the family would pack together inside their automobile and head ten miles west "all the way over" to the big city of Clovis, New Mexico. Previously the home of

Native Americans, Clovis is situated high atop the Llano Estacado Mesa on land that is as flat as buckwheat pancakes on a level griddle- much like its immediate neighbor, the Texas Panhandle. The Atchison Topeka and Santa Fe Railroad ran through the town making it the primary hub for both people and commerce.

Folks would ride their horses or drive their automobiles for miles to do their shopping or to experience the merriments in one of the biggest cities in the area. High above the New Mexico skyline stood the magnificent ten-story Hotel Clovis building, exhibiting a beautiful cream-colored Art Deco exterior and deemed at the time, the tallest building between Dallas and Albuquerque. Many evenings were filled with various types of entertainment where showbiz greats could often be seen at some of the area's many nightspots. Among these, the Hotel Clovis had a magnificent ballroom with an unforgettable crystal chandelier hanging from its ornate ceiling. The swanky ballroom brought in such greats as Hank Williams, Louis Armstrong and Glenn Miller. At this point, no one would ever guess Charlie Phillips would be playing here in the very near future.

Sometimes Ma Kate and Jerry Don's mother, Ollie Utsman, would gather the extended family together and head to the city for a whole day of shopping. Ma Kate and Ollie would send the kids to one of the three local movie theaters, specifically the Mesa Theater, whose cinemas only cost a dime to view. The kids would sit there all day watching a double feature and eating big five-cent bags of popcorn. With any luck, the double feature might include a western.

Clovis sported large department stores as well as intimate family-owned businesses. Folks still remember businesses like J.C. Penny, the House of Music, Levine's clothing store, Woolworth, Barry's Hardware, the Busy Bee Café, and Montgomery Ward, which even had a second floor with an elevator- a big deal in those days. Charlie swears his very, very frugal mother would spend the whole day shopping and would only leave Clovis with a small package of bobby pins or possibly a pair of unmentionables. Maybe those gals were just window-shopping, or maybe they just needed a much-deserved break from the kids.

Right next to the Mesa Theater was a local joint called Coney Island, which was a shotgun-type diner with a long narrow row of barstools, just wide enough to fit the bar, the stools, and a couple dozen people. Like its New York counterpart, their specialty was hotdogs, and the kids would get their fill of the most delicious frankfurters costing a whopping 15-cents per dog. No matter what the festivities in Clovis, it was always a grand treat to visit. "Some of my fondest memories during my childhood were right there on Main Street in Clovis during the 40's and 50's," Charlie recalls, "it was my New York City."

Every now and again, the Phillips family might enjoy the luxury of a vacation. There weren't very many fancy two-lane highways in those days, so most folks of that era stayed within driving distance of their hometown on most occasions. Carlsbad Caverns was in proximity to Farwell, so one time the whole family crawled up in the car and headed for southern New Mexico. Located in the middle of the desert and hotter than blue blazes, the Phillips household drove up to the yawning opening at the mouth of the caverns and began their long descent down the winding and treacherous raw path. Charlie, still a young boy at this juncture, began crying after a couple of hours inside the cave and his older brothers, Carthon and Bunk, carried him on their shoulders through the remainder of the cavern. "I think that's the scaredest I've ever been," said Charlie, decades later. "I was never so glad to get out of a place in all my life," he adds, "to this day I'm kinda claustrophobic. I'm wondering if that ain't what caused it all."

When asked about a small scar on his forehead, Charlie reminisces about another infamous road trip taken years after the Carlsbad trip, to Ruidoso, New Mexico with his family once again crammed into a 1937 gray Chevy sedan. Child-locks hadn't been invented yet, so most families purchased sedans with only two doors, so the kids didn't fall out of the backseat! Anyway, the initial plan on the Ruidoso trip was to take some family vacation pictures with their new Kodak camera, which was a big, solid-incased box weighing quite a few pounds. Before arriving at their destination, whoever was driving, slammed on the brakes and the heavy camera flew through the car hitting Charlie, who had turned around and was standing up between the seats, square in his forehead. He laughs about the event now while touching the scar.

Growing up in West Texas was certainly an endless adventure. There was nothing too terribly special about eastern New Mexico or West Texas for that matter. Farm folks and city folks all intermingled with each other forming a very tightknit community. Residents just moved on with their daily lives. No one could have possibly anticipated the sudden surge of musical talent creeping upon Clovis and her surrounding towns. An unsuspecting movement was sliding in like a thief in the night. It would soon steal the hearts of millions worldwide.

Chapter 3
Rising from the Dust

The Phillips residence on the old Donaldson place was like many rural farm homes of the time- it didn't have the luxury of electricity. Frank purchased a brand-new Zenith battery-powered radio for the family that ran off old six-volt car batteries, which were electrified by a small wind charger located on top of the house. Boy, you had never seen such a beautiful radio with its big frequency-dial positioned directly in the center of its wood-paneled facade. The speaker was covered in cloth, topped with an intricately carved music note. The whole family was very proud of that radio. A ground wire ran from the back of the radio to the outside the home and deep into the hard earth.

Oftentimes the dry Texas weather would cause some static electricity buildup on the ground wire, whereby one of the kids would be ordered outside to pour some water on it. This essentially meant they'd often run outside and pee on the wire, unbeknownst to Ma Kate who would often holler at the kids, "What's makin' that smell behind the house? Have you kids been peein' out there again?" In no time at all, the radio would be up and running again. If for some reason the radio had been playing too long and the six-volt battery completely lost its charge right before their favorite radio program came on, Frank would run out and remove their car battery. He'd then hook it up to the radio so the family wouldn't be without entertainment for the evening.

The *Grand Ole Opry* was transmitted out of WSM's powerful Nashville AM radio station and was heard by tens of thousands of national listeners each week and was certainly a sweet luxury for a farm family. The Saturday night event at the Phillips home, if there wasn't a neighborhood or church get-together of some sort, was to sit in front of the radio often until midnight listening to the programming on WSM. As a young child, Charlie recalls listenin' to and talkin' about new upcoming country stars like Roy Acuff, Ernest Tubb, Minnie Pearl and the marvelous Uncle Dave Bacon. Little did young Charlie know he'd soon be performing with some of these folks.

Notwithstanding, Frank was quite the music aficionado himself. Whistling, humming and singing around the homestead lightened the mood of backbreaking farm work. In the early Arkansas days, folks entertained each other by singing in groups or quartets. If you couldn't play an instrument and you had a decent voice, then you sang. Frank participated in various singing conventions with a local favorite music quartet and sang anywhere he could share his bass voice with others. He continued singing for pleasure, which provided an important early role model for young Charlie.

Hearing the bravura of music both from his father and the music transmitted by WSM, young Charlie soon began imitating the sounds and musical styles of his favorite artists while working on the farm and at school. One of Charlie's earliest memories was his father lifting him up and placing him on the dining room table where he could entertain family and guests in their home. "Now, sing son, get up there and sing us a song!" Frank would prompt and encourage Charlie. While perched on the dining room stage, young Charlie would melodically croon to his eager listeners singing an early tune like "The Prisoner's Song" as performed by Vernon Dalhart.

He loved the attention but felt like a bit of a showoff. In addition to his first living room or kitchen guest appearances, it can be said Charlie's first audience was the copious chickens lined up in the chicken house who appeared to sway back and forth, clucking with approval and flipping their heads, to the sound of music as young Charlie warbled out a melody. No one remembers if the chickens ever gave a standing ovation or not.

Elaine Phillips was the only girl born into the Phillips family. With four brothers at the helm of the household, she held her own pretty well. Ma Kate dressed her in some of the cutest outfits and dresses. Elaine had beautiful flowing blond hair and was one of the prettiest girls in the county. With her striking good looks, she had an angelic voice to match and could be heard humming and singing melodies, just like her father; however, she primarily saved her voice for Sunday church and singin' conventions.

Like Arkansas, the bustling town of Farwell conducted singin' conventions that were usually situated somewhere in town. The ladies of Farwell would each cook something delicious and bring their foods for an all day celebration of singing and eating. The kids joked that the conventions were called, "Dinner All Day and Singin' on the Ground," but they were really named, *Singing All Day and Better on the Ground*. These events were suitably named because Farwell did not yet have any public parks- so they were all literally singing and eating on the ground. Residents of the town would take turns performing their memorizing acts, whether solo or in groups like quartets, if they felt so inclined.

Another talented voice in the family came along after several years when Charlie's sister, Elaine, had a daughter of her own named Mary Charlotte. Charlotte had a beautiful singing voice, but more importantly, she was interested in playing the piano. Since she spent so much time at the Phillips home, Ma Kate decided to buy a piano for the house. This gave Charlotte the opportunity to take piano lessons. An alluring spinet mahogany Wurlitzer piano was the newest extravagance added to the Phillips home.

Mrs. Vineyard was the local piano instructor who soon began teaching young Charlotte how to read music correctly and to play musical notes. It wasn't long until Charlie begged for and was granted lessons, or you could say *a* lesson, as it only took one before realizing reading music notes was not for him. However, having a piano in the house gave Charlie ample opportunity to sit down, bang a few notes out, and eventually learn to play the piano strictly by ear.

Church was another place for the family to display their musical talents. With pillars and large bannisters leading up the steps of the red-bricked building, The Hamlin Memorial Methodist Church, named after Judge Hamlin who was the man that got the railroad through the county line, was located across the tracks from Farwell in Texico, New Mexico. It was here the family sang together, and it was here Charlie was baptized. "My mom was not a religious fanatic, but she came from the old school- you got to be saved," Charlie held. The Methodist church remained in Texico until it was finally demolished, and a new building was erected, this time on the Farwell side of the tracks.

As years passed, Frank continued to purchase land in the general vicinity until he had amassed close to three sections of farmland. Frank, now more commonly known as A.F., once again became a respected leader within his community. The Second World War had broken out, and men from across the nation enlisted once again to fight Germany oversees.

Carthon Phillips had already left home and was attending college when he was called to duty. The whole country was rallying behind the war efforts, and general supplies were in short demand for civilians still living on the home front. It became necessary to ration many daily foods and other commodities at home, so the U.S. government initiated a "stamp rationing" program. Known for his honesty, integrity and also a reliable member of the local community, A.F. served on the Ration Board for the Farwell area. He continued his duties throughout the remainder of the War.

The Phillips family spent many years as sharecroppers on the Donaldson place and their hard work finally became fertile, so to speak. In 1946, A.F. was able to purchase some 320 acres of land on the south side of Farwell and, after the War when building materials became more plentiful, built the family a new modern "mansion." A.F. moved the family from their old shotgun house into their new ranch-style home, which was a pretty good size considering their humble beginnings. Within a few short years, A.F. was elected County Commissioner. They were truly increasing their lot in life.

Long hard days driving his father's powerful Minneapolis Moline tractor on the farm gave Charlie ample time to sing and create various tunes in his head. In the late 1940's and early 1950's several of his first melodies were fashioned while plowing the fields. The lurid sound of the tractor forced Charlie to sing louder than usual so he could hear his voice on top of the roaring engine. Norman Petty, Charlie's first music producer, would laughingly recall years later he'd have to remind Charlie to quiet his voice while in the studio for fear of overloading the tape-recording equipment. It was on a tractor Charlie learned to sing loud and proud, which would come in handy in the near future when he began singing at various venues- often without a microphone. His singing was always improving as he imitated his idol, Hank Snow, as well as another popular country artist at the time, Marty Robbins, who had a smooth, trailblazing sound in his voice.

In addition to the Minneapolis Moline, Charlie drove a four-row, cherry-red, Farmall Tractor. It would be on top of this piece of machinery that the hit song, "Sugartime," would be rehearsed and pre-written. Plowin' in the morning, plowin' in the evening- but never at suppertime- that was for eatin'! "If you've ever been on a farm, you know they have those mile rows," Charlie once explained to reporter, Jim Crawford. "You plow down here for a mile, then turn a corner and plow a mile that way. Anyway, I'd get bored and make up songs. When I got home, I'd write them down and start fooling with them on the guitar and piano." This became his music-writing protocol.

It's no secret, but Charlie was not the best academic student in school. He took the usual classes and played some sports, but didn't excel at any of them. His real passion was music, and as luck would have it, Charlie would be "discovered" by his music teacher at Farwell Junior High School. Mrs. Jobes took a keen interest in him after hearing his tuneful, boisterous voice in class. Mrs. Jobes worked relentlessly with Charlie and helped refine him into a true musician by any sense of the word. Soon Charlie began performing as the featured act at school assemblies and was able to put together his first band and, within no time, he began composing his own songs.

Once he started to perfect his unique talents, Charlie and his friends put together a small group of ragtag teens in 1952 from their freshman class and formed their first band. The band was comprised of Dudley Hughes, James Norton, Jimmy Schell and Charlie; together forming a group they outlandishly named Hornando's Hideaway. No one quite remembers how the designation of Hornando's Hideaway was coined, nonetheless, they paraded themselves as a musical comedy act, often dressing in eccentric raggedy clothes with big hats- appearing like something from a carnival. Occasionally, Dudley or the guys even put on a grass skirt or dress for comic effect. Charlie explains, "There were various school and area talent shows in these small communities. This was our own brand of entertainment. That and the movies are about all we had." He continues, "We couldn't play very good and to tell you, we weren't that funny either. We looked funny," but often that was all one needed to entertain a crowd.

Gloom would soon fill the horizon. The year was 1949. Charlie was sitting in his Agriculture class (Ag class for short) on a windy Texas day and he could see the Superintendent of the school, Jack Williams, through the classroom window walking towards his building. Jack asked the Ag Teacher, Prof Morton, to step outside. After a moment, both Prof and Jack entered the room and made a disturbing announcement. He ordered all of the kids in the class, except Charlie, to report to study hall. Charlie's first thought was, "Oh heck! What did I do now?" Charlie was told to get in the car as Prof broke the news about Charlie's dad, A.F. "Charlie, your father's been killed in an automobile accident."

Just recently, A.F. had purchased a brand new 1949 Chevrolet truck and was pulling an implement trailer. He and Charlie's brother, Bunk, were heading to Amarillo to pick up a new tractor, which had recently been purchased from the International Tractor dealership. They had been driving east on Highway 60 and had gotten as far as Friona, Texas when a woman driving a 1940 Hudson pulled out into oncoming traffic and hit the Chevrolet head-on. She was drunk. Frank was thrown from the vehicle, and Bunk was fused behind the truck wheel as the pressure from the trailer and the Hudson crushed the automobile, causing it to catch fire.

A truck driver happened to be passing by and used a fire extinguisher to douse the flames and was somehow able to get Bunk pulled from the wreckage, thus sparing Bunk's life. In his last moments of final hopelessness, A.F. uttered these haunting last words to his boy, Bunk, "Son, you're gonna hafta take care of things now." Within seconds, he was dead. His services were held at the Hamlin Memorial Methodist Church, the very building where the Phillips family once sang joyfully- now the valediction building for the family patriarch.

Bunk escaped the accident with burns on his hands, scars on his face and more significantly, a brain aneurysm. For the duration of Bunk's life, he endured the guilt of the accident because he was the person driving behind the wheel. He lived for many years after the unspeakable incident; marrying, raising a family, and with the help of Glenn and Ma Kate, was able to keep the farm-operations successful after witnessing his father's tragic death. He fulfilled his father's dying words. The family always gave him credit for stepping up to the plate during such troubling times and soon he will lovingly name one of his children after Albert Frank in remembrance and respect for his father.

Almost three decades later, Bunk arrived at his house after leaving a business in Clovis, and was unexpectedly attacked from behind in his own home as he was struck in the back of the head with a bottle. A Shirley MacLaine special was playing on television as Bunk scrambled to call for help. Not wanting to worry his mother, Ma Kate, he elected not to call the Sheriff's office, but instead called family to take him to the hospital. There were no witnesses to the crime, or at least none with the guts to come forward. He died years later in 1977 from the brain aneurysm caused by either the blow to his head or the former auto accident- no one knows. Unfortunately, the case remains open to this day as an unsolved New Mexico homicide.

Back in those days, when someone in the community passed away, the funeral home would bring the body into the house where friends and neighbors would sit with the corpse all night. When Charlie's father died, people were at their home for several days. A.F. had been killed on a Thursday, yet his service was held on a Sunday; therefore, friends, neighbors, and kinfolk stayed at the house until Pa Frank was buried in the Mission Garden Cemetery three days later. The most disturbing thing Charlie remembers during his teenage years was seeing his father's body, dead as a doornail, lying in the casket right next to the big picture window in the living room.

One would think Pa Frank's unexpected death would have launched the Phillips family into turmoil; however, Ma Kate was a hard-hitting pioneer woman with a strong sense of God, family and duty. She quickly took over the farming operations with the help of Bunk and her other children. "Tough as nails" is a common Texas expression and it describes Ma Kate perfectly. The fourth kiddo, Glenn Phillips, had been attending Texas Tech in the footsteps of his older brother, Carthon. He too stepped up to the plate, quitting college and returning home to help the family on the farm following the death of his father.

As strong and independent as Ma Kate was, she had a tough challenge brewing. In addition to her new job overseeing the farm, she now had to raise a rambunctious teenager named Charles Phillips, alone. Notwithstanding, she kept him working, she kept him in school, and she encouraged his music, which is exactly the structure a budding young man and musician needed in the 1950's. Charlie, however, unknowingly didn't make it easy on her. With his father now absent, Charlie spent much of his time concentrating on his music- and partying. "I don't know how my mother put up with it. I was basically a rotten little kid…but in comparison to teenagers today, I was probably a saint, but I started drinking or 'partying' at a very early age… and 'course, Clovis was dry so as soon we got our drivers license, everybody was makin' runs to Grady, New Mexico to pick up liquor or beer. It seems like the late 40's, and all during the 50's was a kind of up and down time for me musically, life-wise and everything else," he recollects.

Every blue moon, Charlie and his friends would even make their own homebrew. One fine day, Carroll "Lash" LaRue, another childhood romping buddy of Charlie's, decided to concoct a mixture of his own somewhat resembling beer. The boys bottled up their potion in some canning jars and set the liquid gold out in a cornfield underneath some shade so it wouldn't get too hot. Homebrews were known to explode if the temperature got too warm. Well, Ma Kate had purchased herself a brand spanking new Mercury two weeks earlier and Charlie and the boys borrowed her car to take to a party. They stored the homemade beer in her trunk and pulled an all-night drinking binge. They returned the next morning to drop off the car so Ma Kate could make it to church on time. A few of those beers were still in the trunk, and as she sat in church on that warm sunny Sunday morning, each and every one of those beers exploded in her vehicle. That could have been forgiven, but the church windows were open and the aroma from her trunk blew through the church like a dead body. She wanted to kill the boys for the embarrassment it caused.

Buffalo Lake was the closest and only picnickin', waterskiin', fishin' and waterin' hole near Farwell. It was situated off Highway 60 east of Hereford, Texas. Most any boys who hailed from this area would often hitch up their boats and make the hour drive to hang out, drink beer and spend the day roughhousing in its waters. Charlie and a group of high school buddies loaded up his boat as well as a friend's 14-foot aluminum boat with a 25-horse powered engine and headed for the lake one sunny morning. After an afternoon of fishin' and skiin', the boys elected Charlie to make a beer-run to the closest package store, which was a long drive to Amarillo.

His mother had purchased a new Ford work truck that Charlie had adopted as his own, and Charlie drove the truck to retrieve potations for the motley group of teenagers. Back in those days no one really cared if you were of age to purchase alcohol or not, but Charlie wore a hat and sunglasses to disguise his youthful appearance nonetheless. He was a tall kid for his age so most places wouldn't even check his identification. Charlie would say in his deepest voice, "Five cases of Coors please!" and would hand them the money. As he drove back to the lake, he partook of several beers before arriving back at their campsite.

As he neared the other boys who were sitting near the shore of the lake, Charlie stuck his arm out the window holding an open beer can and screamed "Whooee! Look what I got boys!" as he drove straight past the campsite- and smack-dab into the lake! The boys all tried to retrieve the truck, which was knee-deep in water. It was to no avail. Charlie even attempted to double-clutch the truck, but as soon as he let the clutch out, the transmission exploded. It was a silent day back at the Phillips farm and as one can imagine, Ma Kate was none too happy. She must have been a saint for putting up with all she did.

When ginnin' season began, Charlie found himself working at either the local cotton gin or for grain dealer, Mr. Roberts, who'd hire him when the harvest season peaked. Charlie never did really like farming. For one thing, he had allergies, which were aggravated by farming chores. Even though he'd been raised on the farm and all of the many animals, at times he found it very difficult to breathe, especially during wheat-thrashing season. Often during cotton harvest, Charlie and his brothers, along with black laborers and Mexican braceros, would spend most waking hours toiling in the hot sun pulling the white, fluffy fibers from the sharp, finger-slicing bolls and filling their gunnysacks. "I always did my chores, but I wasn't good at it…couldn't get much done," Charlie recalls. "I don't know if I didn't have the energy or the interest, or if I was just lazy, but I wasn't cut out for that kind of work."

The cotton stripper came into style during the 1950's. It was hooked to the back of a tractor, shedding the cotton automatically from its hull and spewing it back into a trailer, thus eliminating the need for as many workers. Unfortunately though, someone had to be in the back of the darned trailer to pack the cotton down as it flown in, which was one of Charlie's chores. He winces when he speaks of the responsibility, "Them durned ole' burrs hittin' you in the face and with the dirt… I mean I would sneeze and cough and wheeze!" "So, anything I could do to get off the farm," was exactly what he was looking for.

Charlie began singing with a high school quartet in addition to the unseasoned group, Hornando's Hideaway. After a few successful local shows, Mrs. Jobes, the high school music teacher, suggested the boys take their disparate group on the road and to a talent show in Muleshoe, Texas. They were offering a grand prize of $20 for the winner. That was a lot of money, so the boys agreed and entered. Various acts arrived for the Muleshoe talent show, respectively. This would be the first time Charlie met a fledgling musician by the name of Waylon Jennings.

Jennings had been playing guitar since he was eight years old and performing since he was 12. He was barely a teenager at the time he entered the contest in the small Texas town. It didn't take long for Charlie and the boys to see Jennings was somber about his music. Both Hornando's Hideaway and Jennings put on a great show for the Muleshoe crowd, but neither won the $20 grand prize. The award went to a four-year-old little girl who sang her rendition of "Jesus Loves Me" to a cheering, awestruck crowd. Perplexed and angry by the audience's decision, Waylon Jennings stormed off the stage in disgust. Charlie and the guys wouldn't see Waylon again for many years.

Chapter 4
Petty Days- The Clovis Music Scene

Charlie had caught wind that a famous group he loved was gonna be playing in Amarillo one Saturday night. Since he didn't have school the following day, he'd borrow the family pickup and take off for the big city in the northern plains of the Texas Panhandle. The Clover Club was a trendy dancing establishment in Amarillo located near the historic Route 66 on the eastern side of town near the Amarillo Air Force Base. Because he was still in high school and too young to get into a bar, Charlie dressed in his Sunday best making himself appear a little older. If his big hero was Hank Snow, then The Maddox Brothers and Rose would have pulled a close second. Having only heard them on the radio, Charlie couldn't wait see them in person as he drove over 100 miles for the opportunity.

Billed as "America's Most Colorful Hillbilly Band," The Maddox Brothers and Rose consisted of Fred, Cal, Henry and Don Maddox as well as their sister, Rose. The group had come from unbelievably humble beginnings as migrant fruit and vegetable pickers in the 1930's who traveled from crop to crop working for little wages in an attempt to feed their family. Life was tough for so many folks in those days, but the Maddox family turned their attention towards their love of music. Rumor has it Fred became tired of picking fruit and wrangled the family a radio spot on a California station, KTRB, out of Modesto. Well, this was just the start they needed to advance their career in music. It took them until the 1950's to develop a noteworthy following, and now here they were in Amarillo.

Charlie had no problem getting through the door at the Clover Club since many of the dance halls in those days couldn't be bothered with checking ID's and whatnot. Boy, but when the music group entered the stage and began playing, it seemed all mayhem had broken loose. The group was notorious for playing country standards, cowboy tunes, folk music to jazzier style songs, Boogie Woogie and perhaps even a taste of what would later be classified as rock 'n' roll. It was on this night Charlie would hear the song, "Big Balls in Cowtown" played for the first time, and he went wild. "I thought that was the best country song I'd ever heard in my life!" Charlie exclaimed. With the excitement of the crowd and the unbelievable performance given by the group, Charlie got so rambunctious he was told to leave the establishment and wasn't even able to see the end of the show. No matter, he had the time of his life and it would be this one-night experience that would shape his future music career.

Charlie continued working on the family farm throughout high school taking up some of the slack from his father's death. He often joked farming was his first paying job, but he never actually made any money doing it. It seems after expenses there was never much money left to go around. To make extra dough, Charlie and some of his friends put together music groups of various sorts, and began their night job by playing gigs at some of the unscrupulous bootleg joints in Clovis, New Mexico. You see, Clovis was dry when it came to alcohol so folks wanting to dance or party would have to travel to one of the outlying towns or take their chance at one of the seedy, illegally-run speakeasies situated throughout Clovis.

Since the boys were still in high school, they continued to perform local talent shows or almost anywhere an audience would gather. Charlie and the guys once performed their act at a local talent show in Bovina, Texas and it was there Charlie met a woman by the name of Betty Hawkins, a gal who had put together a country band of her own. She intently watched Charlie on stage and excitingly approached him after his encouraging performance, requesting he be the male lead singer in her burgeoning country group. More gigs equal more practice and more money, so in no time he agreed and began performing with her in addition to the various other groups he was already accompanying. With lots of practice, Charlie began developing an active voice as well as a unique sense of style and people immediately began to take notice.

Betty had booked another gig at Bovina's next high school talent show. Playing at this venue would prove to be a pivotal moment in Charlie's growing music career. A man by the name of Odis "Pop" Echols was the Master of Ceremony (MC) and in charge of the show. Pop had recently gotten into the radio business and owned a soon-to-be favorite radio station in Clovis, with the call letters KCLV. During this time in the 1950's, there was a popular program airing nationally across America called the *Breakfast Club* hosted by Don McNeil. Pop decided his new radio station needed programming of this genre and popularity, so he mimicked McNeil's original and commenced Clovis' very own radio version of the *Breakfast Club* that was broadcast live out of the Silver Grill in Clovis. Always on the lookout for free talent to perform on his new show, Pop witnessed Charlie's strong stage presence and invited the singer to perform and co-host his live radio show.

Charlie agreed, and each Saturday morning he and a couple of guys would set-up inside of the diner. Pop would entice folks to come to the restaurant by offering some prizes each week, and he kept them entertained by talking to them and interviewing them on-air. Every week the restaurant was packed full of the cutest, little ole' blue-haired ladies Clovis had ever seen. Having had a lucrative and long career in the music business, Pop was able to invite many regional and national celebrities who appeared on the program. This certainly gave folks in the small New Mexico town something worthwhile to gossip about. The show even boasted appearances by New Mexico politicians, Senator Clinton Anderson and Governor Jimmy Davis.

It was at one of these diner appearances Charlie would make his first live on the radio howler. As a special promotion for the listeners of KCLV Radio, the station would be giving away a case of Dr. Pepper for a special listener. It was up to Charlie to announce the big giveaway. As he geared up for his huge pronouncement, his tongue slipped ever so slightly and he publicized to all of the ladies present and to the hundreds of people listening in the area "that the winner of a case of Dr. Peckers is…!" Though mild, Charlie had inadvertently said his first curse word on the radio and the more he tried to correct his speech, the funnier folks thought it was, and the more he blundered. Even 60 years after Charlie's mistake, people in Clovis are still talking about the case of Dr. Peckers they could have won from Charlie that day as they chuckle and laugh.

Loving the attention, Charlie approached Pop with a proposal: would Echols allow Charlie and a few guys to get together and have their own live radio show on Saturday afternoons? Pop listened attentively as the boys spoke and lightheartedly agreed, but said, "I'm warning you though! It cost money to put stuff on the radio. But, I can sell you some time if you guys wanna put your show on," meaning if the boys wanted to go on-air, they'd have to come up with enough money to pay for the time themselves. "That's it?" Charlie thought. So if they could raise enough money and pay for their airtime, they were guaranteed their own show on the radio.

"Well, hell, all I did was go back to my hometown of Farwell where I knew all the gin operators, the elevators, and the banks. I'd tell them I needed something like fifty bucks for a thirty-minute segment on the show. It might have been a hundred, but it wasn't that expensive to have a show in those days," Charlie avows. Most of the local businesses said, "Sure, we'll sponsor you," knowing they'd be receiving some good advertising for their investment. And just like that, Charlie and his close friends, Dudley Hughes, Jimmy Schell and James Norton received their very own live radio show on KCLV.

At the time, KCLV was primarily playing 1950's rock music. It, however, had received such good reviews concerning the boy's country segments, Pop decided to expand the country music show to include more hillbilly and country music as well as country-themed commentary. He offered Charlie a job as one of the first country music disc jockeys on KCLV- making a whopping $60 per week. This may not seem like much by today's standards, but that equates to almost $500 per week in today's money. This wasn't too shabby for an ole' country farm boy with no real education; besides, he would do anything to escape farm life and "keep the burrs from blowing in his face." It was time to learn a new business.

In and of itself, Clovis was rich in musical history beginning in the early 1900's. The sheer amount of local talented musical groups and individuals would be almost too numerous to name in this book; however, it's relevant to note some individuals and establishments who called Clovis home. With musical venues like the new Lyceum Theatre, the La Vista, the Hotel Clovis with the Rainbow Ballroom and the Mesa Theater being built, Clovis was sure to see its fair share of musical talent.

From 1912 to present, Clovis played host to an array of individuals and bands like: The Baker Brothers Orchestra; The Clovis Cowboy Band; The Harley Sadler Tent Show; Glen Barris and the Blue Jackets; The Musical Grays; Gordon Fitzhugh and the Hotel Clovis Orchestra; Ralph Emerson and his 10-piece Kansas City Orchestra; Bob Wills and his Texas Playboys; Hank Williams; Arizona Wranglers; Jimmie Rodgers; Clyde Miller; Smiley Burnette; Roy Rogers; Gene Autry; Jimmy Wakely; Eddy Arnold; Ray Price; Ernest Tubb; Tennessee Ernie Ford; Lefty Frizzell; Hank Thompson; Waylon Jennings; Sheb Wooly; Roger Miller; and eventually Charlie "Sugartime" Phillips, Reba McIntyre and Vince Gill- to name only a handful.

By all accounts, Clovis, New Mexico should have been no more important to the music world as a fly on a goat's ass. The small town wasn't close to any big music cities like New York or Nashville, and it had no ties with the music industry whatsoever. Clovis did, however, have a couple of secret weapons, which would soon rock the music industry to its knees. With the onset of radio programs like the *Grand Ole Opry* and the *Louisiana Hayride* being broadcast into rural homes across America, youngsters were picking up the classic music genres and trying their hand at impersonating and performing songs heard on these radio programs. Additionally, Elvis Presley was gaining national popularity and young people from across the country were attempting to imitate the hot young celebrity. Over the next few decades, an imaginary triangle was established stretching from Amarillo, Texas to Clovis, New Mexico to Lubbock,

Texas birthing some of the finest, most talented musicians the world would ever know.

Norman Eugene Petty was born in the small town of Clovis on May 25, 1927, at the Petty family home on Thornton Street. He secretly commenced playing and mastering the piano by five years of age where he soon began performing for family get-togethers and eventually filled-in for some of the talented local groups in the area. By 14 years old, little Norman produced and presented his own 15-minute show on Clovis' local KICA radio station called *The Norman Petty Show*, quickly becoming a regional favorite. Shortly thereafter, he formed his first musical group consisting of four men, christened the Torchy Swingsters, by the time he attended Clovis High School.

To help the Torchy Swingsters develop a better sound, young Norman began recording their sessions and using the playbacks to help the group improve their practice sessions. After high school, Norman would join the United States Army Air Corps and eventually meet Colonel Bill Leach at Langley Army Air Field in Langley, Virginia, who would teach him all about electronics. Within a few years of serving honorably in the Air Corps and returning to his hometown of Clovis, he began working as a radio announcer at KICA. Eventually, after a move to Texas, he became a recording engineer thus developing a keen sense or "ear" for the way music could be recorded.

Having immense talent not only as a recording engineer, but also as a piano and music aficionado, Norman founded the Norman Petty Ensemble. He played the organ, his high school sweetheart and new young bride, Violet Ann "Vi" Petty played piano, Jack Vaughn performed on guitar and eventually Vi's cousin, Georgiana Veit, joined as a vocalist. When Georgiana left the band to marry, Vi took over the responsibilities of singing and the group became the Norman Petty Trio. While still performing and practicing with the trio, Norman created and opened his first recording studio at 1313 7th Street in Clovis. He then formed a new record label appropriately named NorVaJak, encompassing the names (**NOR**man, Violet Ann, and **JAcK** Vaughn), which became their launching pad, so to speak, for future endeavors.

Norman Petty's former Air Force colleague and friend, Colonel Bill Leach, would make several trips to Clovis assisting Petty with proper installation of the electronics in the new studio. Meanwhile, D. William Boner of the University of Texas and Richard Evans from Radio KSL in Salt Lake City would assist with the acoustics. His sound workshop was well on its way, but just as importantly, the newly formed Norman Petty Trio became wildly successful and landed a recording contract with ABC- Paramount Records. Success would soon follow as *Cashbox Magazine* named them "Most Promising Group of 1954." By 1956, they had sold a half million copies of Duke Ellington's original "Mood Indigo," which was their first successful venture.

Halfway across the nation, Bill Haley's "Rock Around the Clock" enlivened American audiences and was soon followed by Elvis Presley's single, "Heartbreak Hotel." Rock 'n' roll was peaking over the horizon and appeared to be emerging as a viable music genre by way of musicians developing their own personalized style and rhythm. Miles away in Nashville, a man few people had ever heard of with a virtually unknown band, at least in the music industry, was unsuccessfully recording songs with a company called Decca Records.

He and the musically talented group were becoming increasingly unhappy with the sounds produced by their Decca recording studio and lack of interest by their record label. They subsequently were released from their contract, thus freeing the boys to record at another venue- perhaps even a spot a little bit closer to their hometown of Lubbock, Texas. It would be a pivotal move for young Buddy Holly and his gifted band, The (Chirping) Crickets, as they made the journey to Clovis, New Mexico in search of a better sound, and maybe even success.

Country music was still king, but lighter, more effervescent sounds of pop music, as well as rock 'n' roll, would soon begin evolving into an industrialized commercial success shadowing its country music counterpart. Norman first released "Mood Indigo" on his NorVaJak label and then leased the song to RCA, who issued it on their Label "X," subsequently making the melody a popular sensation. The Norman Petty Trio then released their next big hit in early 1957, "Almost Paradise," which became outrageously admired after Roger Williams and Lou Stein covered the tune.

Originally the Petty's were disappointed with Stein and Williams' cover versions, but then royalties started arriving. Conceivably this was an epiphany for Petty, as he primarily realized artists make money off their own recordings, but composers and publishers make money no matter who records their song. The trio soon reaped the benefits of fame, financially allowing Norman to begin the expansion of his Clovis recording studio. Within the next decade, he would turn his small $200 initial investment and recording hobby into a budding recording empire.

Even though the Norman Petty Studio hailed as the largest and most professional recording studio in the area, the small and often musically insignificant town of Clovis boasted two other recording studios. Jimmy Self was a local deejay at KICA and had set up a dexterous recording studio in his garage. Jimmy was a well-known local musician and recording artist in his own right and often worked closely with Norman on various musical projects. Self was an Amarillo transplant to Clovis and worked as a concert promoter, deejay, drummer and singer. He drummed for a season with Hank Thompson's Brazos Valley Boys and also for Merl Lindsay and His Oklahoma Night Riders. His work with radio stations included the KICA Clovis station, KENM in Portales, the purchase of KZOL in Farwell, and eventually manager of Norman Petty's future KTQM-FM and KWKA-AM radio stations in Clovis.

Moreover, a man named Bob Tucker, well, everyone just called him "Tucker" for short as they also referred to his recording workshop as the Tucker Studio, formed another workspace in his home garage. Tucker was also a local, professional country-pop musician who donned a 1950's custom-made Bigsby steel guitar and was already performing gigs around town.

He most notably performed at the nearby Cannon Air Force Base. Tucker, with his conceivably hillbilly-sounding band called Bob Tucker and His Sky Riders, once cut a record with Virgil Hume on lead vocals and released a single on acetate. Very few recordings of its kind exist although a few recorded tracks of Tucker's have surfaced with Virgil Hume on vocals and Jack Vaughn of the Norman Petty Trio playing drums.

Nonetheless, like Petty, Tucker also welcomed young musicians to record at his small studio and charged a nominal recording fee. With three venues to record music in Clovis, ample choices were available for young and old musicians alike to try their hand at potentially becoming the next Bob Wills or Hank Snow. But, it would eventually be the Petty Studio thrust into the limelight and remembered for eternity. Shortly, the Norman Petty Studio would be dubbed one of New Mexico's best-kept secrets.

Still in his twenties, the visionary Petty had evolved from a young boy who liked to tinker with electronics into a man who understood the inner-workings of what can only be described as fundamental electronic recording equipment (by today's standards). Norman painstakingly sought to capture recordings of music so distinctive it will later be labeled as the "Clovis Sound." A reserved and sometimes quiet man, Petty sought to create an environment substantially contrary to the inner workings of Nashville and New York recording studios. Keeping stride with the idea that a calm, hometown work environment would embolden artists to be more creative, he encouraged his artists to relax and get comfortable within the studio atmosphere.

The back of the studio exhibited comfortable living quarters consisting of a bedroom, sofa, armchair, two daybeds, a television and fireplace- all decked out in the modern motif of its day. A small workable kitchen with all amenities was a stone throw from the living quarters. It was truly designed to be a musician's best friend. Petty's unique style of management and the small-town impression of the Norman Petty Studio would prove to be a caldron for artists to bubble creative excellence in the near future.

Norman created a very special policy at the Norman Petty Studio. He believed *all* musicians and composers deserved the chance to be heard. He listened to all recordings from individuals, groups and bands, often sent in on amateur home recording tapes, even if he would only accept a small percentage of them. It's been said, Norman possibly only accepted and recorded one out of every hundred tapes received in his office. This "hearing" policy had all but been forgotten in most New York and Nashville recording studios and it would possibly provide Norman a slight edge in the race to find the "next big hit."

Since young Charlie Phillips had already been playing musical gigs in the area and had become familiar with other bands and musicians, he decided he wanted a chance at becoming a recording artist. Mother's Day was right around the corner, and he made a crucial decision to record a special song for his mother, who had tirelessly supported him after his father's untimely death. Charlie had already met the owners of the local recording studios but elected to drop by Bob Tucker's garage studio and ask Bob to give him a chance to cut a demo. Tucker agreed. Tennessee Ernie Ford, one of Charlie's favored recording artists and idol, had a song on the radio written by Cindy Walker called, "Put Your Arms Around Me," which was a sad, yet beautiful song about a fever-induced man crying out from inside a prison cell for his beloved to hold him. Even if these weren't the words every mother wants to hear, Charlie thought the song was attractive and his mother would enjoy listening to it.

Charlie figured since records had two sides to them, he'd go ahead and also pay to record a song called "Courtin' in the Rain" on the backside. This would be the first acetate recording Charlie would make. Although it took him a couple of tries, he sang out the notes as beautifully as Tennessee might, well, maybe we shouldn't go that far, but it was his first try and he did an unbelievable job for a first-time recording artist. Upon completion, Charlie paid to have two copies pressed- one for his mother and one for the radio station. The radio station you say? He cut a few other acetates during these early years like "Almost," "Too Old To Cut The Mustard," "Release Me" and

"Bully Of The Town," yet these early recordings were not vast sensations for the unnoticed musician.

As expected, Ma Kate adored her Mother's Day gift. Almost as importantly, Charlie had the impudence to take the second disc over to his acquaintance, Jimmy Self, at the KICA radio station in Clovis. After listening to the track, Self simply said, "Man. I'm gonna play that." And play it he did. Charlie's cover version of the song was broadcast to all of the neighboring towns as far as Amarillo and Lubbock seeping into people's homes within a 100-mile radius of Clovis. Charlie was blown away to hear his voice on the radio for the first time. He thought to himself, "Well, my gosh if that's all there is to this...then...this is my career." From that day on, he began writing and composing his own songs and it wouldn't be long until a star would soon be born, so to speak. If it had not been for Jimmy Self, Charlie might have never realized his dream to be played on the radio.

Norman Petty was always concerned with "the sound" his studio recordings produced, and he worked tirelessly to fine-tune the workshop and the equipment using materials available to him at that time. At his original location, the main room or the live room was specifically retrofitted with a hard, wood-paneled wall, specially curved with varying degrees of waviness to capture the best sound possible, leaving NO flat walls in the room. As a musical engineer, Norman placed differing amounts of insulation inside the walls to catch specific resonances he desired from certain sections of each panel, thus almost eliminating low-frequency sounds from live recording sessions.

The acoustics alone were phenomenal. The room he created was not what one would call a *dead room* but it wasn't an *echo room* either as the sound design was as close to perfection as one could achieve in those days. Petty filled his studio with state-of-the-art recording equipment and added unique instruments including an Austrian celeste, a Hammond organ and a $25,000 Baldwin piano purchased for Vi. Additionally, he did something quite prolific for the time. He suspended his Oklahoma manufactured, Altec-Lansing speakers, powered by a state-of-the-art McIntosh amplifier, from the ceiling in mid-air eliminating unnecessary noise and vibrations from being heard on a recording or album giving recording artists a clear, clean, smooth sound. He went to great lengths to ensure only the finest and crispest music would be recorded at his studio, even ingeniously perfecting an "overdub" process that would soon be mimicked by studios throughout the world.

With a proper studio in place, Norman publically opened for business charging up to $75 to cut one side of a record or up to $150 for both sides. This was important because he never charged by the hour as many studios did at that time and still do today. He didn't believe creativity came by the clock, and an artist was never to feel pressured to hurry and get out. In fact, the Petty Studio was designed with special accommodations tailored to an artist's music like: a full eat-in kitchen, a 10-cent Coca-Cola machine and an apartment in the rear of the building that could be closed-off from the rest of the building giving artists much needed rest and privacy. Many an artist over the years ate, slept and worked in the recording studio.

Having a full-service working environment was also important because recording sessions often began in the evenings around midnight, partially because Norman and the Trio had traveled extensively over the years and had become accustomed to a nocturnal lifestyle, but more practically, the studio was situated off busy Highway 84 and the streets became more conducive to recording as traffic dissipated in the evenings. Soundproof rooms were not common in those days, so most studio sessions began late. Additionally, there were fewer chances of power outages or surges in the evenings as the numerous electrical mechanisms needed for making musical recordings drew a considerable amount of electricity. With this being said, entertainers are often night people with their full musical potential peaking while most folks are dreaming, tucked soundly into their beds.

Music was brewing all around Clovis and the Texas Panhandle. In retrospect, the sheer number of creative individuals and bands who developed in this area during the following decades baffles many folks. One such young man and his group moseyed into

Norman's studio not long after he opened the doors to the public. Buddy Knox was a young musician from Happy, Texas and had been attending West Texas State College in Canyon, Texas some 90 or so miles away from Clovis. He had organized a band called Buddy Knox and the Orchids and had been traveling the area performing gigs, and as fate might have it, he and his band members ran into another up-and-coming musician backstage at a show they were performing at the WTSC campus.

Roy Orbison, who's now known for his hit songs like "Crying," "Oh, Pretty Woman" and "Only the Lonely" had already recorded a master tape of his song, "Ooby Dooby," at Norman's studio and was familiar with Petty. Norman had even tried to place "Ooby Dooby" with a pal of his, Mitch Miller, at Columbia Records, but the song fell on unresponsive ears. It wasn't until young Roy ultimately recorded with Sam Phillips at Sun Records in Memphis, Tennessee that the song gained attention. As the story goes, Orbison encouraged Buddy and his band, which had no recording experience, to travel to the Norman Petty Studio and cut an album. So with $60 in their pockets, all three greenhorns, Knox, Jimmy Bowen, and Don Lanier packed their belongings and set out for Clovis with a dream.

Knox and the Orchids had a style of music Petty, whose primary background resembled more of a classical jazz sound, probably wasn't too familiar with yet. However, by using his keen ear accompanied by the boys' unbridled talents, recorded a couple of songs over the next three days. Dave Alldred had now been added as the Orchids' drummer. Interestingly, Norman didn't have a clue how to record the newfangled rock 'n' roll drum sound, so he used a Quaker State Motor Oil cardboard box in place of a drum kit to muffle and redirect reverberations.

With musical substitutions and a lot of finagling on Norman's part, a completed record was created. The boys originally released their tracks on the Triple D label, but soon Roulette Records purchased the tracks and re-released the songs on their label subsequently changing the band's name to the Rhythm Orchids. It was out of that one 1956 session that Buddy Knox would go on to receive two Gold Records the following year for the songs, "Party Doll" and a song he co-wrote with his WTSC classmate, Jimmy Bowen, entitled, "I'm Sticking With You," both singles selling over a million copies.

It's safe to say Knox's career was now well on its way, but just as importantly, Petty's mark on the rock 'n' roll recording industry had also been inaugurated. Knox and the Rhythm Orchids were the first big act Charlie Phillips witnessed birthed at the Petty studio. Although Knox's music was in a completely different category than his own country music style, Charlie sensed he could achieve the same success.

While Buddy Knox and the Rhythm Orchids were making their hits, young Charlie Phillips was busy on the farm, at the radio station, and chasing skirts around the Clovis and Farwell area. He was a bit of a cutup or comedian and not many folks took him too seriously. A local family with the last name of Christian had five girls and Charlie made a point to date ALL of them. Now, when we say dating, it means something different today than it did in the 1950's. As a gentleman, Charlie would take a special young lady to a movie and perhaps grab a soda or maybe some dinner. He never really went steady or became an item with any of the neighboring young ladies. He was mostly traveling in a crowd of rowdy boys runnin' around tryin' to find bootleg whiskey. The closest he came to ever having a steady love at this juncture in his childhood were the two Betty's. Both Betty Hillhouse and Betty Deaton were young girls Charlie fancied, but nothing ever transpired from the close friendships.

Around the time of Charlie's early dating days, he developed yet another peculiar nickname given to him by those close to him. Having been poor his whole life, he developed a particular attitude towards money, perhaps indirectly taught by his late father, Frank, or maybe even the frugal Ma Kate. Charlie felt it wasn't how much money you could earn, but how much you could save that determined success. He was still wearing hand-me-downs specifically from his older brother Glenn and began tightfistedly tucking away every penny, dime or dollar he could get by placing the coins away in one of his grandpa's (or grandma's) old coin purses. Thus, his peers began calling him Scrooge, suitably named after the miserly antagonist from Charles Dickens' story, *A Christmas Carol*.

During that time in American history, a penny was still worth something. A nickel was still worth something. A person needed a container to sock away one's change lest it be lost forever, so Charlie began sporting his tiny coin purse, also a handy place to store his guitar picks. "Nobody else in high school, not even the girls, carried a coin purse," Charlie laughs and recollects, "I'd open up my little coin purse and say, 'I'll give you a penny, but'…[in a miserly voice]" he'd stash and place the penny deeper inside the purse.

Pop Echols once took Charlie and the guys with him on a business trip to Nashville. At the restaurant breakfast table, the guys were all chipping in their fair share when Charlie pulled out his man-purse. The always image-conscious Echols screamed in a hushed voice, "Charlie! Put that danged ole' purse of yours away! It's embarrassing!" Poor Charlie received a lot of good-natured ribbing from his peers not only during high school, but also close friends of his still rib him about that coin purse over 60 years later.

The opportunity finally arose for Charlie to leave the farm, but not in a way he anticipated. The Korean War began in 1950 and came to a close in 1953; however, all able-bodied young men were still required to report for service. Charlie and one of his best friends, Dudley Hughes, were both drafted and couldn't wait to report for service. This was their ticket out of the small farming community, and Charlie could finally follow in the footsteps of his three older brothers, who had all served valiantly in the United States Military.

Knowing this would be one of the last times he would see his friends for a great while, the boys decided they would throw one last shindig before their enlistment. Charlie and the guys tossed one heck of a party the night before they were to drive to Amarillo and perform their military physical. After staying up and drinking half of the night, they arrived right on time for their physical; however, things didn't go as planned. The night of heavy drinking had elevated both boys' blood pressure to an unacceptable beat. They were both deprived of entry into the U.S. Military. There was no getting around an official denial, so the guys dejectedly returned to Farwell and Clovis to continue doing the only thing they could, farming and making music.

In the summer of 1956, another gifted singer and songwriter traveled from Farmington, New Mexico to Clovis to record a couple of songs with the rising star, Norman Petty. Sonny West was a rock 'n' roll fella and sought Petty's tutelage recording his two original tracks, "Sweet Rockin' Baby" and "Rock-Ola Ruby," which would be some of the first tracks released on Norman's newly formed NorVaJak label. The songs met with some regional success, but never took off on the national level- in part because Norman did not yet have proper connections within the music industry.

Clovis was certainly considered to be in the middle of nowhere. Perhaps in many ways the isolation away from major cities could have been a contributing factor why many local musicians from West Texas and eastern New Mexico recorded at the Petty Studio. Many artists had day jobs and could easily take off one evening for a recording session. Had they recorded in a larger metropolitan area, they might be forced to take off work for several days accounting for travel time. The convenience of Petty's secluded studio could have been a causative reason reflecting the number of area musicians who chose the Clovis studio for their recording needs; however, the most likely scenario orbited around the success of Buddy Knox and the Rhythm Orchids and their smash hit, "Party Doll." Very soon, musicians would begin flocking into Clovis in attempts to emulate the accomplishments of Norman's next big protégés.

Petty continued performing, writing and recording with some top notch people and bands, yet he still struggled to get records distributed on a national level. After seeing his own success with "Mood Indigo" and "Almost Paradise" and subsequently fulfilling his last contractual agreement with RCA by releasing his final album called *Corsage*, Petty yearned to find a successful niche within the monstrous music community. It was then Charles Hardin "Buddy" Holley entered Petty's studio for the first time, ready to record his next hopeful record. Little did anyone know these two gentlemen would soon make history together.

Chapter 5
My Buddy- Holly

Buddy Holley had gotten a contract with Decca Records after sending a sample of four Acetate discs to Nashville, which were previously recorded at the Nesman Studio in Wichita Falls. At the time, it was Buddy, Sonny Curtis and Don Guess who first went to Nashville to make records. All of the guys who traveled in this music crowd were excited to see their peers recording in a big Nashville studio. Jerry Allison was still in high school and stayed behind in Lubbock while his musical colleagues traveled to Music City.

After recording a few songs, in addition to, "Blue Days- Black Nights," the boys couldn't wait for their song to be released. The song did get released but met with dismal sales. The boys took Allison back with them in the summer and recorded even more songs for Decca. Whether it was a lack of promotion or lack of interest from the general public, the records just didn't generate very many transactions. The trip wasn't a total loss, however, as they did take the time to see the *Grand Ole Opry* and also encountered well-known artists like Webb Pierce and Marty Robbins.

Vi Petty didn't think too much of Buddy Holly (the "e" had now been dropped from Buddy's last name because of a clerical misprint at Decca records), or the Crickets when she first laid eyes on them in the Norman Petty Studio sometime around 1956. The youths, by all accounts, were clean-cut budding musicians, but typified the rebellious look present in young people during those days; however, having grown up in the Panhandle of Texas, they were respectful, courteous and soon won the hearts of both Petty and his classically trained musical wife. They often wore identical white t-shirts, blue jeans and donned slicked-back hair reminiscent of James Dean's insurgent appearance. Their professional demeanor in the studio and fervent love of music perhaps intrigued both Petty and Vi, who at this time undoubtedly knew very little about rock 'n' roll and the unique style of music created and performed by Holly and his friends. Vi Petty noted, "They didn't look like musicians, but when they played, they showed otherwise." Holly and the boys were becoming seasoned studio musicians after all.

Elvis Presley had been on the scene for only a couple of short years and was entertaining audiences with his upbeat southern, perhaps gritty compilation of country meets rhythm 'n' blues sound. Just two years earlier, the guys from the not yet formed Crickets opened for Presley in Lubbock, Texas at the Fair Park and imaginably became hooked on Elvis' performance, style and newfangled sound. After their fallout with Decca records, the boys were looking for a new music-based home and quickly found it after meeting Norman Petty, who, although less than ten years older than the trio, was able to provide stability, mentorship and a creative work environment the boys were seeking.

Having already seen the success affiliated with Buddy Knox and the Rhythm Orchids, Jimmy Bowen, and Roy Orbison after their recording sessions at his Clovis studio, Norman was ready for his next big soundtrack. Likewise, Buddy Holly and his recently dubbed band, The Crickets, were prepared for a new beginning. Just a few short years earlier in the 1950's, a popular Cleveland disc jockey at WJW known primarily for spinning jazz and pop hits of the day, Alan Freed, had publicly coined the term rock 'n' roll to describe the spiritual up-tempo music primarily targeted to black audiences of the late 1940's and early 1950's.

Little did many know at the time, but racial barriers were about to be crossed as white artists would adopt the style and sound of their black counterparts. Freed would later be quoted in the 1956 film *Rock, Rock, Rock* saying, "rock and roll is a river of music that has absorbed many streams: rhythm and blues, jazz, rag time, cowboy songs, country songs, folk songs. All have contributed to the beat." This new genre fit Buddy Holly and the Crickets and Norman Petty to a T.

Technology was leaping forward. Solid-body guitars could now be plugged into 100-watt amplifiers creating the newer and louder electric sound of the day. The Norman Petty Studio sported the best acoustics and the latest equipment tailor-made for this promising innovative style of music. Innovative? Yes. Would the new creation of music be well received by the general post-World War II adult? Not yet.

By the mid-1950's, most of our soldiers had returned from Europe. The United States was experiencing a period of accomplishment as many families relished new prosperities like home ownership and plentiful work opportunities for both men and women, giving rise to a unique breed of individual- the American teenager. With many families having adequate income and ample opportunities for teens of the day to work, slick, fresh automobiles gave a new sense of freedom to American adolescents. The days of the massive home radio were vanishing and music could now be heard from more portable-style radios, jukeboxes and more importantly, car radios. Ice-cream shops, soda shops, sock hops and drive-in diners became hot spots for gathering teens to meet with friends and listen to their favorite music. This unprecedented pump of rock 'n' roll was considered dangerous by many, but would soon win the hearts of teenagers as well as their adult counterparts throughout America.

A far cry from rock 'n' roll, Charlie Phillips continued polishing his skills as a country music singer. The latest craze of music sounded interesting to Charlie, but his heart lay with the traditional, time-tested sounds of country music greats. His heroes really were cowboys and the pure sound achieved by a few guitar chords and smooth vocals would drive him to press forward with his own style of music. Country music itself was progressing as well.

Up until this time, drums were considered taboo in many country music circles, even though western swing big band leader, Bob Wills, had added a drummer to his Texas Playboys as early as

1935. By 1955, drums were being added to most country music groups; however, the stigma of the impure sound were kept out of the public eye as promoters of the *Grand Ole Opry* and the *Louisiana Hayride* sometimes hid their drummers offstage during live recorded performances. The dobro guitar, an alternative to the Hawaiian steel guitar, was now introduced into country music by the famed group, Flatt and Scruggs, performers of the hit song, "The Ballad of Jed Clampett." Innovation and opportunity would soon lead Charlie Phillips back into the Petty Studio to record yet another record.

Both "Put Your Arms Around Me" and the flipside of the acetate record, "Courtin' In The Rain" were still being broadcast on the airwaves of the New Mexico and Texas Panhandle regions thanks to Charlie's buddy, Jimmy Self. Charlie was proud to hear his singing on the radio almost daily and hankered to get more records made. With Norman Petty's studio being incessantly booked with young new artists, Charlie thought perhaps he could slip across town to Bob Tucker's Garage Studio to record a couple of new songs he had written and with which he was relentlessly tinkering.

However, as luck would have it, an opening arose at Petty's studio and in early 1956, Charlie took his best friends and primary band mates, Pete Wallace, Jimmy Schell, Dudley Hughes and Gerald Brown to the Petty recording studio. It was here the boys recorded "One Faded Rose" and a demo of an upbeat song Charlie named "Sugartime" for the very first time. Petty loved the songs, but he didn't like the musical accompaniment so he suggested Charlie return at a later date to use "different, more accomplished" musicians- something that would cost Charlie more money. The first recording session of "Sugartime" produced a test-acetate; whereby copies were manufactured allowing Charlie to send duplicates to radio stations, record companies or anyone else that would listen. The first known acetates of "Sugartime" were recorded on an Audiodisc and a Soundcraft recording disc. The earliest date printed on the recording is April 4, 1956, signifying Charlie and the guys recorded the very first demo of "Sugartime" on or before this date. It was immediately registered with the U.S. Copyright Office on April 25, 1956, under the name of Charles Don Phillips.

Since the Petty Studio had a comfortable apartment at its rear, as well as an apartment over the adjacent building, and provided a freestyle artistic environment, Buddy and the guys had all but moved into the location working on a variety of songs they had been fiddling with. Just a year earlier, Holly and Allison had written a song inspired by the words of John Wayne in the classic movie, *The Searchers*, called "That'll Be the Day." The song had previously been recorded in Nashville for Decca Records on June 22, 1956, but like many of the group's songs at the time, "That'll Be the Day" had possibly been ignored by record executives. The song remained unissued until September 2, 1957, when Decca definitively released the tune. Petty, however, re-recorded the song and continued working with the young men on other creative projects. Who could have known Petty and the group had just recorded a rock 'n' roll classic?

It's safe to say the Crickets and their front man had become somewhat permanent fixtures at the Norman Petty Studios. Groups of musicians started to hear about the genius of Norman Petty and began pilgrimages to the tiny New Mexico town with hopes of recording with Petty and even perhaps having the next million record-selling tune. Gangs of all different makes and models migrated through the Petty Studio in those days, but it was the Crickets who were selected by Petty to unofficially fill-in as staff-musicians. It's important to realize that although Holly and the band were seasoned young musicians and had performed a variety of tours and shows, they were still largely unknown to the general populace. Petty not only recognized their raw talent, but also acknowledged their work ethic and ability to blend smoothly musically with other artists of varying talents. Quite naturally, they worked well with others.

Billy Walker was a country music singer touring the country on a Columbia music circuit and was contacted by his label with a request he cover the song "On My Mind Again" written by Slim Willett, Dean Beard and Elmer Ray. He was unable to return to Nashville while touring and so on a stop to perform in Clovis, the record label contracted the Norman Petty Studio directing Walker to record the song there. Billy was an eastern New Mexico native, who as a teenager had won a talent contest and was hired by the KICA radio station in Clovis where he performed his own radio show.

After jumpstarting his music career, Walker left Clovis and joined an upcoming show in Dallas, Texas called the *Big "D" Jamboree*. He would later land a recording contract with Columbia Records and become a member of the *Louisiana Hayride* in Shreveport, Louisiana where some folks say he, along with Slim Whitman were partially responsible for Elvis Presley's first appearance on the radio program. By 1955, Walker teamed up with Elvis and a young man named Tillman Franks and toured through West Texas before he moved on to become a cast member on Red Foley's *Ozark Jubilee*. Walker became outrageously popular in the Nashville music scene, securing him a regular spot on the *Grand Ole Opry* later in his career.

It would be at the Petty recording session Walker would meet Buddy Holly for the first time, as he and the guys were the studio musicians hired by Norman to support various bands who were recording at the Petty studio. The plan was to record up to four songs. Buddy recorded "Words of Love" and "Mailman Bring Me No More Blues" and Billy recorded his cover of "On My Mind Again." Norman fancied some backup vocals on Billy's song, so Holly and one or more of the Crickets were hired to harmonize in the background. By the end of summer, "On My Mind Again" had worked its way up to the No. 12 spot on *Billboard's* country disc-jockey poll. Buddy and the Crickets were increasingly proving they could not only create great music on their own, but they could work with some of the best musicians in the business.

During the same month of March in 1957, Roy Orbison returned to Clovis for yet another recording session, and he brought with him a future favorite singing group. Roy had met the guys who had formed the group, The Roses, while attending Odessa Junior College together. They had already traveled with Roy to Memphis, Tennessee to Sam Phillips' Recording Studio where they performed backup singing on two of Orbison's songs, "Devil Doll" and "Sweet and Easy to Love." David Bingham, Bo Clarke, Robert Linville and

Ray Rush were a skillful performing group out of the West Texas region.

It was on this trip to Clovis The Roses officially met the mastermind in the middle of nowhere known as Norman Petty. David Bingham recalls, "I thought Norman was an extremely young person to be the owner of a recording studio... Norman was a very well-mannered, soft spoken, and easy going man." A lifelong professional camaraderie would eventually develop between the group and Norman, as The Roses would soon be added to an extensive list of recording accomplishments through the Norman Petty Studio. It was during this same trip The Roses would most likely meet Buddy Holly for the first time, striking up a phenomenal, yet short-lived musical bond.

With an onslaught of new artists traveling from far and wide to record at the Petty Studio, Norman continued business as usual. The Norman Petty Trio's song, "Almost Paradise" was being covered by some well-known acts and was receiving a lot of airplay throughout the nation. The band itself was already considered a triumph; however, as sales of the song and sheet music grew, Norman Petty would be thrust into the limelight when ABC-Paramount notified him and announced he had received one of the most coveted awards in the music industry, a BMI certificate. This achievement was often considered a songwriter's greatest trophy in 1957.

After winning the desirable BMI award and with his close association surrounding the triumphant recording of Buddy Knox's "Party Doll," Norman began to culminate valuable contacts within the music business. It's a fact, no matter how great a musician or band is, no matter how wonderful their music sounds and no matter how terrific their recordings are, the odds of their music ever being heard by the general public were next to nothing, *unless* one had a principal connection in the music business.

By the mid-1950's, the five top record labels were Capitol, Columbia, Decca, Mercury and RCA Victor- the fundamental forces behind most of the music heard in America. Without a connection within one of these great dynamisms, one's music would simply fall on deaf ears. This practice is still the status quo even in today's hectic billion-dollar world of music.

The traditional "Almost Paradise" had been placed with one of the largest publishing giants in the industry, Southern Music, a business owned by Ralph Peer. Because of the song's enormous success, a relationship crowned between Norman Petty and a Peer-Southern Music executive by the name of Murray Deutch. Deutch respected Norman's professionalism both as a pop performer and as a record producer and gave Norman the opportunity to sign a "sole selling agent" agreement between Petty's NorVaJak Music company and a subsidiary of the Peer-International company called Melody Lane Publications. They would split the profits fifty-fifty. This simple relationship and "connection" within the music industry giant would soon open the door for the small, primarily regional Norman Petty Studio to do something few studios in the nation could. Pretty much, up until now, Norman Petty could record some of the finest music, but getting the songs heard on radios across the country was almost unmanageable. From his little enclave in Clovis, Petty would now promote songs internationally with recognized national record labels.

It's safe to say, Deutch's new business relationship with NorVaJak would soon put him at a distinct advantage over his competition. He had the foresight to understand rock 'n' roll would soon emerge as one of the hottest new genres in America. From his swanky office in the Brill Building located on West 49th and Broadway in New York City, Deutch could stretch halfway across the country and gain a stronghold on the untouched talent radiating from Clovis and West Texas. Deutch had a close relationship with the Coral/Brunswick record label folks and would soon begin sending them unbridled talent via Norman Petty.

Since recording "That'll Be the Day," Buddy and the Crickets had been painstakingly writing and sound-tracking other songs. At the direction of Norman Petty, the group had been recording tirelessly and had been stockpiling their tunes inside the vault at the studio. Several songs were recorded with the hopes of releasing them. A few ditties in the extended repertoire of songs amassed in the Petty treasury included: "Words of Love," "Mailman Bring Me No More Blues," "Maybe Baby," "Last Night," "I'm Looking for Someone to Love," "Brown-Eyed Handsome Man" and "Peggy Sue." With a variety of songs under their belt, it would give them some ammunition if they ever landed a record deal.

While primarily living in the apartment at the back of Norman's studio, Buddy and the guys worked with other artists and became sort of the private studio band. By playing on other folk's songs, they could earn some much-needed cash paid in exchange for their contributions to other artists as well as hone their skills in the studio environment. Exchanges were commonly made between many of the close-knit Clovis or West Texas music communities, including Buddy and the Crickets to "scratch other's backs and in return, they'd scratch yours." Buddy Knox and Jimmy Bowen, two guys no one had heard of a year before, were still basking in the triumph of their hits, "Party Doll" and "I'm Sticking with You."

On April 7, 1957, Knox, Bowen and The Rhythm Orchids appeared on *The Ed Sullivan Show*, the biggest variety show on television at that time. One cannot help but wonder if many of the young artists who were working so hard on their music didn't witness the appearance of Knox and Bowen on *The Ed Sullivan Show* and think, "I should be up there." The highly driven, highly motivated and highly talented Buddy Holly must have been itching to squirm free of his cage.

Charlie Phillips and his young friends thought their songs, "Sugartime" and "One Faded Rose," which they'd recorded months earlier at the Petty studio, were good enough for the big time. However, Charlie's employer at the radio station, Pop Echols, and DJ Jimmy Self were not convinced. Something just didn't seem right. Pop had an ear for music and made Charlie an offer. Echols would pay to have the two songs re-recorded in a more professional environment under the tutelage of Norman Petty, but in exchange, Charlie would put Pop's name as co-writer on the "Sugartime" song to recoup any initial expenses Pop incurred. Charlie excitedly agreed.

Pop Echols, with Charlie's permission, took on sort of a management role as the two agreed if Charlie was going to start making records, then he'd need someone to manage him. Pop had always been so good to the boy from West Texas and had always been somewhat of a fatherly business figure, that a professional relationship seemed wise at the time. After all, it was Pop who had noticed Charlie's talent onstage, and it was Pop who gave the young hick his first job in the radio business. Echols supported Charlie's ideas and he was about to bankroll Charlie's music career. Echols then called up his business acquaintance, Norman Petty, in April of 1957 and arranged an appointment for Charlie to record "Sugartime" and "One Faded Rose" again; however, time was short for Petty as he was inundated with the numerous artists pouring into his studio. The guys all decided to record just one song Charlie had written called, "Be My Bride," which he and his band members had previously recorded at the Petty studio with Charlie's original band.

By all accounts, Norman had a lot of irons in the fire and probably had little or no interest in recording more hillbilly music, but business was business and Pop was not only a paying customer, he was also was a beneficial party for Norman's studio because he owned the local KCLV radio station and often traded services in exchange for advertising. On that warm spring afternoon, Charlie and his band members enthusiastically began loading their instruments into their automobiles in preparation for an evening recording session. It was an exciting time for the boys.

When Charlie and the guys walked into the studio on 7th Street, Norman and Vi's secretary, Norma Jean Berry, politely greeted them. She directed the boys where to setup in the studio and offered them some refreshments. The guys hauled their instruments in from the bustling road outside and began arranging them in the studio. Pete Wallace opened his guitar case and began fiddling around with the strings, Dudley Hughes worked to get his bass set up and prepared as Gerald Brown started to haul his drum set in; however, there was already a set near the back wall of the main studio room so Gerald wondered if he could just use those drums. Jimmy Schell didn't come with the guys on this particular gig.

After haphazardly getting most of their instruments into place, Norman Petty, who had been conspicuously absent, quietly walked into the control room and made a few adjustments to the machinery. He walked out of the control booth and said hello to the boys as he began rearranging all of the instruments and microphones. He agreed to allow Gerald to use the drum set already established in the studio.

No matter who was recording in Norman's studio, everything had to be formulated perfectly. No one knew how to arrange the studio setup better than Norman. He knew every instrument placement, the best mics to use and where, the perfect positioning of the musicians and every soldered piece of the recording equipment. He then silently left the main room and took a seat in the control room, positioning himself where he could reach and adjust the instruments while peering through the small window dividing the two rooms from each other. He pressed the speaker button piped into the main room and calmly said, "Ok, let's get started."

The band composed themselves for a moment, and just like they'd practiced, began the song. Charlie belts out, "I've been looking for days and I can't find my girl. I've been looking so hard, that my heart is in a whirl!" Suddenly, over the loudspeaker right on top of the song was Norman's unruffled voice, "Uh, Charlie. Uh, Charlie? Listen, the microphone can pick you up just fine. There's no need to sing so loudly into the mic. Ok?" It had never dawned on Charlie that after spending years on a tractor and forcing himself to sing over the roar of the engine, Charlie had become accustomed to singing with a bit of a yell. Other than the live concerts they performed and the two other times they had ever been in a studio, Charlie and the guys were proving they were truly greenhorns when it came to studio recording. Once Charlie composed his voice, he once again stepped up to the imported, German-made Telefunken microphone as they began playing "Be My Bride" again.

Once the boys had completed the song, they began smiling and congratulating themselves on a job well done. They were thinking, "Well, that's a wrap" so they might as well get packed up and move on to another project. However, Norman had a special surprise for the guys. Always the perfectionist, Norman silently walked out of the control room and without saying a word, slipped right beside the guys and traveled through the door leading to the back of the building. After waiting for what seemed like forever, Norman walked back in and told Charlie, "I'd like to try something new." Suddenly, a couple of lanky guys popped through the door like they owned the place. Norman introduced Charlie to Buddy Holly and Niki Sullivan.

"When I first laid eyes on Buddy Holly, I thought he was a big star. Just he was... he carried himself- he gave off the look of someone who was some big-time musician," Charlie describes after meeting Holly on that April night in Clovis. It might be significant to note, Holly or the Crickets didn't yet have any big hits on the radio. They were pretty much anonymous at this time and yet, Holly and Petty had created quite a stir around town as Buddy had performed with the now famous Elvis Presley and countless other musicians. Charlie was impressed with Holly from the get-go.

After the guys all shook hands and said their howdy-dos, Norman explained to Charlie that he liked the song they had just played, but it was missing something. He asked Buddy and Niki to listen to the song again and give their advice on how the tune could be improved upon. Buddy was a quick learner when it came to just about anything musical, so it didn't take long before he, Niki and Norman came up with ideas for the unique backup beat to accompany Charlie's song. They began the song again, but this time with Buddy and Niki's suggestions. After a few glitches, the song was performed flawlessly. Norman was pleased with the outcome of "Be My Bride" because it wasn't the usual hokey country song he was accustomed to hearing, but a very upbeat, almost familiar sounding melody, which probably appealed to Norman's pop music sensibility. If "Sugartime" knocked on the door of rockabilly, "Be My Bride" opened the door and walked in. It would be only three short months until Norman would get Charlie scheduled in again to record a couple of more songs.

In May of 1957, Petty presented Buddy Holly and Jerry Allison's song, "That'll Be the Day" to his contact on the east coast, Murray Deutch. It was Norman's hope he could help Buddy and the guys land a recording contract with a big label. Deutch had a close connection with Coral Records and happened to be one of the biggest A&R directors in the business. Deutch's friend and colleague, Bob Thiele, took a listen to "That'll Be the Day" at the prompting of Deutch. Thiele wrote years later in his autobiography *What a Wonderful World*:

> When Murray played the recordings for me, I became rabid as soon as I heard "That'll Be the Day." I said, 'Jesus Christ, this is fantastic,' and wanted to release it immediately. (The record label wasn't sold on the idea of releasing what they considered hillbilly garbage)... 'Meanwhile, I was enthusiastically playing Holly and the Crickets for a lot of people in the company, and everyone again said, 'This record absolutely cannot come out on Coral. It'll destroy the image of the label. We have great and beloved artists like Lawrence Welk, Debbie Reynolds, the McGuire Sisters, Teresa Brewer, and now you want to come out with this horrible music by something called 'The Crickets."

Thiele was ultimately able to convince the folks at the record company to sign Buddy, and the band known only at the time as The Chirping Crickets, to contracts with both the Coral and Brunswick labels. "That'll Be the Day" was pressed and released on the Brunswick label. It wouldn't be too long until the song reached radio stations throughout America although it wasn't going to be an easy task. Norman Petty had now proved he could get artists who recorded at his small studio in the middle-of-nowhere-America, a record deal. The connection between Clovis and New York had been sealed.

On June 29, 1957, Buddy and the band popped back into the studio to record more songs. With a potential hit song on the horizon and a record deal in place, the guys would begin recording songs in addition to the several they had already stockpiled in the Petty vault.

On this trip to Clovis, they would record the songs, "I'm Gonna Love You," "Peggy Sue," "Listen to Me" and "Oh Boy!" which would be some of the most prolific music they'd ever create.

After Roy Orbison had virtually introduced the unknown band from the Odessa area, The Roses, to Norman Petty, they had become quite the fixture at the Petty studio. With Buddy and the Crickets signing recording contracts and the possibility of them hitting the national spotlight, Norman increasingly began using The Roses in the studio as a backup band or staff musicians. They backed up a variety of groups, but most notably Buddy Holly songs like, "It's So Easy," "Think It Over," "Lonesome Tears" and "Fool's Paradise." The Roses signed a contract with Petty making them the official staff musicians at the Petty studio.

The Norman Petty Studio was bustling with entertainers, yet Petty somehow found the time to juggle numerous recording sessions and now, adding fuel to the fire, he had become the manager for Buddy Holly and the Crickets. True to his word and after the successful recording of "Be My Bride," Norman scheduled Charlie Phillips to record his newly written songs sometime in the evening of early July 1957.

The two songs Charlie really wanted to record were "One Faded Rose" and "Sugartime," but at the prompting of his new manager, Pop Echols, a fancier version needed to be cut in order to increase both songs' appeal. Once again, Charlie and his band members hauled their instruments over to the Petty studio and unloaded them into the workspace. Charlie showed up wearing a white V-neck short-sleeved t-shirt rolled up a bit on the arms, reminiscent of how Buddy and the guys were wearing it in those days. Since Pop was paying for the session, he attended as managerial support. In true Pop style, he arrived in a full dress suit with a white button-down shirt and tie. His hair was slicked back, and he donned his trademark sporty mustache. Almost always present on Pop were gold and diamond rings and an unlit cigar in hand. Norman, of course, would have never allowed smoking in his studio-domain.

The guys set up just like last time and Norman began his usual recording regimen; however, after a couple of trial runs, Norman stopped the studio session. With Pop's money on the line, it's possible he talked Norman into upping the ante, or more likely, it appears the trained ears of Petty had something much bigger in mind for these two songs.

With so many more-seasoned and perhaps more talented musicians at his disposal, Norman gathered a variety of guys who were scattered throughout the compound. Norman rounded up Buddy Holly and Jerry Allison. Jack Vaughn, the guitarists for the Norman Petty Trio, was in town and was asked to join the session. An accomplished steel guitar player and Roswell, New Mexico radio personality, Jimmy Blakely, was also at the studio doing some recording work with Norman and was asked to join in on the session. George Atwood was an unbelievable bass player who had worked with Buddy Knox and Roy Orbison and had been working with the Petty studio as a session musician. He too was persuaded to join the group. Even Vi Petty was called from their home to run down to the studio and help play the piano. Suddenly, Charlie Phillips found himself with all new musicians and his own guys were eliminated from the recording session. Hindsight always being twenty-twenty, Norman Petty knew exactly what he was doing. He was there to create the best music possible and that's precisely what he did.

Charlie didn't know how to read or write musical notes very well. To bring the band up to speed, he played and sang the songs so the other guys in the room could get a feel for the compositions. Odis Echols created some lead sheets to help the other musicians with the arrangements, but much of the music was played by-ear. After a few practice runs, under Charlie's direction, everyone involved felt they could recreate the sounds Charlie was after.

The first song recorded was "One Faded Rose" which was a slow, calm cowboy-type song reminiscent of Charlie's hero, Hank Snow, or perhaps a sluggish Hank Williams tune, which Charlie had written about the loss of one's favorite gal. Heard on the record is Charlie singing in almost a calm whine, accompanied by the pleasant sound of Norman on the Hammond organ and Vi lightly keying her piano. Jimmy Blakely casually slid his steel guitar while Jack Vaughn strummed guitar and George Atwood plucked his bass quietly. An almost silent snare drum can be heard from Jerry Allison as Buddy Holly accompanies Charlie's voice.

At the end of the song, Vi Petty was almost drawn to tears. The music had been so beautifully executed, probably imparting feelings from her training and career in classical music, drawing from the sounds of this country ballad. She glanced over at Charlie and gave a reassuring smile of approval. The guys all relaxed for a bit while Norman entered the control room to listen to the final take of the song. After what seemed like forever, Norman announced from the control booth, "Ok everyone, that's good."

Of course "Sugartime" was inversely written and would need to be recorded much differently than "One Faded Rose." After a break, the guys all regrouped in the studio. It was approaching around 1 a.m. or so, and everyone was attempting to get his or her second wind. Needless to say, the guys were all tired. Early morning would soon be approaching, and it was important to finish the next song before normal-working folks woke up and began their bustling journey to work. Buddy Holly was going to play lead guitar on "Sugartime" so some practice was needed to get the riff just right. No one knew history was in the making, and the song they would all create together would become a standard music classic.

Charlie began working with the fast-learning Buddy on the opening guitar riff. He talked with Buddy about the beginning guitar solo that excitedly starts the up-tempo song, "Sugartime." Charlie asked Buddy if he could begin the song out as he mouthed the beat, "Dida- dida- dit- dit- dida- dida- dit- dit- dida- dida- dit- dit- ta." Norman asks Buddy over the loudspeaker, "Buddy, can you do it?" With a quick wit, Buddy replies, "Sure, Dida- dida- dit- dit- dida- dida- dit- dit- dida- dida- dit- dit- ta," as he too mouthed the words to the intro instead of playing it on his guitar. The guys all had a good chuckle and Holly immediately played the riff on his guitar. The band all commenced their first recording of "Sugartime" and then Norman removed his headphones and quietly announced over the loudspeaker again, "Charlie, you don't have to sing that loud. The microphone will pick you up." Once again, Charlie had to dial his voice back.

The fast moving "Sugartime" was recorded, and because of the efforts of the rock 'n' rollers who sacrificed their time and talents to help Charlie fashion a masterpiece, Charlie had written and created not only a classic, but also another rockabilly composition. Coming from a country-only background, all Charlie knew was country music and "Sugartime" was indeed written as a fast paced country ditty, but would soon take on a life of its own. At the end of a long night of recording, Charlie thought to himself, "My God!" as he was quite surprised by the length of time spent recording just *two* songs.

His only other recording sessions were accomplished by playing a couple of times through per song while recording and voila, they were done. This would virtually never happen during one of Norman's recording sessions as he would keep the guys playing over and over again until the song, in his mind, was perfect. "Norman Petty was a perfectionist. I mean, he could hear one little thing that wasn't right, we'd need to cut it over," remembers Phillips. Pop Echols stayed with Charlie and the group until the early hours of the morning while Norman wrapped up the final session.

As promised, to help Pop Echols recoup his initial investment in Charlie, Pop's name was placed on the record as co-writer, even though he hadn't contributed anything to the composition other than financial backing and moral support. This was perhaps a very common practice, though controversial, in the early music-recording days. It was not uncommon for a manager or producer, no matter how unethical it might sound, to add his name to a song receiving a cut of the sales should the song ever become successful. Although the initial recording of "Sugartime" was already registered with the U.S. Copyright Office under Charlie's name alone, on September 18, 1957 Pop had the new recording re-registered under Charlie's name and his name.

Shortly one month after recording "Sugartime," Norman Petty and Murray Deutch prompted Buddy Holly and the Crickets to travel to The Howard Theater in Washington, D.C. It would be around this time the band experienced widespread exposure. Murray Deutch and Bob Thiele were both masters of promotion, and in August of 1957, sales of "That'll Be the Day" skyrocketed. All of Jerry Allison and Buddy Holly's hard work and discipline (with the accompaniment of several other artists) would soon create the allure and legend of Buddy Holly and the Crickets.

The Crickets began touring the country on *The Biggest Show of Stars of 1957* tour. Since the triumph of "That'll Be the Day," the boys had the privilege of traveling with some of their great idols like Fats Domino, Chuck Berry, Eddie Cochran and Little Richard. The tour would take them to Tulsa, Oklahoma where on September 28, 1957, the Norman Petty Trio was booked nearby at the Officers Club at Tinker Air Force Base in Oklahoma City, Oklahoma.

Norman wanted to record their performance, so he took his portable recording equipment. Since Buddy Holly and the Crickets were in proximity to Norman, they met him later that evening at the base. Buddy had a few more songs they had been fiddling with, so Norman set up his recording equipment and PA system in the main hall. In the wee hours of September 29, Buddy and the Crickets with the assistance of Norman Petty recorded "Maybe Baby," "An Empty Cup," "You've Got Love" and "Rock Me Baby." The Crickets returned to their tour. Norman took the tapes back to the studio and asked a band named The Picks to record backup vocals for the songs. It would prove to be a celebrated recording session.

Chapter 6
Sugar in the Morning

With the recent success of "That'll be the Day," Norman Petty recognized running his operation solely from the Clovis studio in New Mexico was ineffective and it was now necessary to have a proper base operation in New York City, closer to the action. Petty realized he needed a loyal associate to deal with licensing agents, promoters, publishing issues and tour engagements so he opened up a NorVaJak Music office in New York. No longer a greenhorn and now a novice, Petty hired a friend of both he and Vi, Jo Harper, who had little experience in the music business. She was, however, someone he could trust to handle operations when he wasn't in the Big Apple. Jo, or "Josie" had attended college at the University of New Mexico and had now become quite the Greenwich Village socialite. She would become an even more trusted friend and ally for Norman as the years progressed and handled much of the business for the Norman Petty Agency from the New York office.

Decca Records was the parent company for both the Coral and Brunswick record labels. Bob Thiele worked industriously as the artists and repertoire (A&R) man and additionally, Norman Wienstroer began working with Norman Petty as the director of sales connection for the record label. The trio of Murray Deutch, Bob Thiele and Norman Wienstroer were all seasoned veterans in the business who understood excellent records needed massive promotion. And promote they did.

Working closely with Southern Music Publishing, the guys developed a cooperative relationship where Norman Petty would produce the music in his Clovis studio and Deutch, Thiele or Wienstroer would polish the end product seeing it through to completion. Petty could now build songs from his hometown, and the New York offices would stimulate and develop songs to be distributed and promoted nationwide or even perhaps worldwide. Artists from across America began their pilgrimage to the tiny town of Clovis with hopes of becoming the next success story out of the Petty studio.

Norman Petty had now worked with some great artists, and he felt Charlie Phillips would be a terrific pawn to introduce into the country music market. Deutch trusted Petty's opinion, so Norman took the recently recorded demo record of "One Faded Rose" and "Sugartime" to New York with hopes of creating another star performer. Deutch loved the songs immediately and thought the crisp sound of "One Faded Rose" would be a good fit with Coral Records. Additionally, the fun rockabilly sound of "Sugartime" would certainly be a crowd pleaser.

A thought-provoking story as rumor has it, Sonny Curtis was at Norman Petty's home in 1957 when Bob Thiele was in town for a stopover. Sonny sang Charlie's version of "Sugartime" to Bob who took Charlie's record back with him to New York and straightaway began arranging for the McGuire Sisters to cover the tune in New York with Neil Hefti arranging the song. According to speculation, Thiele had the Sisters originally cut "Sugartime" with a sixteen-piece big band but eventually stripped the accompaniment down to just a rhythm section. Whether Petty *or* Thiele took the song back to the Big Apple is unknown, but it would be Thiele who got the ball rolling with Coral.

By November of 1957, Coral released both melodies on the same record and promoted the songs to the country music industry. "One Faded Rose" and "Sugartime" began to crawl up the charts almost immediately giving Charlie his first national attention. The ole' country boy from Farwell, Texas was now being heard on radios and jukeboxes throughout America.

It was of course "Sugartime" that traveled up the country music charts the fastest. Within a few short weeks, the song had reached a position somewhere around the thirty-something spot on the coast-to-coast charts while enjoying higher success on some regional charts. The song was mildly popular in country music circles. Murray Deutch and Bob Thiele were, however, masterminding an alternative plan for "Sugartime." Unbeknownst to both Charlie and Norman Petty, they were covertly communicating with a famous group of gals who were already contracted under the Coral label.

The Ohio-born McGuire Sisters were an accomplished melodic trio of siblings who began their singing careers at the First Church of God in Miamisburg, Ohio where they regularly sang for weddings, funerals and church revivals. Within a decade, the girls branched out and began singing at veteran's hospitals and, like the Norman Petty Trio, entertained at various military bases. They quickly became proficient enough to sign and become recording artists with Coral Records by 1952.

During that same year, Christine, Dorothy and Phyllis McGuire appeared on *Arthur Godfrey's Talent Scouts* and were so well liked, Godfrey hired them for his other shows where they regularly performed for the next seven years. The dazzling girls were tailor-made for television as they moved beautifully when they sang and danced to choreographed productions for the television audience. They unquestionably became a national sensation and were instantly loved by the universal public.

By 1954, the trio had recorded numerous songs for Coral Records and had their first big hit with "Goodnite, Sweetheart, Goodnite." The following year saw great success as their sweet and melodic song, "Sincerely" propelled to the No. 1 single in the country. "Sugartime," as sung by Charlie Phillips, had been on the charts for several weeks when the record executives at Coral prompted the sisters to do a cover-version of the song.

Bob Thiele introduced the idea of the traditional sisters recording the country tune with a more pop version and contacted Norman Petty. Norman, in return, contacted Pop Echols. No one could conceivably argue any reasons against making this type of arrangement; after all, the McGuire Sisters were at what seemed like the top of their musical game. They had already accomplished a No. 1 single reaching the charts a couple of years previously. The arrangement was struck and Pop filled Charlie in on the agreement. "Why not?" he thought at the time without paying any more attention to it.

Lots of folks don't realize, but Charlie's original version of "Sugartime" had marginally different lyrics than the version sung by the McGuire Sisters. It's not clear which studio person made this astute decision, but after working with the song in the studio, it's likely one of the executives at Coral Records thought some of the lyrics needed to be changed in order to appeal more to the popular music following the gals had already amassed over their clean-cut careers. "Sugartime" imaginably needed a lighter, more pleasant sound. Most likely someone within the Coral network reworked the tune, changing the music composition; however, there is one other rumored possibility.

A dissimilar account of the lyric change involves a young musician who traveled to the Petty Studio to record an original record entitled, "Hypnotized." Terry Noland was a talented Lubbock musician who hooked up with Petty around 1957 and landed a record deal with Brunswick Records through Norman Petty's connections, Murray Deutch and Bob Thiele. Noland heard Charlie's song and anticipated recording it, thus he and Norman began work on re-writing the lighter version. Noland would quickly find out the song had been flagged and was destined for the McGuire Sisters, so recording it would be fruitless. Whether the McGuire Sisters' studio musicians at Coral changed it, or Terry Noland did, is unclear; nevertheless, it *was* re-written and the new version would become the staple of American society.

The original version of "Sugartime," as written and sung by Phillips, was arranged as follows:

Sugar in the morning
Sugar in the evening

Sugar at suppertime
Be my little sugar
And love me all the time

Like the stars above me
I will always love you
And call you mine
So be my little honey and love me all the time
Won't you say you love me?
Like the stars above
And forever be mine
In a haven of love

Well, honey in the morning
Honey in the evening
Honey at suppertime
Be my little honey
And love me all the time

(Guitar riff)
You went away
Last Saturday
And you thought
You'd make me pay
Well you did
But now you're back
So we'll never
Leave our little shack

Well, honey in the morning
Honey in the evening
Honey at suppertime
Be my little honey
And love me all the time

"Sugartime" by Charlie Phillips and Odis Echols Copyright © 1956, 1957 by MPL Communications Inc. Copyright Renewed Used by Permission All Rights Reserved

After the lyrics were re-written, the girls recorded the following version in 1957:

Well, sugar in the morning
Sugar in the evening
Sugar at suppertime
Be my little sugar
And love me all the time
Honey in the morning
Honey in the evening
Honey at suppertime
So be my little honey
And love me all the time

Put your arms around me
And swear by stars above
You'll be mine forever
In a heaven of love

Sugar in the morning
Sugar in the evening
Sugar at suppertime
Be my little sugar
And love me all the time

Now sugartime
Is anytime
That you're near
'Cause you're so dear
So don't you roam
Just be my honeycomb
And live in a heaven of love

Sugar in the morning
Sugar in the evening
Sugar at suppertime
Be my little sugar
And love me all the time

Be my little sugar
And love me (love me)
All (all), all the time

Sugartime, Sugartime, SUGARTIME!

"Sugartime" by Charlie Phillips and Odis Echols Copyright © 1956, 1957 by MPL Communications Inc. Copyright Renewed Used by Permission All Rights Reserved

Of course, the latter version would develop into the rendering that would become the standard version heard and adored by most Americans. The cleaner, sweeter style was recorded in New York City in late 1957 with another colorful McGuire song, "Banana Split" on the flipside of the record, which was made available for immediate release. Within weeks, the song rose on the national pop charts and for the third and last time, "Sugartime" was registered yet again with the U.S. Copyright Office on December 17, 1957. It's possible either Coral Records or perhaps the McGuire Sisters' management re-recorded the copyright to cement their claim on possible future royalties generated. The song was then released onto the airwaves.

On December 9, 1957 *Billboard* stated under the McGuire Sisters headline: "Sugartime' is the strongest by the chicks recently. It's a fine cover of this semi-folk rocker, which was first cut by Charlie Phillips. It could put them back on top." Then *Cashbox Magazine* noted, "The McGuire Sisters delve into the country music catalog and come up with a choice gem that should come up with a heap of loot. It's far away the most inviting side the gals have offered in months and should be a tremendous hit. 'Sugartime' is a cornball foot stomping novelty with contagious melody chanted with wonderful harmony. Great sound which jocks will go for in a big way."

On December 23, 1957 *Billboard* reported action on the McGuire's version was heavy in all markets and the song was destined to be a smash hit. It entered the pop charts the following week. By January of 1958, some newspapers reported "Sugartime" as one of their most requested songs alongside "At the Hop" and Buddy and the Crickets' "Peggy Sue" and "Oh Boy." It had already worked its way up the charts into the top-10 position. Phones were ringing off the wall as teenagers throughout America called their local radio stations requesting their favorite new song. "The girls have invaded the country field with this one: 'Sugartime' is a corny but promising novelty item, while the flip side has definite teenage appeal," wrote one California newspaper. The journalist who wrote the blurb probably had no idea what was in store for the song.

Both with the sale of records and sheet music, as well as the continuous airplay, "Sugartime" reached its destination on the charts. By February of 1958, it became the No. 1 song in the United States on the *Billboard* charts and topped off at the No. 7 position with *Cashbox*. The McGuire Sister's version of sheet music stayed on *Billboard's* Top 15 spot for 24 weeks. The loving sound of "Sugartime" rang in the ears of almost every American. With Coral's connection overseas, the song moved up the charts, perhaps more slowly than in the U.S., but topped at the No. 1 position in New Zealand, the No. 14 position in the United Kingdom and charted in the Top 20 in Australia, Canada and Germany. U.S. sales skyrocketed as "Sugartime" bumped other artists like Perry Como's "Catch a Falling Star," Pat Boone's "April Love" and Elvis Presley's "Baby I Don't Care" from the top positions.

Charlie's older brother, Carthon Phillips, was deployed to Hawaii after finishing an assignment in Washington D.C. He always remembered listening to his younger brother in Ma Kate's living room where Charlie routinely played some of his premature versions of "Sugartime" for Carthon- who'd reassure him and express how much he liked the song in a brotherly way. The older Phillips wouldn't think another thing about the song after leaving the dusty town of Farwell.

Carthon had begun his flying assignment around the Pacific and as he lay in bed one evening listening to *Hit Parade*, he could hear music being broadcast through the leisure radio as he heard the

McGuire Sisters singing their version of "Sugartime." Carthon said out loud to one of his bunkmates, "That sounds like a song my brother wrote and used to sing." He couldn't be sure because it sounded so much different than when Charlie would pound out the notes on his mother's piano and roughly belt out the melody. His shipmates scoffed, "Oh come on Phillips, you're saying your brother wrote that song?" Yes. Carthon was right, it was Charlie's song and it would soon become one of America's most beloved melodies. The McGuire Sisters now had their second and final number one hit.

Perhaps "Sugartime's" rise to the top seemed slow going at first, but quickly picked up steam. An Indiana newspaper wrote in March of 1958, "Their latest hit is 'Sugartime' and the other side, 'Banana Split,' isn't through selling yet. Dotty, Phyllis and Chris McGuire are currently starring at the Waldorf-Astoria in New York." If anyone could have made "Sugartime" a hit- it was the McGuire Sisters. By this time, "Sugartime" had produced more money than any other rock 'n' roll song published by NorVaJak and was added to the British catalog, making Norman Petty's company a recognized independent publisher in the U.K.; however, Petty is not often credited for any foreign music.

By summer of 1958, the McGuire Sister's version of "Sugartime" had sold over one million records. The company that collects the licensing fees and royalties on behalf of musicians, Broadcast Music Inc. or BMI for short, sent Charlie Phillips, Odis Echols and Norman Petty notification that "Sugartime" had reached the one million seller status and Norman, Charlie, Pop as well as the McGuire Sisters would all receive a Gold Record for their accomplishment. Charlie's notification came from BMI then-president and CEO, Frances W. Preston, on official BMI stationary. It reads:

Dear BMI Million-Air:

It gives me great pleasure to send you the enclosed Certification of Million-Performance Status. Each certificate represents BMI's official recognition of exceptional achievement in American Music, and a grateful acknowledgement of your part in making BMI licensed music part of America's past, present and future.

Songs which have reached this coveted status are in a very select group of worldwide favorites. This award honors the superb creative ability of songwriters and composers who have given these musical gifts to all music lovers, and the dedication of the publishers who have nurtured the writers and promoted the songs.

On behalf of all of us at BMI, and the millions of people around the world who have derived pleasure from this work, we offer our special congratulations and heartfelt thanks.

Sincerely,

Frances W. Preston

The actual certificate reads:

Special Citation of Achievement presented by BMI to Charlie Phillips in recognition of the great national popularity measured by over 1 million broadcast performances attained by Sugartime. Signed, Frances W. Preston

News quickly reached Clovis as well as Norman Petty, who in his own silent way, was elated by yet another hit to originate from his Norman Petty Studio. 1957 had seen Jimmy Bowen's "I'm Sticking with You," Buddy Knox's "Party Doll," and the Crickets "That'll Be the Day," which were all the culmination of talented young artists respectively plus the "ear" of Norman Petty, soar to the top of the charts. Now in 1958, other Petty releases would include the Crickets' "Oh Boy," and Buddy Holly's "Peggy Sue." Concurrently, the McGuire Sisters' version of "Sugartime" would conclusively cement itself on the charts as the number twenty-sixth best song of 1958. "Sugartime" would be the best-selling song to ever originate from the NorVaJak label. Norman would receive the Gold Record as publisher and Charlie and Odis "Pop" Echols would receive the Gold Record as writers.

This new claim to fame quite frankly caught Charlie off guard. His dream was to make music and get on the radio. It had barely been over a year since he first heard his version of "Put Your Arms Around Me," sung purely for his mother, played on the local radio station. Now, he had a No.1 hit he'd written being heard by millions. An invitation was extended to both Charlie and Pop Echols to fly to New York and receive their prestigious award and Gold Records; however, it would be Pop Echols and his son, Odis Echols Jr. , who would make the momentous trip with Charlie. Maybe.

For whatever reason, Pop Echols decided it would be more beneficial for Charlie to stay at home and for he and his son to make the trip to the east coast. As Pop's employee and one of the primary deejay's at KCLV, it was decided Charlie would stay behind and continue his daily radio program. No. 1 song or not, Charlie still had an obligation to the radio station and like most southern men of his time, one's responsibilities were to be honored above any fancy award ceremony. As time to receive the award drew near, Pop told Charlie something along the lines of, "We'll go pick up the award, you don't need to go."

Additionally, Charlie had a regular Saturday night gig in the neighboring town of Kenna, New Mexico, about thirty miles southwest of Portales. The Pioneer Bar and Lounge was owned by a rancher with the last name of Denton and was located outside of the alcohol-banned town of Clovis, but close enough the locals, as well as stationed service men, could drive over and tie one on to the music of a live band.

The Pioneer Bar was more of a dance hall decked out with a unique motif of wood. The establishment itself was built of wood and decorated with all things fashioned from knotty pine. The façade was ornamented with knotty pine, walls were covered in knotty pine, chairs were made from knotty pine, the tables were created from knotty pine and the centerpiece of the lounge boasted the most beautiful bar made from, you guessed it, knotty pine. With such a unique look complemented by now-famous musicians like Charlie Phillips, the Pioneer drew packed crowds every weekend.

With no alcohol, Clovis was as dry as the dirt and wind blowing through it. The Pioneer Bar was only one of four close establishments Clovisites would venture to in the early and late evenings. Directly to the north on Highway 209 was Grady. It had the closest liquor store to Clovis and it also had a modern legal dance hall owned by Ed Pedigrew aptly named Ed's Place. When the boys weren't playing at some of the other spots in and around Clovis, Ed's Place was a trendy venue to perform. Directly to the west off Highway 60, miles past Cannon Air Force Base, was the small New Mexico town of Taiban, which also housed another trendy legal dance hall.

The popularity of dance halls and live music venues were at an all-time high during this era in the 1940's and 1950's. With so few entertainment options available as well as few venues in which to meet and court a guy or gal, either one's church or a dance hall would be the best chance for such an encounter. With the popularity of "Sugartime" and the fantastic performances by Charlie Phillips and his newly dubbed Sugartimer band, getting gigs at some of the numerous Texas and New Mexico clubs became second nature as they were always in high demand. People would drive from the small Texas towns of Farwell, Muleshoe, Bovina, Friona and even as far as Dimmit and Hereford to hear the sounds of the Sugartimers.

Pop's trip to New York City would have Odis "Pop" Echols and Odis Echols Jr. packing their finest duds. They would be staying at the famous Waldorf Astoria Hotel located on posh Park Avenue. Like today, the Waldorf was one of the premier hotels in the world catering to the financial elite with luxurious rooms and amenities. The guys flew into La Guardia airport and took a cab into the city. BMI spared no expense on their award ceremony, and Pop Echols graciously accepted his honor along with the award afforded Charlie

Phillips, who worked tirelessly back in New Mexico. This would be Pop Echols' first brief encounter with the famous trio, the McGuire Sisters, who also showed up to receive their Gold Records for their achievement.

Up until this time, the McGuire Sisters had performed their No. 1 hit "Sincerely" and attained great success, but it would be "Sugartime" that would reinforce them as one of the biggest acts of their era. Already highly gifted musicians, the McGuire Sisters would continue their careers recording over one hundred charting songs after the onslaught of "Sugartime," momentously endearing them to America and imaginably the world. "Sugartime" was their biggest hit of all time and as Charlie reminds, "The [my] song made them even bigger."

At the height of their "Sugartime" success and shortly after the announcement they had sold over one million records, the girls appeared on the NBC-TV television program, *The Perry Como Show*. On this episode, Perry Como sits in his dark suit while the three girls surround him wearing their glittering dresses with big smiles on their faces. Perry starts out the segment with a scripted act saying, "Well I'd like to do the song, er, your latest called 'Sugartime.' And I have a very special reason for doing that. Because the Coral Recording Company, you know the people you know, the people you record for? They sent me a record they want me to give to you for selling one million copies of 'Sugartime' and that's a lot of sugar isn't it?"

Perry reaches behind his back and retrieves a gold 45 record to show the girls. The McGuire Sisters thank Perry as Dorothy takes the record from his hand. Suddenly, Phyllis reaches over and grabs the record from Dorothy's hand and thanks the host. Chris turns and snatches the record from her sister Phyllis and thanks Perry.

The entertainers pass the record back and forth each claiming possession. To solve the sister rivalry, Perry retrieves the record that is now back in Dorothy's hands and places it behind his back as he simulates breaking the record into pieces as the audience hears a loud crackle sound. Como then presents the gals with three pieces of the record so they each have their own. The audience laughs hysterically. Phyllis looks sheepishly at Perry who is still sitting beside her and says, "That's Perry! Always breaking records." Perry, the girls and the audience all have an uproarious laugh as everyone claps.

Perry Como announces the girls have already sung "Sugartime" on the show before but will be performing it again as Phyllis reveals she's seen Perry sing it himself a couple of times on his show. Como articulates, "Yeah, we've done it a few times, wrong tempos, Mitch always does the wrong tempos" then he asks, "What say we do this thing together?" as the music begins, and the girls harmonize perfectly to "Sugartime" Perry Como joins in. At the end of their number, the authentic framed Gold Record is brought out and presented to the three. Perry gives brief instructions on how to keep the record looking shiny and new. He states to rub some Noxema on it, and they all laugh. The following Saturday evening, NBC-TV also aired Jimmy Rodgers and Gisele MacKenzie singing "Sugartime" on *The Gisele MacKenzie Show*.

During their long careers, the McGuire Sisters will perform live for five Presidents of the United States- notably Richard Nixon, Gerald Ford, Jimmy Carter, Ronald Reagan and George Herbert Walker Bush. They will also perform for Queen Elizabeth II. The gals continue making television performances for many years most especially for Red Skelton, Dean Martin, Perry Como, Milton Berle and their last performance later in 1968 will be on *The Ed Sullivan Show*.

Do opposites attract? Of the three McGuire Sisters, it will be the youngest, Phyllis McGuire, who will be scandalously cast into a different spotlight when she meets and befriends the infamous mobster, Sam Giancana, a fixture both from Chicago and in the Las Vegas casino scene. After being wooed by the gangster, the two begin what can only be seen as a courtship.

The showbiz confection's love affair with Giancana lasts for many years, an account she vehemently denies, suggesting their friendship was just that- merely friends. Rumors abound and Phyllis perhaps becomes caught up in one of the most well known scandals of her day. Even Sam's daughter made the claim Phyllis was having a concurrent affair with President John F. Kennedy; however, whether any of these allegations were true, damage had been done and the wholesome McGuire Sister image had conceivably been tainted.

Phyllis told *People Magazine* in a 1986 interview, "All of a sudden my friends told me, 'Do you know who you are seeing? He's murdered people' I was all wide-eyed. I didn't know what they were talking about. I just knew I liked the man. His wife had passed away and he was very nice to me. And if he had done all of those things they said he did, I wondered why in God's name he was on the street and not in jail." Perhaps no one will ever really know the true extent of Phyllis' relationship with Giancana, but for a brief time in history when good girls didn't do certain things, Phyllis allowed a different type of spotlight to shine on her life. Imaginably, love really is blind.

Over three decades later in 2000, an original Home Box Office (HBO) movie was released, loosely chronicling the bizarre relationship of the beauty and her beast, starring John Turturro as Sam Giancana and Mary-Louise Parker as Phyllis McGuire. Of all of the titles the movie creators could have chosen for the film, they aptly entitled it after Phyllis and her sisters' biggest hit, "Sugartime."

"Lewd" was how Phyllis described the portrayal of herself in the movie, *Sugartime*, during an interview with *TV Guide*. She passionately objected to much of the film saying, "It was malicious" and "It never happened" in comparison to what she describes as "my quite conventional" romance with Giancana. According to the author of the *Sugartime* movie, Martyn Burke, much of the dialog he wrote for the script came directly from FBI wiretaps.

Mary-Louise Parker, who portrayed Phyllis in the film, defended both herself and the McGuire Sisters stating, "You'd just be laughed at today if you got up onstage and did what the McGuire Sisters did... But there was something so pure about them, and when you have struggled like they had to reach success, and then you're able to give people something really nice [back]...well, why NOT smile, showing two rows of teeth." Parker continues, "She was so positive in so many ways." Possibly because of the stigma attached to Phyllis' love affair, the McGuire Sisters wouldn't perform again until 1986 after their *Sullivan* appearance in 1968.

For decades now, there's been a discrepancy regarding the number of Gold Records actually distributed for the two "authors" of "Sugartime." Assuming both Pop and Charlie received only *one* Gold Record to be shared between them, Charlie has not seen the actual award since the 1960's. After Pop Echols' meeting with the McGuire Sisters and after receiving the Gold Record for he and Charlie, Echols and his son, Odis Jr., traveled back to the sleepy town of Clovis and resumed life as usual. Pop never really mentioned the Gold Record much to Charlie; he simply hung the award on his office wall behind his desk at the radio station. To this day it's not known if Odis Jr. or Pop kept a second record or if only one existed in the first place, but other than seeing the honor hung in Pop's office, Charlie never saw his Gold Record again.

As money goes, "Sugartime" sold far more than a million records, and money quickly began arriving in Clovis through BMI and the Coral label. It seems everyone got his small cut from the song. Coral split money through Peer Publishing and with the NorVaJak label; the McGuire Sisters received their cut of the profits, both Charlie and Pop Echols received and split their slice of the pie. As Charlie explains, "The pieces of the pie were getting smaller and smaller 'til there wasn't much pie left to eat."

It was around this time Pop Echols, still acting as Charlie's manager, would receive notice from Peer Publishing and Norman Petty that a New York law firm was suing Charlie's publishing company for copyright infringement. Chico Marx, of the Marx Brothers fame (or possibly his guardians in the latter years of his life), had heard "Sugartime" on the radio and believed the beginning melody of the song was too similar to an obscure song Chico had written years earlier possibly in the 1920's called, "Animal Crackers," which surprisingly had a similar melody. Lawyers got involved and brought suit against Charlie and everyone connected to "Sugartime," insisting royalties be paid to Marx and his folks.

Pop notified and explained the dilemma to Charlie, who, by the way, had never to his recollection heard Chico's song. It was decided a lengthy court trial would not be in anyone's best interest, so an agreement was reached to pay Chico a settlement out of court, with Mr. Marx and his people receiving 20-percent of the writer's rights to "Sugartime." The arrangement was finalized and everyone moved forward. Norman Petty had been in the music publishing business long enough and explained to Charlie that when a hit-song makes lots of money, "leach publishing companies" come out of the woodwork and try to take a piece of the gravy train. Charlie's pie was now even smaller than ever, but with this being said, enough money was still making its way back to Clovis for all to enjoy a better lifestyle than they ever enjoyed before.

Although fame was now within Charlie's grasp, he was still just a country bumpkin from Texas. His radio program on KCLV resembled his life as his cornball hick accent on the trendy local radio segment sent listeners into laughter. It was entirely acceptable in those days for the DJ to create a silly and wild persona for the country music audience, as would later be seen with the antics of popular shows like *Hee Haw* and heard on programs like the *Grand Ole Opry* and the *Louisiana Hayride*.

Never before had Charlie seen so much money at one time. His pay from playing live gigs, his weekly pay from the radio station, and now his royalty checks trickling in from the record company now afforded Charlie the opportunity to do some things he never dreamed possible. Ben Franklin was right when he said, "A penny saved is a penny earned," and Charlie had certainly learned how to sock away a penny, but now he was introduced to something contemporary- investing.

Although Pop Echols served as Charlie's manager, he was also a mentor of sorts. After Charlie's father was killed, Pop took on a sort of fatherly role, offering advice where needed both personally and professionally. With the advent of money falling into Charlie's lap from royalty sales, Pop met with Charlie suggesting he invest some of his newfound proceeds.

His advice to Charlie was to purchase five small houses that had come on the market in Clovis. Charlie would be able to buy the homes ranging from around $5,000 to $15,000 each. After the initial purchase, Charlie would resell the homes, but would receive a down payment and carry the remainder of the note for a specified time with interest. This early induction into the real estate business would prove wise advice from Pop and would eventually become a lifelong source of income as Charlie purchased many more properties over the years and ran what might be considered his own personal real-estate mortgage company.

Of course, no advice is ever perfect, especially when it comes to financials. Pop tugged Charlie into his office one morning and explained that a good ole' boy from Portales, New Mexico and also a friend of Pop's was going to open up a dairy farm outside of Portales. He was looking for some guys to get in on the ground floor of this golden moneymaking opportunity. As the story goes, both Pop and Charlie each put in $5000 of their money to help get the dairy farm off the ground, but alas, no dairy farm ever existed and the investment money was lost forever. Charlie pondered years later if Pop had duped him out of the money or if they had both, point of fact, lost their money in the transaction. "Who knows what actually happened with that deal," Charlie reminisces.

Not yet in his mid-twenties with a what seemed like a lifetime of music under his belt, weekly local gigs, investment properties and the author of the No. 1 song in the country, Charlie began looking outwardly from both West Texas and the Clovis area, closely observing what many other artists were doing at the time. Several pickers and stringers of the day flew their personal airplanes and Charlie thought that was just what a big star of his caliber ought to have. With some of his royalty earnings, he and bass player, Dudley Hughes, chipped in together and purchased a small two-seater Ercoupe.

On January 22, 1959, the boys would pay the handsome sum of $3452.20 for one 1946 Model Ercoupe, the "grandmammy of all your Coupes" from Murray-Davis Aviation Inc. located in Curry County, New Mexico. The guys split the purchase down the middle with Charlie paying his half in cash and Dudley conveniently financing his half totaling $1726.10 payable for two years at 7-percent interest tallying $71.93 per month. That two-seat coupe had 60 horses of power and could cruise at a speed of about 90 MPH, about the same darned speed Charlie would usually drive!

Charlie's good friend, Doyle Vaughn, had gotten his pilot's license at a young age and had become a skilled flyer. Doyle would sometimes dash the guys in his personal plane on Sunday afternoons from Clovis to Ruidoso, New Mexico for the horse races, which was exciting for Charlie and his young friends. Not surprisingly, Doyle would eventually leave the dusty plains of New Mexico and would become the personal pilot for Robert Maheu, an early confidant and advisor of industrialist Howard Hughes, acting as Hughes' chief executive. Maheu was also closely associated with the Kennedy family and occasionally would request Doyle fly he and the Kennedys to and from places. Eventually, Doyle Vaughn would become a commercial pilot for Southwest Airlines based out of Love Field in Dallas, Texas- a far cry from running Charlie and the boys to and from their party destinations.

Charlie began taking lessons from a seasoned local pilot and started flying his plane from the Clovis Municipal Airport to and from the Phillips farmland located only a few miles away from each other. In order to land the aircraft on his family's property, Charlie hired an ole' hillbilly boy originally from Oklahoma, Mr. Barnes, to use a road grater pressing down a landing path through much of native grass and Bear Grass located across the grazing and pasture land. Charlie had Barnes grate the road in a big "X" across the property to cover enough room in case the wind changed directions, or there was a dangerous crosswind.

Charlie's new toy would prove to be quite the contrary as on several occasions he experienced many near misses or collisions. The Phillips' property located just outside of Farwell had an 80-foot television antennae built right beside the house that made navigating a landing somewhat complicated. Charlie positioned his new airstrip to circumvent a potential collision of said antennae, but in doing so, had to locate the strip in such a location it would be surrounded by the farm's barbed wire fencing.

Charlie's first close call occurred one afternoon when on a quick trip to Clovis, he cranked up the engine and took off from the family farm. He had gotten a mile or so away from the house when smoke began billowing from the engine while ascending. His first thought was, "Oh my gosh, what's goin' on here!" He pressed his head against the cockpit window and could see flames shooting out from the left side of the plane and over the wing of the small aircraft. He circled the plane around and veered back towards the homestead. He knew he'd need to land the plane as quickly as possible, but could only think, "Well, this is where it's over… this is how it ends… I'm done for."

Charlie navigated the plane to his makeshift runway and initiated an emergency landing. As the plane set down, the massive landing gear began smashing the Bear Grass and native cactus as the aircraft bounced recklessly until it completely came to a stop. Charlie quickly exited the burning plane and began preparing for the worst, a possible prairie fire!

After a few minutes, the smoke died down, and Charlie was able to look inside the engine. The problem became apparent immediately. A sparrow had built her nest right on top of the manifold and had caught fire when the engine heated. Ma Kate had been watching from the house and began running towards her son when she sensed something was wrong. She ran directly up to the fence and exclaimed, "What in the world is wrong with you- you are as white as a sheet?" It would be many years before Charlie would tell his mother what had actually happened that day. It was a terrible close call, but both the plane and Charlie survived.

Most of Charlie's flying was for local trips and perhaps funny shenanigans. It was a novel idea to take the aircraft up and buzz over his friends' farmhouses, but mostly the plane was used for quick and limited trips. He would often fly to Plainview, Texas or Amarillo or Lubbock, but this was about the extent of his excursions- never traveling long distances. Possibly because of his near-death experience, Charlie wouldn't even get in someone else's small plane much less fly his own plane if the day wasn't beautiful or if there was a single cloud in the sky.

With the plane sheltered at the farm, one weekend Charlie and Dudley Hughes made a beer run to Grady, New Mexico just a few miles north of Clovis. They picked up a few cases of beer and the ever-vigilant Charlie filled-up the tank on the plane. He was often in fear the plane might run out of gas. Their plan was to fly the airplane to Clovis for a party. With a full tank of gas, two men in the front seat, and a backend full of cases of beer, the plane had difficulty gaining the momentum necessary to ascend the runway.

It was a hot summer afternoon and Charlie firewalled the engine in an attempt to get the plane traveling the minimum of 55 or so miles per hour on the runway. The plane just wouldn't lift as both Charlie and Dudley quickly neared the barbed wire fence at the end of the runway. Charlie could see Dudley, seatbelt intact, sinking further and further into the cockpit in anticipation of a crash. With room running out, the plane finally started its ascension and narrowly cleared the fence as the two young men breathed a sigh of relief. Having a good but dry sense of humor, Dudley slowly reached behind the seat of the plane, grabbed a hot beer from the stack of cases in the back, popped the top of the can stating, "I think I'll have a beer." Wiping the sweat from his brow, Charlie said, "Well, while you're at it, better get me one too."

With several near-catastrophic flying incidents, one would think Charlie would have enough sense to stop flying, but it would be the deaths of other friends and pilots that would finally end his hobby. A distant cousin of Charlie's by marriage, James Norton, often played guitar for the band and owned a four-seat over-wing plane. James was a superb pilot and planned a quick trip to his neighbors at the nearby Lankford place. James, his young son, and the Lankford's son all loaded themselves into the plane and traveled towards their destination. However, something went critically wrong and according to witnesses, the plane flew too low and crashed, killing all three in this terrible accident.

To top it all off, the gentleman Charlie had purchased his plane from through Murray-Davis Aviation, a World War II pilot, was leaving on a trip in his personal Beechcraft Bonanza with his wife and two friends when an early morning fog set in. They had gotten off the ground just fine, but it's possible he became disoriented and ironically crashed his plane onto James Norton's property off Highway 60 just outside of Farwell. All four were killed instantly. With these looming plane crashes weighing on his mind as well as his own near misses, not to mention Ma Kate's concerns, Charlie and Dudley hung up their pilot's dreams never to step inside a small craft again.

After witnessing the deaths of so many close friends and acquaintances, who were all accomplished pilots, Charlie decided, "Well, I ain't gotta chance. I better quit while I'm still alive." This wise decision possible saved Charlie's life as more and more musicians began using small planes traveling to and from long distance gigs. Also, Charlie's friend and colleague, Buddy Holly perished tragically in a plane crash while on tour. Soon after Charlie's days as a pilot, Patsy Cline was killed near Camden, Tennessee and the following year, his dear friend and associate, Jim Reeves, perished in a plane crash similarly in Tennessee. It was decided all of the Charlie Phillips and his Sugartimer Band gigs would be traveled by car or bus, but never in a small craft.

Up until this time, Charlie and his band were playing to packed houses, even more so after the success of "Sugartime." Most of the gigs the band performed were put together by either Pop Echols or suggested by Norman Petty. Although they kept the band busy, and some were quite lucrative, Charlie wanted to start branching out and form his own gigs. The first real concert he put together himself, he rented the old American Legion Hall located at the end of Main Street near downtown Clovis, next to the Mesa Theater. Jimmy Schell and Pete Wallace were playing with the band at that time, and the group decided to create their unique dancing venue, playing only on Friday nights. They packed the house! Every teenager in the area who wasn't dragging Main Street was jam-packed into the dancehall.

Of course with teenagers in the late 1950's, came teenage drinking. Although Clovis was dry, and the American Legion didn't serve alcohol, youngsters would either sneak booze into the venue or leave to drink alcohol in their cars. Finding the magic elixir wasn't too difficult, even for a kid in those days. The neighboring town of Grady was a short drive from Clovis and the liquor store would sell to anyone- well, anyone with cash. Young people would sneak around and pick up their booze for the Friday night dance. Many of the dance attendees were respectable kids looking for a good time on Friday evening, but some became drunken buffoons and quelled the efforts Charlie had worked so hard to achieve. Unfortunately a band of brothers who lived close to the venue, known mainly for being the town ruffians, continually disrupted the dance and started fights, thus cutting the event short and eventually butchering the whole project.

Charlie and his friends were certainly not innocent when it came to partying. If the saying, "work hard and play harder" was true, the guys all fit the bill. Late nights were, and probably still are, the norm for musicians who play gigs deep into the darkness and until the bars closed. After they finished playing, they loaded their equipment up and left the establishment because the party didn't have to end. Waking one's parents up to bring a bunch of hooligans over at four in the morning was certainly out of the question; so the boys all decided to chip in and rent a small furnished apartment in Clovis specifically used for late hour parties as well as a place to crash once the festivities ended. Boys will be boys.

At the height of Charlie's popularity, Norman set up a recording session through Bob Thiele and his connections at Coral Records that would beckon both Charlie and Odis Jr. to New York City in order to record a new record. Charlie had already been working on a fresh tune he wrote entitled, "Be My Bride" he had previously tested on his dancehall audiences. They received the song enthusiastically. Charlie and his band mates, Jimmy Schell, Dudley

Hughes and Gerald Brown had already recorded a version of "Be My Bride" in 1957 at the Norman Petty Studio, but Coral wanted Charlie in their studios for a different version.

Pop Echols made the necessary arrangements for Charlie and Pop's son, Odis Jr., to travel up to the Big Apple. Up until this point, Charlie, who had lived all of his life in Farwell, Texas, had only made a few trips outside of New Mexico and the Texas Panhandle, but was prepared to enter the big-time as he'd be recording at one of the biggest label studios. Dressed in their Sunday best, Odis Jr. and Charlie boarded an airline in Amarillo, Texas bound for Coral Records.

They landed at the busy La Guardia Airport in Queens, NY and traveled into Manhattan via cab. Never before had Charlie seen such a sight. There were so many buildings in New York and Charlie couldn't fathom all the traffic. Of course, he had seen the bustling streets of Clovis but never had his eyes seen a sight like this. Odis Jr. had booked them into the posh Warwick New York Hotel, a luxury hotel on West 54th Street just south of Central Park, originally built by publishing mogul, William Randolph Hearst. It's rumored Elvis Presley had mentioned how beautiful the hotel rooms were to Odis Jr. when they talked in Lubbock. The young Echols wanted to see what the entire hubbub was about, but most likely, Coral records probably booked them there because of its proximity to the studio.

The cab pulled up to the ornate exterior of the Warwick, and Odis Jr. instructed Charlie to pay the cabby for the ride from the airport. Having never even been in a cab, Charlie proceeded to give the driver his money. There was 25-cents left over, so Charlie told the cab driver to, "Keep the change," which was very uncharacteristic coming from the boy nicknamed, Scrooge. The cabby looked at the quarter and tossed it back at Charlie's chest and yelled something along the lines of, "Looks like you could use this more than me buddy!" Dazed and confused, Charlie didn't understand why the cab driver had said that until much later.

Charlie walked up to the ornate brass entryway that stood glistening in the sun. The two brass doors were like bookends being caressed by the black-marbled façade. A large brass revolving door with thick plate-glass centered itself separating the foyer from the streets of New York. The vestibule of the Warwick was magnificent. It was decked out in high extravagance the likes of which Charlie had never seen. White and black marble floors led to the brass elevator doors. The guys made their way up to their shared room. Having grown up in extreme poverty, this was the current highlight of Charlie's life thus far; *until*, they entered their room. "I think that room was the size of my closet back home!" Charlie exaggerates after seeing two twin-size beds crammed into what appeared to be a broom closet. As beautiful as the hotel was, Coral apparently *did* spare the expenses for their young new artist.

The Warwick was within just a few blocks from the Brill Building where Norman Petty secured an office. It was also in proximity to the Waldorf Astoria, where Odis Jr. would have a special surprise for Charlie later that evening. The McGuire Sisters were still playing at the Waldorf and Odis Jr. had obtained tickets to see the girls perform live. Charlie had never actually met the lassies who made his song so popular. In true form, the girls played to a packed house and received a standing ovation following their last number. Odis Jr. asked Charlie to join him as they made their way through the crowd into a side foyer where the McGuire Sisters met them holding a cake. They were thrilled to meet the man who had written their second No. 1 single. After pleasantries had been exchanged, a photographer snapped a photo of Chris, Dorothy, Phyllis, Charlie and Odis Jr. The sisters then waved goodbye as they as they were ushered back inside the famed Empire Room so they could begin their second act for the evening.

The following day, the recording session at the Coral studio was less than eventful. It was a far cry from the relaxed atmosphere of the Norman Petty Studio. Charlie wasn't able to bring any of his own musicians on this trip as the studio was providing everyone needed. "Be My Bride" was Charlie's latest creation and had already been recorded at Norman's studio using his own musicians, but Bob

Thiele thought a fancier studio with more accomplished musicians would produce a better product. Boy did they have someone in mind.

Milton Delugg was a talented accordionist who flourished into a successful composer, arranger, bandleader and producer for numerous albums and television programs throughout his long career. Delugg would compose many of his own songs, but would probably be more known for compositions like the closing theme for the television show, *What's My Line* and shows like *Broadway Open House*, *The Bill Cullen Show*, the *Winchell and Mahoney Show* and *The Tonight Show* with Johnny Carson. Milton also produced Buddy Holly's legendary record, "Rave On!"

Milton Delugg was assigned to Charlie's new record, but unlike Norman's studio based solely on the perfection of a singular recording, Coral's Bell Sound Studio, was founded on an hourly, in-and-out rate. "Be My Bride" was recorded as the lead song and was brilliantly directed by Delugg with studio musicians and orchestral music. Charlie had planned on using one of his own songs for side-two, but it was decided a melody written by George Green named, "Too Many Tears" would be a good fit. Under this new and stricter approach to recording music, Charlie would observe how to record outside of the stress-free Petty environment and would learn quickly the habit of recording the song right on the first try. Some performers and producers would later christen Charlie with the name, "One-Take Charlie."

While the McGuire Sisters enjoyed the benefits "Sugartime" had generated throughout 1958, a famous female singer from England covered Charlie's already famous American single. Alma Cogan, sometimes known as "The Girl with the Giggle," was a successful British female entertainer who had already seen achievements after covering popular songs by artists such as Rosemary Clooney, Georgia Gibbs and Dinah Shore. Her version of "Sugartime" would add to her popularity and would be one of her best-selling singles.

While the McGuire Sisters' version topped at No. 14 on the U.K. charts, Alma's would top at No. 16 respectfully. The beautiful and fashionable Alma would distinguish herself and be voted "Outstanding British Singer" four times from 1956-1960 in the *NME* reader's poll; however, by the early to mid-1960's, her popularity waned. Even Cynthia Lennon, John Lennon's Beatle wife at the time, remarked, "John and I thought of Alma [as] out of date and unhip." Plagued with stomach cancer in 1966, humble Alma's life would be cut short as she succumbed to the illness at only age 34.

Johnny Cash spent some of 1961 recording an album entitled, *Now Here's Johnny Cash* with songs like: "I Couldn't Keep From Crying" by Marty Robbins; "Hey Porter" by Sam Phillips; "Cry! Cry! Cry!" by Cash; "Oh Lonesome Me" by Don Gibson; "Home of the Blues" by Cash, Glen Douglas and Vic McAlpin; and was finally able to release his version of "Sugartime" he recorded with Sun Records in May of 1958. Cash had very much enjoyed Charlie's tune and used the song to introduce his album. Throughout his career, Johnny would sing his cover version on radio shows, television programs and live in concert. Kitty Wells once joined Johnny Cash on television singing their duo version of "Sugartime" and Kitty would even do her own tribute to the song. Johnny Cash's cover-version of "Sugartime" would eventually peak at only No. 47 on *Cashbox* and has since charted on several *Sun Greatest Hits* album packages.

Many folks might remember English-born actor, voice artist and singer-songwriter, Jim Dale. Jim would fashion an attractive version of "Sugartime" sung in high English technique during 1958. His version of the song would reach No. 25 on the U.K. charts but wouldn't become highly popularized; however, it would grab attention as he released a songbook with his boyish good looks on the cover, thus selling thousands.

Jim is seen on the songbook looking picturesque with coiffed jet-black hair wearing a plaid country-like shirt, holding his guitar with his right hand and extending his left arm towards the reader as he sings "Sugartime." After covering Charlie's song, Jim would enjoy a long and illustrious career in film, theater, television and voiceovers. Of the twenty-six awards he'd receive over the course of his career, most noticeably will be a 1980 Tony Award and a 2001 and 2008 Grammy Award for his voice work on the popular *Harry Potter* series. In 2009, Jim was inducted into the esteemed American Theater Hall of Fame.

"Humph, in my generation we had dinner time and we had suppertime. Nowadays as I hear they have a new one- Sugartime. My guess would be that that's shortly after suppertime (audience laughs). Here is Larry and Lorrie Collins. Give 'em a hand" was the exciting introduction announced by the host, Tex Ritter, on his wildly admired television program, *Tex Ritter's Ranch Party* in 1958. Ritter was one of the most celebrated country artists and cowboy movie stars of his day. His television program frequently featured country entertainers, cowboy singers, and even a few cutting-edge rock performers. The show was shot in front of a live audience who laughed and clapped for the easygoing and fun-loving Tex.

Several years into his career, Charlie would run into Tex Ritter in the elevator at the Andrew Jackson Hotel in Nashville, Tennessee for one of the well-known Deejay conventions. Tex shook Charlie's hand and said in a jovial voice, "Pleased to finally meet you young man" and briefly described how much he enjoyed the song, "Sugartime." Tex was wearing his traditional and elaborate garb of a Nudie Suit made popular by many country artists of the day.

Charlie recalls later that evening, Tex was smoking a pipe after dinner and inadvertently placed the still-lit pipe into the inside coat pocket of his Nudie Suit. He probably just forgot about it as he returned to his hotel room and put the suit in the closet. After no time, the suit coat caught fire and was billowing smoke into the room and hallway. Charlie recollects seeing smoke pouring into the corridor as he and many of the guests thought the hotel was on fire, but after the hotel staff arrived and pinpointed the cause while extinguishing the fire, everything returned to normal.

The Collins Kids were a brother and sister rockabilly-singing duo and regularly performed on the *Ranch Party* from 1957- 1959. They played their version of "Sugartime" retitled, "Be My Little Honey" with young Larry characteristically strumming his double-neck Mosrite guitar and his beautiful sister, Lorrie, singing the lyrics while receiving thunderous applause at the finale. Larry was quite the energetic performer as he danced a jig while belting out the words to "Sugartime." Both Lorrie and Larry also enjoyed lengthy careers in the music industry. Lorrie even dated Ricky Nelson and appeared on an episode of *The Adventures of Ozzie and Harriet* while young Larry grew up and wrote a number of hit songs including "Delta Dawn" and "You're the Reason God Made Oklahoma."

In 1977, Linda McCartney with the help of her band, Wings, created their interpretation of "Sugartime" with Linda singing lead vocals and her Beatles husband, Paul McCartney, sounding backup vocals while playing his Wurlitzer. Linda was both a musician and photographer and later became an animal rights activist and businesswoman. Just a few years before recording "Sugartime," Linda photographed Eric Clapton and became the first woman to have a photograph featured on the cover of the May 11, 1969, *Rolling Stone* magazine. She and her husband Paul would also appear on the cover of the magazine in 1974. "Sugartime" was one of Linda's favored tunes, thus probably the reason she chose to record it for her Wings album.

Her husband would enjoy a long career in the music industry even being knighted, Sir Paul McCartney, by Queen Elizabeth II of Great Britain for his contributions to music and his philanthropy. Sir Paul, later in the 1970's, would actually purchase the publishing rights from the NorVaJak label obtaining the rights to Buddy Holly's music. Linda McCartney's life would, regrettably, be cut short as she was diagnosed with breast cancer in 1995 and succumbed to the disease at age 56, passing away on April 17, 1998.

Although short, her life was one full of vivacity as an artist, musician and mom. The Linda McCartney Centre opened as a cancer clinic at The Royal Liverpool University Hospital in 2000. In 1998, twenty years after Linda's first recording of "Sugartime," Sir Paul

McCartney's company released an album named *Wide Prairie* with "Sugartime" as one of the album's song compilations. It's important to note, Sir McCartney also produced and hosted the 1985 documentary, *The Real Buddy Holly Story*.

The Wilburn Brothers' cover of "Sugartime" saw some success in the U.S. also. Furthermore, Dutch sheet music was created for interpretation in the Netherlands aptly named "Kommer Du I Aften." This would be one of the first times international cover tunes would become an integral part of Norman Petty's business. Petty stated in a 1959 newspaper interview, "We have records of 'Sugartime' and 'Peggy Sue' in several different tongues... The two were big hits overseas." Back in the 1950's it was extremely difficult for small independent publishers like Norman Petty to get songs distributed abroad, yet with the popularity of Buddy Holly and the McGuire Sisters, doors opened for Petty- even if for a small frame of time.

Mama's Family was a television sitcom broadcast on NBC in the 1980's starring Vicki Lawrence as the feisty, old, straight-shooting fictional grandmother, Thelma Harper. Her initially juvenile delinquent grandson, Bubba, came to live with her later in the series. Some of the show's skits featured her giving wisecracking and cantankerous, yet grandmotherly advice, supporting his upbringing. Bubba enjoyed music and perhaps had dreams of being a rock 'n' roll star especially when he hooked up with his friends, Dwayne and T-Boy. On a particular episode entitled "Bubba's House Band," teenage Bubba and his gang called the Bone Crushers all decked out for their big rock performance in Thelma's living room as they prepared for their practice session. Always getting involved with her grandson's activities, as she herself wants to be part of the group, Thelma takes her place at the piano for the Bone Crusher's rendition of "Sugartime," an extremely unlikely song to be sung by a rough group of teenagers.

No longer the sweet and innocent unblemished sound of the McGuire Sister's 1958 version of "Sugartime," the song has become known as an industry standard, instantly recognized by millions of folks around the world. Just the use of "Sugartime" on a nationally broadcast television sitcom shows its influence on American society.

Many folks reading this might be endeared to the McGuire Sister's rendition or even Charlie Phillips' much-sung version of "Sugartime," but young folks reading this might recognize a much different and more commercial version of the song with the lyrics completely overhauled. In fact, "Sugartime" was remade for an actual commercial- the theme music for Bagel Bites. Currently owned by the Heinz and Ore-Ida food producers, Bagel Bites ran an illustrious television commercial in the 1980's geared towards American teens and youth with the catchy jingle:

Pizza in the morning,
Pizza in the evening,
Pizza at suppertime!
When pizza's on a bagel,
You can eat pizza anytime!

The commercial was a success not only for the food company selling the product, but also for Charlie as each benefitted from the resurgence of the appealing ditty. The song written from his father's tractor had now been covered by big stars like the McGuire Sisters, Johnny Cash, Linda McCartney and was currently reintroduced, granted in a small way, to the new youth of America in the form of a commercial jingle selling small pizzas. As time marched forward, not only has the original rendition been covered, but also folks are now actually covering the pizza jingle. Stars like Jimmy Fallon and singer, Meatloaf, would perform their spoof of the song in the video production of *Late Night With Jimmy Fallon* as Fallon and Meatloaf jokingly crooned a rock operatic remake entitled "Ode to Bagel Bites."

Although mostly unrelated, ABC-TV introduced a sitcom in the 1970's about three girls who are aspiring rock singers, aptly named *Sugartime*. The show starred three beauties of the day, Marianne Black, Didi Carr and the illustrious Barbi Benton who was often synonymous with her once boyfriend, Hugh Hefner, of the *PLAYBOY Magazine* fame.

It's virtually impossible to count the number of times "Sugartime" was re-recorded and performed by other artists. There are no actual numbers available through BMI, but the estimate of individuals and groups would be in the thousands. It's not uncommon to hear church functions, schools, theater groups, and choirs singing their interpretations. It seems so many people jumped on the "Sugartime" bandwagon over the years. A headline in a 1958 Oklahoma newspaper, the *Miami Daily News*, reads, "Sugar Time Promised," regarding Senator George Miskovsky: "His latest effort to get attention makes use of the song to the tune of "Sugartime" which suggests there would be money from morning to evening to suppertime if voters would go for George." You know you've arrived when politicians are using your music to coax votes outta folks.

When Charlie was asked about his feelings regarding his country version of "Sugartime" being bumped off the charts by the McGuire Sisters version, he simply stated, "The McGuire's version was great; you can't feel bad about an act that makes your song the biggest hit of the year. Of course, as an artist, cover versions are disappointing but as a composer the more people who cut your material, the better it is."

In 2015, a popular Rap artist from Singapore, ShiGGa Shay, covered his version of "Sugartime" with the accompaniment of Inch Chua. Their rap/reggae rendition of the song saw fresh new words and beats, reviving the tune for the youth of today, albeit with a few explicit, sexually charged lyrics. When Charlie Phillips was asked his reaction to the renewed genre, he simply states, "Well, that's not my favorite type of music, but I love to see young people doing something fun with my song. That's what 'Sugartime' was all about. Good times."

Who knows what the future holds for "Sugartime." Imaginably there will be another resurgence of the song if covered by additional artists or companies, or maybe the song will slip quietly away into the recesses of the music vaults. Time will tell. Most likely the upbeat happy song written by a poverty-stricken boy on a farm in West Texas will live in the hearts of many for generations.

Chapter 7
Talk About Pop's Music

It probably wouldn't be a stretch to say if it weren't for one Odis "Pop" Echols, then there may have never been a Charlie Phillips. True, if Pop hadn't seen Charlie playing at the Bovina talent show, it's possible Charlie might have found his way to the Norman Petty Studio sooner or later, but one thing's for certain, Charlie might have never entered a career in the radio business. Pop Echols' tutelage of Charlie would prove to be the catalyst of great things to come in the music industry. "I suppose I owe Pop my whole career," Charlie would say 60 years after first meeting Pop. Here's the fascinating story of Pop Echols:

If one thing could be said about Odis "Pop" Echols, he was a masterful storyteller and had a colorful personality. It's difficult to discern fact from fiction when chatting about the incredible life Pop lived, and the voluminous culmination of his life's experiences. Odis Echols was born on May 7, 1903, to Mr. and Mrs. W.L. Echols in Enloe, Texas. Little Odis began his career in music by age seven, where he started directing songs at conventions while singing in his family's quartet. By age 13, young Odis began leading the religious choir at the Methodist Church in his hometown. Growing up, the fledgling Odis contended with his nine brothers and sisters who all liked to sing as each became interested in gospel music- perchance an early indication of the direction his life would soon yield.

Odis married the love of his life, Grace Traweek in Lubbock, Texas and shortly moved just west of Clovis to the now extinct town of Blacktower, New Mexico around January of 1922. Echols would join his first quartet and soon begin studying and teaching music in schools that had no public school music program. He was often seen driving his T-Model automobile throughout Eastern New Mexico and West Texas. Echols once told a newspaper, "I'd go and teach one hour a day in public schools, and then the whole community would come back to the schoolhouse at night, and I'd teach them how to direct songs and lead music."

By 1926, he auditioned for Frank Stamps' Stamps Quartet and secured a place possibly as the group's baritone singer. He and Grace moved with the quartet boys to Chattanooga, Tennessee where Odis continued to sing with the assemblage, even after Frank reorganized the group and changed the name to the All-Star Quartet. At Odis' prompting, the favorite foursome added a fifth musician to its group, a jazz pianist named Dwight Brock. Brock would later become famous for his unique rhythmic playing style in gospel music. It's thought the All-Star quartet was the first to integrate a fifth musician, which later became the staple for modern gospel harmony groups.

The group squeaked out a living from the price of admission for attending the singing event as well as from the sale of their printed songbooks as they traveled from church to church throughout the South. "We were called modern, and we almost were thrown out by some churches," Echols once recited. "Some people thought we were too rhythmic. We were the first gospel singers to do rhythm type spirituals." Yet, audiences eventually fell in love with the group and frequently gave Echols standing ovations for his rendition of "Ol' Man River."

Around 1927, talent scout and record producer, Ralph Peer, who was with Victor Records, contacted the group and had the singers travel to Atlanta, Georgia to audition for a promising recording session with the record company. After meeting with both Stamps and Echols at the Biltmore Hotel, Peer decided to record the men, suggesting the two popular songs "Bringing in the Sheaves" and "Rescue the Perishing." After recording those two songs, the group persuaded Peer to allow them to record "Give the World a Smile" and "Love Leads the Way," both audience favorites at the time. This was a wise move as "Give the World a Smile" would purportedly be the first gospel record to sell one million copies. An early affiliation with Ralph Peer would cement a future business relationship as Peer founded the Southern Music Publishing Company and would later be instrumental in publishing acts like Buddy Holly and the Crickets and Charlie Phillips.

Echols left the Stamps family and the quartet around 1929 moving back to Clovis where he began working in the music department at Fox Drug Store. While he was there, Pop sang in a trio formed with his brothers, Horace and Coy Echols, calling themselves the Fox Trio. Also, he prearranged another quartet he named the Melody Boys Quartet, but as fate would have it, the Great Depression set in and Echols moved back to Lubbock opening the Stamps-Baxter Music Company songbook store. He would additionally work closely with the Stamps family and J.R. Baxter Jr. in the Stamps-Baxter School of Music for several years.

Baxter would later ingratiate himself to Echols and even wrote an endorsement for Pop as an introduction to a booklet designed and sold for 50-cents entitled, *The Melody Album of Odis Echols and his Melody Boys, A Collection of Songs, Poems and Pictures*. Baxter writes:

> *It affords me pleasure to indorse the work that Odis Echols and his Melody Boys are doing and have done thru the years. He is a tireless worker and has achieved the distinction of being one of the best entertainers in the ranks of Gospel singers. He has a fine family and thousands of loyal friends all over the land...*

Echols taught ten-night singing lessons for various churches in the area and surrounding towns. Certainly one claim to fame was his tutelage of a young Jimmy Dean, who lived in Plainview, Texas and sung at his father, George Dean's, Seth Ward Baptist Church. Young Dean could often be seen hanging around his mother's beauty shop when not in school or church and, as rumor has it, sometimes would give a haircut to some of the young men who popped into the shop for a quick restyling. Of course, Jimmy Dean would have his first music hit, "Bummin' Around" in 1953, and would go on to music fame eventually forming the Jimmy Dean Sausage Company by 1969. (Dean would meet Charlie Phillips sometime in the 1960's where the two developed a lifelong musical friendship).

By the mid 1930's, Echols would move yet again to Abilene, Texas after starting the Odis Echols' All-Star Texans Quartet and joining Harley Sadler's 18th Annual Tour, which was a traveling revival tent show seating up to 2500 spectators. However, the Great Depression hit folks hard, and Sadler was unable to meet expenses and decided to close the shows. Echols returned to Abilene and begin working at Hall Music Store and would also start a singing school.

Pop Echols began yet another quartet, but this time he stepped aside as one of the stars. The N.B.C. or Neighborhood Boys Cut-up Quartet was made up of four boys from seven to 12 years of age. The talented group of youngsters would see success as they were featured on an amateur talent contest in Ft. Worth, Texas at the Ringside Club and won first- prize out of 22 contestants. The boys subsequently auditioned for a screen test at the Casa Mañana Theater for scouts from the Hal Roach Studios and Universal Pictures.

Keeping in mind the financial hardships and devastation families were still feeling from the Great Depression, it was important for American families to move where they could to feed their kinfolks. Frank Stamps had joined Echols in Abilene helping Odis with the singing schools and the two reorganized their once successful assemblage, the Stamps Melody Boys. In an attempt to revive their careers, they moved their singing group and families to Hot Springs, Arkansas just miles from Pencil Bluff, Arkansas where Charlie Phillips' grandparents, the Massongills, had just recently departed in their attempts to find a better life in Texas.

The Stamps Melody Boys showed hope as they performed their classics on the local KTHS radio station for 14 months. While in Arkansas, Echols purchased ownership in the Hartford Music

Company, one of the major gospel songbook publishing companies in the South, and sold songbooks when the quartet was on the road.

Because of the KTHS gig, Echols would be asked to move to Nashville, Tennessee hosting the *Saturday Night All Gospel Show* on WLAC radio. Towards the end of the Korean War, the Melody Boys sang "When the Battles are Over" and "The Boys Come Marching Home" bringing the audiences to tears after hearing the beautiful, touching songs. The Stamps Melody Boys would move on and relocate to Louisville, Kentucky where they continued to perform for audiences and for WHAS radio station where they were broadcast on 35 different stations and later on the Mutual Radio Network that broadcast from coast to coast.

A national drug company sponsored 25 stations, and the other ten were on the Old Kentucky Home Evangelistic network. For 52 weeks at WHAS, the boys were serendipitously known as Odis Echols and his Faultless Melody Boys because they were under a sponsorship contract with the Faultless Starch Company. Though lucrative for a year, new groups and materials arose on the radio scene and the boys would need to seek employment in a fresh new environment. Odis, the boys and their families would move yet again as work opened up in other towns.

Around 1946, Echols sold his interest in the Hartford Music Company and moved to Shreveport, Louisiana with his renewed group, The Melody Boys Quartet. The group was able to land a spot on the favorite radio station KWKH where they performed their gospel ensembles Monday through Saturday. While in Shreveport, the Melody Boys with Odis at the helm, rented the Shreveport Municipal Auditorium and began a Saturday night show broadcast over KWKH-AM radio station. Echols emceed the weekly show and was introduced to some of the finest musicians and potential hopefuls like Jim Reeves, Faron Young, Webb Pierce and a young Tommy Sands.

Odis Echols moved several more times over the years, forming and teaching music classes as he continued singing for one quartet or another, once even appearing on *Los Angeles' Club 15* hosted by Bob Crosby on his CBS radio show. After another move back to Lubbock, Texas Odis would meet a promising young lady in one of his singing classes at the Four Square Gospel Church.

Charlene Condray would be an early discovery of Echols, as she would sing at local churches and talents shows. By age 16, Charlene would perform on Lubbock's television station KDUB on the *Circle 13 Dude Ranch Show* and soon became known as "Lubbock's Sweetheart." Western Swing bandleader, Tommy Hancock, saw Charlene perform and asked her to join his band, the Roadside Playboys- she did, and the two musicians eventually courted and married.

The Melody Boys Quartet was dissolved by 1952. After a few years in Lubbock, Odis had the opportunity to purchase the KCLV radio station in nearby Clovis, New Mexico. Short on cash, Echols approached his brother, Coy, who loaned him the money to make the purchase and after a long hiatus from New Mexico, Odis "Pop" Echols officially moved to Clovis in 1953. He had made numerous connections in the music business, and it seemed appropriate he could now capitalize on his many years in the music trade.

Pop Echols was a handsome, dapper individual who learned early in his career that appearances meant everything. Since 1935, Echols had been sporting a well-coiffed mustache and even claims he started the trend of men in gospel groups growing prominent mustaches to single themselves out to an audience. "The Beatles started long hair. I started the mustache," Pop said in an interview. "You could always see Pop dressed in his Sunday-best no matter what time of the day," explained Charlie Phillips. "I don't think I ever saw him in anything but a three-piece suit and loaded with gold rings and jewelry." One of the greatest perks owning KCLV radio station was Pop's knack for working out trades with local businesses throughout the Clovis area. In exchange for radio advertising, Pop would eat at some of the finest places in town and could always be seen driving the latest Lincoln Towncar. It wouldn't be long until he gained notoriety in the community as a business owner, leader and supporter of his township.

Arthur Godfrey was a popular radio and television entertainer on CBS-TV and having heard the music of the Stamps Quartet and Odis' creation, The Melody Boys, invited Odis Echols to New York City for a brief interview on his television program, *Arthur Godfrey's Talent Scouts*. The two could be seen on TV chuckling it up while sitting in front of the curtain gabbing into the large CBS microphone as they talked about music. Interestingly, this is the same program that would help launch the career of the McGuire Sisters and also be the folks who turned down Buddy Holly after auditioning for the platform.

Even though Odis was enjoying his position in the limelight, the radio station hadn't yet taken off. So to make ends meet in the beginning, Pop and his son, Odis Echols Jr. , hosted a variety of programming on KCLV, keeping primarily with a pop music format. They also produced shows out of Clovis they took on the road to many neighboring towns like Muleshoe and Plainview, Texas. Pop emceed the shows and as various performers like the Crowder Family, the traditional Lubbock quartet, and the Commodores took the stage.

The shows were met with success and helped supplement the income of the Echols family. In 1956, Pop and Odis Jr. were able to produce the *Pop Echols Reunion Show* held at the Lubbock fairgrounds. Waylon Jennings had come a long way from his talent show days and was a popular Lubbock disc jockey on KLLL radio station serving much of the Texas Panhandle. Jennings interviewed Odis Jr. for the show and soon established many connections and friendships in Lubbock.

The Echols men met "Pappy" Dave Stone and "Hi Pockets" Duncan at another radio station in Lubbock with the call letters KDAV. This station would later be dubbed "the Buddy Holly Station" because they were the first to broadcast music of Buddy Holley before he became famous. All in all, the shows became prosperous since they featured local musicians as well as those with more notoriety like the Commodores, Roger Miller, a budding Willie Nelson, a young Roy Orbison to even more accomplished stars of the day like Johnny Cash and eventually Elvis Presley.

Having already lived a full and exciting life, Pop surprisingly received an invitation in 1957 from NBC television producers asking him to appear on the television program, *This Is Your Life*, hosted by Ralph Edwards. The young actor and singer, Tommy Sands, who Odis had basically discovered while in Shreveport, requested the former quartet singer appear on the program being filmed in Los Angeles. Echols obliged and performed on the national program.

If Odis Echols discovered Tommy, it would be Elvis Presley's manager, Colonel Tom Parker, who would sign the teenage Tommy to RCA Records. After some success, Echols would often invite Tommy to the small New Mexico town of Clovis to appear on KCLV radio, or even to hang out at the newly popularized Norman Petty Studio. Charlie Phillips, who was around Tommy's age, would often be asked to entertain the young Sands when visiting, especially after "Sugartime" propelled to the No. 1 song in the country. Tommy and Charlie would be seen driving the streets of Clovis hopping from one party to the next when Sands would visit Pop in Clovis.

Sands had movie star good looks and not only became a singing success, but also joined movie fame after being asked to sing at the *Academy Awards*. Tommy's unfortunate decline would occur shortly after divorcing Nancy Sinatra, music mogul Frank Sinatra's daughter, who would ostensibly have him blacklisted from the entertainment industry. Curiously, Tommy won't be the last guy in our story slighted by the all-powerful Frank Sinatra.

Odis Echols was a celebrity of sorts in the gospel market, but now enjoyed his own celebrity as two television appearances popularized the small town resident. Having made the acquaintance of Arthur Godfrey, Eddy Arnold, Tommy Sands, Elvis Presley, Roger Miller, Roy Orbison, Faron Young, Jim Reeves, and even comedienne Minnie Pearl as well as many others, Pop seemed at home around fellow accomplished musicians and entertainers. Popular 1950's pop star, Rusty Draper, once crashed Pop's KCLV studio in Clovis to plug his new record.

It seems this was finally Pop's time, and he had earned it. His life of moving from town to town was now over as he enjoyed a much-longed sense of stability while working in the music business in Clovis for the remainder of his life. Young Odis Echols Jr. would graduate from Texas Tech University in Lubbock, Texas and serve as a State Senator from the great state of New Mexico for 11 years. It was a life well lived and Charlie Phillips owed Pop his radio career.

Chapter 8
The Grand Ole' Louisiana Heydays

The latter part of the 1950's showed great promise for Charlie Phillips as he'd now written a No. 1 best-selling record, had a recording contract with Coral Records, was an accomplished radio deejay on a regional station and was extremely busy performing shows at the abundant dancehalls and event centers throughout West Texas and eastern New Mexico.

With the advent and success of "Sugartime," Charlie found himself in high demand. Clubs, halls and shows in the area were requesting him personally. His group capitalized on the sensation of Charlie's hit song and was dubbed, Charlie Phillips and the Sugartimer Band. A popular radio program that broadcasted out of Shreveport, Louisiana on a 50,000-watt station was targeting one of the largest country music listening publics in America. The *Louisiana Hayride* was at the top of their game by 1958 and were featuring new up-and-coming music artists as well as exhibiting tried-and-true celebrity country stars of their day.

Horace Lee Logan had disembarked in Shreveport by 1932 at barely 16 years old. His voice was so deep at a young age he'd won the honor of becoming an announcer on Shreveport's KWKH-AM radio station. After a successful decade on the radio, Horace launched a three-hour Saturday night program recorded in front of a live audience at the Shreveport Municipal Auditorium he christened, the *Louisiana Hayride*. Rumor has it the creator of the *Hayride* obtained the name after reading a 1941 book entitled the *Louisiana Hayride* by Harnett Thomas Kane chronicling an incident from 1939 – 1940 that tarnished the image of great state of Louisiana as scandal arose involving James Monroe Smith, President of Louisiana State

University and George Caldwell, former Louisiana building superintendent, both of whom were sentenced to prison for some under the table misgivings.

The first broadcast of the *Hayride* debuted on April 3, 1948 with a star-studded cast comprising of: the Tennessee Mountain Boys with Kitty Wells, Johnnie and Jack, the Bailes Brothers, Harmie Smith, the Mercy Brothers, Curley Kinsey and the Tennessee Ridge Runners, the Four Deacons, Bob Wills and His Texas Playboys, and the Ozark Mountaineers. Mirroring the style of the already popular *Grand Ole Opry*, the show quickly gained popularity and was heightened by adding a regional 25-station network broadcasting over an enormous area, which was even heard overseas on Armed Forces Radio. The show eventually was broadcast via CBS to 191 stations across 13 states in the South.

Unlike the *Opry* that required an artist to have a hit record before performing on their program, Horace "Hoss" Logan encouraged and welcomed greenhorns so long as they had actually taped or pressed a record. Logan often encouraged experimentation and even allowed amplified guitars and other untried instruments and singing styles. This simple leniency would give rise to the introduction of drums being used onstage during a country music set, an almost unheard of thing even though the drums were sometimes hidden backstage and out of view of the audience. Bob Wills had already introduced a set of drums in his act by this time, but it was still an untried instrument among country folks. The powers that be allowed a drum sound to be played as long as the audience essentially didn't see the drummer, an almost unheard of thing in present times, but nonetheless, it would be Logan who'd set the stage, opening doors for such experimentation.

Additionally, with the introduction of rock 'n' roll on the scene, artists, even country musicians, were beginning to use amplified guitars when performing. The *Opry* had banned the use of electric guitars, but Horace's coincidental forethought regarding this innovative instrument would give rise to one of America's greatest superstars, the teenage Elvis Presley, who, by the way, had been turned away from the *Grand Ole Opry*. Elvis would see mammoth reactions the year following his first performance on the *Hayride* on October 16, 1954.

Horace Logan believed in giving a person a chance, or in some cases, imaginably a second chance. When Hank Williams was fired from the *Opry* for his drinking problem, Horace welcomed him back to Shreveport and gave him a job. The *Opry* had once told the young Elvis Presley to stick to truck driving, but good ole' Horace could see past any hurdles and understood his talents. Logan chronicled his early beginnings with these two artists in his 1998 memoir, *Elvis, Hank and Me: Making Musical History on the 'Hayride.'* After hearing Elvis' debut of his song, "That's All Right Mama," Horace signed him to a one-year contract making appearances on the program for a whopping $18 per weekly appearance.

Hank Williams, Kitty Wells, Faron Young and Webb Pierce were among some of the first artists to catch a break and reach a large audience from the *Hayride*. It had been only a couple of years before the first broadcast of the *Hayride* that Pop Echols performed his gospel shows at the same Shreveport Municipal Auditorium. While in Shreveport, Pop had met some up-and-coming musicians and was introduced into some of the same circles. Not to mention, he had kept a close relationship with former co-workers at KWKH radio, most notably Horace Logan.

As Charlie's manager, Pop arranged for him to have his national debut on the *Hayride*. Charlie's version of "Sugartime" was already on the country music charts and was doing exceedingly well, not to mention the McGuire Sisters hadn't yet released their cover-version of the future No. 1 single. Thus far, Charlie had only recorded nine songs in the studio since 1954, but was receiving significant airplay, so the *Hayride* was delighted to have him on their very popular program.

Pop set the date for October 26, 1957. Charlie loaded up his guitar and some clothes into Pop's 1956 Lincoln Premiere and they embarked on the road trip with Pop's wife, Grace, and Charlie's close friend, Doyle Ford, tagging along for moral support. The distance from Clovis, New Mexico to Shreveport is over 600 miles, but the almost ten-hour drive would be instrumental for Charlie Phillips to increase his exposure for a national audience.

The closer Charlie got to Shreveport, the more he noticed the heat and humidity. Even though it was already autumn, the difference in temperature amid the windy plains of the dry Panhandle compared to the more humid region of the deep South is often stifling. "Thank God Pop's car had air-conditioning, or I might of melted on that trip," he remembers. Yet, the drive went smoothly and they pulled into Shreveport early Friday afternoon.

Once the group had settled into their motel, Pop took Charlie directly to the KWKH studio where the former gospel singer had formerly broadcast. Charlie had heard the *Louisiana Hayride* so many times on the radio and, of course, admired the show's overall presentation, but not much could prepare him for his first introduction to the one and only, Horace Logan, who gladly shook Charlie's hand as soon as he and Pop entered the KWKH radio station. "I was so excited," he said, "It was like shaking the hand of God" he lightheartedly joked.

KWKH had a rich and interesting history. Its original owner, William Kennon Henderson, purchased and aired the first radio broadcast from Shreveport in 1926. Henderson was often in trouble with the Federal Radio Commission because of some on-air expletive-laced outbursts against chain stores moving into the area, as well as the United States government. Of course, we're used to hearing these types of outbreaks today with the arrival of "talk radio" programming, but in the early days of radio it was highly uncommon to be so opinionated on-air. Financial problems ultimately plagued Henderson, and he was eventually compelled to file for personal bankruptcy, negatively affecting his radio license. Within a couple of years, W.K. eventually lost his radio station, and new ownership was transferred to a sizeable publishing company.

After Pop, Grace and Charlie caught up with Horace about their lives and music, Pop drove the group to the Shreveport Municipal Auditorium, later dubbed The Muni, a few miles across town just west of downtown Shreveport on Grand Avenue and Milam Street. The auditorium itself was constructed with a beautiful dark-bricked façade with ornate stonework and limestone friezes wrapping the fringe and erected with an Art Deco theme. It had been dedicated to the soldiers of The Great War on Armistice Day, November 11, 1929 commemorating troops who used the building as barracks during The War as it also housed an early radar warning system for incoming aircraft.

With an equally fantastic Art Deco interior, the design was a bit of an architectural marvel exhibiting superior acoustics under its 54-foot proscenium arch facing the audience. The auditorium boasted one of the largest stages in the area. Large crowds could quickly gather in the viscera holding more than 3,000 spectators. The hall is five stories tall, taking up much of the city block with its 129,000 square feet interior. It once advertised on its programs the building was not only fireproof, but also out-of-town visitors could be assured of good seating.

It was just two years before Charlie's introduction to Horace that Colonel Tom Parker saw Elvis Presley's performance on the *Louisiana Hayride* and quickly signed young Elvis to a management contract and initiated his promising recording career. Parker bought out Elvis' $18 per weekly performance contract for the princely, or should we say the kingly sum of $10,000, freeing Elvis to pursue his soon to be lucrative career.

Already nicknamed the "Cradle of the Stars," celebrating the vast celebrity performances and hopeful newcomers, the *Hayride* had already seen famous country music superstars like Hank Williams, Johnny Cash, Tex Ritter, George Jones and blues musician, Huddie Ledbetter, perform on its stage. Now Charlie Phillips would have his opportunity to wow audiences with his panache.

After meeting Horace Logan, Charlie's next introduction would be to a lesser celebrity of sorts, but a star in his own right.

Bruce Jones opened his first Southern Maid Donut shop in Shreveport, Louisiana in 1941. People would drive from all around to taste and smell his hot glazed sweet donuts. Upon entering the store, folks were uncharacteristically greeted, not by a friendly checkout clerk at the hostess stand, but by two rowdy gentlemen dressed as Mynah birds often throwing insults at unsuspecting customers. This was most comparable to Heckle and Jeckle from the admired cartoon series. Jones was a huge lover of music and became one of the first sponsors of the *Hayride*. His sizeable banner prominently hung alongside the KWKH radio station banner on the backside of the stage just above the performers. The banner read, "Southern Maid HOT DONUTS FROM 4 OCLOCK ON, NOW THREE CONVENIENT LOCATIONS."

An enormous hit with locals as well as visitors, Jones would appear onstage during a concert break and bring a box of hot glazed donuts to give to Horace Logan or Frank Page, who was the other *Hayride* announcer. Folks couldn't wait to get their hands on one of these translucent covered confectionaries after watching the announcers devour the delectable. Bruce Jones was the second person Charlie would meet after arriving for his night on the *Hayride*, who welcomed Charlie with his usual southern hospitality.

Since Charlie wasn't able to bring his band, he was required to use some the staff musicians present that early evening. Since the band members had never played with Charlie before, they spent some of the early evening practicing two of Charlie's most attractive, yet virtually unheard of songs, "Sugartime" and "One Faded Rose." Tommy Tomlinson was a staff musician and was on-hand to backup Charlie for his evening gig even though Johnny Horton was to head the regulars for the night.

Gerald Delmar "Tommy" Tomlinson was one of the most gifted musicians to ever grace the stage of the *Louisiana Hayride*. Tomlinson was raised on a farm quite close to the Cash's family farm near south-central Tinsman, Arkansas. Although he was not a native of Shreveport, you'd be in a pickle if you told a local Louisianan that- as they've claimed him as one of their own. Like Charlie

Phillips, Tommy had begun his first band by age fifteen and played at bar dances and social events. By the time Tomlinson had reached the *Hayride* in 1954, he had already played with the likes of Hank Williams and had previously performed on the *Hayride's* facsimile show out of Dallas called the *Big "D" Jamboree* before he joined the Marine Corps.

While deployed to Korea, Tomlinson was wounded in both legs during combat yet, he would continue to serve until his honorable release in February of 1954. After the military, Tommy returned to Louisiana and almost immediately began playing guitar on the *Hayride*. It wasn't long before he'd meet two other legendary musicians at the *Hayride*, both Tillman Franks and Johnny Horton. The trio would develop a musical connection and friendship. On this fall evening in 1957, Charlie would become acquainted with Tomlinson and they would perform together for the first of many times, as they too would develop a musical relationship lasting for years.

Present at the *Louisiana Hayride* this evening was also another country music star who would perform on his own segment following Charlie. Benny Barnes had gotten his big break while playing guitar during a George Jones recording session. Barnes recorded his first big hit, "Poor Man's Riches," which peaked at No. 4 on the country music charts the same year he appeared with Charlie on the *Hayride* show. Charlie had played Benny's big hit record on his radio platform and was excited to actually be onstage live with such a performer.

Hank Williams Jr. once noted, "If the *Opry* was the Promised Land for country musicians on their way up, then the *Louisiana Hayride* was Heaven's Gate." It had been less than three months since Charlie had recorded "Sugartime" and "One Faded Rose" at the Norman Petty Studio with the accompaniment of Buddy Holly, who perhaps gave him the confidence to appear onstage in front of 3,000 country music fans, not to mention the thousands of at-home listeners. With a sure-accomplished guitarist like Tommy Tomlinson leading the charge and a talented backup band, Charlie's first national appearance was an anticipated hit. Pop Echols and his wife,

Grace, couldn't have been more proud and Charlie, well Charlie, was on cloud nine.

Thousands of people from all across the South heard Charlie play that evening. Even Ma Kate was delighted to hear her son on the radio, but of course, was more concerned about the crew driving safely back to Texas and was inquisitive as to when her son would be returning home. After that boastful night, Charlie and the gang would return to Clovis for business as usual. It would be only one short month before the McGuire Sisters would reintroduce "Sugartime" to the world thus making Charlie an even bigger sensation. This opened up the door for him to appear on other national programming.

Charlie returned to Louisiana several more times over the next few years. He appeared on the *Hayride* a couple of occasions during 1958 at the height of the "Sugartime" fuss and would also perform various times during the 1960's. The *Hayride* requested he play many times over the years; however, Charlie usually declined. When asked why he didn't appear more often, he states, "Well, for one, it was a long drive from Farwell, Texas and another, they didn't really pay that much. I had money comin' from my gigs, and the radio and such, plus some of the money was comin' in from the record sales...so there wasn't much use drivin' all that way just to get exposure."

Interestingly, there were two other Phillips' on the country music scene during the late 50's who were of no relation to Charlie. Bill Phillips was a good ole' boy from North Carolina who had built up his career on the *Old Southern Jamboree* out of Miami, Florida. Around the time Charlie was appearing for the first time on the *Hayride*, Bill was working in the Nashville area and was doing some traveling throughout the country with Johnnie Wright and Kitty Wells. Stu Phillips was another country singer on the scene. Stu was a Canadian-born singer who was on his rise to the top around the same time as both Bill and Charlie. Stu would see success over his career performing regularly on the *Grand Ole Opry* and would ultimately be inducted into the Canadian Country Music Hall of Fame.

With three famous country singers with the last name Phillips touring the country and being played on the radio, a precarious hitch arose. Folks were getting the men confused! Charlie might attend a performance and be introduced as Bill Phillips, or vice versa, and Stu Phillips might be in Nashville and someone says to him they just love his song, "Sugartime." Bill Phillips and Charlie were at a performance in Dallas, Texas and Bill told Charlie that so many people thought he (Bill) wrote "Sugartime" that family and friends were asking him for money thinking he'd become a big rich songwriter. So as fate would have it, and because of the popularity of "Sugartime," Charlie added the widespread title of his song as his middle stage-name and for the first time Charlie became, Charlie "Sugartime" Phillips- thus alleviating any confusion during introductions. This was around 1958, and his new nickname would stick with him throughout the remainder of his life.

In 1958, Charlie was asked to perform on a television program broadcast from Springfield, Missouri. Red Foley was one of the top country music personalities in the United States and hosted a program on KWTO radio and on ABC-TV most commonly called, Red Foley's *Ozark Jubilee*, which was the first nationally televised country music program reaching around 25 million listeners and viewers across America each week. Some of the most known personalities appearing as regulars on the *Ozark Jubilee* at this time were the 14 year old Brenda Lee, Webb Pierce, Porter Wagoner, Sonny James, Wanda Jackson, Jean Sheppard and The Browns. The *Ozark Jubilee* is often acknowledged as having a substantial influence on television and for country music, bringing a taste of the Ozarks into many American homes.

Red Foley began asking on the program, "If you folks want us to come and visit at your house like this every Saturday night, why don't you drop me a line in Springfield, Missouri?" The following week over 25,000 cards arrived in Springfield! By the time Charlie played the *Jubilee*, the show was being carried by 150 affiliate stations across the country and had one of the largest viewing audiences on American television.

At the time, Springfield had become the center of country music and ranked third only behind New York City and Hollywood for originating television programming. Folks from all across America can hear the sound of Foley's theme song, "Sugarfoot Rag." Red's program featured his own staff musicians, so Charlie left his band back home in Texas and set out for the 650-mile trip to the Ozark region. Although Charlie had reached thousands of homes with his radio appearance on the *Louisiana Hayride*, this would be his first national guest appearance and his initial television network debut. Charlie arrived on Friday and situated himself in a nearby motel and dropped by the filming location to get acquainted with the staff musicians.

Red Foley was one of the first guys to make his introduction as he shook Charlie's hand. "He just seemed very nice and mild-mannered," Charlie recalls. The following day would be reserved for rehearsals, or so Charlie thought, as each guest performer's time was segmented out so the staff band could practice their music. This would be Charlie's first encounter with an adorable young talented artist named Brenda Lee. Little Miss Dynamite was the nickname given to this four-foot nine-inch boisterous singer from Georgia after she recorded the song "Dynamite" the previous year in 1957. Charlie wondered silently how such an energetic voice could come out of such a small frame.

Little Miss Dynamite may have been small in stature and only a teenager at the time she and Charlie met, but she would go on to do some very amazing things in the near future. Havin' gotten her big break on Red Foley's show, she became the youngest regular to make consistent appearances. The first time Red saw her on stage he remarked, "I still get cold chills thinking about the first time I heard that voice...There I stood, after 26 years of supposedly learning how to conduct myself in front of an audience, with my mouth two miles wide and a glassy stare in my eyes."

Who could have known at the time, but Brenda, the little girl from Georgia, would go on to record dozens of albums and sell tens of millions of records. Years later in 1997, she will be inducted into the Country Music Hall of Fame. Lee is also in the Rockabilly Hall of Fame, the Hit Parade Hall of Fame and was voted into the Rock and Roll Hall of Fame in 2002. Little Miss Dynamite furthermore has a Lifetime Achievement Grammy Award. "She just seemed so professional for a young lady when she performed onstage," Charlie recounts after seeing her for the first time. This won't be Charlie's only encounter with Little Miss Dynamite, as they'll perform on the same stage several times and tour together shortly.

The *Jubilee* performance would be unlike any Charlie had made to date. The band never rehearsed Charlie's biggest hit, "Sugartime" that afternoon because Charlie wouldn't actually be *singing* with the accompaniment of a live band that following Saturday evening. The *Ozark Jubilee* was filmed before a live audience and Charlie was asked to do something he had never done before. Lip-sync! He wouldn't even know what that word meant. Of course in today's music world, this type of performance is commonplace. Yet Charlie never really understood the reasoning behind this; however, he performed as he was told and stepped onstage mouthing the words to "Sugartime" as a record played over the speakers before the live audience.

Not knowing a lot about how television worked, Charlie would actually be convening at home with his mother and friends the following week as the *Ozark Jubilee* aired on their local ABC station and Charlie was able to watch himself on television for the first time. He had learned the difference between a show being taped before an audience and a show that was aired live.

Phillips would appear only one more time on Red Foley's *Ozark Jubilee* as the show's final episode aired on September 24, 1960. He would carry with him many fond memories of his very first television appearance. At the very least, the *Hayride* taught him how to play before an audience of thousands, but the *Jubilee* trained him to perform for an audience of millions of listeners and viewers.

Local gigs around the Clovis and Texas Panhandle were Charlie and the Sugartimer's bread and butter. But occasionally, Charlie was called to make guest appearances farther from home.

Although shows like the *Hayride* and the *Jubilee* barely paid enough money to cover the price of gasoline, which, by the way, was around 31-cents per gallon, or even a motel room, they provided an artist with indispensable, free publicity. If an artist had a new record he or she wanted to promote, an appearance on a large regional or national program could provide enough exposure to push record sales and create a hit record or album. It was for this reason Charlie continued to drive long distances at the prompting and assistance of his manager.

By the early 1960's, Charlie was already a veteran after just a few short years of recording and performing, and his star-status was rising to the ranks of many of his childhood heroes. "Sugartime," his first penned song, was opening doors that might have otherwise been closed. There was a lesser-known show southeast of Clovis broadcast from the Dallas Sportatorium in Dallas, Texas called the *Big "D" Jamboree*. Originally called *The Lone Star Barn Dance*, the *Big "D"* was carried on the CBS Radio Network and was broadcast throughout the region. It was the only country music program in the Dallas area, so it became wildly popular.

Charlie would debut in the summer of 1960 and would return that December at the request of the *Jamboree* producers. A program advertisement for this event read, "Few people have made an impression like the one Charlie Phillips made when he debuted here last summer. The talented Texan who is responsible for the all time hit, 'Sugartime' as made famous by the McGuire Sisters will return Saturday to head up a 'special' New Years Eve type program." Charlie performed his country version of "Sugartime" for the crowd and it's likely he performed his latest recording of "Welcome to the Wedding," to name a few.

At the time Charlie played the Sportatorium, Al Turner and Ed McLemore produced the show. They advertised as *Ed McLemore's Big "D" Jamboree- Biggest & Best Country & Western Show in the Entire Southwest*. The December lineup boasted headlining artists like Ernest Tubb, Johnny Cash, George Jones, June Carter, Leroy Vandyke, the Louvin Bros. and Charlie Phillips who would be opened for by Johnny Riels and Sisters as well as Lana Parker and Cowboy Weaver. Phillips would return to the *Big "D" Jamboree* only three more times over the next few years. His first return would be on March 24, 1962. By this time, Charlie had left Coral Records and began working with Columbia Records at the prompting of his new boss and manager, Ray Winkler. Charlie performed again on March 9, 1963, and would return for his final performance in Dallas on January 11, 1964.

By 1960, Charlie's innovative manager, Ray Winkler, decided it was time for him to start playing with the big boys, so he asked Columbia to get Charlie an appearance on the *Grand Ole Opry* in Nashville, Tennessee. If you were a singer or performer during this era, you dreamt of one day being an artist on the *Opry* and as a matter of fact, some still do even to this day. It too was Charlie's dream.

The *Grand Ole Opry's* roots ran deep watered by the music of its era. It began in November of 1925 when WSM radio announced fiddle player, Uncle Jimmy Thompson, would be the first performer on a brand new show called *The WSM Barn Dance*. The rest, as they say, is history. Many folks don't know, but in the earliest of days, the *Opry* was housed in the National Life & Accident Insurance Company building for almost a decade before moving to the Hillsboro Theatre. After a couple of years, they moved the show to the Dixie Tabernacle. Then within a few years moved to the War Memorial Auditorium. In June of 1943, the *Grand Ole Opry* relocated into a more permanent location housed inside the Ryman Auditorium; formerly the Union Gospel Tabernacle built in 1892, where they would stay until March of 1974. The Ryman came to be known as the "Mother Church of Country Music" and rightfully so as it would be virtually unrivaled in country music listenership.

Opry members in the 1940's would include notables like Eddy Arnold, Minnie Pearl, Little Jimmy Dickens, Grandpa Jones, Ernest Tubb, Hank Williams and George Morgan naming just a small sample. These were the men and women the young Charlie Phillips had grown up listening to. By the 1950's, the music show had added the likes of Kitty Wells, Lefty Frizzell, George Jones, Webb Pierce,

Marty Robbins, Johnny Cash, Ferlin Husky, Ray Price, Jean Sheppard, Porter Wagoner, Faron Young, Chet Atkins, Jimmy C. Newman, Jim Reeves and Charlie Phillips' all-time hero, Hank Snow, once again to only name a few of the talented artists associated with the *Opry* at this time.

By the early 1960's, Charlie's penned song, "Sugartime," had already become a household standard recognized by millions worldwide and Charlie was popping onto the country music charts under the direction of Columbia Records with songs like "Welcome to the Wedding," "No More Sugartime," "I Guess I'll Never Learn," "Now That It's Over," and "Cancel the Call." He was ripe for the *Grand Ole Opry*. By this period, the *Opry* had incorporated stars like Stu Phillips, Dottie West, Patsy Cline, Loretta Lynn, Whisperin' Bill Anderson, and Dolly Parton to their repertoire of hit makers.

Charlie worked closely with Ray Winkler at KZIP radio station in Amarillo, Texas and was developing quite a following, not only as a singer and songwriter, but as a distinguished deejay as well. The *Grand Ole Opry* welcomed Charlie to Nashville to hear him perform, but perhaps most importantly, Charlie's prowess as a deejay endeared him to many of the *Opry* performers because he could do something very special for them- he could get their records played on the radio reaching much of West Texas, Oklahoma, Colorado and New Mexico. It might be construed as an "I'll scratch your back if you scratch mine" scenario, but it was necessary for artists to befriend deejay's from across the country so they could keep their record sales high.

Nashville today somewhat resembles Nashville of the past with the moniker "Music City, USA." With WSM radio station still airing just as bright as it did when it began its first broadcast in 1925 and the Ryman Auditorium still standing a block north of Broadway sandwiched between 4th and 5th Avenue North, one can still take a walk down memory lane and reminisce about days of country music's past. Live music venues were and are still scattered throughout the city, but many at that time were concentrated off

Broadway and also several blocks away in an area known as Printer's Alley.

Charlie was excited to make the trip to the *Grand Ole Opry* for the first time, packing only a night bag and his guitar to make the Nashville flight sometime in the early 1960's. After settling into the Andrew Jackson Hotel, he left for the Ryman Auditorium acquainting himself with the *Opry's* staff. It would be then he would receive the surprise of his life. His all-time hero, Hank Snow, would be appearing on the *Opry* that very evening. Charlie couldn't believe his ears, as he was already slightly nervous about his first appearance on what could only be reasoned as the greatest country music show in the world at that time.

The *Grand Ole Opry* operated pretty much the same way in the 1960's as it does today. The show was divided into two separate portions, the first show beginning at 7 p.m. and running for a couple of hours. The crowd would be cleared out for another show to start around 9 p.m. and run until around 11 p.m. Artists that were regulars had their own special 30-minute segment broadcast out on WSM radio and guest artists like Charlie would play with that particular artist on their segment.

Roy Acuff, also known as the "King of Country Music," played on his 30-minute portion and then Hank Snow began playing his. After what seemed like forever and with butterflies in his stomach, the announcement was made for Charlie to join Snow onstage where he played behind Charlie's music. It was a dream-come-true and went off without a hitch.

Dale Woods was a regular on the *Opry* back in the day and appeared on the same show as Charlie. She had a big hit record released called "Down Yonder on the Piano" and was enjoying high success from it. Charlie was young and handsome and remembers Dale flirting with him the first time he appeared with her on the program. She was quite the tease, but also very professional. Charlie was photographed with her behind the stage and lovingly remembers Ms. Woods and her charismatic personality. Charlie appeared at a later time with Ernest Tubb whose big hits, "Blue Christmas" and

"Waltz Across Texas" were a national sensation. As far as anyone knows, there are no surviving photos of Charlie actually onstage at the *Opry* as Charlie never received one, and the *Opry* itself had a disaster in years past destroying much of their archival material.

Nevertheless, there were always folks coming and going behind the stage at the *Opry* as each act prepared for their time onstage. Back in those days, there was usually a photographer or two snapping photos of each of the artists who were convened backstage. Over the years, Charlie would be photographed with many hit-makers of the day like Roy Acuff, Dale Woods, "Whisperin" Bill Anderson, Jimmy C. Newman or Homer and Jethro to label a few-always standing in front of the renowned backstage brick wall.

After a couple of successful appearances on the popular program, Charlie was asked by the *Opry* administration to become a regular, which, of course, was a huge honor and often a life-changing or career-changing opportunity. This would present the young singer and songwriter with a dilemma. He could now be a steady fixture on the greatest country music show of the century. However, it would come with costs. Charlie would have to move further from his mother who was concurrently living close by on the farm she was still operating in Farwell. He would have to quit his permanent job at KZIP radio station in Amarillo and he would have to sell his home-all to move to Nashville and as he's quoted saying, "to live on the doorsteps of Columbia records with dozens of other musicians at the time." It was quite a conundrum.

On his third trip, he was going to give the *Opry* his answer, which by the way, he didn't even know what his response would be. His boss and friend, Ray Winkler, was leaning towards him taking the position, but Charlie himself wasn't yet sold on the idea-although it sounded really lucrative. It would be an inexplicable occurrence that would make up his mind.

Charlie and his band mates rode the long trip to Nashville making what would ultimately be Charlie's final appearance on the show. The boys were to check into their hotel room within walking distance from the Ryman Auditorium. As they entered the hotel, they were met by screaming teenage girls who mobbed them as they entered the foyer. Unbeknownst to them, the legendary Elvis Presley was in town and hundreds of girls were overcrowding various hotel lobbies with hopes of seeing rock 'n' roll's bad boy. Charlie and the guys maneuvered through the crowded lobby of screaming girls with their luggage in tow. After signing some autographs, they cleared a path to the elevator. Charlie knew he had arrived at stardom but was still undecided as whether or not to leave his comfortable life in Texas to take the position for a chance to start again in the dog-eat-dog world of Nashville.

Suddenly, the elevator door opened, and the boys witnessed a sight they had never seen before. A popular country music artist who they recognized immediately was laying on the floor of the elevator either drunk or possibly even on drugs. The sight of the artists' twitching body scared the onlookers. Charlie looked at his friends and said, "Boys, I don't want to end up like this guy. I think I'll turn down the Nashville job." And he did. This might or might not have been a troubling decision for Charlie; it just raises questions as to "what might have been" if he had taken the *Opry* position.

In addition to playing music, there was always some time for fun while in Nashville. Ask any artist who's ever played the Ryman Auditorium in the early days and they'll tell you just 37 steps outside the rear exit of the Ryman would take you across the alley and into the backdoor of perhaps the most famous country music bar in Nashville called Tootsie's World Famous Orchid Lounge, or Tootsie's for short. On occasion, Charlie might slip across the alley and meet up with friends or colleagues imaginably like Johnny Cash or George Jones as they talked about music and whatever else was going on in their lives. If one visits Tootsie's today, the walls are covered in thousands of musician signatures from today and yesteryear and if you look really closely, somewhere hidden on the wall is the name of Charlie "Sugartime" Phillips.

Phillips met so many individual entertainers on the *Opry*. Many he stayed friends with over the years, and some were just contemporaries. Charlie even traveled on a short *Opry* tour with

"Whisperin" Bill Anderson. Since Bill had also been a DJ in Georgia at WGAU-AM and WJJC-AM, he understood Charlie's affiliation with the radio business. While traveling on their tour in their preliminary days, Bill had run low on money, so Mr. Tightwad Charlie loaned him a few dollars. Whenever the guys talked again in the future, Charlie often joked, "Hey Bill you still owe me 'X' amount of dollars." They'd have a laugh about it, especially after Anderson became a mega star. Bill used to call Charlie to get his latest record played on the Amarillo radio station and Charlie would, of course, oblige. As Bill's career unfolded, he became one of the most successful singers and songwriters in country music and enjoyed a long career on the *Grand Ole Opry*. He and Charlie lost touch over the years, but Phillips always reminisces the great talks they had and appreciates the camaraderie they shared.

Charlie "Sugartime" Phillips contemplates his days on the *Opry* very fondly. Just like his attitude for the *Hayride*, the long trip and the expense to travel the distance no longer justified the exposure and notoriety received, so he just turned down any future offers to appear on *Opry* programs. Finally, the day came when the *Opry* stopped calling altogether and his times spent in Nashville became just a memory.

Chapter 9
Jolly Cholly and the Radio Biz

Charlie "Sugartime" Phillips' radio career started out as an entirely hands-on experience when Odis "Pop" Echols tossed him onto KCLV radio when he was just a teenager. Thinking back, he probably just seemed like a hillbilly teenager trying to squeak by the best he knew how with an uneducated Texas drawl and the vocabulary to boot. "I wonder if I didn't have Attention Deficit Disorder because I didn't make very good grades; more especially in math. And my English was the worst. And I wasn't a very good reader…I mean I wasn't illiterate, I just wasn't a good reader," Charlie explains.

Back then, radio was done essentially with live scripts. The deejay would sit in front of a microphone and read his script. Sometimes the information would be prerecorded. Early slip-ups on the radio were common including his "Dr. Pecker" announcement. An even worse pronouncement haunted Charlie when describing a movie playing at either the La Fonda drive-in or the Yucca drive-in, both located just outside of Clovis. Charlie got tongue-tied when announcing the flick and inadvertently stated it was playing at the La Fukka Drive-in, which caused quite a stir in eastern New Mexico and Texas. This led some to believe Charlie was a potty-mouth. He knew the damage had already been done when the phone started ringing. "What did you just say?" the caller would demand, "What did you say!" These were just some of the bloopers Charlie committed in his primary radio years.

Anytime the deejay played a prerecorded commercial, it became quite a production of its own, as commercials were only recorded on reel-to-reel tapes and each tape had to be queued up on the reel to a specific spot. Many of the live scripts were read simply out of a spiral-bound notebook or written on pieces of paper. The deejay would look in his logbook and see when the next commercial was scheduled to be played and then he'd just read it off his fancy notepads. The premise of Charlie's first broadcasts was to be a hick or hillbilly show, which wasn't too hard for Charlie as he already sounded like he just fell off the cotton truck. With many of the country shows of the day, the program managers wanted the deejay to sound like as if he'd just wandered in from the hills.

The best thing about country music stations is you didn't have to be Walter Cronkite. You just had to be a good ad-libber and believe you me, Charlie had the gift of gab. By the time "Sugartime" hit the height of its popularity, Charlie was still making $60 a week working full-time for KCLV. He never complained because he was still living on the family farm with his mother and didn't have any substantial expenses yet. Charlie had grown up dirt poor, and Ma Kate always felt sorry for her youngest son who had primarily walked around barefoot and in his brother's third-generation hand-me-downs. Since her son was working, she always made sure he had a newer model car to drive around safely and in style.

Shortly after "Sugartime" won the Gold Record, numerous artists visited the KCLV studio in the sleepy town of Clovis. With Pop's business connections, even non-music types like sportscaster, Dizzy Dean, dropped into the studio to congratulate both Pop and Charlie on their successes. In addition to being a deejay, Pop also trained Charlie to be a newsman, schooling him with skills to slip out of his hick-talk in order to present the news in a more professional fashion. His years as the announcer on Clovis' Silver Grill's *The Breakfast Club* were a success as Charlie often made the announcements and sang something special for his listening audience.

Phillips' big break as a newsman approached when a phone call came into the KCLV station describing a fire on a dirt farm road near Clovis. At that time, KCLV had a special promotion for listeners stating if they called in a Hotline tip, they'd win a free meal.

So this particular day the caller explained they could see a car on fire, and it looked to be serious. It's hard to imagine nowadays, but this was the late 1950's before cell phones and GPS directed you and offered service in an emergency. KCLV had a 1956 Ford station wagon called the News Wagon equipped with a mobile broadcast radio and antennae primarily used to conduct on-air live interviews and news reports. The young reporter was directed to the proximity of the fire via the radio. Charlie could see the smoke billowing up into the air, and although he was a native of the area, he had trouble circumnavigating the narrow, dirt farm roads.

In the middle of what seemed like nowhere, close to a dilapidated old barn, Charlie eventually found the car, still smoking after being engulfed in flames. He radioed the station. The car was propped up on blocks, and the hood was raised suggesting there had been some trouble with the engine. While conducting his haphazard on-air interview, Charlie approached the vehicle. There was a body still sitting in the drivers seat. It had been charred beyond recognition. Making matters worse, the poor soul's head had fallen off and the body sat bubbling on the seat springs. To Charlie's horror, he announced to the radio audience there was a body inside the burning vehicle. The person who had called the station had not contacted the proper authorities- they had instead *only* called the radio station. It was then up to KCLV to notify the sheriff's office and the fire department. The young reporter waited nearly an hour before authorities arrived. It was Charlie's first big experience as a reporter, and it haunted him throughout his life.

The radio station was dubbed "Home of KCLV's Million Dollar Music," but regardless whether Charlie was working at a small station or a big one, he made every effort to put on a good show and play the best country music hits. Even a New York City magazine, the *TV Radio Mirror*, ran an article on the young deejay in their August 1958 edition. Promotional Manager, Howard Greene, wrote in a letter to Charlie, *"Here it is! Your story is featured in the enclosed August issue of TV RADIO MIRROR, which will be on newsstands Thursday, July 3rd. I know you'll enjoy reading the story. I'm sure you will want to tell your many fans about it."*

The burning automobile incident and a couple of years on-air created a seasoned radioman out of Charlie. The hillbilly teenager was slowly growing up before the radio-listening public. With "Sugartime's" success, Charlie agreed to a tour out of Nashville headlining Marty Robbins and others. This is where he would meet a concert promoter and radio station owner by the name of Ray Winkler. Ray co-owned and operated KZIP radio station in Amarillo with his friend, "Pappy" Dave Stone Pinkston. Winkler had just recently dismissed one of his most popular deejays and local performer, Roger Miller.

Miller was a great entertainer and had one of the best senses of humor a person could ever ask for. This is probably one of the attributes that caught Ray Winkler's ear when he initially hired the young man. Roger, however, didn't work too long at KZIP, as he was more of a night owl and most likely despised having to report for duty at the radio station at the crack of dawn each morning. It wouldn't be long before Winkler explained to Miller, "Things just weren't working out."

Little did anyone know, but Winkler had done Roger Miller a huge favor. Miller was born in Fort Worth, but his family moved up to Oklahoma and began farming cotton. He walked approximately three miles daily to attend the one-room schoolhouse. Miller later joked in a politically incorrect statement, "The school I went to had 37 students...me and 36 Indians." Performer, Sheb Wooley, had married Miller's cousin and said, "It's a good thing he made it in the music business 'cause he would have starved to death as a farmer," talking about Roger's daydreaming on the farm. Does this type of artist sound familiar?

Miller spent a few years in the Army after getting caught crossing state lines with a stolen guitar. His sentence would be either the Army or jail, so. He joked his education was "Korea, Clash of 1952." After returning home from the service, he got a job in Nashville as a bellhop at the Andrew Jackson. As he ushered folks up and down the elevator, he'd sing them a song and soon became known as the "Singing Bellhop." He had a song or two out on the airwaves when Ray Winkler first put him on the radio after moving to Amarillo. When his stint at KZIP failed, Miller hooked up with Ray Price and the rest is history.

After leaving Amarillo, Miller would record and release dozens of albums and singles. His release of, "Dang Me" reached the No. 1 position on the charts by 1964 and his mega-hit, "King of the Road" topped the charts at No. 1 in the U.S. and the U.K. in 1965. Roger Miller's long career would garner great success as an accomplished guitarist, fiddler, drummer, singer, songwriter, television star, and even a Broadway composer. When Ray Winkler was asked if he had any regrets about firing Miller after seeing his huge success, Winkler retorted something like, "No, Roger was destined for greater things."

Pop Echols had been on the frontline of the rock 'n' roll movement after witnessing hits churning out of the Norman Petty Studio. He wanted to expand his presence in the marketplace, so he decided to increase the rock format at his station. Starting in 1960, KCLV would be weeding out much of their country music and would play more pop and rock. He called Charlie into his office and told him the new plan followed by, "Charlie you're fired- but not to worry, I found you a job at a more fitting station in Amarillo if you want it." Ray Winkler had been the promoter of the Marty Robbins tour Charlie was currently performing on and Winkler was already aware of his songwriting and singing talents. It's possible Ray contacted Pop Echols in Clovis or Pop contacted Ray in Amarillo to strike a deal regarding Charlie's contract. It was decided Charlie would make the big move to Amarillo and would work at the widespread KZIP radio station.

Amarillo held a rich radio heritage since its first radio station, WDAG, broadcast with its 10-watts of power in 1922. As the population of Amarillo grew, so did the number of radio stations. One would never talk about radio in Amarillo without the mention of the "soft and soothing voice" of Ruby "Lady Cool Breeze" Lewis. Ruby was the first woman and African-American deejay in the Texas Panhandle. She debuted her first show in 1955 spinning rhythm & blues and jazz on Saturday evenings on KAMQ-AM. By the 1960's her studio was located in the downtown Amarillo area just off Polk Street with an alley-facing window to the outside world letting folks see into the life of the real "Lady Cool Breeze."

Known for saying, "Don't touch that dial, we're gonna rock for a while," became her calm mantra. As racial tensions escalated both locally and throughout the U.S., Lady Cool Breeze was a voice of reason in troubled times. During the 1950's and 1960's, Amarillo's Polk Street was a main drag for teenagers to cruise up and down listening to the new pop and rock hits of the day. Lady Cool Breeze was readily accessible as teens could slip her notes under the window requesting she play their favorite song. According to an Amarillo local and historian, Lady Cool Breeze was the Queen of Amarillo Radio and is compared to being Amarillo's own version of Wolfman Jack.

Ruby was one of the first inductees into the Texas Panhandle Broadcasters Hall of Fame. She was a woman who paved the way for other women to enter a field dominated by men. She is credited with being an inspiration not only to women, but African-Americans as well. Charlie didn't meet Ruby Lewis until years later, but claims she was a true inspiration even though their genres were markedly different. Years later in 2001, Charlie would appear on a radio program with Ruby "Lady Cool Breeze" Lewis as well as other local notables like Bob Izzard, Charlie Broomhead, Mike Davenport, Dean Kelly, Jim Richardson, Billy Edd Dixon and Corky Mayberry to raise money for the Bob "Pappy" Watson Memorial Scholarship Fund allowing college students to financially seek work in mass media.

In March of 1960, Charlie would move to Amarillo and start working at his newfangled radio station and begin his new life. He was Roger Miller's replacement and had some big shoes to fill. KZIP was unique in the radio world as it was one of only three stations in the United States supporting a "country music only" format. Folks today might not remember, but prior to 1953, the FCC regulated that radio stations set aside block programming as the general format used by all radio stations. For example, during a specific hour, pop music would be played, and then the next hour, big band music would be played and so forth.

Then in September of 1953, Pappy Dave Stone and his real-estate partner, Leroy Elmore, successfully lobbied the FCC and became the pioneers of America's first one hundred-percent country formatted radio station in Lubbock, Texas with the call letters KDAV. Pappy had another business partner, Bob Clark, and the two also began the "sun-up to sun-down" radio station. KDAV would be the station Waylon Jennings would cut his teeth at and would also be the station first broadcasting the then unheard of Buddy Holley.

Stone got his start in the radio business when be began working as a bookkeeper for KSEL radio, and as chance might have it, a deejay walked out one day without notice. Stone stepped up to the microphone and took his place. By the end of a year, Stone was promoted to general manager of the station, and shortly his new career as a station owner would begin. Eventually Pappy established ownership over other radio stations like KPEP in San Angelo, Texas followed by KZIP in Amarillo and ultimately KPIK in Colorado Springs.

Pappy used to tell stories about booking Elvis Presley for shows paying the future star just $75 per night. He would be the person to introduce Ray Winkler to Jim Reeves launching a lifelong friendship between the two. Pappy was friends with Bill Haley of the Comets and is sometimes recognized as introducing Bill to a Lubbock High School guitarist, Buddy Holley, who seemed so incredibly talented that Bill Haley contacted his record label, Decca, and they signed the future star.

Many years into the future, Waylon Jennings was playing a location in Las Vegas and called Pappy onstage in commemoration to honor his former boss. It would be decades later in 1999 that the Country Music DJ Hall of Fame would induct the man who was the pioneer of the all-country music format.

Ray Winkler was born in Bonham, Texas and began his career in business and radio broadcasting in Dallas before entering the U.S. Navy. After World War II, Ray began broadcasting sports and announcing professional baseball games. In 1955, Ray purchased a share of KZIP radio with Pappy Dave Stone. A few years later, Johnny Hathcock came to work for Winkler and Stone as the future general manager at KZIP. Hathcock would work at the radio station for many years proving he was not only an efficient manager, but also was a good traffic man and great copywriter. Not to mention, Johnny was a prodigious poker player no one at the station dared compete against. He saved it for the bars and nightclubs where unsuspecting or slightly inebriated entertainers would lose their money to the skillful gambler. Just ask Willie Nelson.

The business-savvy Ray Winkler wasn't just looking for a deejay to fill the shoes of Roger Miller. He was looking for a man who fit the description of "a complete package." Yes, Charlie "Sugartime" Phillips was a deejay, but more importantly he was a songwriter and popular performer. The word around the campfire at the time was, "You couldn't get a job for Ray Winkler unless you could write a song." Ray was known for hiring "combo guys" and Charlie appeared like he would be a good fit at one of the only all-country radio stations in the U.S. As part of his new job description, Charlie was assigned as a top radio personality and would also help by selling advertising for the station. This is what he originally accomplished for Pop Echols and it was now time to try his hand in the larger Amarillo market. It was exactly what Charlie did. Listeners who had known him by his on-air handle "Sugartime Charlie" would now know him by his new KZIP handle, "Jolly Cholly," for his on-air wit and humor.

KZIP radio station was located off East Amarillo Boulevard, which was still the same road surnamed Route 66. Since Charlie had only lived on his family farm up until 1960, he would now need to uproot his former life and resettle in a new town. He did not have a place to call home in Amarillo, so Ray Winkler made certain Charlie had a place to stay when he began work. Across the street from the radio station were both a restaurant and the Plainsman Motel that the station had worked a symbiotic trade-out with; swapping radio advertising for food and room. Charlie moved away from the comfort of his mom's home and into a little motel room complete with a small kitchenette. Charlie secretly admitted after he had gotten set-up permanently in Amarillo, his mother kept his room just as he left it. Anytime he would return to Farwell for a night, he always had a place at his mom's place. She kept Charlie's reserved room available until the day she passed away.

Radio stations weren't too fancy back in the day. KZIP was located in a small cinderblock building near a neighboring, mostly dry playa lake. Their transmitter tower was located smack-dab in the middle of a low spot in the lake. The building itself consisted of a lobby and entryway with a couch and chairs, a transformer room, a broadcast room, a sales office, a production studio, a manager's office, a small bathroom and a bookkeeping and traffic office. A couple of the rooms had large glass panels so one could see through into the other rooms and lobby.

As part of the financial arrangement between Pop Echols and Winkler, Ray would not only hire Charlie for the station, he would also act as Charlie's manager. In hindsight, this was one of the best moves concerning Charlie's career. While Pop was satisfied with the success he and Charlie received with "Sugartime," other songs like, "One Faded Rose," "Be My Bride," and "Too Many Tears" had not scored very high on the country music charts and had seen limited sales.

Unbeknownst to them at the time, both Charlie and his friend, Don Guess, had been shelved by the Decca/Coral label. (Much like what probably happened to Buddy Holly and the guys when they were originally with the Decca label). Shelving occurs when a record company executive decides he or she is done with an artist and wants to instead promote other up-and-coming persons or acts. They put their artist on the backburner, usually never to be heard from again. After Charlie's contract expired with Coral Records, he was now free to sign with Columbia Records, a company recruiting only top country acts. With Ray at the helm, Charlie's ship would soon sail much smoother.

A primary perk extended to employees at a radio station was the trade outs. Additionally, radiomen gained access to big stars, as KZIP was a chief promoter of large concerts in the Amarillo area. With Pappy Dave Stone and Ray Winkler's connections, employees of KZIP were often special guests at shows and were offered the opportunity to meet many of the acts scheduled to play in Amarillo including Willie Nelson, Merle Haggard and George Jones.

Ron Peterson was a KZIP deejay known as "Big R" and worked with Charlie in the initial days. He remembers folks going to see shows like Tennessee Ernie Ford, Glen Campbell and even Spiro Agnew, Vice President under Richard Nixon, who was in Amarillo for a talk and press conference.

Often Charlie would be called into the field to interview artists or help promote local businesses. One morning Minnie Pearl was in Amarillo on a KZIP promoted show and was making her rounds for the station when Charlie was asked to interview the comedienne at Lewis Jewelers in Amarillo. She was a real cut-up and kept Charlie in stitches as he attempted some dialog while the two tried to hock a diamond-crest ring. Minnie was a blessing to Charlie as she touted his radio show over the Amarillo airwaves. Always the airplane enthusiast, Charlie fondly remembers Pearl's husband, Henry Cannon, because he was a twin-engine pilot and would fly Minnie to her engagements across the country.

Jolly Cholly soon became a popular fixture in the Amarillo community and became the "go-to" man when big stars traveled through Amarillo. In an early interview sitting, Charlie was directed to a hotel room in Amarillo to interview Victor Borge, a Danish comedian who spoke English with a heavy dialect. Borge was a trained classical pianist and had been on *Toast of the Town* hosted by Ed Sullivan and was also in the *Guinness Book of World Records* when his show, *Comedy in Music*, became the longest running one-man show in history. Of course Charlie didn't know too much about the guy and became nervous during the interview, so he began rattling off questions for Borge.

Phillips had no idea how to pronounce the Dane's name, but was familiar with a neighboring Panhandle oil town called Borger. So in the heat of the moment, he kept referring to Victor Borge as Mr. Borger. This must have amused Borge as he averted Charlie's questioning completely. The witty comedian, known primarily for his tomfoolery, took full advantage of the novice deejay's ignorance as every question Charlie asked was turned back towards Charlie. At the conclusion of the interview Borge said, "I've enjoyed listening to you Mr. Phillips." Charlie recollects, "I had no idea until later but he was pulling his act on me, and I guess I wasn't smart enough to realize he was making a fool outta me."

Of course, this wouldn't be the worst of Charlie's blunders. Years later, Ray Winkler would tell Charlie he had a very special interviewee coming to KZIP. As a baseball man, Winkler announced the baseball player and new country singer, Charley Pride, would be traveling through Amarillo and Ray had arranged an interview. Folks at the station were all excited to have the new RCA recording artist in their studio.

When it came time for the interview, Charlie was on the air and could see three gentlemen enter the lobby. "Right on time," he thought. When he started the next song rolling, Charlie popped into the foyer and invited the men back. As they came towards the door of the broadcast room, Charlie shook the hand of the first guy and said, "Good to meet you Mr. Pride!" and the gentleman replied, "Oh, I'm not Charley." Then Charlie shook the hand of the second guy and said, "It's a pleasure Mr. Pride!" "NO, exclaimed the second man, *this* is Charley Pride," turning to the third man. Charlie Phillips had never been so embarrassed in his life!

To that date, few people had actually *seen* Charley Pride and Ray Winkler had of course not mentioned Charley was African-American. Why would he? Well, Phillips conducted a terrific interview but has always felt disconcerted he made a preconceived blunder assuming all country singers must be Caucasian. He was never able to apologize sufficiently to Pride for his wrong assumption, nor did Pride seem to expect one. Charlie Phillips talked with Pride while performing together at numerous shows in the future, but they never spoke of the embarrassing incident in Amarillo. Of course, Charley Pride went on to become one of the most celebrated country singers in the world.

In addition to making appearances at local retail establishments, Charlie was also commissioned to mark his presence at various happenings around the city. Even special events like *Wrestling, King of Sports* proceedings held at the Tri-State Fairgrounds starring popular wrestlers of the day like Dory Funk Jr., Big Tex McKenzie, Dusty Rhodes, Terry Funk and "The King," Rufus R. Jones. The fly bills would announce, "Renowned Western recording star Charlie 'Sugartime' Phillips will be here at the Sports Arena next Thursday night. PLUS the first 10 LUCKY boys and girls will receive his latest record release '20 Fools Ago,' which has been high on the top 10 charts for several weeks now." Also affirming, "He has also been one of the top D.J.'s at Radio Station KZIP for the past 10 Years."

After serving as a deejay and salesperson, Charlie would be promoted to Program Director in 1965. Winkler had full faith in Charlie at the station, but he also saw a potential star in the country singer. It was Winkler who made the initial connections for Charlie to be on the *Grand Ole Opry* for the first time. Additionally, as a deejay, a trip was planned yearly to attend the annual Deejay Convention in Nashville. This probably doesn't ring a bell with most folks, but this convention is essentially what the modern day Country Music Association has evolved into (The CMA Awards Show).

On July 6, 1962, Charlie would receive the honor of becoming WSM's Mr. Deejay U.S.A. The annual Disc Jockey Convention was held every year, and all of the stars and music moguls would congregate in Nashville joining their fellow deejays. Alongside winning a Gold Record and receiving the BMI Award, this would be a highlight in his career, as he was called onstage at the Ryman Auditorium to receive his award. Charlie appeared as a guest on the *Grant Turner Radio Show* on WSM in Nashville that Friday night, and then appeared as a special guest disc jockey on the *Grand Ole Opry* on WSM-TV on Saturday. Charlie was a well-respected deejay and was now being billed by some newspapers as one of the nation's top Country Jocks.

Around 1963, a friend of Charlie's who grew up not too far from Farwell in Plainview, Texas (and fellow Columbia artist) was hosting his own show on ABC-TV called *The Jimmy Dean Show*. Dean would often be the master of ceremony on Columbia Record's Showcase at the Ryman Auditorium during the deejay conventions. Phillips was being recognized by Columbia for his recent achievements, and it would be the Texan from the Panhandle who would announce and present Charlie onstage. Dean would publicize, "Here's a good ole' boy who just lived up the road from me." Phillips shook Dean's hand and spoke a few words.

Phillip's songs, "I Guess I'll Never Learn" with "Now That It's Over" on the flipside were released on Columbia Records during this time and appeared to be a hit. His friends, Johnny Hathcock and Weldon Allard, who also penned the song "Wake Up Irene," wrote, "I Guess I'll Never Learn," for Charlie. By all appearances, Charlie was not only at the height of his career as a top deejay but as a music artist as well. Only time would tell the direction Charlie's life would take. The *Music Reporter* announced in a July 28, 1962, article, "Owner Ray Winkler of Amarillo's KZIP, is crowing over the fine job that Charlie Phillips, Columbia artist, did as 'Mr. DJ, USA' over at WSM recently." Ray couldn't have been more proud for Charlie, but just as importantly, all of the attention was great publicity for the KZIP radio station.

The life of a deejay/recording artist wasn't always cracked up to what it might seem. There was a slippery slope between the double role deejay's who were also performers faced, sometimes presenting a serious problem if not handled properly. Although country music deejays that were also performers were not a rarity, especially in the early days, it might be easy for someone to accuse the deejay of promoting their own material over that of others. Charlie will readily admit when he first entered the airwaves as a teenager, he played *his* country music version of "Sugartime" probably far more than he played the more popular McGuire Sisters version. But as his position in the radio business matured and as he matured, he was much less likely to pull such a stunt.

Two of the most known entertainers who were performers as well as announcers were Tex Ritter and Ralph Emery. The two guys teamed up together in the 1960's co-hosting the *Opry Star Spotlight* on WSM. These two were always hesitant to play their own songs on a program they were hosting because they might antagonize listeners or viewers or be seen as bragging about their talents. Emery was quoted in a Nashville publication article entitled, "DJ-Artists' Life Not All Gravy" stating, "A disk jockey is naturally reluctant to toot his own horn." Adding, "That's why I never perform on my own TV show. I'd be tempted to push my record. So I stay in the background and let others perform." Charlie is presented in the same article as an additional person who doubles as an artist and deejay. "I've always tried to [sparingly] play my own music, but if it was on the charts, I would play it like I would any other song," Charlie expounds. Other recording artists like Waylon Jennings, Jim Reeves, "Whisperin" Bill Anderson and Buck Owens all began as radio deejays.

Jolly Cholly would work with some of the best deejays, radiomen and radio women in the business. At KCLV, Odis "Pop" Echols, would show him the ropes while men like Odis Echols Jr. and Mike Mitchell would work with Charlie on a one-on-one basis cultivating an on-air presence. KZIP owners, Pappy Dave Stone and Ray Winkler, taught Charlie professionalism and how to be a contender in the radio business.

Over the next 29 years Charlie worked with Amarillo notables and radio personalities like: Ralph Newton; Dean Kelly; Joe Cooper; Walter T. Crawford; Bob Ferris; Ernie Thrasher; Ron Peterson; Johnny Hathcock; Bob Jackson; Mike Fox; Wayne Whitson; Doc Deweese; Howard Walker; Jim Roberts; Bobby Hughes; Ray Whitworth; Jack Grant; Bobby Roundtree; Terry Niemire; Bob Slay; Janie Kirkland; Corky Mayberry; Steve Rich (Lewis) and Jerry Brown. All these men and women were instrumental to the team, making KZIP one of the most successful country radio stations in the area.

Charlie hired the good-looking Steve Rich as an up-and-coming young deejay. Charlie asked Ron Peterson and Mike Fox to show him the ropes, and they must have done a great job because Rich would eventually leave KZIP and head to bigger pastures. Rich would later change his name to Steve Lewis and work in larger markets like KOMA in Oklahoma City and then move on to be a hot deejay at ABC Radio Network's *Real Country* where he worked until 2009. Steve Lewis conducted hundreds of interviews with top stars over the years and was known for being a professional and a gentleman, a trait he states he learned from Charlie. Steve Lewis speaks highly of Phillips stating, "I don't know if I'd even had a radio career without Charlie."

Ron Peterson moved on over the years and runs a Sunday morning gospel show out of Granbury, Texas at KPAR. Ron was always image-conscious and, even at the threat of losing his job, wouldn't play anything on the radio he felt inappropriate. When the Bellamy Brothers came out with their song, "If I Had a Beautiful Body," Ron lightheartedly refused to play it even if it was on his required playlist. Charlie Phillips wasn't always innocent at KZIP either and had his lesser moments. Steve Rich admits one time when he was playing Billy Swan's hit, "I Can Help," Charlie didn't feel it was country enough for the station and was personally tired of hearing the song, so he entered Steve's broadcast room and took Swan's record and broke it over his knee as a gesture that record would no longer be played at KZIP.

Janie Kirkland worked as Charlie's right-hand woman, and he admits, "I couldn't have run the station without her!!" Mike Fox purchased some of his own radio stations, and after he sold them, began another career at Wells Fargo Bank. All KZIP employees didn't fare well, like hotshot Walter T. Crawford, who suffered a heart attack at home shortly before he was to bring the station on-air. Ron was scheduled to be on the radio at five a.m. that morning. When the radio didn't start broadcasting, people began calling the station. He never made it. There were so many stories originating from the KZIP over the years, perhaps too many to tell here.

Ray Winkler had been dabbling with some songwriting of his own and showed his friend, Johnny Hathcock, some of his scripts. Johnny stated Winkler was getting pretty good. The two collaborated penning various songs, but one would stand out among all others.

Because of their friendship with Jim Reeves, the two composed a song meant for Jim, hopefully, to record. Together, Ray and Johnny would write a song that would immortalize the pair as Titan songwriters for eternity. "Welcome To My World" was written in 1961 and was recorded by fellow radioman, Dean Kelly, backed by the Blue Boys at the KZIP studio. This original demo was played for Jim Reeves, who stated he'd consider making a recording of it.

In the meantime, Charlie was set to make another recording in Nashville with Columbia Records and asked Winkler if he might take "Welcome To My World" with him to Music City to record it under the direction of Don Law. Both Winkler and Hathcock agreed, so Charlie took the song with him and recorded it at Columbia. He presented his version of the song to Don Law at the Columbia Recording Studio, who haphazardly listened to the recording, but told Charlie he had some other songs he thought would better "fit" Charlie. In other words, he didn't want the singer to introduce any new material; rather he'd have Charlie record some pre-chosen songs already in the Columbia catalog, which is what he did.

Charlie often wondered what might have happened if Don Law would have allowed him to record the song composed by Ray and Johnny. Would he have finally gotten the big hit that always seemed an arms length away? Or might the song not have become the great achievement as performed by the great Jim Reeves? No matter, Charlie states he always loved Reeves' version of the song, and he was happy Jim made it such a success.

Of course, "Welcome To My World" would see huge triumph not only for Reeves, but would also get recorded by some top entertainers in the field like Dean Martin, Ray Price, Faron Young, Ricky Nelson, Eddy Arnold and even the legendary Elvis Presley. Throughout the years, over dozens of different artists would record the tune. It sold into the millions and, like "Sugartime," is now considered a standard classic.

Winkler owned Libby Records recording label until 1964 and, the following year began Reveller Records in addition to his music publishing company, Neilrae Music. He sold his interest in KZIP in 1965 and moved to Dallas leaving Pappy Dave Stone at the helm. Charlie was left without his mentor and friend. Before leaving, Ray vehemently advocated Charlie move to Nashville. So much so, a country music magazine wrote, "Ray Winkler, KZIP C&Whirler Amarillo jots that Columbia waxer Charlie Phillips aims the moving van at Music City Apr. 1 to put him closer to his helmsman, Bob Neal. Latest Phillips disc: 'No One To Love." But it was not to be, as Charlie just wasn't going to become the little fish in the big pond. He stuck to his radio vocation, recording and local performances.

By 1979, Pappy Dave Stone sold his interest in KZIP and the rest of his radio chain and Charlie was asked to stay on with the new owners to help make the transition easier. Charlie tried, but knew he simply couldn't keep up his hectic work schedule in addition to performing weekly gigs, especially with new owners at the wheel. He had worked his way up the ranks from a deejay to program manager, to assistant manager, to operations manager, to the general manager. It was finally time to retire from a full career in the radio business, and it was time to concentrate on the one thing Charlie loved *most*- playing to live audiences.

Phillips still made guest appearances on the radio, but no longer broadcast full time. He would now concentrate his efforts at the Aviatrix Ballroom, which was still in full bloom. It would be many years later in May of 1999 that Charlie would be inducted into the Texas Panhandle Association of Broadcasters Hall of Fame. He joined a long line of his respected contemporaries.

Chapter 10
Amarillo in the Evening

When folks conjure up a picture of Amarillo, Texas, one can't help but think of the song co-written by an outstanding Amarillo artist, Terry Stafford, called "Amarillo by Morning" made famous by country music legend, George Straight. Folks who have traveled through Amarillo will frequently talk about the unusually flat terrain and constant and forceful wind, which usually blows from the southwest. If one moves through in the summer, the intense dry heat is immediately recognized, but if traveling through in the dead of winter, the brutal cold is all that can be remembered. And of course, the most haunting commemoration of a visit through Amarillo is what the locals might describe as "the smell of money," which is the overwhelming stench of cow manure in the air. Some folks still think the residents ride horses through tumbleweed-blown streets, but as one might discover, the town has grown into a metropolitan expanse with around 200,000 residents settled into the once grassland plains.

Amarillo is now conveniently situated on Interstate-40 and is a common stop-off between Oklahoma City, Oklahoma to its east and Albuquerque, New Mexico to its west. Of course if a person is traveling upwards or downwards through the United States, Amarillo is the centerpiece between its neighbor to the north, Denver, Colorado and its sister city to the south, Dallas, Texas. Geographic destinations would indeed include the Canadian River, a couple of hours drive northerly, and the Red River, branching into several forks. Most notably however is the magnificent, and second largest canyon in the United States behind the Grand Canyon, Palo Duro Canyon situated a short drive southeast of Amarillo.

With seemingly endless expanses of flat grasslands disbursed in all directions from Amarillo, Paleo-Indian hunters and gatherers first inhabited the area. Locals might describe the first occupants as the Plains Indians as these original peoples included tribes from numerous native societies like the Pueblos, Apaches, Comanche, Kiowa, and Cheyenne tribes. One of the first white settlers in the area was Charles Goodnight, who established his 16,000 or so acre ranch near present-day Palo Duro Canyon. Charles Goodnight's first experiences settling in the new wild country of West Texas can even be viewed when visiting the area through the loosely based drama and musical, *Texas*. *Texas Musical Drama* began production in 1966 and was originally staged inside the beautiful Palo Duro Canyon telling visitors the stories of folks who braved to settle the vast desolate Panhandle.

Amarillo was first named Oneida, but as one early citizen stated, "...the town's name stuck about as well as a half-licked postage stamp." With two railways passing through (the Ft. Worth/Denver and the Kansas & Southern) and a newly constructed post office, the tiny Texas town's name was changed to Amarillo, perhaps because of the yellow grass and wheat planted in the area. They don't call it the "Golden Spread" for nothing! Well, an agriculture reporter named Garland "Cotton John" Smith coined that phrase, but that's neither here nor there. Farming, ranching, gas, oil and a little helium provided early residents with a living, and the town grew slowly at times and perhaps boomed during others.

Amarillo received its first radio station with the call letters, WDAG around 1922. The station was the first in the area to broadcast selected music, local church services, news, advertisements and covered special events. By 1940, the primary commercial street in Amarillo was Polk Street, aptly named after American President James K. Polk. At the time, Amarillo was dubbed, "America's Best-Lighted Main Street" because of the numerous businesses located on its hub lit with vigor, not to mention the town's ornate streetlights. On the southern direction of Polk Street was the opulent Paramount Theater, a venue decked out with magnificent chandeliers, gigantic oil paintings, and a cathedral-size pipe organ. The Paramount Theater was ultimately fitted with an enormous blink-lit neon sign beckoning visitors and residents and inviting them in for whatever event was showing.

The Herring Hotel was situated on the northern side of downtown Amarillo. It was originally built as a result of oil money. The hotel boasted 600 hotel rooms and was a whopping 14-stories high, a practical skyscraper in early days of the Texas Panhandle. The basement of the mammoth hotel housed the very popular Old Tascosa Room, a dining, dancing and entertainment nightclub favorite where oil barons and some of the more affluent folk could gather to discuss business and enjoy a robust nightlife. Artist, Harold Bugbee, created a large Western-style mural proudly stretched across an expansive wall of the basement showing visitors just what the Panhandle was all about. Some Amarillo old-timers say country and western bands would perform within the walls of the Old Tascosa Room late into the nights.

Several blocks south of the Herring Hotel off Polk Street across the street from the original Amarillo High School was one of the most popular eateries. The Double Dip Drive-in was among the first drive-ins in Amarillo initially serving only ice cream, thus its clever name. With its proximity to the first Amarillo High, not to mention its 5-cent and 10-cent hamburgers, the drive-in became one of the most popular hangout destinations in Amarillo. As Amarillo embraced the 1950's and the advent of rock 'n' roll, the drive-in continued to thrive and became a hub for teenagers who listened to the music their parents so adamantly shunned.

Before Interstate-40 had ever been conceived, U.S. Highway 66 or more universally known Route 66, stretched across America connecting the west coast all the way to Illinois. As luck would have it, Amarillo would be the only major town in Texas it would pass through. And if you were getting really picky, Amarillo is located virtually smack dab in the middle of the Route 66, 1122 miles from Los Angeles and 1122 miles to Chicago once making Amarillo the "center of America" so to speak. With time, Route 66 would be dubbed "Main Street USA" and eventually be christened the "Will Rogers Memorial Highway."

With Route 66 passing through Amarillo, came an influx of travelers with automobiles. With that particular combination, the new Amarillo thoroughfare would see the expansion adjacent to the highway packed with gas stations, motels and restaurants, which accommodated folks passing through the Texas Panhandle. In addition to Route 66, Highways 60, 87 and 287 all crossed through Amarillo connecting the municipality with other neighboring towns and states like Oklahoma and Colorado. A local advertisement bragged that Amarillo was the "Hub City of the Land of Modern Pioneers."

Amarillo was growing by leaps and bounds and by 1942, the Amarillo Army Airfield base opened on a 1500-acre tract of land around 11 miles east of the town. It was established for the training of aircrew and ground mechanics servicing B-17 Flying Fortress aircraft during World War II. The base eventually served as basic training, as special courses of instruction were conducted to train technicians and flight engineers for the B-29 aircraft. While personnel were stationed at the airfield's Army Technical School, young men could take "old-fashioned dance instruction," sponsored by the Works Progress Administration Recreation Division. The dance classes were held on Tuesday in the Amarillo Hotel in downtown. This gesture by the government would begin a local pastime, as folks would soon gather by the hundreds to cut-a-rug with many dancehalls soon opening.

The Second World War came to an end, and the Army Airfield was designated as a permanent base, yet would soon close. Within a few short years and as the Korean War accelerated, the Army base was reactivated; however, it was designated the Amarillo Air Force Base and by 1954, boasted around 5000 students centered on training. By 1955, the base was selected for Strategic Air Command B-52 operations. This sudden influx of new residents, in addition to the current inhabitants, would give rise to numerous dancehalls, clubs and music venues being opened on the east side of Amarillo on or near the busy Route 66. The beautiful Amarillo Municipal Auditorium also played host to a variety of early acts.

Charlie Phillips' colleagues, Ray Winkler and Dean Kelly, often joshed about a 1955 performance at the Amarillo Civic Center Auditorium by Elvis Presley. Elvis was being hailed not as the King of Rock, but the King of Western Bop. He was on a nation-wide tour of the states traveling with seasoned artists like Wanda Jackson, Jimmy Day, Porter Wagoner, Jimmy C. Newman, Bobby Lord and Johnny Cash. Presley had been booked into the Amarillo Auditorium earning just a few hundred dollars a night, but by October of 1955 he was making as much as a couple of thousand dollars a night.

According to Charlie's friend and star of the *Grand Ole Opry*, Jimmy C. Newman, when the troupe began their tour, Elvis was just one of several performers joining a long list of famous entertainers. As his songs gained momentum on the radio and the charts, he soon began surpassing the other celebrities in notoriety during the tour. Newman recalled his dreadful 1955 visit to Amarillo stating, "Elvis started out opening up for us, but as the tour went on, he became sort of the headliner. When Wanda or Porter or me would be tryin' to do our act onstage, we couldn't even perform our number 'cause girls were just screamin' Elvis! Elvis!"

Newman continued his story, "I had driven my Cadillac on this tour and I remember going to the back of the auditorium where I had parked my car and them darned ole' girls musta thought my car was Elvis' because they had stripped everything off that car! I had to drive the rest of the tour with no hubcaps, no nothing!" Both Winkler and popular radio announcer, Dean Kelly, would broadcast this story over and over again throughout the next several decades making it wittier as they added their own funny embellishments.

One would never talk about the early days of music in Amarillo without mentioning certain music venues most notably and selectively: The Avalon Ballroom, the Aviatrix Ballroom, Billy Briggs Night Club, the Casa Del Club, the Cattleman's Club, the Clover Club, the Country Barn Supper Club, the Lakeside Club, the Nat Ballroom, the Panhandle Barn Dance, the Playboy Club, the Rainbow Ballroom or the V.F.W. Ballroom. With so many locations within the same vicinity of each other, the grouping of bars was simply known as "the strip." These establishments became mainstays in the community primarily in the 1950's, 1960's and even into the 1970's and 1980's each encountering their own ups-and-downs respectively. As a musician, Charlie's involvement with most of these clubs would stem from the necessity to have a venue to play his music.

After moving from Farwell to Amarillo in 1960 to join Ray Winkler as a deejay for KZIP radio station, Charlie Phillips began using his musical connections moonlighting at some of the local establishments. Since he didn't yet have a formal band of his own in the new town, he began sitting in with some of the most reputable musicians already centered in the Panhandle. The first club he played was the Billy Briggs Nightclub with Billy Briggs and the Chew Tobacco Rag Boys who invited him up onstage on occasion to do a few numbers. Charlie's success of "Sugartime" and his national appearances on the *Louisiana Hayride*, the *Ozark Jubilee* and the *Big "D" Jamboree* opened up the doors for him to perform with some of the finest bands and entertainers in the area. Not to mention, he was a deejay on one of the most exciting country music radio stations in the area. He wouldn't be the wrong person to get to know if a musician wanted to get their song played on the radio.

Charlie began scouting other venues but played at Brigg's club on numerous occasions throughout the short life of the organization. Briggs eventually sold the club to another individual who commenced booking various acts of some type or another. Charlie's least fond memory of the club after Brigg's departure was a night Jim Reeves was scheduled to play. Jim was friends with Charlie's station owners, Ray Winkler and Pappy Dave Stone, and would occasionally be booked to play some of the smaller clubs as a favor to Winkler or Stone (not to mention he could make some money on the side).

Reeves would typically drop by the KZIP studio during the day and Charlie, or one of the other deejays would interview him on-air and would promote the evening's show. Reeves and the Blue Boys traveled to Amarillo on November 22, 1963. While Charlie and

Ray anxiously awaited Reeves' arrival, an announcement began streaming into KZIP. President John Fitzgerald Kennedy was dead.

Reeves and the Big Blue pulled into the parking lot of the Plainsman Motel across from the KZIP studio around three in the afternoon. Jim was visibly shaken by the sad news. Reeves was scheduled to play that evening at the Briggs nightclub, where Eddie McDuff, Lana Parker and Charlie Phillips were all to help Reeves open the show.

Putting the horror of Kennedy's death aside, Ray Winkler and Jim Reeves were forced to decide if the show would go on that evening as the country and Amarillo cried in shock. Flags were at half-mast. The murder had occurred just over three hundred miles south in Dallas and fellow Texan, Lyndon Baines Johnson, had been sworn in as President. The two decided to cancel the show; however, as nightfall neared folks who had purchased tickets for the evening's festivities began calling the station confused as to what they should do. The people of Amarillo needed, if only for a night, to take their mind off the tragedy, and perhaps the best decision would be to allow Jim to play. The show should go on.

Ray spoke with Charlie who agreed. The country stood at a standstill. According to some accounts, Winkler and Reeves got on the radio and asked folks if they still wanted Jim to play and if so, to please contact the radio station. Charlie remembers that he, Ray Winkler and Jim Reeves all got on-air at the station and asked the Amarillo listeners if they wanted the show to continue. The station became flooded with phone calls with a resounding "yes." That evening Jim performed one of the most touching and respectful shows of his career with Lana, Charlie and Eddie leading the way. There was no room to dance as the old Billy Briggs Nightclub was standing room only and packed to capacity.

Reeves had been a fellow radio announcer and once landed a job a KWKH-AM radio out of Shreveport. Jim first saw success as a performing artist as early as 1953 with his hit song, "Mexican Joe" followed by his No. 1 hit, "Bimbo." Then in 1957 "Four Walls" would rise to No. 1 on the charts trailed by "Billy Bayou" in 1958.

Reeves would contribute another hit in 1960 with "He'll Have to Go" and would release his single, "Welcome to My World" in 1963 written by friends, Ray Winkler and Johnny Hathcock.

On July 31, 1964, Jim's life would tragically be cut short, as his Beechcraft Debonair aircraft he was piloting would crash en route to Nashville. Jim's fans would enjoy six more No. 1 hits from Reeves, some even after his death. Charlie would be instantly reminded of his decision to quit piloting his small airplane. He, Ray Winkler and Johnny Hathcock were forever saddened by the loss of their dear friend and superstar performer, simply referred to as "Gentleman Jim."

Charlie would play the Clover Club in latter years, which was the dance establishment he had visited while still in high school in order to see the Maddox Brother and Rose. The Clover Club had been completely remodeled in 1953 to meet the expectations of Bob Wills and his Texas Playboys who moved to Amarillo to do a six-week concert for KGNC radio. Jack Jackson owned the Clover Club and still booked some of the finest acts in the area. While playing the club, Charlie would reminisce about the night he got half-drunk as a minor and was tossed out of the establishment after hearing the Maddox Brother's play "The Big Balls in Cowtown." Depending on who was booked at the Clover Club, Charlie and his newly formed Sugartimers band played with or onstage with acts like Webb Pierce, Wanda Jackson, Ferlin Husky, George Jones or Willie Nelson, to name a fraction of the musicians retained at the club.

The Casa Del Ballroom was another dance establishment situated on the east side of Amarillo. An ole' fella named Bob Collingsworth and his wife owned it. Lou Walker was the staff musician and had done some work with Bob Wills as a Texas Playboy, but had branched out on his own commanding his personal band, the Western Playboys. After Charlie Phillips moved to Amarillo in 1960, Lou would often call Charlie up onstage at the Casa Del, announcing, "Let's bring Jolly Cholly up onstage!" Since Charlie worked at KZIP, Lou would sometimes bring his newly recorded records in for Charlie to play on the radio. Charlie did perform as a guest musician making numerous appearances with Lou Walker at the Casa Del over the years.

The Playboy Club was an establishment located a little further out from the other nightclubs, as it was illegal to sell liquor in Amarillo on Sunday. Jerry Basden built his dancehall from an old army barrack just outside the city limits so he could sell alcohol to his patrons on Sunday afternoon. Basden called Charlie out and explained he was going to build a larger dancehall onto the building and would do so if Charlie and the Sugartimers would play for him on Sundays.

The location that started as a small bar became quite the destination with its huge dancehall in the back of the building. Charlie was asked to be a staff musician for the Playboy Club working first on Sundays, but soon began performing on Friday and Saturday nights as well. As the club expanded, Basden began bringing in some top-notch entertainers. Charlie was asked to open up for Ray Price on a couple of occasions at the Playboy Club sometime in the 1960's when Ray still toured smaller clubs in the Panhandle. Playing three evenings a week, in addition to working full-time at KZIP, began wearing on Charlie. Then Basden asked Charlie if he could begin playing seven nights per week, which of course was too much for him. So at Charlie's suggestion, Jerry hired a good friend of Phillips' from Lazbuddie, Texas and topnotch musician from Clovis, New Mexico, Larry Trider to take his place.

The Lakeside Club was known as everybody's club as both young and old showed up to dance. It did quite well during its heyday, but like other bars in the area, it began taking business away from the other establishments. Other club owners couldn't have that. It was commonplace in those days for club owners to hire a group of thugs to visit their competition and start fights, wreaking havoc on the place, thus chasing out crowds of people. Although Charlie was the bandleader, he was often charged with being a bouncer and charged with ejecting many of the troublemakers. It was sad, but if the thugs were sent in enough times, a business would drastically lose customers and eventually close.

Although Charlie played and booked artists at virtually every dancehall in Amarillo, about the only place he never really played on a regular basis was the Avalon Ballroom. The Avalon was a very popular Amarillo establishment entertaining hundreds of folks weekly. Many of Charlie's Sugartimers like Tiny Duncan, Vic Ashmead or Bobby Hughes either played there on a regular basis or were staff musicians. Billy Briggs played there for many years before he opened up his club and regional favorite, Jess Williams, was a staff musician and bandleader who enjoyed decades of playing in the Amarillo area.

The Avalon was the only Amarillo nightclub open five nights per week closing only on Sundays and Mondays. The other clubs in town were geared more to couples dancing, but the Avalon catered to the older single crowd especially as time passed lending it the unprincipled nickname, the "Menopause Palace," which of course was a nasty description of what was a very nice establishment with nice people who were all "looking for love in all the right places."

Tiny Duncan was Charlie's longtime friend and colleague and regularly played the Avalon. On nights Charlie wasn't working, he made the rounds to several bars playing or sitting-in with whoever was performing. One particular occasion before Charlie could make it over to the Avalon, an ole' boy no one had ever seen before went up to Tiny during his break and introduced himself and asked, "Yes sir. My name is Charlie Phillips and I'd like to sit-in with you boys if that's ok?" Tiny asked, "What Charlie Phillips are you talking about son?" The stranger replied, "I'm Charlie 'Sugartime' Phillips," as the crowd of musicians all looked at each other and laughed. "Well, I hate to tell you this son, but you're *not* Charlie 'Sugartime' Phillips because he lives here and we know him!" Well the outsider turned white as a sheet and scrambled out the door. According to Phillips, it wasn't unreasonable in the days before the Internet for guys to travel the country pretending to be someone they weren't in attempts to earn a few bucks and be treated like a celebrity for the night. "Unless you were some big-named star, no one would have a clue what you looked like," Charlie recounts.

Originally dubbed the Natatorium, the Nat Ballroom had opened in the 1920's as a health club with a swimming pool situated in the middle of the latter enclosed great room. As time progressed, it was converted into a ballroom atmosphere by covering the pool with 10,000 feet of hardwood maple flooring turning the former health facility into a dance palace. While almost all of the other clubs in Amarillo were located off Route 66 on the eastern side of Amarillo, the shortened-named "Nat" was located off Route 66 just west of downtown Amarillo. Because of its large dance floor, the Nat became popularized during the rise of the big band era hosting numerous acts like the Dorsey Brothers, Harry James, Guy Lombardo, Benny Goodman as well as Duke Ellington, who frequently made appearances.

The Nat was popular with the airmen stationed at the Amarillo Air Force Base and as musical tastes changed, would host musicians playing the new style of music christened rock 'n' roll. Buddy Holly would make an appearance or two at the Nat as well as his colleagues, Little Richard and Roy Orbison. The Nat saw much early success because while other clubs in town primarily played country and western swing, the Nat branched out and welcomed other genres.

The Nat Ballroom closed in the 1960's but remained as a venue for special acts. Years later, Joe Ely performed at the Nat as well as the country group, Cooder Graw. The Dixie Chicks performed a special event concert when local Amarillo favorite and resident, Susan Gibson, won the CMA Songwriter of the Year for her penned song, "Wide Open Spaces." Charlie rarely played the Nat, but would most remember the venue from his childhood when he and his buddy, Donald Joe Pipkin, had their parents drive them up from Farwell to see any number of wrestling matches held in the ballroom. The location slowly fell into disrepair and was eventually purchased and remodeled as an antique store. It is now on the National Register of Historic Places and has even been the site of some paranormal investigations regarding legendary stories of ghosts and hauntings.

While at KZIP radio station in Amarillo, Charlie Phillips, Ray Winkler and Johnny Hathcock decided to open up their own venue inside the Clover Club after it closed. They changed the name to the Rainbow Ballroom and redesigned the interior giving it a fresh new appearance. With Ray and Johnny's connections in the music industry as well as the friends Charlie made while on the road, the Rainbow Ballroom booked top-notch acts in Amarillo.

Willie Nelson was the first artist booked into the newly renovated Rainbow Ballroom. Bob Wills and his Texas Playboys played soon after that. Charlie Phillips and the Sugartimers often backed Wills depending on circumstance or the needs of Wills. Artists like Ray Price, Webb Pierce, Wanda Jackson, Charlie Phillips, Ferlin Husky, George Jones, Jim Reeves, or Willie Nelson were regularly booked at the club just to name a handful. Charlie often brought in his friends like David Houston and Tillman Franks. It's estimated Ray, Charlie, and Johnny booked more than 100 acts during their ownership of the Rainbow Ballroom.

All good things seem to come to an end. Shortly after remodeling and opening the club, the guys realized they had made a fatal mistake at their new venue. They had moved the bandstand from its original location on the far south wall to the easterly wall resulting in poor sound quality, which they were never able to fully correct. Although thriving for a few years, they eventually closed the doors and the property reverted back to the former Clover Club.

Johnny Hathcock was known as quite the poker player and many a night would talk the traveling talent into a "friendly" game of poker back at Hathcock's house after the performance had ended for the night. Many artists were out-bluffed, so to speak, by Hathcock's poker prowess; however, none more than Willie Nelson. Charlie Phillips, still nicknamed Scrooge, wasn't much for gambling his hard-earned money away, but sat-in several nights watching performers try their hand at poker after closing. Hathcock and Nelson would play for hours with anyone else who was willing, and before you knew it, Willie would lose most if not all of the money he'd earned for his night's performance. He'd either have to borrow money to get to his next gig or he'd have to agree to return for a free performance.

Many of the guys remember Willie's then-horrible poker playing skills, but as everyone knows, he got the last laugh, as no one realized Willie would mature into one of the greatest country music icons in history. Perhaps Nelson wasn't as bad of a gambler as one might think. He took a gamble and bucked the Nashville multinational and created a style of music legendary only to the star we all now know as Willie Nelson.

It's important to note Johnny Hathcock would also become one of the most creative music writers in history. He would pen more than 400 songs in his long career and hundreds if not thousands of artists to date would record those songs. "Wake Up Irene" was his first hit and was recorded by Hank Thompson on Capitol Records. He and Ray Winkler teamed up to write "Welcome to My World" successfully recorded and sung by Jim Reeves. This song went on to become the anthem for the country singer, Eddy Arnold, and was covered by more than 60 popular artists including Andy Williams, Dean Martin and Elvis Presley.

Hathcock also became a columnist for the *Amarillo Globe-News* and an editorial writer for the livestock publication, *Record Stockman*. Moreover he worked for radio stations in Texas and New Mexico. Johnny released his self-penned collection of poetry in 1999 entitled *Sweet & Sour*. Charlie Phillips, Ray Winkler and Johnny Hathcock all remained friends until Winkler's unfortunate death on May 9, 1998. Hathcock would soon follow Winkler in 2000 and Charlie would be left with only memories of his good friends and the many adventures they shared over the years.

In the early 1930's, Amelia Earhart experienced a loosened hatch while attempting a non-stop flight from Los Angeles to Newark and after holding the hatch shut for 75 miles, sprained her wrist in the process. She made an emergency landing at English Airfield in Amarillo and this headlining news ostensibly prompted Earl Hooper of Amarillo to name his small drive-in and café located near the airfield, the Aviatrix. In 1939, Carlton Scales and his mother, Iweta, purchased the little restaurant and enlarged the facility turning it into a premiere Amarillo nightspot making it the most elaborate ballroom and supper club in the Texas Panhandle.

Horn man, Carlton Scales, created the family dancehall and formed his own five-piece orchestra leading the charge of his popular big band music of the era, which sometimes consisted of as many as nine to 12 musicians. Charlie remembers Scales occasionally enlisted a whole horn section to dazzle an audience. Stan Kenton did a live NBC broadcast from the Aviatrix in March of 1953. The early years saw band trailblazers like Woody Herman, Les Brown, Harry James, Tommy and Jimmy Dorsey, Spike Jones, Velma Middleton, Louis Armstrong, Billy Strayhorn and Duke Ellington play to the crowds amassed in their large dance hall. In 1952, the Aviatrix burned to the ground joining the list of other clubs like the Avalon, the Clover Club and the Casa Del, which all experienced devastating fires at various times, razing them all. Each was rebuilt to higher standards including the Aviatrix.

Ruth's Steakhouse was located just across the street near the Eastridge Bowling Alley with a large grocery store situated across the boulevard. The fresh Aviatrix sported a new canopy extending from its front door and into the parking lot. The original sign still bore a big A on the Aviatrix sign facing both directions fronting Route 66 or what would become known as Amarillo Boulevard. Local Amarillo Air Base personnel would begin flocking into the new location, which by the 1960's had changed its music format from big band music to primarily country and western swing at the request and prompting of Charlie.

In 1965, Charlie "Sugartime" Phillips was now highly established as a fixture in the Amarillo community and Carlton and Iweta Scales had since closed the Aviatrix Ballroom because it waned in patrons. Charlie asked the two if they could strike a deal. They would still own the nightclub, but Charlie would help them reopen and would become the weekly staff musician. They agreed, and the Aviatrix reopened once again. What probably should have been a temporary gig became a 25-year musical love affair. At the time, the Aviatrix was the largest ballroom between Dallas and Denver. The facility could hold hundreds of people on its large hardwood dance floor with its circular half-moon seating tiers.

With Charlie and the guys using KZIP radio's connections, large acts were brought in to play the Aviatrix Ballroom, just as it'd been done at the Rainbow Ballroom. Fats Domino played the club, and Pappy Dave Stone, Ray Winkler and KZIP were able to book the popular Jerry Lee Lewis, who arrived in full form for an electrifying performance. At the time, the Aviatrix did not have a proper piano for Lewis to play on, so KZIP rented one from a local Amarillo music store named Tolzien's. The evening was packed with dancers cutting a rug to Lewis's powerful music. As Jerry pounded the piano for his grand finale, in his excitement and in true form, he kicked the piano over onto the bandstand to the excitement of the crowd and the shock of the guys at KZIP, who had to purchase that piano from the music store. The radio station lost some profits that evening, but the excited crowd won one of the best shows ever.

Charlie always enjoyed when his friend and colleague from Capitol Records, Ferlin Husky, visited Amarillo. Either Winkler or Hathcock would book him into one of the local clubs. Charlie interviewed him on-air a few times and was always sure to play his recently released records. "I thought Ferlin had a great voice," speaking fondly of the singer. The great entertainer had already been in a few movies like *Mr. Rock & Roll* and *Country Music Holiday*, but was always humble, and the guys enjoyed him a lot. Years later in 2010, Charlie's friend would ultimately be inducted into the Country Music Hall of Fame.

Pappy Dave Stone loved country music singer and songwriter, Sonny James, and would get him booked at the Amarillo Civic Center Auditorium as often as he could. According to Phillips, Sonny was, "One helluva entertainer." The guys might all hang out before or after a show and Sonny would sometimes drop by the KZIP station. According to Charlie, James had such a polite manner and this is the reason he established the nickname, the Southern Gentleman. Phillips remembers on so many occasions Pappy would be talking-up the country star- as he had so many stories to tell. The Southern Gentleman would similarly have an illustrious career in country music topping the charts with a hit song 23 times!

Charlie was set to play every Saturday night at the Aviatrix and in over twenty years, missed very few weekends, unless he was called out of town to perform at a larger venue. Willie Nelson made a couple of appearances before his music truly took off. Charlie booked as many of his friends and colleagues into the Aviatrix first and foremost to make money, but Charlie had an un-talked about ambition that drove him. He always wanted to see his friends working. So as long as Charlie had a band and had a venue to play at, he could always assure his contemporaries they had a place to perform their music and as he is quoted, "So I'd always have someone to play with…You're only as good as the guys you have behind you."

The Scales family was continually happy with the crowds Charlie Phillips and the Sugartimer Band brought in. With the exception of bad weather days, the Tri-state Fair or competing big name artists, the Sugartimers could always draw a crowd, even after twenty-three years of playing. "That's what it's all about," Phillips insists.

As many successful years passed, Amarillo grew. Much nicer venues began popping up in better neighborhoods. Music began changing also. The Amarillo Air Force Base had long since closed and the east side of Amarillo slowly became a ramshackle burrow, especially after Interstate-40 bypassed Route 66 and much of Amarillo. Both Iweta and Carlton Scales succumb to bad health and business slowed to a trickle. By 1989, Charlie and the Sugartimers would perform their swan song and bid Route 66 and Amarillo Boulevard farewell on New Years Eve. They had a long fruitful run.

Charlie's friend and fellow Columbia recording artist would tour the U.S. and have bookings in Amarillo. Ray Price occasionally requested Charlie and his band back him up or open for him at the Rex Baxter Building in Amarillo. Charlie had first met Price years earlier at Clovis at the Air Force Base. They rehearsed and played together for various shows. Usually Charlie and the Sugartimers would play for an hour before Price's lead performance.

He and Price were once booked to play at the Rex Baxter show, but they noticed when setting up at the large Baxter building, their PA system wasn't big enough to accommodate the crowd space. Charlie called his friends at Randy's Music Mart, a popular Amarillo music source at the time, and was provided a new PA system. Randy's worked tirelessly to instate a proper sound system finishing their installation only moments before the show started- to Price's chagrin. It was a very temperamental show. When Ray was interviewed years in the future, he reminisced about the times he and Charlie played together. Priced recounted some of Charlie's career stating, "Me and Charlie played together off and on over the years…I always thought he was one of the most underrated singers in the business…I art [ought] to give him a call." But it was not to be as Price passed away shortly thereafter in December of 2013.

Charlie would reacquaint himself with old friend and singer, Darrell McCall, who did a lot of harmonizing and backup singing for both Price and Willie Nelson. Phillips insists, "Darrell was one of the best harmonizers in the business." McCall assisted Charlie with some harmonizing vocals on his song, "I Guess I'll Never Learn" on a Columbia recording session.

On another instance, Merle Haggard needed an opening act at the Amarillo Civic Center Coliseum, so Charlie rounded up some Sugartimers and obliged his old friend by putting on one heck of a performance. Decked out in all black with silver and turquoise jewelry reminiscent of the time period, Charlie "Sugartime" Phillips and his band played to one of their largest Amarillo audiences.

On June 26, 1999, another Amarillo radio station favorite, KGNC, sponsored a concert held at a baseball stadium near the fair grounds and Dick Bivins Stadium in Amarillo. Charlie and the Sugartimers were to be the guest openers for the then popular band, Diamond Rio. By this time, Diamond Rio had already received the Country Music Association's award for Vocal Group of the Year and had been nominated for several Grammy Awards.

Charlie and the Sugartimers were to install their sound equipment and were instructed *not* to touch anything belonging to the big stars. The soundstage built by the Diamond Rio crew was enormous for such a small location, and Charlie enlisted his roadie, Chris Moore, to help the guys setup their equipment. All of the Sugartimers were now in their 60's or 70's, and it would be a daunting task for them to play in the hot, dry, windy heat of the day. The crowds had packed the stadium seats and were now overflowing onto the baseball diamond with their chairs and blankets.

The Sugartimers put on the show of their life as the crowd applauded and gave them a standing ovation. Upon finishing, the guys were notified that their equipment needed to be removed from the stage immediately and before Diamond Rio made their grand entrance. Charlie and the guys all scrambled quickly to disassemble and exit the stage. Since they were the opening musicians, they were accustomed to sitting backstage while other acts performed, but this occasion would prove quite daunting.

The men were forced by Diamond Rio's security staff to leave the backstage area never to return. Charlie and the guys couldn't believe it. They had never been asked to leave their own venue. "Where the hell were we old guys gonna sit? It's not like we had tickets or anything!" Charlie reminiscences. So they trickled into the baseball diamond with the other spectators. The only exception was renowned fiddle player and Sugartimer, Jimmy Young, who disappointingly thought, "To heck with this!" as he left the facility. This would be Charlie and the Sugartimers' final big-venue show. After a lifetime of playing music and dozens of charted songs, the phone slowly stopped ringing and large-crowd shows playing to thousands of screaming fans, became a thing of the past.

Charlie and a few of the Sugartimers decided it was time to slow things down. They would later join smaller venues like one of the longest-running dance clubs in Amarillo, dubbed the Over-39 Singles Dance Club Country category. As the name implies, single men and women over the age of 39 were welcomed to tie one on to the sounds of live country music and western swing. The guys just headlined once a month. Charlie enjoyed the fresh new faces and put on quite a show until, as luck would have it, the 45 & Uppers Club Country genre called in need of a regular weekly band.

Charlie Phillips and the Sugartimers began playing every Friday night and continued until November 2013 when Charlie had a fainting spell from heart problems onstage and visited the heart clinic shortly thereafter. His heart had slowed down and was in need of some help. His doctors installed a pacemaker. It was time for Charlie to retire temporarily, if only for a bit. After years of playing at the 45 & Uppers, Earl Cliff, head of the dance organization would present Charlie an award plaque commemorating seven years of service to the organization.

Over the century, Amarillo blossomed from a one-horse town into a sprawling metropolitan area boasting just fewer than 200,000 people and perhaps, if one counted the folks from close surrounding towns, the number of persons would topple over 300,000. Throughout the years, many notable people would either originate from Amarillo or a town nearby, or they would simply call Amarillo home.

Carolyn Jones developed into an actress and became the star of the popular television series, *The Addams Family*, playing Morticia Addams. Ron Ely was most known for his role on the television series, *Tarzan*, while Ann Doran played alongside James Dean in *A Rebel Without a Cause*. Danny Elfman hailed from Amarillo and became a rock singer and famous movie composer winning a Grammy Award, an Emmy Award and was nominated for 4 Academy Awards, primarily for his work with film creator, Tim Burton.

Trent Willmon, J.D. Souther, Jimmie Dale Gilmore, Blair Garner, Kevin Fowler and Joe Ely all became well-known country artists. Kimberly Willis Holt, Jennifer Archer, Art Bell and Jodi (Koumalatz) Thomas flourished as famous authors. Todd English became a celebrity chef, and Grady Nutt became a sought after comedian on *Hee Haw*. Ben Sargent won the Pulitzer Prize as an editorial cartoonist, and Gail Caldwell won the Pulitzer as a book critic. Lacey Brown became a folk singer and claimed her fame as an

American Idol finalist. Susan Gibson penned "Wide Open Spaces" performed by the Dixie Chicks, winning her the CMA Songwriter of the Year, BMI Writer of the Year in 1999 and the 2009 West Texas Music Hall of Fame: Entertainer of the Year. John Rich was an Amarillo native with the band Big and Rich scoring success with their tune, "Save a Horse (Ride a Cowboy)." Rich also wrote songs for Wynonna and Jason Aldean, Faith Hill and Gretchen Wilson, as well as becoming a judge on *Nashville Star* and appearing on Donald Trump's *Celebrity Apprentice*.

It wasn't just entertainers and artists Amarillo produced. Billionaire oilman, philanthropist, and corporate raider, T Boone Pickens, hailed from the Panhandle in addition to Texas State Senator, Kel Seliger. James Beverly became the governor of Puerto Rico. Beau Boulter was elected a U.S. Congressman. James Nathan Browning served as Texas Lieutenant Governor. John Marvin Jones became U.S. Congressman and a Chief Judge. Local favorite, Teel Bivins, was appointed the U.S. Ambassadorship to Sweden.

Many sports stars sprung from the Golden Spread including professional golfers, Rex Baxter, Brad Bryant and the people's favorite, Ryan Palmer. Tennis star, Alex O'Brien won the U.S. Open Men's Doubles with Sébastien Lareau and also competed in the 2000 Sydney Olympics. Bum Phillips was an Amarillo High School coach who went on to become coach of the Houston Oilers and New Orleans Saints football teams. Wrestling fans will also remember famous wrestlers/entertainers who called Amarillo home like Dory Funk, Dory Funk Jr., Terry Funk, Mike Knox, Barry Orton, Ricky Romero, Chris Romero, Mark Romero, Steven Romero and Erik Watts. Mixed martial artists, Paul Buentello and Evan Tanner, called Amarillo home. Professional football player, Hurles Scales, played with the Cincinnati Bengals, the St. Louis Cardinals, the Chicago Bears and the Green Bay Packers; William Thomas was a linebacker for the Philadelphia Eagles and the Oakland Raiders; Ken Vinyard played for the Atlanta Falcons in the 1960's; and Pampa, Texas native, Zach Thomas, signed with the Miami Dolphins and eventually opened up a sports gym in Amarillo called Zach's Club 54.

The famous gambler, "Amarillo" Slim, enlightened audiences worldwide with his gambling expertise and card & pool ball tricks, while Fritch native, Ron "Mr. Tater Salad" White kept audiences in stitches with his comedy act while touring with Jeff Foxworthy, Bill Engvall and Larry the Cable Guy on the *Blue Collar Comedy Tour*. Ron's younger sister, Shea White, became a comedienne, author and animal rights activist. Paul Lockhart became an American astronaut completing two Space Shuttle missions. Also, another Amarillo astronaut became a household name when his space shuttle craft, STS-107, tragically disintegrated upon re-entering earth's atmosphere sadly killing Amarillo native, Rick Husband, and all of the crewmembers aboard. Husband received the Congressional Space Medal of Honor for his dedication and bravery. Amarillo honored the fallen hero by renaming the Amarillo International Airport- the Rick Husband International Airport.

Although Charlie Phillips wasn't born in Amarillo, he has called it home since 1960 and has lived in the same house for most of the 55 years he has resided in the Texas town. While in Amarillo, Charlie saw around 27 of his songs enter the country music charts, with only one entering the top-10 position. Even though Phillips was from Farwell, he always considered Amarillo his home. He has played virtually every week at one location or another until 2013 and according to his statement, "I've loved playing this town, and I love these people and I hope I'm not done yet!"

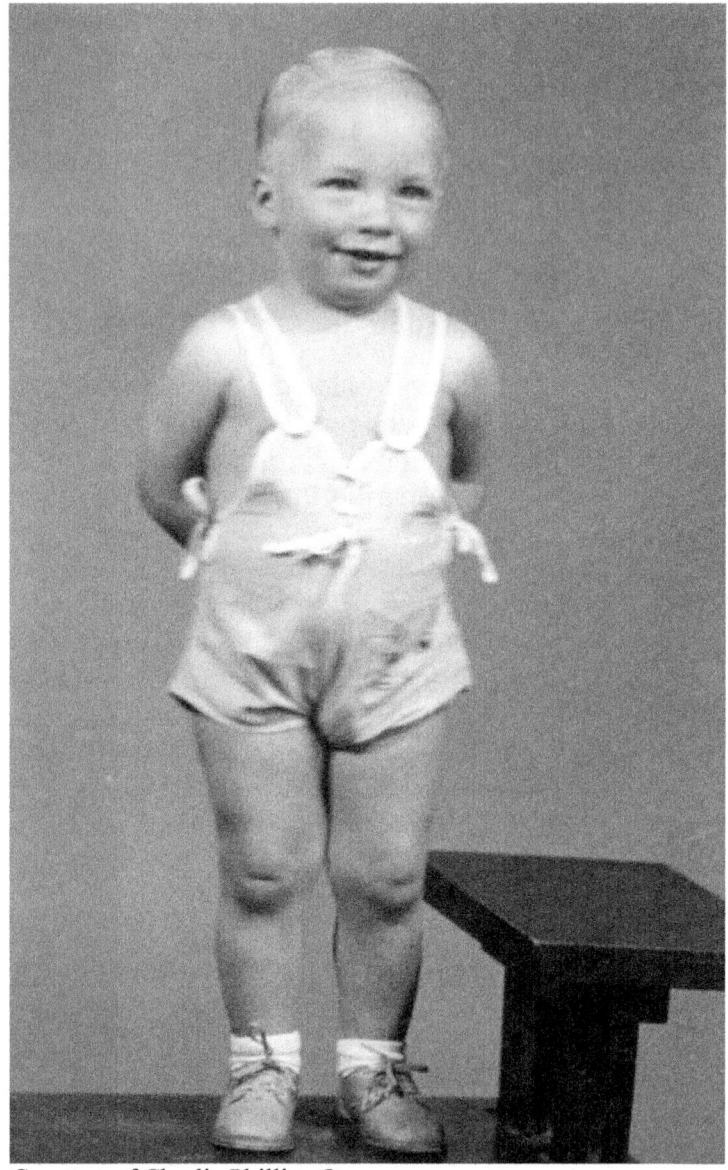

Courtesy of Charlie Phillips ©

Young Charlie Phillips already entertaining for the camera. (1936)

Courtesy of Charlie Phillips ©

Midgie riding along with Charlie on his tricycle. Photo taken on Charlie's sixth birthday at the Old Donaldson farm in Farwell, Texas (1940)

Courtesy of Charlie Phillips ©

Gracie, the goat, was one of Charlie's favorite domesticated farm animals. The goat was traded to a neighboring farm after she jumped on top of the family's new model automobile and blemished the paint. Notice the family bathtub propped next to the watering trough. Photo taken on the Old Donaldson farm in Farwell, Texas. (1941)

Courtesy of Charlie Phillips ©

After a neighborhood tragedy, Albert "A.F." Phillips purchased Charlie's first horse, Paint. Young Phillips exhibits his riding skills while Paint puts on quite a show. Taken on the Old Donaldson farm around 1943- 1944. Notice the newfangled Allis-Chalmers Harvester in the background.

Courtesy of Charlie Phillips ©

Charlie Phillips sports a "P" monogramed tie during his Farwell High School senior photograph in 1952.

Courtesy of Charlie Phillips ©

Jimmy Schell (L) and Charlie show off their new country duds while performing for the camera at the Phillips' family home around 1954-1955. The guys wanted a picture to make them look like stars.

Courtesy of Charlie Phillips ©

Jimmy Schell (L), Charlie Phillips and Dudley Hughes (R) perform for a small crowd at a KCLV sponsored show around 1957.

Courtesy of the Dudley Hughes estate ©

Taken the night of the official "Sugartime" and "One Faded Rose" recording session at the Norman Petty Studio in Clovis, New Mexico with Buddy Holly accompanying. Odis "Pop" Echols paid for and supervised the evening while Charlie made music history.

Courtesy of Charlie Phillips ©

"Sugartime" won the Gold Record after the McGuire Sisters took it to No. 1 on the charts. "Ma Kate" proudly sits with Charlie in Odis "Pop" Echols' KCLV office, all enjoying the benefits of "Sugartime's " success. (1958)

Courtesy of Charlie Phillips ©

Charlie coiffed and singing proudly on this *Louisiana Hayride* stage appearance while Dudley Hughes plucks the bass, beaming from ear to ear. Most likely this was Charlie's second appearance on the KWKS sponsored show. (1958)

Courtesy of Charlie Phillips ©

Charlie driving a young Tommy Sands to and from party locations throughout Clovis, New Mexico in his 1958 Mercury Monterey. Bass player, Dudley Hughes, can be seen peering over the car. (1958)

(NEW YORK) . . . Odis and Charlie Phillips celebrate one million record sales of "Sugartime" with the McGuire Sisters at The Waldorf Astoria Hotel prior to their Empire Room Appearance (1958).

This 1958 newspaper-clipping photo was taken inside The Waldorf Astoria Hotel between the McGuire Sisters' two shows in the Empire Room. Odis Echols Jr. surprised Charlie with tickets to the show and a visit with the girls. The trio wanted to meet the man who wrote their No. 1 tune. Photo Courtesy of the *Clovis News-Journal* ©.

Photo courtesy of R. Peterson ©

Minnie Pearl chuckling it up during a Charlie Phillips interview at Lewis Jewelers in Amarillo, Texas early in Charlie's KZIP radio career around 1960. The two laughed while trying to hock a diamond-crest ring to the adoring public.

Photo courtesy of R. Peterson ©

Charlie boarding a Braniff Airline flight to Nashville for an appearance on the *Grand Ole Opry* in the early 1960's.

Photo Courtesy of Janie Kirkland ©

Charlie sits in charge of the control room at KZIP radio station in Amarillo, Texas. Gone were the days of the reel-to-reel tapes, as records and more portable tapes were primarily used at more advanced stations. (Early 1960's)

Photo Courtesy of Charlie Phillips © Promo Photo

Jimmy C. Newman (L) and Charlie in casual conversation backstage at the *Grand Ole Opry* at the Ryman Auditorium in Nashville. Young Jimmy had only appeared on the *Opry* for a few short years before this picture was taken and of course, he became a legendary star. Notice Newman's name etched onto his guitar. (1961)

Photo Courtesy of Charlie Phillips © Promo Photo

Legendary performers, Homer and Jethro, pose with Charlie backstage before their *Grand Ole Opry* appearance at the Ryman Auditorium in Nashville, Tennessee. (1961)

Photo Courtesy of Charlie Phillips © Promo Photo

Charlie posing for a serious promotional headshot. (1960)

Photo Courtesy of Charlie Phillips ©

The "Sugar Timers" trailer carried the band's equipment to their many scheduled gigs during the Columbia Records days. To help pay for the initial costs, Pepsi co-sponsored the two-wheeled trailer. (1961)

Photo Courtesy of Charlie Phillips, Royce Brantley, gifted from Webb Pierce ©

Webb Pierce (L) posing with Charlie and his new mustache. This photo was taken in the basement of Pierce's Nashville mansion during a party thrown for the annual DJ Convention. Although Charlie had several records out with Columbia Records, he was now well regarded as a radioman. This trip would see embarrassment, as Charlie would inadvertently squish a pimento cheese sandwich into the hand of Tennessee's governor. (Early 1970's)

Photo Courtesy of Charlie Phillips © Promo Photo

Charlie waving from a stagecoach during a mid-1970's promotional photo-shoot at a Big Texan Classic in Amarillo, Texas.

Photo Courtesy of Charlie Phillips © KZIP Promo

George Jones (L) and Charlie "Sugartime" Phillips joke around after a show at a downtown Amarillo restaurant in the latter 1970's. Notice Jones' jacket embroidered with GGJ, George Glenn Jones, while Charlie sports the latest turquoise jewelry.

Photo Courtesy of Charlie Phillips © KZIP Promo

A beardless Merle Haggard (L) and radioman, Jolly Cholly, pose backstage at the Amarillo Civic Center after a KZIP sponsored show in Amarillo, Texas. Photo most likely taken in the late- 1960s.

Photo Courtesy of Charlie Phillips and Stull ©

Phillips singing and reviewing lyrics during a 1970's recording session at the Billy Stull Studio in Amarillo, Texas.

Photo Courtesy of Charlie Phillips © Promo Photo

Charlie "Sugartime" Phillips accompanied by the Sugartimers opening for Merle Haggard at the Amarillo Civic Center Coliseum in the 1980's.

Photo Courtesy of Bella Bird Photography

Charlie "Sugartime" Phillips at around 80 years of age. Taken at the Bella Bird Photography Studio in Amarillo, Texas.

Photo Courtesy of Cy Cushenberry ©

The Norman Petty Recording Studios located at 1313 7th Street in Clovis, New Mexico was the birthplace of notable musicians like Charlie "Sugartime" Phillips, Buddy Holly and the Crickets, the Fireballs, the Roses and many others. The building still stands preserved in its original location.

Photo graciously loaned by the Phillips family ©

One of the only surviving photos of the Phillips family slightly restored for clarity. (Standing L-R) Glenn Phillips, Carthon Phillips, Albert Frank Jr. "Bunk" Phillips (Seated L-R) Elaine Phillips, Albert Frank "A.F." Phillips, Katherine Luella "Ma Kate" Phillips and baby Charlie.

Chapter 11
The Music Man

Since his first recording sessions between 1954-1955, Charlie recorded an estimated 200 songs during the following six decades. Few of these were released to the public, and many sit dormant on reel-to-reel tapes and recorders, never to see the light of day. Some were even destroyed by disasters, and others were just lost. With only one top-10 hit under his belt, the record companies moved on to other hopeful artists leaving behind only memories for Charlie and his fans. He's become the forgotten country music legend. "Sugartime" would become his ultimate legacy. If it wasn't for a schoolteacher who encouraged him, a man who believed in his talents and gave Charlie a career in radio, and a legendary music producer, Charlie may have lived out his days toiling on his dusty family farm.

If a person is going to talk about the rise of pop and rock 'n' roll, it would be safe to start with Horace Logan. After hearing him sing, "That's Alright Mama" later recorded by Sun Records, Horace gave the young Elvis Presley a chance to prove himself on the *Louisiana Hayride*. As Elvis began touring, young acts like Buddy Holly and the Crickets would soon emulate his sound and style of performance. This perhaps led Buddy and the Crickets to Norman Petty who produced what is now retrospectively known as the "Clovis Sound." It would be Norman Petty who used his skills in the studio to record music that had never been heard at the time. With Buddy and a Cricket or two on one of the first cuts of "Sugartime," Charlie's record could now be presented to Coral Record executives. This created a whirlwind and an unexpected ascent, crafting Norman Petty into a force to be reckoned within the visionary concept of rock 'n' roll- after selling millions of copies.

Through Norman's connections with Decca/Coral, Buddy Holly's voice and style illuminated the airwaves worldwide. This would catch the ear of a young band overseas that would model their name-concept after the tight-sounding Holly. The Beatles would begin with their own style, admittedly because of Buddy Holly. Alongside the Beatles, would march the Rolling Stones who visited the States in 1969 to record at another virtually unknown independent recording studio, the Muscle Shoals Sound Studio in Sheffield, Alabama. Without Sun Records, the Norman Petty Studio and the Muscle Shoals studio, the world of music might sound quite differently today and imaginably be much less exciting.

Phillips' first two acetate records, "Put Your Arms Around Me" and "Courtin' In The Rain, " were thought to be lost to time; however, in August of 2015 the last remaining original copies surfaced after childhood friend, Jerry Don Utsman, passed away. It was the recording of these two songs that gave Charlie the courage to visit his friend, Jimmy Self, at the KICA radio station in Clovis- the first deejay in the country to play Charlie's music. Jimmy did something else for the young artist. He told Phillips to start writing his own music, telling him he couldn't make a living covering other people's songs. This was prophetic advice. Thanks to Jimmy, Charlie did write many of his own tunes. With Self playing some of Charlie's songs on KICA radio, the singer developed self-assurance enough to confidently play in bars throughout Clovis and the surrounding region.

Only a few copies of the unissued demo of "Sugartime" and "One Faded Rose" would survive. Pete Wallace, Jimmy Schell, Dudley Hughes, Gerald Brown and Charlie probably had no idea they had made music history together. "One Faded Rose" was a simple song that had originated with a friend of Pop Echols, Nita Bryant. Nita had written a few lyrics on a piece of paper, and it would be up to Charlie to arrange the music and compose the words. Phillips sent the "Sugartime" and "One Faded Rose" record to various radio stations in the area, but unfortunately it fell on deaf ears. Neither song possibly ever received any airplay and Charlie never received word from any of the stations or deejays.

Thank goodness for Pop having the faith in Charlie, enough to advance the initial funds needed to record "Sugartime" suitably. Charlie was excited Buddy Holly and the Crickets, whom he had heard so much about, would be playing on his compositions. Buddy and the guys were just plain ole' talented musicians to Charlie. They weren't superstars. Who could have possible foreseen the Buddy Holly and the Crickets craze that would soon follow- then tragically end so abruptly? Over the years, some have speculated the long-drawn-out guitar riff leading to the introduction of "Sugartime" was the work of Buddy, but Charlie laughs and contends it was *his* riff and Buddy simply played it as instructed.

The recording date often listed for this particular demo of "Sugartime" is July 26, 1957, but it's unlikely this was the actual date as there is evidence to support recording artist, Sherry Davis, recorded her two songs, "Humble Heart" and "Broken Promises" at the Petty studio on this date. It's most likely "Sugartime" as well as the flipside were recorded on July 17 and July 18, 1957 during one long overnight session. Davis was certainly not present during this session, but interestingly she would base one of her primary future acts on the McGuire Sister's version of "Sugartime."

Shortly after the original taping of "Sugartime," Norman Petty flew to Miami on July 27, 1957 for a Columbia sales convention. It's plausible he introduced the newly recorded song to record company executives on this trip; however, it would be the Coral executives ultimately committing to Charlie.

It did not take Norman exceedingly long to place Charlie's future hit. It helped that Buddy Holly and the Crickets were now well received and starting their journey onto the charts after being placed with Decca/Coral. By September 16, 1957 just a few short months after the first professional recording of "Sugartime," Norman arranged a recording deal for Charlie's masters and Coral released them in November 1957. Intriguingly though, Charlie's first appearance on the *Louisiana Hayride* would be announced in the *Shreveport Times* dated October 26, 1957- a full week before Coral released the record to the public.

It was probably Pop Echols who sold Charlie's potentiality to Horace Logan, undoubtedly telling Horace that the young artist was about to have a big hit with Coral Records. It would be this fall evening at the *Hayride* Charlie debuted his song to a national audience. Every *Hayride* show was recorded, but unfortunately no material has yet surfaced of Phillips' early shows. All that remains are the photographs of Charlie singing and playing guitar under the famed Southern Made Donut sign.

On November 4, 1957, only one week after his first national appearance, *Billboard* gave Charlie a C&W (Country and Western) Spotlight Review stating, "New artist opens with two great sides which establish him as a potential star. 'Sugartime' is a swingy chant that gets a fine performance. 'One Faded Rose' is also potent with overtures of salvation. Good cat. It's a solid coupling which can also break in the pop market." This review reveals more than meets the eye and requires rationalization.

Charlie Phillips was familiar with the term rock 'n' roll when Buddy Holly and the Crickets helped back his cut of "Sugartime." Bill Haley and Little Richard were all over the airwaves and even Charlie and the guys emulated some Elvis songs at their own performances. Between the era of big band music and rock was what would be commonly referred to as pop music, the shortened word for popular music. Charlie would rarely describe himself as anything other than what he thought he was- a country music artist. *Not* a pop artist. But because of Buddy Holly and the Crickets' involvement on Charlie's album, in addition to the pop vocal group, the McGuire Sisters, taking his song to the top of the charts, a colossal problem ultimately arose for Charlie.

Was he a country singer? Was he a pop singer? Can we hear some rockabilly in there? Even Coral record executives were confused about where to place Charlie and within what genres? Now, if anyone has ever heard "One Faded Rose" played, there's no mistaking the pure country sound. Although Charlie was very contented to be recognized as a recording artist with a national record label, other folks in the industry often became confused as to what type of artist Charlie actually was.

Phillips' version of "Sugartime" was heavily plugged by the deejays in the late 1950's, but the McGuire Sisters would soon overpower the success of his version. Since the sisters were one of Coral's top acts, word soon went out to cease the play on Charlie's version. In fact, it's very difficult to even find a copy of the actual record today.

By March of 1958, the McGuire Sisters were heavy on the charts, as were two other cover versions by British artists, Alma Cogan and Jim Dale, each performing their own version of "Sugartime." Both Cogan and Dale scored well on the British charts. Also, Coral released Holly and the Crickets' "Maybe Baby," "Oh Boy!" "Peggy Sue," and "Listen To Me." This sudden saturation of song releases opened the eyes of record executives as Norman Petty now had seven songs out of the top 30 places on the charts.

While Charlie was recording other songs, he and Norman attempted to revive "Sugartime" around 1962 as they introduced their version of a dance song called the "Sugartime Twist," which was once again released by Coral with the McGuire Sisters singing the lyrics. In all probability, the song was undoubtedly released too little too late as Chubby Checker's "The Twist" had already begun to fade from the radio's at this time. The record topped on the *Billboard* charts at a meager No. 107; however, the song would soon be revived and covered by the popular Edwards Twins followed by Duane Eddy on his *Twistin' & Twangin'* album in 1962. Years later the song would appear on the album, *Wanda Jackson Rockabilly Party Girls*. Regardless of its lack of sales, the song's catchy tune was well played by many artists no matter who sang the cover.

After "Sugartime Twist," Charlie returned to the Petty studio and recorded a dub of "Be My Bride" at Norman's in the early months of 1957. A copy was sent to Coral asking their approval. By Christmas of 1957 he would return to the Norman Petty Studio and cut a new version of "Be My Bride" with his personal band, hoping this version would entice Coral to release another record. Jimmy

Schell and Pete Wallace backed up Charlie on guitar with Dudley Hughes on bass and Gerald Brown on drums. This version would never be issued to the public and did not meet with the approval of Murray Deutch or Bob Thiele.

Yet, here's the oddest circumstance requiring interpretation. Although this version was of high quality, Coral requested Charlie travel to New York in order to cut yet another, better dub of the song. One might not have seen it at the time, but this was a first step in the process of perhaps, "cutting out middlemen like Norman." It's been documented in various books, the exec's in New York saw Norman Petty as a hick from the sticks and they both rightfully and wrongly assumed they could cut Norman out of the picture completely, securing themselves with more profits and maintaining more control over the artists and songs they released. Yes, Norman *could* be eliminated from the picture and yes, the record companies wouldn't have to pay him royalties. They simply needed to lure artists away from Petty and re-cut the artist's songs in their own studios; however, they left something very important out of the mix.

The *only* person who could create the "Clovis Sound" was the man who invented it, Norman Petty. And it took the record execs too long before they figured out this equation. Yes, Buddy Knox was talented. As was Roy Orbison, and Buddy Holly and the Crickets, and Charlie Phillips- yet without Norman Petty at the helm- studio recordings from other workshops were just that, recordings- usually not masterpieces. Neither Charlie nor Norman could have foreseen what the Coral executives had planned at the time, so Charlie recorded yet another version of "Be My Bride" at the Bell Studios in New York City as well as the flipside, "Too Many Tears."

Phillips was a young and fresh recording artist and couldn't figure out why the record label wanted him to re-record a song outside of the Petty studio. In true fashion, Charlie always did as he was told and followed their orders. The only highlight of this trip was being introduced to the McGuire Sisters, the very gals who made "Sugartime" such a success. The sisters were delighted to meet the boy who wrote their biggest hit.

By April 1958, the new record was released. *Billboard* wrote: "Be My Bride." "This up-tempo folk effort receives a strong vocal from the country based singer and it also has a chance for some coins in the pop market. The lad sings with spirit. 'Too Many Tears' is a country styled ditty about a broken love affair and also receives a good vocal but the flipside should get the action." Although "Sugartime" is often heard in the music world as having a rockabilly feel, it was "Be My Bride" Charlie would be accredited with for creating a unique rockabilly sound. Surprisingly, just after the song's release, Pop Echols notified Charlie announcing Dick Clark, host of *American Bandstand*, had played "Be My Bride" on his popular teen program. Charlie had unexpectedly become popular with the younger generation, even though he was only in his early 20's at the time.

Since Charlie was having vast pop-music appeal with a younger audience and was being featured in teen magazines, Bob Thiele and/or Murray Deutch thought Charlie would be considered too old for his new youthful listeners. They "suggested" Charlie secretly lower his age by three years, which was a common occurrence for singers and movie stars. Of course young Phillips agreed with whatever the music executives said, so with the stroke of a pen, Charlie became a teenager again- at least on paper. One wouldn't think this to be a big deal, after all, many folks fib about their age, but as Charlie matured and began getting older, he continued living with a lie spelled out by the record company. Oddly, decades later, some of Charlie's closest friends actually believed he was three years younger than he truly was. It was a successful ploy.

Charlie was invited to a three-day Fireman's Benefit in Houston, Texas and took his new single, "Be My Bride" on the road. This package trip would feature Phillips playing onstage with Marty Robbins, Ray Price, Brenda Lee, Kitty Wells, as well as Johnny and Jack. His new single was popular with the audiences and was also receiving substantial play on the radio, but sales were dismal and within months had dropped off the charts. "Be My Bride" wouldn't be seen again for decades until it was once again released on several rock 'n' roll compilations, not on country albums as one might think. Charlie probably didn't know too much about the rockabilly genre, but his up-tempo song about proposing to a woman was straight-up rockabilly and the first of its nature penned by the songwriter. Although it's never been written about, it's possible Buddy Holly and the guys might have inadvertently influenced the creation of "Be My Bride" as a more upbeat country song.

Charlie had recorded at the Norman Petty Studio and had now recorded at the Bell Sound Studio in New York City, but Coral requested he travel to Nashville and cut yet another record at the Castle Recording Studio. In 1958, he had been transferred to the Decca country label from Coral at the Nashville office under the direction of Paul Cohen and at times, Owen Bradley.

Cohen was a record producer who had been with Columbia, but joined ranks with Decca in 1934 heading their country division. Ernest Tubb and Red Foley were the first two successful artists produced by Cohen as he soon began lining up other stars, thus creating quite the sensation in Nashville as his Midas-touch for finding new and exciting musicians culminated into what would later be dubbed, the "Nashville Sound." It would be Cohen who would popularize such legends like Kitty Wells, Brenda Lee, Webb Pierce, Patsy Cline and many others. Yet, it was not to be for Charlie.

The August 1958 Nashville session was nothing compared to a Norman Petty session. Contrary to a usual Petty recording session, the Nashville recording would be done on the clock and everything was very rushed. Thankfully, "One-Take Charlie" had become accustomed to recording by this time and could usually sing any song on the first try.

The Nashville session developed with Thomas Grady Martin on guitar, Charlie's friend Don Guess on bass, William Whitley "Bill" Purcell on piano and a few other musicians to cut the songs, "Faker" and "I Won't Be Around." Not long after recording these two songs, Charlie felt the writing was on the wall when these tunes by Coral were never assigned a master number suggesting the songs had been rejected. Years later, they burned in the MCA/Universal Studio vault fire, destroying the original masters.

The original cast of Sugartimers, Pete Wallace, Jimmy Schell, Dudley Hughes and Gerald Brown all moved on to greener pastures yet Jimmy Schell continued as lead guitarist and Don Guess was brought in on bass or sometimes lead guitar. Often Hughes filled-in if needed, but Charlie primarily kept a smaller band with the same lineup, after all, this is how Johnny Horton and Elvis Presley operated. If Charlie needed a bigger sound, he might bring in Larry Welborn on guitar and he would bring in drummer, Doug Roberts, before Doug officially began tapping away for the Fireballs.

Charlie and the Sugartimers would be asked to drive to Lubbock as part of a *Grand Ole Opry* package on January 3, 1959. The guys would perform onstage with Johnny and Jack, Minnie Pearl, Kitty Wells and Little Jimmy Dickens. The Lubbock Municipal Auditorium was packed with concertgoers and the men played a fascinating show.

The following month in February, they finished another performance in Midland, Texas. Phillips gloomily explains, "I had recently done a show with the Big Bopper on the *Big "D" Jamboree*," and adds, "While driving back from Midland we were listening to the radio and the most unbelievable news was announced. Buddy Holly had been killed! It was just so hard to believe." He had died in a small plane crash near Clear Lake, Iowa on his way to Moorhead, Minnesota while on tour with *The Winter Dance Party*. Buddy, J.P. "The Big Bopper" Richardson, Ritchie Valens and pilot, Roger Peterson, were all catastrophically killed.

Yet again, Charlie couldn't help being reminded of his decision to quit flying; it was probably the wisest choice he made during his whole career. Years later when asked to talk about his feelings after he heard the grave news, Charlie only says, "That's probably the question I get asked most often by Buddy Holly enthusiasts, but I really don't like to think about it much," he continues, "It was sad for all of us. But mostly for Norman and Vi who, I guess thought of him as their own son."

After Charlie's last two songs had been "shelved" by Decca, his contract wasn't renewed and he was free to bargain with another label. Charlie decided to return to the Petty studio and record yet another record. In September 1959, he wrote and cut the follow-ups to his big hit called "No More Sugartime" backed by "Welcome to the Wedding." This would be the first time Charlie would work closely with Ray Winkler from KZIP in Amarillo. Ray co-wrote "Welcome to the Wedding" with Norman Petty and another KZIP radio employee, Dean Kelley. Word around the campfire is Kelley was instrumental in developing Buddy Knox's song, "Party Doll" into the sensation it became. "No More Sugartime" was played in true rockabilly fashion.

Pop Echols soon sold Charlie's management contract to KZIP co-owner, Ray Winkler, who suggested Charlie sign with Columbia Records after the Decca debacle. Norman Petty had some pull at Columbia and it's very likely he put in a good word for Charlie. After Phillips recorded "Welcome to the Wedding" and "No More Sugartime," Ray became interested in signing the popular artist and bringing him onboard at the radio station. Winkler had moreover seen Charlie on a KZIP sponsored show in Amarillo where he opened for Marty Robbins. He thought Charlie was just what he needed for his station. Charlie had been touring with Robbins from Lubbock (Sponsored by Ray and Pappy Dave), to Oklahoma City and Tulsa and also toured with Robbins to El Paso, Texas. Charlie's work ethic greatly impressed Winkler.

Ray was instrumental in getting Charlie a new record deal and this time with one of the biggest labels in the business. He felt honored to get a recording contract with Columbia because he was seen as a Nashville outsider. It was very difficult to get a contract with a major label unless you knew someone. Although Norman Petty had a lot of clout at the time, it was Ray Winkler who talked Don Law, head of Columbia's country music division, into signing the young singer and songwriter.

Petty would arrange the "Welcome to the Wedding" and "No More Sugartime" session at his 7th Street studio in Clovis. Jack C. Smith played lead guitar on the record, Jack Vaughn played rhythm guitar, Cricket, Joe B. Mauldin played bass, Mike Mitchell played drums, as well as Norman Petty personally appearing followed by Bill Pickering and a few other musicians.

To help explain the difference between the usual recording session at one of the big important studios as opposed to one at the Norman Petty Studio, one only needs to hear Charlie speak about an ordinary session in this John Ingman interview: "Most studios operate a closed-door policy. Nobody is allowed in the studio unless they are active participates. Petty had very different ideas; he always encouraged other musicians to watch. When you're recording, you have to concentrate on your own contribution and can miss the overall picture. Sometimes an observer can say, 'I've a riff that might fit this tune...If it worked, we had an improvement that wouldn't have happened if the observer hadn't been present." Instead of egos flaring, many times musicians assisted other bands always with the hope of producing the best sound. This is an essential element missing from some of the larger studios.

Both "Welcome to the Wedding" and "No More Sugartime" would be released under Charlie and Ray's new contract with Columbia Records. Both songs would hit the charts, but a familiar pattern emerged once again. The Edwards Twins were moved in to cover "No More Sugartime" and Charlie's version silently slipped off the charts. Conceivably in hindsight, a man wrote both "Sugartime" and "No More Sugartime" but the songs were probably enhanced when women artists sang them. Nonetheless, Columbia enjoyed some success with their bright new artist and was satisfied with their new singer/songwriter.

Charlie spent all of 1960 and much of 1961 acclimating himself to his new job at KZIP radio off the east side of Amarillo's Route 66, now more commonly called Amarillo Boulevard. As mentioned, Charlie replaced the ever-popular Roger Miller at the radio station. Although uncharacteristic for Ray Winkler, Miller was purportedly fired on-air; however, there have been no witnesses to corroborate this sensationalism. During his early stint at KZIP, Charlie kept touring and making appearances on the *Grand Ole Opry*, the *Big "D" Jamboree*, the *Louisiana Hayride* and Red

Foley's *Ozark Jubilee*. Charlie also toured for a season with Johnny Cash and Danny & The Juniors on a Columbia package deal.

Phillips loved touring with Cash, but often complained on this particular tour, Cash was drinking excessively and even remembers while performing in Albuquerque, Cash would stop in the middle of a song, walk offstage, do what he went to do, and come back to finish his song. "That's just one of the things I remember, but mostly we had some really good times," reminisces Phillips. He and Cash worked well together on various occasions and was always a joy to be around probably because he had so much musical talent.

According to Phillips, Ray Winkler was always delighted for Charlie to take time off for touring and TV appearances because it added some credibility to his deejays and to the KZIP radio station. Charlie boasts it was the perfect job for him as Ray was his perfect boss. Charlie always made a point to plug the radio station whether in or out of town in attempt to boost listenership and since Ray was his booking manager, touring was more profitable for both men.

By September of 1961, Columbia requested a new recording session be completed in Nashville at the Bradley Film & Recording Studio. Charlie would once again work with some top musicians during this session. It seems Columbia went all out and hired a lot of terrific and talented people. Charlie provided vocals while studio musician, Harold Bradley, played guitar in addition to Raymond Q "Ray" Edenton also playing guitar and more so Thomas Grady Martin on guitar. Joseph S. Zinkan played bass for the session and while Murray "Buddy" Harman Jr. drummed. William Whitney "Bill" Purcell played piano and Darrell McCall sang some harmony. The group recorded two songs during this session, "I Guess I'll Never Learn" and "Now That It's Over" and the new record was soon released to the public.

For the first time in Charlie's recording career, he broke into the top-10 on the charts with a song written by Johnny Hathcock and Winkler. "I Guess I'll Never Learn" entered the *Billboard* C&W chart on April 14, 1962 and five weeks later peaked at No. 9. To date, it was his highest-reaching record on the national charts in which he himself performed. With popularity soaring, he would be summoned back to Nashville for the annual Deejay Convention. This time and to his surprise and astonishment Charlie would be honored with an award bestowed a top deejay; he received Radio WSM's Mr. DJ, USA award.

With his acceptance soaring this particular week in Music City, Charlie would make guest appearances on Grant Turner's *WSM Breakfast Show* and also gave live performances in the station each evening. On August 4th, he again made a guest appearance on the *Grand Ole Opry*. Ray Winkler soon became concerned with his own obligations and suggested it was now time Charlie have a proper agent, so he introduced his artist to Bob Neal of Wil-Helm Talent Management where Charlie signed on with the firm. Bob was able to get his new artist some high-status tours as Charlie juggled his time between the radio station and new touring schedule.

In February of 1962 Charlie first recorded an incredible tune written by Ray Winkler and Johnny Hathcock christened, "Welcome to My World." Charlie was currently at the top of his game and it seemed possible he could take the tune to the top-10 just like he'd done with "I Guess I'll Never Learn." Charlie took the recording with him on his next trip to Nashville and presented his idea to producer, Don Law. Immediately Law rejected the new proposal. It was not meant to be as Columbia executive, Don Law, had other plans for Charlie. He wanted Charlie to record only music written by songwriters in the Columbia repertoire and only songs he had handpicked. Charlie reluctantly agreed. Even though "Welcome to My World" eventually became a worldwide hit for Jim Reeves, it was Charlie who recognized the song's potential before it ever became a hit. Of course Winkler, Hathcock and Dean Kelly envisioned the song's hopeful success.

His next recording session would take place in June 1962 at the Columbia Recording Studio in Nashville. This recording session would have all of the same session musicians as the previous session, but this time Floyd Cramer would be added on piano and Anita Kerr Siners would contribute harmony vocals. Cramer was one of the busiest studio musicians in the business. He was already playing piano for stars like Elvis Presley, Jim Reeves, Eddy Arnold, Brenda Lee and Patsy Cline on the shortlist.

Many years later, Cramer would be inducted into the Country Music Hall of Fame, the Rock and Roll Hall of Fame and the Louisiana Music Hall of Fame, but right now he simply added the magic touch to Charlie's songs. This time Charlie would record four songs for Columbia instead of the usual two. Phillips recorded "No One To Love," "'Til Sunday," "Cancel the Call" and "You're Moving Away." Of these four, "Cancel the Call" would rise to No. 42 on the *Cashbox* chart and the other three would see mild success slightly lower on the charts.

At the height of his popularity the inevitable happened. Charlie began receiving more fan mail than he could answer and couldn't possibly keep up with marketing engagements. Additionally, he could no longer adequately contact other radio stations with his new songs. His mailbox at home and at the station was flooded with requests for autographs and memorabilia. It was then a young female fan offered her assistance. Mildred "Millie" Darnell became the first and only fan club president for Charlie "Sugartime" Phillips. Millie was also in charge of Jim Reeves' fan club so she gladly offered her services to Charlie and soon relieved the stress from a demanding fan base.

Millie received and answered letters as she developed into a marketing expert whilst writing letters to organizations and to various radio stations informing them of Charlie's new songs and his whereabouts. Millie was probably one of the greatest country music fans alive and relished the idea of being around some of the biggest country stars. Her association with both Charlie and Jim Reeves opened many doors for her. Every trip she took to the *Louisiana Hayride* allowed her to collect one of her favorite things, country music star autographs. She would be seen carrying the same *Louisiana Hayride* program each time she went, in hopes of collecting yet another autograph.

Millie had autographs from people like: Don Davis and Felton Pruitt from Buddy Attaway & Soko Sokolinski and the Lump Boys; Jim Edward and Maxine Brown; Carolyn Bradshaw; Jack Ford; Jeanette Hicks; Hoot & Curley; Johnny Horton; Horace Logan; Jimmy C. Newman; Jim Reeves; Slim Whitman; Balin' Wire Bob; David Houston; Tom Perryman; and even Elvis Presley when he made an appearance on the early *Hayride*. Millie certainly loved her job. She served Jim Reeves until his death in 1964 and she ran Charlie's fan club until the 1980's when Charlie no longer needed it. Millie and Phillips remained close friends throughout their lives until she was invariably placed in a nursing facility, where Charlie visited her virtually every week until her death on November 21, 2015. During her life, Millie never received any pay for her work; she did it solely because she loved country music.

By December of 1962, Charlie was one of the most plugged artists on the *Opry* touring package primarily at the City Auditorium in Albuquerque. He was playing onstage with Johnny Cash, George Jones and Willie Nelson. Just the night before, they had sold out the *Big "D" Jamboree* and packed the house at the popular Dallas honkytonk, the Longhorn Ballroom. Although he enjoyed being part of the Columbia family and decisively had some records hitting the charts, Charlie stopped writing music for the first time since he was a teenager.

It seems other Columbia artists or friends of the executives shot down every song he took into the Columbia studios as they had already pre-selected the songs they wanted Charlie to record- their songs. Remember long ago when Charlie's friend Tucker told him to write his own material? "You can't make money covering other people's music," he said. Suddenly Charlie felt he had to do just that, as the Columbia execs were no longer interested in hearing his original melodies. In hindsight, Charlie should have stood up to the record executives. He should have insisted it be his way or the highway. Merle did it. Willie did it. Waylon did it. They all became the outlaws of country music. But it wasn't in Charlie's nature to buck authority or the system.

In 1963, Charlie performed on another tour sponsored by the Sir Walter Raleigh Tobacco Company, and the crew would head to Denver, Colorado. It would be an easy trip because of its proximity to Amarillo. He worked primarily with Webb Pierce, Hank Snow, Bill Anderson, George Morgan, Kitty Wells and Johnny and Jack, most of who were flown in from Nashville to be on the show.

Charlie was able to take the Sugartimers along on this tour. Everyone was excited to have the opportunity to play with such recognizable musicians, but the guys' excitement soon turned sour. They were awkwardly faced with a dilemma where they felt like they were forced to walk on eggshells. Webb Pierce *never* did a sound check, at least on this tour. He'd enter the stage and just start singing and playing. Webb didn't even tune his guitar with the band and didn't seem to notice what key he was playing in, or at least the Sugartimers didn't know what key he was playing in. The guys felt it was almost impossible to follow Pierce as he scratched out song after bloodcurdling song. Webb was so popular, and no one dared say anything to him, as they were afraid of being removed from the show- so everyone kept their mouths shut. Some of the guys still talk about this particular show today, wincing at the thought of Webb's performance.

On another Colorado trip, Charlie and the Sugartimers were hired to open for George Morgan and would be making a stop in Cañon City, Colorado at the Cañon City College. The guys drove from Amarillo in Charlie's 1960 Lincoln Premiere pulling their Sugartimer trailer proudly sponsored by Pepsi Cola. They arrived in Cañon City, turned to the gymnasium, and set up their equipment. They got situated in their motel rooms and began heading to the show. Rex Terry was driving the Lincoln with Charlie, Bill Craven and Gary Thurlow riding as passengers. Suddenly, their car struck a young man in a 1960 model Chevy Corvair 4-door car who had run the red light. The Corvair went sliding across the street and crashed through a plate-glass drugstore window. Fortunately, none of the musicians or the other driver was seriously injured. However, they were late arriving at the show, all visibly shaken by the accident.

George Morgan had wondered what happened to the guys and was about to send out a search party.

This same year, Charlie flew to Springfield, Missouri to be a guest on Red Foley's *Ozark Jubilee*. Additionally, he was touring as far west as California and Las Vegas where he would play gigs at a few casinos. Although Charlie enjoyed the travel and the touring, he preferred it in small doses. Home was where his heart was, and he appreciated arriving back in Amarillo after a tough touring season.

His next recording session was held in May 1963 in Nashville. Once again the same Columbia session musicians accompanied Charlie on four different songs. Unbeknownst to Charlie, this will be his last recording session with Columbia. This sitting will produce "The Street of Loneliness," "Later Tonight," "This Is the House" and "Please Help Me Believe." Only "This Is the House" will show the most promise although all of the songs made it to the charts. "This Is the House" would peak at No. 30 on *Billboard* spending only a week on their chart.

With low-showing numbers, it was decided Charlie would drop Columbia as his record label. When asked if he was bitter about the Columbia experience, Charlie just replied, "No, not really. I was disappointed they wouldn't let me record what I wanted, but I charted more with Columbia than with anyone else. I knew it would be tough to be successful in Nashville if I didn't live there and have the connections...I'm grateful for the experience and I'll probably always cherish them days."

After his stint with Columbia, Charlie decided to take time off from recording and concentrate his efforts more towards his Amarillo gigs and also into promoting concerts at assorted establishments in Amarillo. Charlie not only booked acts into the neighborhood nightclubs, but would also reserve acts into the Amarillo Civic Center Auditorium. George Jones and Charlie had known each other for years, and Jones had developed quite the reputation for being late or not even arriving at all. George was given the infamous nickname, "No Show Jones." Charlie had been the opening act for one of Jones' shows and the star never even appeared. Newspapers remarked, had it not been for Charlie Phillips and other gifted musicians, the crowd might have revolted.

In the future, when Jones was booked into an Amarillo venue, Charlie routinely sent Ron Peterson, who was the sales manager and DJ at KZIP, to George's previous location picking him up and making certain he arrived at the concert. Phillips is sometimes known to say, "Poor George" years before former Governor of Texas, Ann Richards, began jokingly belittling her rival, George W. Bush during an election year. Years later when Jones began getting ill, he said in an interview, "There was a time when I was pretty messed up, and I gotta be honest, Charlie [Phillips] [and Ron Peterson] was there for me. I 'member a time when hardly anyone wanted to book me in 'cause, see, I had a drinkin' problem. I 'member Charlie'd always come through for me." Of course, no one can refute George Jones' contribution to country music as he's considered one of the greatest stars of all times.

Sometime in the early 1970's, George Jones and his wife, Tammy Wynette, invited Charlie and his radio colleague, Ron Peterson, to a party at Tammy's sprawling estate in Nashville. When they arrived, it was obvious Jones had a bit too much to drink. They all had a great visit talking about country music and the music business itself, but during the festivities, George thought the party needed more alcohol, so he propped himself up on a riding lawn mower and snuck off to the liquor store. Phillips laughs as he recollects the vision of Jones heading out on the dirt trail, shirtless, bouncing up and down on the lawnmower.

Sadly, Jones and Wynette experienced a short-lived marriage divorcing shortly in 1975, but not before they had a beautiful baby girl they named Georgette, who eventually became a musician in her own right. Phillips and Jones remained occupational friends until George eventually passed away. When Jones died on April 26, 2013, Charlie was in his late 70's and was unable to attend the funeral. "George had one of the best voices I'd ever heard," Charlie remarks. Even the legendary Waylon Jennings said, "If we could sound the way we wanted, we'd all sound like George Jones."

By 1964, Charlie was once again without a proper manager and a record label for the first time in his career. Ray Winkler offered Charlie a suggestion. Ray referred Charlie to ole' friend and colleague to handle future bookings. Tillman Franks played with Charlie on his first trip to the *Louisiana Hayride* and agreed to the task. Tillman once worked with Tommy Tomlinson and Johnny Horton and assisted the men with managerial duties. It wasn't until the three men became involved in an untimely auto accident in November of 1960 that their lives would be irrevocably changed. Johnny Horton lost his life. Grievously Tomlinson lost his left leg in the crash and Franks suffered some head injuries.

Franks wholeheartedly agreed to manage Phillips and tried to keep him working. Charlie stayed busy in Amarillo with his position at KZIP. As mentioned earlier, by 1965, he, Ray Winkler and Johnny Hathcock reopened the Clover Club in Amarillo renaming it the Rainbow Ballroom. They ran the club booking weekly acts with Charlie playing most weekend nights and filling-in on nights they booked top country acts. The guys ran the club for a few years until they finally decided it wasn't lucrative enough to keep the doors open.

Early in 1965 Tillman Franks booked Phillips for a recording session at the Robin Hood Brians studio in Tyler, Texas. The studio was new and had only been in operation for about two years when Charlie first recorded there. Tillman produced David Houston's "Mountain of Love" released on Epic Records and would now try his hand at producing Charlie. This project would take more effort than previous recording sessions. Tillman gave Charlie free reign as to what songs he would record. Phillips had always wanted to record "Big Balls In Cowtown" ever since the day he saw the Maddox Brothers and Rose perform it so many years ago in Amarillo at the Clover Club.

But to cover the song, permission would need to be granted from its creator. Charlie had been a recording artist for over ten years and had a few connections in the business, namely a woman he befriended at BMI, the folks who collect the royalty money for artists like Charlie. (They also make sure an artist gets their money after a song is played or after a record is purchased). Charlie called his BMI friend, Frances Preston, and asked her if she knew where "Big Balls In Cowtown" was placed, and she stated they had it in their catalog there at BMI. Charlie asked her to look up the song's creator, which she did, and she relayed back the song was a PD song, or was quite simply in the Public Domain, meaning the song had been released so long ago the copyright had run out, therefore anyone could record it without paying royalties to its author. "Well, hot dog!" Charlie thought. He wouldn't need to go through all of the motions to contact the writer.

They proceeded to Tyler, Texas and recorded his version aptly retitled, "The Big Ball Is In Cowtown" in addition to another cover song, "Rainbow in the Valley." Although they weren't his songs, he had always felt a particular connection to these melodies and finally had the opportunity to give the songs his special flair. The recording session went quite well, but after the completion of the recording session, something just didn't sound right. Charlie's ear was catching some anomalies on the tapes, so he did what any guy who had ever recorded in Clovis would have done. He took the tapes to Norman Petty to remix and edit.

The sound on the "The Big Ball Is In Cowtown" and "Rainbow in the Valley" recording sessions were repaired by Petty and became some of the best recordings Phillips had ever produced to date. Tommy Tomlinson played lead guitar, and Tillman Franks played bass while Charlie concentrated only on his vocals. Norman Petty filled-in on piano with Ben Qwick playing steel guitar. It's rumored the Gary Dale Singers also provided phenomenal backup singing but this statement hasn't been corroborated.

After their achievement, they needed a label to release the record. Charlie took the songs to an ole' friend of his from Dallas, Dewey Groom, who owned the famous Longhorn Ballroom where Charlie had played on so many occasions. The two, with the assistance of former boss, Ray Winkler, struck a one-off record deal on Groom's record label, Longhorn Records. Like many of Charlie's songs, the record received enormous airplay on radio stations across the country but dawdled in actual record sales. After all, many musicians had already covered the song over the years; however, to Charlie's knowledge, this was the first time the song had ever been released on a 45 RPM nationwide.

Suddenly, a quandary arose. Charlie was made aware "Big Balls in Cowtown" was apparently *not* a PD (Public Domain) song as BMI had informed him; it had been registered to a longstanding country music artist, Hoyle Nix. They suddenly clambered to make sure Nix was credited for arranging the song; however, some damage had been done and with the record still making dismal sales. The truth of the matter is, this was probably *not* the case at all. Gid Tanner would record one of the earliest releases of "Big Ball in Cowtown" on October 31, 1927 and several other artists like the Delmar Brothers recorded a similar derivation of the song, "Big Ball in Texas" in the 1930's. So in all actuality, the song most likely *was* in the public domain; however, Hoyle Nix most certainly changed wording and composition of the tune and is now credited with having written the cowboy anthem.

The following year Charlie ran into Hoyle Nix's son, Jody Nix, at the annual Bob Wills Day celebration in Turkey, Texas. He wanted to talk with Jody and explain how the mix-up occurred, but as he began to introduce himself and extended his arm to shake Nix's hand, Jody looked down at Charlie's hand and simply walked off. Charlie never knew if Nix was angry about the mix-up or if he thought maybe Charlie was just an anxious fan and didn't have time to talk that day. The official cowboy anthem of "The Big Ball Is In Cowtown" would be one of Charlie's crowning achievements vocally, but would turn into one of his strangest recording situations.

Before Red Steagall performed for President Ronald Reagan at the White House, before he became a movie star, and before he was named The Official Poet of Texas, he was simply known as "Rusty" to all of the guys. Charlie had known Rusty for a considerable time and even played many of his songs on the radio at KZIP. Steagall would occasionally pop into the KZIP radio station and see if Charlie wanted to record any of the songs he'd written, or the two would simply catch up on the world of country music.

Steagall had heard Charlie's version of "The Big Ball Is In Cowtown" on Longhorn and appreciated the new version, so he handed a copy to his friend, Jimmy Bowen, a producer and A&R man for Reprise Records, which had been founded years earlier by Frank Sinatra. Charlie had known Bowen from the early Norman Petty days when Jimmy wrote and recorded, "I'm Sticking With You," which was the B-side to Buddy Knox's "Party Doll."

Steagall suggested he produce Charlie's records and in March of 1967, Charlie traveled to Hollywood in Los Angeles recording four songs for the Reprise label at Western Recorders. Before this time, the record label primarily consisted of Sinatra's friends and colleagues including Jo Stafford, Rosemary Clooney, Nancy Sinatra, Bing Crosby and comedian, Redd Foxx. Bowen set the session at Western Recorders on Sunset Blvd. and invited some local musicians to join the session.

An all-star cast was assembled for the Hollywood session including Leon Russell, who primarily played some guitar and harmonies for Charlie on this session. Leon, of course, would have a very fruitful music career during his life, and his talents were such he could play a variety of distinctive styles from country, rock, R&B to gospel. Russell performed with numerous elite musicians including Gram Parsons, Doris Day, Ray Charles, Eric Clapton, Barbra Streisand, Sinatra, Bob Dylan, the Rolling Stones and he even had a hit song with Elton John.

Glen Campbell was hired to play lead guitar and provide Charlie with harmony vocals. Al Casey also played guitar for Charlie on this recording session. As a studio musician, Al worked on sessions with Elvis Presley, Johnny Cash, the Beach Boys, Eddy Arnold, Sinatra and his daughter Nancy when she performed, "These Boots Are Made For Walking." Louis Morell was a young guitarist on this session and would soon record for MGM Records, Impulse!, Capitol Records, Columbia and Decca.

Carl West played steel guitar for Charlie. Carl had played for years with Wynn Stewart's West Coast Playboys and would later record with notables like Bobby Vee, the Byrds, Eddie Drake and Jerry Inman. Additionally, Chuck Berghofer played bass for Charlie, and he too enjoyed a lengthy career in music, primarily as a jazz musician. Chuck often played as a studio musician in the movie business where he made over 400 appearances and was eventually awarded the National Academy of Recording Arts and Sciences Award.

Hal Blaine was an additional session musician who drummed on Charlie's sitting. No one knew it at the time, but Hal would later be considered one of the most prolific drummers in recording history and would become a member of the Percussive Arts Society Hall of Fame, the Musicians Hall of Fame and the Rock & Roll Hall of Fame. Michael Melvoin played piano on Charlie's session. He too was part of this all-star cast as an inexhaustible jazz pianist, song arranger and composer playing with such notables as Sinatra, John Lennon, the Beach Boys, Natalie Cole and the Jackson 5. Melvoin would also be nominated for a Grammy Award later in 2003.

With the best of the best backing him up on his new records, both Charlie and Rusty might have speculated the songs would be successful. "The Bridge I Can't Burn," "Souvenirs of Sorrow," "Be Careful, Go Easy, Walk Slow" and "I'm Trapped" were all recorded during this session. Charlie remembers Glen Campbell was probably one of the best singers and guitarists he had ever worked with. "He had one of the most beautiful voices I had ever heard," recalls Phillips. The same year Campbell accompanied Charlie on this recording session, Glen won four Grammy Awards and, of course, would go down in history as one of the greatest musicians and artists of all time.

"Souvenirs of Sorrow" and "I'm Trapped" would see noteworthy airplay nationally, and "Souvenirs" would see significant sales, yet the other songs fell flat. Bowen poured money into the promotion of the records yet to no avail. This leads one to ask, what was the problem? The quality of music and vocals on the records were top-notch and could rival any record currently being played. Is it possible Charlie just didn't have appropriate representation or management or perhaps didn't have the proper connection within the country music conglomerate?

It's recognized during this time, major Nashville labels kept tight control on C&W charts, which were based on airplay. Even record companies like the west coast Capitol Records struggled for hits. Buck Owens didn't get a No. 1 hit until 1963 although he had been releasing songs since 1956. A relatively minor west coast label with a limited country output wouldn't garner much credit in Nashville no matter how high the sales. The Maddox Brothers & Rose were reputedly the most popular country band in the nation but never even entered the charts. With insufficient sales and a change in direction by Warner Bros. Records, who had purchased Reprise from Sinatra in 1963, Charlie was dropped from their label as Bowen was purportedly told, "Reprise does not waste money on country music."

The following year in late 1968 and through some of 1969, Charlie returned to Nashville to the Columbia recording studio cutting another album, but not for Columbia Records this time. He would be recording for a smaller label named K-Ark, owned by John Capps. Phillips was armed with an arsenal of fresh music accompanied by a new staff of musicians supplied by Capps.

Booking management was no longer being handled by Tillman Franks and had now been assigned to Jack Turner, who offered Charlie a substantial advance payment to make more recordings. On this session, Charlie worked closely with the piano player, Hargus "Pig" Robbins. Robbins was a renowned blind keyboardist and pianist who had recorded with stars like Merle Haggard, Roger Miller, George Jones, Dolly Parton, Loretta Lynn and Kenny Rogers to name just a few. The group worked closely together and initially produced six songs for airplay.

"Your Going is Coming," "Just Let the Flowers Grow," "Twenty Fools Ago," "Blue Blue Bottle," "Ballad of Bill Jones" and "Before the Next Daybreak's Gone," were all recorded during this session. "Blue Blue Bottle," was a song written by his childhood friend, Tiny Lynn, and then spruced up by Charlie. It would be the bestselling from these six songs and almost became a hit record, but alas tragedy surprisingly struck again. Unbeknownst to Charlie and many others in the music business, K-Ark had been accused of the unscrupulous activity of underpaying their studio musicians. They would soon lose their license to operate in October of 1971. This would cease any future releases of Phillip's music on K-Ark. Charlie dusted his britches off from this unforeseen experience and once again concentrated on the Amarillo night scene.

Phillips was playing weekly at the Aviatrix while booking guest artists and was still employed full time at KZIP working his way up the ranks when he received a call from Norman Petty. Petty now owned KWKA-AM and KTQM-FM radio stations in Clovis and was endeavoring to modify their layout to an all-country format. Petty asked Charlie if he would manage the stations and help make the conversion. Phillips had already invested so much of his life with KZIP after leaving Clovis and still had his weekly gigs at the club, plus he continued to tour and record. It would not be in his best interest to change radio stations, so he humbly declined Norman's offer. Besides he needed to devote more time to his music.

Charlie "Sugartime" Phillips wouldn't record again until October of 1974 when producer Tom Hartman purchased the song catalog from the now defunct K-Ark Records. Hartman signed Phillips as an artist on Hartman's Artco label. Charlie traveled to Hartman's studio in Oklahoma City where he would record several new songs, but this time in a different manner. Tom asked Charlie to dub his voice over some prerecorded tracks rather than using expensive house musicians. Charlie agreed and sang along to seven different songs.

Phillips re-recorded "Sugartime" and already owned the masters to "Rainbow in the Valley" and "The Big Ball Is In Cowtown." Artco used original masters on the new issues of these songs. "I'm Giving Her Love" and "I Walk Alone Tomorrow" were also recorded and available for distribution as was "Bend me Straight Again," "Who Are You," "Twenty Fools Ago," "Your Going Is Coming," "I Am Giving Her Love," "Blue, Blue Bottle," "Just Let The Flowers Grow" and "Before The Next Daybreak's Gone."

Sometime in later years after these songs were released, Hartman became extremely ill and was forced to abandon his record business, leaving Charlie with only one choice. He purchased all of his K-Ark and Artco masters from Hartman. This was the only way Charlie could control his own music at this point. The masters were first cut onto 8-track tapes in the 1970's, and when 8-tracks lost their appeal, Charlie had the songs converted to a cassette in 1981 primarily using the copies to sell at his gigs.

K-tel International was a company who distributed music compilations for an "As-Seen-On-TV" audience and in the late 1970's offered Charlie a one-time-fee to re-record three songs for one of their music assemblages. They promised extensive television advertising, so Phillips recut "Sugartime," "The Big Ball Is In Cowtown" and "I Guess I'll Never Learn" for the organization. To this day, he doesn't know if the tracks were ever released or if he ever received any money if they sold. Discouraged, he then turned to an old friend asking assistance to record a few more releases.

Royce Clark was a friend and colleague of Charlie's he had known for many years from the Norman Petty Studio days. He was a big ole' boy with a brash laugh. He loved to tell the story about the day he and Charlie met the governor of Tennessee in the party-room inside Webb Pierce's mansion basement. As the story goes, Governor Ray Blanton was walking down the stairs when Pierce began hollerin' for Charlie to meet the governor. Phillips was at the base of the stairs talking to Royce and quickly turned around with a pimento cheese hors d'oeuvre in his right hand and a drink in his left hand. The Governor extended his hand for he and Charlie to shake. Forgetting he had the sandwich and in the quickness of the moment, Charlie reached out and squished the sandwich between his hand and the Governor of Tennessee's! Both men were completely embarrassed as pieces of bread and pimento cheese fell to the carpet. If Charlie or Royce ever told this story, uproarious laughter would fill the room, and Clark would laugh so hard he'd fall onto the floor.

Royce Clark Bentley or Clark Bentley originally hailed from Muleshoe, Texas and went on to see some stardom in movies like,

Coal Miner's Daughter, *They Call Me Renegade* and *The Night the Lights Went Out in Georgia*. Royce was now a record producer for Plantation Records and asked Charlie to meet him in Nashville to cut a few songs at the Shelby Singleton Studio. He met his friend at the studio and they recorded "Wild Side of Houston" and "No Greater Love." These songs were released on the obscure Spirit (Of The 21st Century) label. The tunes were of very high quality, but regrettably they too saw very few sales in the marketplace.

Phillips had spent just under thirty years in the radio broadcast business and knew it was time to retire. Pappy Dave Stone had sold his radio station, KZIP, as well as its sister stations and was retiring himself. The new KZIP owners were changing their format, so Charlie saw this as his opportunity to resign from the radio biz and concentrate exclusively on recording as well as his weekly live appearances. Charlie remained a few weeks at the station to allow the new owners time to make the progression. By this time, Norman Petty had sold all of his interests in his radio stations and was using his time to install state-of-the-art equipment in his opulent studio he built inside of the old Mesa Theater Building in Clovis.

After his official retirement from radio, Charlie began doing radio specials in the area and became a part of the *Cracker Barrel* series, which initially broadcast locally from Amarillo. Charlie was joined by many of his friends and colleagues in the business like Dean Kelley, Jim Richardson, Corky Mayberry and Doug Collins. The series was eventually broadcasted to many armed forces stations in the country. It was the hope of the sponsors the show be syndicated nationally, but it never developed beyond its initial scope.

Around 1980, a musician friend of Charlie's and a former Sugartimer, Jon Sisco, approached Charlie with the idea of recording a full album of Phillips' music using some of Charlie's best hits in addition to having the singer cover some popular songs from yesteryear. Jon and Charlie traveled down to the Norman Petty Studio and presented their idea to Norman, who agreed to co-produce the album with Sisco. Norman and Charlie talked about old times, as Charlie hadn't recorded with Norman in several years. Norman told Charlie that he had made more money as the publisher of

"Sugartime" on the NorVaJak label than off of any song he had since produced, including any of Buddy Holly's songs. That statement might now be refuted. Charlie concurred and told Norman "the only real money I ever made was on my recordings at the Petty studios."

In hindsight, Norman was probably just sending out some puff or was simply talking about the money he made strictly from the NorVaJak label as it is well documented Petty received substantial royalties from his composer credits in the Holly/Crickets catalog. In addition, it's believed his biggest money earner was royalties received from his composition of the instrumental song, "Wheels," which has since been recorded by others more than a couple of hundred times earning him substantial profits. Nonetheless, both Charlie and Norman once again struck up a business relationship with hopes of triumph.

As they began their newest project, Phillips would drive from Amarillo to Clovis regularly recording songs with his long-standing mentor. "You could get no better sound than what Norman could put together in the studio," claims Phillips. The first four songs on this album they recorded together were "Goin' Away," "Love Queen," "Shambles of My Home" and "Souvenirs of Sorrow." Amarillo musician and recording studio guru, Billy Stull, would play guitar on this session with Scott Nelson on bass, Lynn Williams on the drum with Mike Price accompanying. It wouldn't take long until these two songs were allocated to Ray Ruff's Oak Records out of California. George Tomsco from the Fireballs and his wife Barbara had composed "Goin' Away," which had been previously recorded by various artists in the Petty Studio, but unfortunately the powerful song had failed to substantially hit the music charts. Even Charlie's version of the song failed to garner much attention.

Charlie and Jon spent the next three years traveling to and from Amarillo and Clovis recording various compilations for Charlie's new album. All of Charlie's previous songs had only been released on 45 RPM's, 8-track or cassette tape. The journey would be slow going during this time especially as Norman Petty received the news he was stricken with leukemia and his health was failing.

Jon Sisco recalls during these sessions Norman was constantly amazed at the range and power of Charlie's voice, which is said to reach a four-octave vocal range where Charlie can sing *all* of his own background harmonies. Jon states Norman would just grin as Phillips was able to capture his voice on the first recording- leading Norman to describe the singer once again as "One-Take Charlie." According to Sisco, on some of the recordings, Charlie was singing anywhere from two to four different vocal parts leading Norman to shake his head and joke, "It sounds like the Charlie Phillips Singers are in very fine voice tonight."

Popular country music disc jockey and actor, Sammy Jackson, contacted Norman Petty for an on-air interview in the early 1980's before the producer became too ill. Sammy was known for his guest appearances on television but was most known on Los Angeles' KLAC radio station. Jackson had previously been awarded "Radio Personality of the Year" by the acclaimed Country Music Association by the time he contacted Norman for their interview. The first question he asked the Clovis producer was, "And you have found Charlie Phillips, who was extremely hot back in the late 50's and early 60's- you brought him out of retirement and put him into the studio up in Clovis, didn't you?"

Norman responds, "Well, Charlie's always been an excellent singer. He's probably one of the best country singers I've ever had in the studio, and he feels like that this is full circle for him." Norman continues, "Charlie had some hits with Columbia…and he's been sort of knocking around from label to label and so he and a young producer by the name of Jon Sisco came over to Clovis." Petty elaborates on the conversation with Sisco explaining, "Well, this is where it all started for us- why don't we try it again."

Shortly before Norman succumbed to Leukemia at only 57 years of age, the team had finished six completed masters, yet their sound had not been finalized. It would be several years before Jon and Norman's former engineer, Billy Stull, would finish much of the work. It seems after Norman's death, no one had the drive to complete what they had so vigorously started years earlier. It took almost twenty years before what would be christened, "the last Norman Petty sessions," were completed.

It took many people's efforts to complete the *Full Circle* album keeping in mind several songs were re-creations from Charlie's early career. The musicians credited on this album include (realize some had already passed away): Woody Key on electric guitar; Billy Stull on electric guitar, acoustic guitar, mandolin; John Gairett on acoustic guitar; Darrell Gairett on bass; Shorty Spang on drums; Norman Petty on synthesizers, piano, Hammond organ; Jim Gairett on steel guitar; Don Bristow on steel guitar; Blair Camp on drums; Bob Fletcher on bass; Susan Bagwell on vocals; Mike Price on harmonica; the Gary Dale Singers on background vocals; Ben Qwick on steel guitar; Tillman Franks on bass; Tommy Tomlinson on electric guitar; Jack Vaughn Acoustic on guitar; George Atwood on bass; Jerry (J.I.) Allison on drums; Jimmy Blakely on steel guitar; Buddy Holly on electric guitar, harmony vocals, background vocals; Niki Sullivan on background vocals; Pete Wallace on electric guitar; Dudley Hughes on bass; and lastly Billy Stull's "Big Band," respectively.

After Norman's death, Sisco sought out people he felt qualified to finish production on the album. He used Carey Wise from the 4th Creation Recording Studios in Conroe, Texas to complete an analog-to-digital transfer of the songs. Also, he used 4th Creation for the audio restoration and mixing of unmixed multi-tracks on the masters. He then chose Billy Stull, who now owned Masterpiece Mastering in South Padre Island, Texas to complete the masters. Brenda Wise at 4th Creation Graphic Studio created the album graphics while Sugartimer, Gary Thurlow, crafted the label graphics.

Full Circle was finally released in 2008 after twenty years had passed. Both Jon and Billy Stull spent countless hours producing the album for Sugartime Music Group. Jon Sisco's plan to record Charlie's album would finally be realized and the *Full Circle Album-The Last Norman Petty Sessions* would be released to the public. For the first time, Charlie had a release on a compact disc (CD). To date, this album would be a stirring creation encircling Charlie's talent.

Billy Stull had recorded a local western swing legend, Windy Wood & New Sons of the West. Wood had planned to release an LP album and had an all-star cast to play and sing on the compilation, but encountered that a couple of songs needed a stronger male vocal range. Charlie was recruited to assist Windy on two of the songs to complete the album. Phillips performed on "Has Anybody Seen Me Lately" and "Where Do I Go From Here?" Stull produced the album, and it was eventually released on the Rimstone label. It's unknown if this album met with any success. In 2003, Windy Wood accepted his induction into the Pioneers of Western Swing Hall of Fame and Honor Roll for his numerous contributions to music.

Of the abundant songs Charlie wrote over the years, only one was explicitly intended for another artist. "Graveyard Waltz" was composed for Charlie's lifelong friend and colleague, Tiny Lynn, and is included on Lynn's *Tinymite* LP. Though the song is now considered Lynn's, Charlie often performs the tune live around Halloween. It was unfortunate, but his songwriting days predominantly died while he recorded with Columbia Records, remaining six-foot underground.

Phillips would only allow one more album to be released after Jon Sisco's *Full Circle* album and after assisting on the Windy Wood LP. Phillips had been in contact with two men from Europe who would eventually guide him towards a re-release independent record label based out of Hambergen, Germany. Both John Beecher and John Ingman would become an integral team assisting Charlie in the revival of his earlier songs.

John Beecher had taken over the Buddy Holly and the Crickets (U.K.) Fan Club in 1960, which incidentally became the second largest fan club in the U.K., subsequent only to Elvis Presley's. John was in recurrent contact with Norman Petty back in Clovis and made attempts to obtain promotional information regarding Holly and the Crickets; however, Norman had become overly protective of any Buddy Holly dealings after the singer's untimely death.

Norman Petty was inexplicably evasive with Beecher during most of their early encounters. It wasn't until Norman planned a trip to Europe where he visited Beecher's London base of operations when his outlook began to change. After a few fruitful trips to Great Britain, Norman became captivated with John, who was wholeheartedly endeavoring to promote Holly's retrospective releases. John's marketing could turn into an advantageous affiliation for Norman, so perhaps in some way the isolated producer slowly lowered his guard. With their relationship improving, by 1964 Petty recommended Beecher to a friend who needed assistance running his U.S. publishing company in the United Kingdom.

Norman eventually requested John visit him in Clovis and Beecher did just that, stopping over sometime in the 1970's. When John visited the quiet New Mexico town, Norman had already closed the original studio on 7th Street and was now recording at his newer location in the old Mesa Theater building on Main Street. John truly wanted to see the 7th Street studio where all of the magic happened years previously, but Petty vehemently denied him access stating the longstanding building was used only for storage; however, one particular day when Norman left for an appointment, Vi Petty agreed to show their guest the previous location. Beecher anticipated seeing the studio that launched the careers of so many musicians. Because of Vi Petty, the three ultimately became friends as the approachable Vi acted resourcefully as the liaison between Beecher and her often-reserved husband.

Norman had a unique sound to his recordings that appealed to the Brit. Beecher began seeking out specific records that could be re-recorded for sales in Europe, importantly Charlie Phillips, in addition to numerous Buddy Holly releases. Because of Beecher's involvement and successes with the Buddy Holly Fan Club, Norman suggested John Beecher should possibly begin yet another fan club in Europe, but this time for the Fireballs. John declined but found another person qualified to create the organization. Shortly after the fan club was founded, the Fireballs encountered their first big hit in England entitled, "Quite A Party."

John Ingman had joined Beecher's Buddy Holly Fan Club in the early 1960's. He too realized many artists besides Buddy Holly recorded at the Petty studio and ultimately became interested in preserving the history of the Norman Petty Studio and the music it created. John had first visited the U.S. in 1982 to attend the Buddy Holly Music Festival in Lubbock, Texas and it was there he would meet Vi Petty for the first time. It took some doing, but Ingman was eventually able to enter the original Clovis studio and assist Vi in cataloging and refurbishing much of the music.

After Norman's unfortunate passing, John Beecher would be responsible for taking a BBC film crew to Clovis where they filmed Vi, who after years, finally agreed to free up music archives Norman had kept hush-hush during his life. Paul McCartney, along with the BBC, was sponsoring a documentary called, *The Real Buddy Holly Story*. John Beecher was charged with consulting the assemblage. At long last, archives and film canisters that had remained closed for over 20 years were conclusively unveiled.

In 1985, Vi had a get-together for some of her Clovis studio musician friends and invited them to meet Ingman and his friend, Jerry MacNesh. John had met Charlie the previous year and on this visit they would get acquainted with each other and begin what would become a longtime musical friendship. This trip would be exceedingly fruitful, as Ingman and MacNesh would assist Vi in cleaning the original 7th Street Studio and help her organize what had become an untidy storage facility. Thanks to the efforts of a small group of people like Ingman, the original studio was completely refurbished and reopened just in time for the restart of the annual Clovis Music Festival. For the first time in decades, the public would be allowed to visit the original Norman Petty Studio.

Both John Ingman and John Beecher became honorary saviors of the preferred music, which once emanated from the Norman Petty Studio. They dedicated much of their life to the preservation and distribution of both the music and facts concerning

Norman and Vi's dedication. John Beecher had first spoken to Charlie over the phone in the late 1980's where they discussed possibly releasing a country compilation album hopefully on Richard Weize's German-based label, Bear Family Records. Charlie had mentioned to John Ingman he had innumerable tapes at his house but had no means of playing them. Ingman passed this information along to Bear Family Records, and they arranged to have digital copies created. Charlie contemplated the symbiotic pairing between the two Johns in conjunction with Bear Family Records and ultimately agreed they would be a good fit.

Bear Family Records is most known for reissuing older, mostly archival country music and rock 'n' roll, primarily from the 1950's. Eventually through Beecher's hard work and Charlie's willingness, they were able to license some tracks and obtain some publishing rights. John Beecher ultimately involved John Ingman together with the Bear Family group and began work on creating an entire CD compilation for Charlie. Ingman worked diligently with Charlie for years starting around 1984 and conducted numerous interviews, correspondences and telephone calls over the next twenty-five years. It would be John Ingman who would meticulously write the inner booklet for Charlie's last album release recapping Charlie's life in a nutshell.

The Bear Family Records collection of Phillips' music would include many of Charlie's songs from his earliest recording days. The new album would comprise tracks from the Norman Petty Studios, the Bradley Film & Recording Studio, the Columbia recording studio, the Robin Hood Brians studio, Western Recorders, and the Shelby Singleton Studio. All in all, Bear Family Records' release of *Charlie Phillips Sugartime* would contain 35 various tracks recorded in truly superb sound quality including a 70-page booklet with information and photos from Charlie's long career. In 2011, the *Charlie Phillips Sugartime* CD would be the final album released by Charlie at the time of this writing. It was a success.

Both John Beecher and John Ingman agreed, "Charlie has a superb voice." Beecher resumes, "...I do love his down-home personal style...and I doubt he has any regrets about not becoming a big country music star...Of course, 'Sugartime' has done him proud...I have found him to be one of the easiest artists to work with...I love Charlie because right from the start he treated me like an old friend." Charlie responded to the two John's claims stating, "Those guys were always so easy to work with. They were always straightforward and honest with me and that's a rare quality in the music business."

Shortly after the album release, a 7" EP (extended play) record was released using tracks from his Clovis titles namely, "Sugartime," "Faker," "Be My Bride" and "One Faded Rose." The bright orange record sleeve features Charlie singing proudly into the KWKH microphone stamped with Roller Coaster Records- The Sound of High Fidelity.

After 60 years in the music business, Charlie reflects in a 2010 published quote captured by John Ingman:

> ...I didn't tour as much as I might have; probably not as much as I should have. I wouldn't give up on the security provided by my radio show as I've always accepted the 'bird in the hand' philosophy. Looking back I think I should have toured and pushed myself a lot more, but who knows? ...There's so many artists who were really hot superstars but nowadays you never hear of them. I still have my health, a decent home and income; and enough dance bookings to keep me happy and occupied whereas non-stop nationwide touring cost Buddy Holly, Johnny Horton, Patsy Cline, Jim Reeves and so many others their lives. I've no regrets about the way my life turned out.

Charlie spent a lifetime playing to live audiences and had worked with some of the most talented men and women in the business. His last few years of playing, he performed every Friday night at the 45 & Uppers Dance Club with some of the musicians he had been playing with off and on for more than 40 years. His principal ensemble of musicians would consist of Jimmy Young on fiddle, Tiny Duncan on piano, Chet Calcote on bass, Dwight Cook on steel guitar and Ted Czechchowski on drums (Including Vic Ashmead, Rick Sudduth and Lee Barlow). Although there were many other band members who filled-in as part of the Sugartimer gang, these guys would be the steadiest. The men were all in their 70's or 80's by now and were still playing the music they loved. Charlie would finally receive another prestigious honor. In 2004 Charlie "Sugartime" Phillips was inducted into the Western Swing Music Hall of Fame in Sacramento, California. This would be one of his last crowning achievements.

It was now time to slow his life down. In early 2013 after months of negotiations and planning, Charlie agreed to allow the author, Cy Cushenberry, to begin writing his life story. "I'm not even sure what there is to write about," Charlie humbly explained continuing, "I haven't really done much with my life." His long radio career, his musical connections and his influence on the world of country music were only secondary in nature. Nothing he ever did was that special to him; it was all in a days work.

Chapter 12
Sugartimers at Suppertime
An All-Star Troupe

It would be hard to talk about the undying success of Charlie "Sugartime" Phillips without the dedication and support of the men and women who accompanied him as Sugartimers over the last 60-plus years. No matter how small a role or how large a role, these talented musicians were all an integral factor in keeping the world of country music and western swing music alive.

This chapter was created to honor the men and women who either served as Sugartimers or were in their own capacity instrumental (or at the very least inspirational) to Charlie Phillips' career.

Acciaioli, Carmen- Acciaioli is a steel guitar and fiddle player with an impressive resume. Carmen filled-in on steel guitar occasionally when Charlie Phillips needed his expertise. He was a member of Michael Martin Murphey's Band from around 1980 to 1988. A current resident in the Amarillo area, Acciaioli has played with Michael Hearne and *South by Southwest*. According to a Chip Chandler interview at the *Amarillo Globe-News*, Acciaioli moved to Amarillo to be closer to his wife's family and began hooking up gigs with local musicians stating, "...all of the musicians here are great, great players." Acciaioli played a limited number of engagements with Charlie at the 45 & Uppers Dance Club. In addition to playing with Charlie Phillips and the Sugartimers and other Texas country bands, Carmen is a father and has worked as a librarian for a local middle school.

Adams, Dustin- Dustin was a good-looking young man who was eager to learn and is certainly worth mentioning. He played with the Sugartimers on a few occasions. He was more of a jazz and pop musician, but he picked up on country music and the swing life like a pro. He's remembered years later as a great guy and was always a professional musician to be around.

Allard, Weldon- Weldon Allard was a talented singer, songwriter and musician who played bass for the Sugartimers when needed. Weldon's friend, Johnny Hathcock, had moved to Amarillo, Texas in 1947 to work for KAMQ radio station. The two teamed up and wrote a variety of songs like: "Tears Are Only Rain," "Wake Up, Irene," "What Will I Do Next Monday," and "When Your Love Burns Low." Hank Thompson recorded a few of the duo's songs for Capital Records, but most notably "Wake Up Irene" was a hit among fans. Johnny Hathcock claimed later that Allard had written this melody as a parody of the song, "Good Night, Irene" written by Huddie Ledbetter in the early 1900's. It's rumored the song took around ten minutes for Allard to write. "Wake Up, Irene" was also recorded by one of Charlie Phillips' idol groups, Maddox Brothers and Rose. Bob Wills recorded Allard and Hathcock's tune, "Gotta Walk Alone," which was released many years later in 1992 on the *Country Music Hall of Fame Bob Wills Compilation* CD. Then in 2010, Willie Nelson released "Gotta Walk Alone" on his country music album. Allard was also a lead vocalist in the Billy Briggs start-up band, the XIT Boys. Charlie's biggest solo hit record on Columbia was a collaboration between the writings of Johnny Hathcock and Weldon Allard called, "I Guess I'll Never Learn."

Allm, Harold- Harold worked a few times as a Sugartimer. He played drums as a fill-in guy. Harold was most known in the Panhandle as an employee of a local television station.

Ammen, Drexal- Ammen was a stylish drummer who played with Charlie and the Sugartimers on a relatively regular basis over the years when they performed at the Aviatrix Ballroom. Although he was not a regular with the Sugartimers, Ammen could always be counted on and according to Charlie, "was an excellent drummer."

Drexal Ammen played with various bands throughout the years, most notably in current days with a local group called Young Country.

Anderson, Dub- Charlie Phillips first collaborated with Anderson in the early 1960's after they met and played together at the Playboy Club located on the Fritch Highway just outside of Amarillo. The duo worked well together and built a lifelong friendship with each other. Anderson and his wife, Helen, worked together at the Aviatrix Ballroom with Dub regularly playing onstage and Helen working the door. Anderson was also a regular player at the Casa Del Ballroom working five days a week entertaining large expecting crowds. Charlie and Dub were playing together and additionally helped open the Lakeside Club off Eastern Street in Amarillo. Dub Anderson was instrumental to the success of the Sugartimers over the years as he was not only a terrific bass player, but also added to the harmonies of the boys, reaching the high notes like no other. Dub was more of a guitar guy in the beginning, but Weldon Allard suggested he pick up the bass and sold Dub his standup, which began a lifetime preoccupation with the bass. Although Dub would play with many, many bands over his long career, some of the most notable people he played or stood in with was Curtis Marchbanks, steel guitarist Harry Coffman, Weldon Allard, Blackie Foster and Lou Walker. Dub Anderson and his wife would retire from the Aviatrix Ballroom in 1985, but he would resume playing off and on for the next three decades.

Anderson, Larry- Larry Anderson was a part-time bass player who filled-in for his cousin, Dub, when the Sugartimers needed someone to accompany them. Anderson always showed up with enthusiasm and a good attitude. Over the years, Larry became the Western Swing Music Hall of Fame vice-president.

Anthony, Buck- Buck became a regular fiddle player for the Sugartimers in the early days at the Aviatrix Ballroom. He was a quiet, laid-back guy with a dry sense of humor, but boy when he got on the fiddle, he could play some melodies. "Mr. Smooth" was what several of the guys called him because of his glassy fiddle playing abilities. He moonlighted with his fiddle during the evenings but worked commonly during the day as the manager of a local implement store.

Ashmead, Vic- Vic played steel guitar and could also play the violin. At the time of his death, Vic Ashmead was one of the most distinguished steel guitar players in the world. His playing prowess shall always be recollected, but just as importantly, Ashmead will be remembered by thousands of once-young students for his honesty and fair dealings as the vice-principal of one of the largest schools in Amarillo, Texas called Palo Duro High School where he spent 29 years. Vic admired education and completed his Master of Education degree in 1963 following his completion of a Bachelor of Science degree from the local West Texas State University in Canyon, Texas. Of the Sugartimers inaugurated into the Western Swing Music Hall of Fame, Vic Ashmead would be the second of the bunch inducted, following Jimmy Young. Ashmead began his musical career at age 13 for some area bands and never stopped playing during his life. He was inducted into the Western Swing Music Society of the Southwest Hall of Fame on July 21, 2001, and the Western Swing Society of Seattle Hall of Fame in August 2002. Ashmead worked with the Rogers Twins in the 1950's. He and Charlie collaborated with each other regularly, playing at the Over-39 Singles Dance Club as well as the 45 & Uppers Club in Amarillo. He continued playing as a Sugartimer until 2008. Vic usually played the Avalon Ballroom with the likes of Tiny Duncan and Merl Lindsay. His daughter, Victoria (or more familiarly known as Vicki) lovingly remembers she and her childhood friend, Janet Funderburk, loading Vic's equipment into their automobile at the Ashmead neighborhood home for Vic's next big gig. Vic was a very devoted husband to his wife, Nelda June. Vic once declined his 1998 attendance at a Hall of Fame award ceremony because his adoring wife fell ill with cancer, so he sent his daughter and best friend, Vicki, as well as his son, Rodney, to accept the award in his stead. Although Vic was always known as one of the Sugartimer gang, he also played regularly with Windy Wood and the Sons of the West and "Honest" Jess Williams and the Cavaliers during his career.

Bailey, Bob- Bob Bailey was a drummer who sometimes filled-in with the Sugartimer boys during the Aviatrix days. Folks eternally remember him as a nice guy who was always eager to make the drive accompanying the Sugartimers. Bob forever had some huge shoes to fill, as his father, Jack Bailey, was one of the finest fiddle players in the region.

Bailey, Jack- Originally from Muskogee, Oklahoma, Bailey began playing violin at six years old and developed his skills performing professionally by age 16, accompanying Jack Beasley on KOMA radio out of Oklahoma City. After honorably leaving the Army after World War II, Jack went to work with Odis "Pop" Echols and the Melody Ranch Boys at KWKH radio out of Shreveport, Louisiana. By the 1950's, Bailey traveled to Gallup, New Mexico where he worked with the Benny Martin Band and it's rumored he was featured in a couple of movies. He later played with Merl Lindsay and the Oklahoma Night Riders, a band that eventually evolved into the Ozark Jubilee Band for Red Foley's program. Bailey toured in the 1950's with the likes of Pee Wee King, Little Jimmy Dickens, Minnie Pearl, and the Wilburn Brothers to name a few. His fiddle playing became legendary while complementing prominent individuals like Ernest Tubb, Lefty Frizzell and Ray Price as well as Frankie McWhorter and the Over The Hill Gang who regularly performed at the yearly Bob Wills Day in Turkey, Texas. Jack Bailey graduated in 1963 with a degree in music from Panhandle State University, afterwards teaching in both public schools and also privately. Although not a full-time band member, Jack was an occasional special guest on fiddle at the Aviatrix. Bailey would join the long list of Sugartimers to be inducted into the Western Swing Society Hall of Fame in 1997.

Barlow, Lee- Lee played bass for Charlie and the Sugartimers quite frequently and also played some fiddle under the tutelage of Jimmy Young. Over the years, he filled-in for his friend and musical colleague, Chet Calcote, and also played as a roving fiddle player for the Big Texan Steak House (Home of the FREE 72oz. steak if eaten in one hour) in Amarillo. He also played the Coors Cowboy Club Ranch Rodeo. Lee performed for Bob Wills Day in 2014, which is held yearly in Turkey, Texas. Lee was once quoted, "I love this type of music," continuing, "This is a release from the stress. This is my workout." Lee Barlow's older sister worked at KZIP radio station with Charlie.

Beevers, Gary- Gary was a favorite and magnificent steel guitarist who played with the Sugartimers in the Clovis days. By age ten, he began loving and playing music as he heard the western swing sounds of Hank Thompson and Bob Wills broadcast on the radio. Gary did a few shows with Charlie in the 1950's both before and after "Sugartime" became a hit. He would also join the Sugartimers at the Aviatrix in Amarillo. It was said Gary "could blow most steel guitar players away." He also played for various bands and individuals over the years including the Lehman Denison Band (later the Tiny Lynn Band), Curley Cook, Harold Reddin and the Reddin Bros. Band, Jim Bowman and his Roadrunners, the Western Ramblers, the Fireballs, the Western Rainbows, Tommy Haney and the Rainbow Ramblers, Johnny Mulhair, the Santa Fe Band, and for Larry Trider on the *Larry Trider Show*. Gary Beevers created a distinctive band called the Cold Country Band and regularly played at Clovis' Lyceum Theater. Johnny Mulhair handpicked Gary in 1995 to perform and record LeAnn Rime's *Blue* album and *Unchained Melody, the Early Years*, at the Norman Petty Studio in the old Mesa Theater on Main Street in Clovis. When he performed with the Santa Fe Band, Gary stepped out and played steel on Hank William Sr.'s song, "Cold, Cold Heart."

Benjamin, Jimmy- Jimmy Benjamin served in the U.S. Navy where he learned to play the drums, and he learned to play them well. By the time he was 30, Benjamin had hooked up with a favorite musician who would later be dubbed "The King of Swing," Mr. Bob Wills himself. Jimmy would first appear on Bob Wills' November 1956 Music City Recordings album, *Bob Wills & Texas Playboys*, as the drummer and would record over twenty songs with Wills within the year. He then played drums on the February 1957 Wills album recorded on Decca Records out of Hollywood, California. Benjamin would play with Wills intermittently throughout Wills' life, and he would continue playing with the Texas Playboys off and on for the rest of his musical career. Jimmy also worked occasionally through the years with Merl Lindsay. Mr. Benjamin worked as a Sugartimer off and on for countless years. Before many rock 'n' rollers began the showmanship of throwing their sticks into the air while playing, there was swing drummer Jimmy tossing his sticks up during a set. Many of the guys he played with lovingly joke that as Benjamin got older, his hearing got worse- and he refused to wear a hearing aid. He never missed a beat, but as he aged, his flawless drumming got louder and louder and louder. His playing became so intense during gigs that Charlie built a pin around Jimmy's drum stand made from foam rubber to absorb some of the beats. Well, this *did not* set right with Jimmy, so he stopped playing with Charlie and the guys during his latter years. When asked about Jimmy Benjamin's skills, Charlie Phillips contended, Jimmy was "one of the best western swing drummers of all times."

Blackburn, John- John was an ole' boy Charlie was friends with for a long time. He was an excellent guitar player and an all-around crowd pleaser. His specialty was playing the Flamenco guitar. Although not considered an actual Sugartimer, John was often hired to perform at the Panhandle Broadcasters Association. John was friends with and recorded an album with famous philosopher and cowboy poet, Buck Ramsey.

Blair, Teddy- Teddy was a Clovis native and although not considered a Sugartimer, sat in with Charlie at Elkins' Bar just past Kenna, New Mexico during Charlie's early playing days. He did play with the Sugartimers a limited number of times while in Clovis. Blair laughs he only knew three songs in the beginning of his music career and was sometimes dubbed, "3-Songs Ted," but he soon learned and began performing with more local area musicians eventually touring with bands all over the world. He would ultimately play with Kitty Wells and Ernest Tubbs on Red Foley's *Ozark Jubilee*. Teddy enjoyed a musical career spanning more than 35 years.

Bowerman, Bruce- Bruce was an occasional drummer for the Sugartimers and played with various local bands in the Texas Panhandle over the years. He was always available when Charlie and the guys needed him and according to Charlie, "Bruce was one heck of a drum guy." Bruce Bowerman tapered out of the ballroom scene over the years and began playing for his local church band.

Briggs, Billy- There are steel guitar players, and then there is Billy Briggs. Billy was birthed in Ft. Worth, Texas in 1919. He interned under groundbreaking electric steel guitarist, Bob Dunn, of Milton Brown's Musical Brownies, as Briggs joined the Hi-Flyers. He soon moved to Amarillo where he joined up with the Sons of the West. The pioneering Briggs built his personal nine-string steel guitar, and it's rumored *he was the first person to attach legs to a steel guitar and perform standing while he sang and played guitar at the same time.* He formed his first band called Swinging Steel in 1939 and later fashioned the XIT Boys in 1946 initially consisting of: Briggs on steel guitar and trumpet, Freddy Beatty on sax, J.R. Chatwell on fiddle, Herschell Marson on drums, Loren Mitchell on piano, and "Honest" Jess Williams playing bass and offering vocals. Briggs' most popular regional hit was "Chew Tobacco Rag" released in 1951. Musicians like Pee Wee King, Spade Cooley and even R&B artist, Lucky Millinder, would later cover this song. The XIT Boys' most known songs include, "The Sissy Song," "North Pole Boogie," and "Freckle-Face Snaggle-Tooth Gal." Briggs' style of playing would gain the recognition and admiration of producer, Norman Petty, as well as fellow artists like Roy Orbison, Buddy Knox, Jimmy Bowen, Ray Ruff and Buddy Holly. When Charlie Phillips moved to Amarillo in the early 1960's, it would be at the Billy Briggs Nightclub where Charlie would begin playing as a guest artist for Billy's band. Briggs is perhaps one of the most progressive and innovative musicians of the current century, yet because of lack of record sales and exposure, he has been widely overlooked and undervalued. Although not actually a Sugartimer, Billy and His Chew Tobacco Rag Boys were significant contributors to the Sugartimer band.

Bristow Don- Bristow was a natural musician mastering many instruments. He was a world-class banjo player by age 12 and then mastered guitar picking. It's said Bristow could manipulate the sound of an electric guitar making it sound like a steel guitar. After moving to Amarillo, Bristow began working with Doug Collins, a radioman now inducted into the Texas Panhandle Association of Broadcasters Hall of Fame, who prompted him to take up the steel guitar. Don Bristow will always be remembered as a valuable guitar picker for Charlie Phillips and the Sugartimers, especially during the Aviatrix days.

Brown, Eugene- Eugene played with The Electra's alongside Hubert Heatherly, Bob Hacker and Jon Sisco. He also played in a band called The Chips with Tommy Euton, Don Carpenter and Bobby Hacker. Don quit and was replaced on bass by Chet Calcote. Eugene was a Sugartimer during the Rainbow Ballroom era playing guitar and contributing his strong vocals.

Brown, Gerald- Gerald Brown can be considered one of the first drummers to join the Sugartimers during Charlie's early days in Clovis. He regularly drummed with Pete Wallace, Jimmy Schell and Charlie (on the banjo) at the Pioneer Club in Kenna, New Mexico. Gerald was kin to Pete Wallace through marriage and the two regularly played together. Some remember Gerald Brown as a very handsome guy with coal black hair and always an eye pleaser for the ladies. Brown played drums on the first ever-recorded version of "Sugartime" and the unissued demo, "One Faded Rose." Gerald was one of the few musicians who later grew up and weaned himself away from a career in music.

Byers, Kirby- Charlie Phillips became acquainted with Byers in Nashville at an awards banquet. Kirby would travel to Amarillo and play with the Sugartimers for a period at the Aviatrix. He was a fantastic musician playing both guitar and drum. Byers performed with a lot of groups over the years even recording several records of his own, yet never seemed to make it big despite his immense talent.

Calcote, Chet- One of the longest standing Sugartimers would indeed include Chet Calcote, who played bass and provided vocal support. Chet began singing as well as playing both the guitar and harmonica at age four. Having grown up around ranch hands that taught him to pick the strings on a guitar, young Chet would expand his repertoire to include a variety of instruments like the banjo, the fiddle and the bass. By age 10, Chet was offered a position as host of a live, Saturday-morning program on KOKO radio in Colorado. He regularly performed on KLMR radio by the time he reached high school. He also entered television as the musical co-host of *The Colorado Corral* where he would meet his future wife, Maureen McKenna. Calcote soon toured with Leon McAuliff's Western Swing Band based out of Tulsa, Oklahoma and acted as musical director and road manager for the group. Through the years, Calcote would share the stage with notables like legendary Bob Wills. He would tour many local and regional venues throughout his long career, also incorporating a USO tour of Europe as well as stints at various Las Vegas venues. Calcote directed the album entitled, *Windy Wood- The Classic Sound of Western Swing.* Primarily known for his country music expertise, Calcote learned to appreciate and play a variety of musical genres like- big band, Celtic, cowboy, Dixieland, jazz and western swing. He also led such notable bands like The Classics, The String Technicians, Texas Rhythm and Starjazz. Calcote served as bandleader and bass player for a musical show at the Amarillo Little Theater called, *Can't Get Enough of Texas*. Like many of the all-star cast of Sugartimers, Calcote would be inducted into the Western Swing Music Hall of Fame in Sacramento and the Western Swing Society of the Southwest.

Caldwell, Aubrey- Aubrey Caldwell played horns with the Sugartimers on a limited basis. Aubrey had a strong voice and could easily imitate and sound like one of his favorite singers, Hank Thompson. (Buddy Holly toured the country with *The Hank Thompson Show*). Aubrey could also mimic the style and sound of Charlie Phillips as Charlie could also mimic Aubrey- almost indistinguishable from each other. Aubrey was a farming and ranching guy from the northern Texas Panhandle and could always be counted on to fill-in with any horns during the Aviatrix days. Later in life, he performed in his own one-man band.

Campbell, Don- Don Campbell was a bass player who worked jobs with Charlie on an as-needed basis. He once led the group at the 45 & Uppers Dance Club. He's remembered as one heck of a Sugartimer. To read a great story concerning Don Campbell at a

West Texas State University fraternity gig, read over Shorty Messer's biography in this chapter.

Capranica, Larry- Larry was introduced to Charlie by Chet Calcote and filled-in with the Sugartimers on a limited basis. Charlie remembers Larry as a "great trumpet player." Larry may have worked a bit at the Aviatrix Ballroom and also collaborated with Charlie playing the horn for the Over-39 Singles Dance Club.

Carpenter, Harold- Harold was a distant relative of Charlie's through marriage and knew Charlie since he was born. Charlie thought he was one the funniest man who ever lived. Carpenter played ragtime piano and gladly showed Charlie a few things about music during Charlie's early upbringing. Harold was not a Sugartimer but was certainly instrumental as a musical mentor for the then budding Charlie Phillips. "I think he could play anything on a piano," Charlie recollected.

Carter, Marion- Carter played bass with the Sugartimers on a limited basis when they performed at the Aviatrix Ballroom and also worked with Charlie at the 45 & Uppers Club which assembled at the senior-citizen hall located south of downtown Amarillo inside of the Amarillo College North Polk Street campus. Marion worked with Rick Sudduth in the band, Blue Denim.

Cartrite, Richard- Richard Cartrite only played a couple of times as a Sugartimer, but his excellent skills as a bass player and trumpeter deserve a mention. He worked with Charlie and the guys on a *Western Swing Showcase*. He drove into Amarillo from Clarendon, Texas where he worked at a Chevrolet dealership. He sometimes performed with Chet Calcote similarly. Cartrite's most notable skill was he could play two horns at the same time in full synchronization.

Casso, Carlos- Carlos Casso is an accomplished musician and saxophonist living in Amarillo, Texas. He's known for filling-in for bands that require his talents. Depending on the type of venue and the music chosen, Carlos performed with the Sugartimers when an expert sax player was needed and he also recorded the entire *Cracker Barrel Show* in his studio- produced by John Hodges who was the founder of the Texas Panhandle Association of Broadcasters Hall of Fame where Charlie is also inducted. Although musically talented, Casso is probably more recognized in the West Texas community as the owner of Audio Refinery Recording Studio in Amarillo. Casso began in the recording business around 1978 and handles hundreds of artists' recordings. Charlie would record several songs at the Casso studio. Most notably, Carlos Casso has been the producer for the Audie award-winning modern children's audiobook series entitled, *Hank the Cowdog*.

Chandler, Fred- Fred is not a Sugartimer, but Charlie played with him during Clovis' Border Town Days with the Border Town Days Band. Fred was a Farwell native and was an instrumental force behind keeping the Border Town Days celebration festival afloat.

Clay, Don- Don Clay played fiddle and sang vocals with the Sugartimers for a couple of years at the Aviatrix. He was a superb singer with a broad range of vocals. Don was a sturdy man who worked in concrete as his day job. "He was one of the hardest workin' men I knew. He owned a very big and successful concrete contracting business," Charlie recollected. The two musicians went skiing together a time or two in Red River along with Don's family. Don worked with other great bands before he retired from the music business, but would eventually be talked into returning at the prompting of Charlie and other band members.

Cliff, Earl- Earl Cliff was a terrific vocalist and played both lead and rhythm guitar occasionally with the Sugartimers. Earl was the man responsible for hiring Charlie "Sugartime" Phillips to play on a regular basis at the 45 & Uppers Dance Club. Of the many folks on this list, Earl was not actually a Sugartimer, but he did sit-in on several sessions as the group welcomed his skills. Charlie was always happy to have a long-term member of the club accompany his band and do a few numbers. Earl Cliff presented Charlie with an award for Charlie's seven years of service to the group.

Coffman, Harry- Coffman was a splendid steel guitar player who filled-in with the Sugartimers on an occasional basis. He would play with various bands throughout the years and would endear himself to the western swing world by co-founding and serving as treasurer of the Western Swing Music Society of the Southwest Hall of Fame. Harry played with many area great bands during his career.

Cook, Dwight- It was on the back of comic books Cook first saw advertisements to begin selling seeds for a nickel a package. He walked all across Childress, Texas selling his seeds to earn $3.25 plus $2 shipping in order to purchase a brand new Gene Autry guitar, which he realized after it arrived wasn't worth a darn. He learned how to play it nonetheless. Dwight grew up next door to his uncle's crew, the Jimmy Reece Band, a clan of Western swing pickers, thus sparking his interest in dance music as they taught him rhythm guitar and how to maneuver a lap Sears steel guitar. Cook would become gifted in guitar, steel guitar and bass. After honorably leaving the Army in 1957, Cook would begin working at an aircraft factory, but continued playing gigs with groups and musicians in his downtime. Over the course of his musical career, Cook played with: Bill Wimberly's Band; Curley Chalker; the Albert Talley Band; Maurice Anderson; the Texas Playboys; Tommy Morrell; George Richey; Skeets McDonald; the Merl Lindsay Band; Hank Thompson; Leon McAuliffe; Rick Sudduth; Tiny Duncan; Bobby Wynne and the Khiva Shrine Temple Western Swing Band; John Mann and the Magic City Cowboys and Little Jimmy Dickens to name a few. Cook played steel guitar and bass for the Sugartimers for many years and credits musicians like Vic Ashmead, Jimmy Young, Kenny Williamson, Tiny Duncan and Chet Calcote for his musical development. Dwight filled-in for Chet Calcote when Calcote was summoned to play with another band led by Patrick Swindell, an Amarillo musician and attorney. Cook was ultimately recognized in 2001 as a "Pioneer of Western Swing" at the annual Pioneers of Western Swing Music in Everett, Washington. Dwight Cook would be the guy to nominate his friend and colleague, Rick Sudduth, for the Western Swing Music Society of the Southwest Hall of Fame, where Rick would eventually be inducted.

Cornelius, Corky- Corky performed drums with the Chew Tobacco Rag Boys playing and accompanying Billy Briggs at his self-penned Billy Briggs Nightclub on the Fritch Highway just outside of

Amarillo, which is where Charlie first encountered Corky. He worked with Charlie and the Sugartimers at the Aviatrix Ballroom. Although Corky loved country and swing, he preferred drumming to the sounds of pop or jazz.

Cornelius, David- David Cornelius worked at the 45 & Uppers Club before Charlie and the Sugartimers arrived on the scene. David was an excellent piano player and could reinforce his playing with solid vocals.

Couch, Benny- Benny played steel guitar for the Cattleman's Club as a staff musician for many years. His job entailed him often playing six to seven nights per week. Couch filled-in on steel guitar when the Sugartimers needed a good player but only when he was available. Benny worked with various groups throughout the years and often played with Tiny Duncan when needed. He was once married to drummer, Judy Couch.

Couch, Judy- In a world dominated by men, Judy could do more than hold her own. She was an excellent sought-after drummer in the region. She was good-looking and the men who worked with her remember her top-notch drumming expertise. She was once married to steel guitar player, Benny Couch. Judy Couch had a regular gig as the staff musician for the Cattleman's Club off East Amarillo Boulevard.

Craven, Bill- Bill Craven was a lifelong friend of Charlie's who grew up with him in Farwell, Texas. Bill lived about three miles north of Charlie on a farm and grew up as a sharecropper's son in much the same fashion Charlie did- poor. Bill moved to Amarillo a few years before Charlie did, but the two caught up with each other in no time. The guys worked together on various gigs, and Bill worked closely with Charlie as a Sugartimer at the Aviatrix. Bill sang and played rhythm guitar. Craven was an excellent singer and even did some songwriting of his own. Bill was a comical guy and always had a joke. "Blabbering Bill" was what some of the other musicians would jestingly call him. He often began telling a joke from the bandstand, forgetting he was in public, and would tell an "off-color" joke, which sometimes wouldn't be too well received by the audience. Rumor has it Bill named one of his children after Charlie.

Czechchowski, Ted- Good ole' Ted Czechchowski was a Polish immigrant who arrived in New York City during the Cold War in 1968. While in the Big Apple, Ted began filling-in as a drummer for the renowned Tom Jones. He played around the area doing many gigs throughout New Jersey also. Ted's father was a jazz and pop drummer who taught his son how to beat those drums. Ted toured the open seas as a traveling drummer on cruise ships but left New York permanently after folks kept unconsciously giving him objects with "Texas" on them, or he kept seeing the word, Texas. Ted took this as a sign he needed to be in the Lone Star State. Shortly after arriving in Amarillo, he met a lovely girl, and they married. It didn't take long after disembarking in Amarillo before Czechchowski realized if he wanted to make some money playing music, he'd better learn some country and western styles. Ted began his tutelage with Charlie in the latter years at the Aviatrix. In no time, Ted absorbed the sound and style of western swing. He took a job at the local weapons disassembly plant, Pantex, just outside of Amarillo for his day job, but continued knocking out the beats in the evenings. Unlike some musicians, Czechchowski could read music, which would allow him to teach drums and percussion at the local Amarillo music store, Tolzien Music. Ted would continue a lifetime of teaching and playing western swing, hooking up with Charlie for many years at the 45 & Uppers Club. He would also join Amarillo jazz musician, Patrick Swindell. Of all of the members of Charlie's Sugartimers who played western swing for almost half a century, Ted Czechchowski will be the *only* member not officially inducted into the Western Swing Hall of Fame; however, Charlie and the rest of the crew made him an honorary member.

Darby, Marc- Marc Darby played piano with the Sugartimers on a limited basis. Those who knew Marc know he had a "fine tuned" ear when it came to a piano and in fact, he was intended for it. Not only was Marc an accomplished pianist, in recent years he has made a living using his honed hearing tuning pianos for churches, organizations and individuals.

Deweese, Doc- Robert Kevin "Doc" Deweese was a very likable guy in the Panhandle, especially in the Amarillo and Pampa areas. He was a graduate of Lubbock Christian College and played drums on a limited basis for the Sugartimers. Doc and Charlie worked together at KZIP radio station in Amarillo. Doc received numerous awards from the Amarillo Advertising Association and was known in the radio business for his original voices on local commercials. Doc was a top on-air personality, as well as promoter and music director. Popular regional publication, *Accent West Magazine*, highlighted Deweese in a feature article, "Pilot of the Airwaves."

Dodd, Bobby- Bobby Dodd was an Airman from Louisiana and was stationed at the Amarillo Air Force Base. Dodd asked to audition for Charlie and claimed he had worked with "so and so" from the *Louisiana Hayride* so Charlie somewhat hesitantly gave him a chance. Bobby Dodd blew Charlie's socks off when he began playing guitar. "Man could he pick!" Charlie brags. After his service to our nation, Bobby moved to the Nashville area and has continued to play.

Dolman, Andy- Andy was a versatile musician playing both saxophone and fiddle with the Sugartimers. Coincidentally, Andy moved to Texas from New York City and was introduced to Charlie by Ted Czechchowski- a man who had arrived to Amarillo in precisely the same manner. Andy was an Army man. Dolman worked various times for the Sugartimers primarily for the 45 & Uppers Club. He also worked at with the Sugartimers at the American Legion in Childress, Texas. He performed on various occasions with fiddle player, Jimmy Young.

Duncan, Tiny- As one can surmise, there was nothing minuscule about Tiny Duncan. He was pinned with the nickname by a saxophone player, contending Rupert M. "Tiny" Duncan couldn't pronounce his own name. Tiny began his piano-playing passion after his sisters began showing him how to pluck out the ivory keys at the ripe ole age of three. His hands were so small. Tiny jokingly purports, "they never got much bigger." In fact, he went to a piano teacher and was told his hands were too small to master the instrument. It's a good thing he didn't listen because master the piano he did. As years progressed around the 1950's, Tiny began playing professionally by hauling an upright piano from dance to dance in the back of his truck. Like many musicians, he learned to play his instrument by ear, learning during jam sessions. In 1956, young Tiny played at the National Guard Armory and realized he might etch out a living doing what he loved. He was paid a whole $20 for the session- a far cry from the $1.56 ½ per hour he was used to making working hard labor in the oil field. He continued playing gigs throughout the Texas and Oklahoma Panhandles for three years and finally embarked on a long journey to San Jose, California where he hooked up and played with Clyde Arnold and the Blew Boys and at the Crazy Otto's Club. He also began performing with the Jimmy Rivers Band at the 23 Club in Brisbane, California. Soon after that, Tiny played for Merl Lindsay and the Ozark Jubilee Band. Duncan returned to Amarillo and began working with "Honest" Jess Williams and the Western Cavaliers, a paying gig that lasted intermittently at the Avalon Ballroom from 1960 to 1987. In addition to also being a regular and longtime Sugartimer, the little kid with hands that were too small to play piano, would back up some of the biggest names in show business. Over the course of his career, Tiny would play with or accompany onstage: Archie Campbell, Glen Campbell, Patsy Cline, Freddy Hart, Ray Price, Johnny Horton, David Frizzell, Lefty Frizzell, Waylon Jennings and George Jones, as a small sample. Local Texas musicians Tiny played with include- Vic Ashmead, Jimmy Benjamin, Chet Calcote, Ted Czechchowski, Frankie McWhorter and Windy Wood & The New Sons of the West. Although Tiny primarily played at the popular Avalon Ballroom (the bar once burned down with his equipment inside), he also performed at the Ace of Clubs, the Caravan Nightclub, the Clover Club, the Rainbow Gardens and the Star Night Club. He regularly worked with Charlie at the 45 & Uppers Club. Like select Sugartimers, Tiny is inducted into the Western Swing Music Society Hall of Fame in Sacramento, the Western Swing Music Society of The Southwest out of Oklahoma, and the Hall of Heroes out of Ft. Worth, Texas. Charlie Phillips was quoted in the *Amarillo Globe-News* stating, "Tiny is just a natural musician, and a good vocalist… he can play just about anything." Charlie adds, "I can't think of anyone more deserving to be in the (Western Swing Society) Hall of Fame." It's been said there was not a song Tiny couldn't play and not a key in which he could not play it. The man with "little hands" proved to be one paramount piano player.

Felty, Gregg- Gregg played drums with the Sugartimers on a limited basis. He worked with various bands throughout the Panhandle and was considered by his peers to be a gifted musician.

Foster, Blackie- One could say Blackie Foster was just a natural musician as he cultivated music within his family. The retired truck driver played bass for the Sugartimers on a limited basis, partially because of the hours he spent running his family-atmospheric music store in Amarillo called Foster's House of Strings. Blackie loved all sorts of music but was especially fond of bluegrass, even fronting his own band, Blackie Foster and his Blackhawks. The band did quite well in the 1950's as they appeared on local television and radio shows and booked gigs throughout the area. Blackie's daughter, Billie Foster Palmer, was once quoted as saying; "We didn't go to Disneyworld like the other kids. We went to bluegrass festivals." Panhandle local musicians remember Foster's House of Strings fondly because Blackie held weekly jam sessions open to any local musicians who wanted to participate. Sugartimer and all-star fiddle player, Jimmy Young, often repaired musical instruments for the Foster's business customers, but could also be seen sharing his fiddle playing for the weekly jam sessions.

Goad, Paul- Paul Goad is a talented Clovis instrumentalist who regularly played piano accompanied by his vocals when the Sugartimers needed him. In addition to piano, acoustic guitar, harp, drums and even keyboards, the multi-talented Paul was a terrific bass player and performed with several Panhandle bands over the course of his musical career. Paul was an original member of Gary P. Nunn's Sons of the Bunkhouse Band. Over the years, he shared the stage with artists and bands like Rusty Weir, Jerry Jeff Walker, Willie Nelson and the Fireballs. In most recent years, Paul played with The Texas Blues Rangers incorporating Jay Weeks, Marc Durham and Johnny 'Reverb' Holston. In 2012, Paul Goad was involved in a project by Texas Music For Life presenting Pink

Floyd's *Dark Side of the Moon*, which was performed live onstage with Goad playing bass and offering vocal support. Goad presented his talents to the group, Home Cookin' Band, comprised of musicians like Brad Billingsley, Gary Beevers, Johnny and Jill Mulhair, as well as himself. Jill stated the band was "named among the top 10 in the Country by Nashville's *Music Row Magazine* in 1996 and 1997." It's rumored Goad and members of the Home Cookin' Band worked on LeAnn Rimes' album in 1994- 1995. Goad has also played with the Fun Brothers Band and has continued his career as a songwriter, studio musician and sound technician for Mulhair Studios.

Griffin, Jim- Jim Griffin played saxophone with the Sugartimers on an as-needed basis. A bit of a music aficionado, Jim's love for music would be hard to surpass. He studied and performed music for decades and learned to play some eighteen different instruments. Among these include: saxophone, flute, piano, bass guitar, lap steel guitar, clarinet, duduk (an Armenian double reed instrument), sitar (a stringed instrument much like the lute), swarmandal (the Indian harp), santoor (an Indian stringed instrument), tabla (Indian drums), African barrel drum, bansuri (a transverse flute), thumb piano (an African instrument like an idiophone), bass clarinet, classical guitar, electric jazz guitar, and shehnai (like an Indian double-reed oboe). One could never argue Jim wasn't a hardworking, industrious music man.

Guess, Don- Don Guess was born into a musical family. His household moved to Clovis, New Mexico when Don was six years old. His mother and two sisters had a show singing on KICA radio and were among the first to record at what would be known as the Norman Petty Studio under the name, The Guess Sisters. Then the family performed under the name, the *Guess Family Gospel Show*. Very early in his life, Don would pick up pointers on piano, steel guitar, bass and guitar. One would be hard-pressed to have a conversation about the origins of Buddy Holly without mentioning his Hutchinson Junior High musician friend, Don Guess. Four youngsters, Buddy Holley (born with the 'e'), Bob Montgomery, Jerry Allison and Don Guess would each craft their own musical distinctiveness cementing each individually in the history books.

Two early groups associated with Buddy Holley are The Rhythm Playboys with Don Guess and Bob Montgomery and The Three Tunes with Jerry Allison, Sonny Curtis and Don Guess. The guys began playing country and bluegrass primarily, but after seeing a young Elvis Presley in Lubbock, Texas during the 1950's, the guys tried a more rock 'n' roll approach in their music with Guess primarily playing steel guitar and bass fiddle. Guess would write or co-write a number of songs including, "You Are My One Desire," "Baby Won't You Come Out Tonight," "Flower Of My Heart," "Modern Don Juan," "Queen Of The Ballroom," and "Girl On My Mind." Over the next decade, Don will record several solo singles at the Norman Petty Studio. This is where he will meet a young Charlie Phillips. Years later in Nashville, Don will play bass on Charlie's recording of "Faker" and "I Won't Be Around" in August of 1958. Don will appear on songs recorded by various other artists including: Faron Young, Terry Noland, Roy Orbison, Buddy Knox, Marty Robbins, Sonny James, George Jones, Wanda Jackson and will tour with *The Hank Thompson Show* as would Buddy Holly and the Crickets. As unbelievable as Don Guess' early musical career will commence, Don begins weeding music out of his life eventually settling down as an insurance agent. It would be challenging to speculate the influence Don might have had on the early life of Buddy Holley, Bob Montgomery or Jerry Allison. Don played with Charlie and the Sugartimer gang numerous times over the years. "He was one of the best-darned musicians you'd ever want to meet!" Charlie exclaims. Don toured with Charlie on many occasions including a special appearance on the *Louisiana Hayride*.

Hadaway, Tom- Originally born in Chillicothe, Texas, Tom Hadaway's family moved to the Lubbock area where Tom took up the guitar. He joined the United States Army in 1950 and served in the Korean War as a sergeant. Sgt. Hadaway would provide entertainment while traveling through Europe under the name, the Grand Old Opry. In 1953 while serving his tour of duty, Tom would meet and marry his wife, Dorothy. After receiving an honorable discharge, he would eventually move to Amarillo where he became a plant manager for Star Paper Tube working there until his retirement. Tom loved playing his guitar he suitably named, "Girtie." Tom was an outstanding guitar picker and became a regular sit-in for Charlie Phillips and the Sugartimers. He could always be counted on. Tom Hadaway also had one heck of a musical grandson, Dustin Young, who would also become a Sugartimer (along with his other grandpa, Jimmy Young).

Ham, Earl- Earl was a drummer for the Sugartimers and worked on a limited basis filling-in if a primary drummer couldn't make their engagement. Earl was certainly a swing music lover, and his skills were greatly appreciated by the band. He was also an accomplished jazz and pop drummer. Earl was a very faithful family man and husband to his wife of over 50 years.

Hamilton, Larry- Larry was a BNSF Railroad guy who was always on call, leaving him little time to do what he loved. When Larry could make it over to fill-in as a Sugartimer steel guitar player, he played it like he loved it. Charlie verifies, "Larry was an excellent steel player and very good at what he did." Larry would assist the Sugartimers at the 45 & Uppers Club and the Over-39 Singles Dance Club when available. In latter years, Larry sat in with some bands at the Western Horseman in Amarillo.

Haney, Tommy- Tommy Haney lived just up the road from Charlie further out in the country, which made it easy for the two to hook-up with each other in their high school days for jam sessions. Tommy never actually became a Sugartimer because he was on the scene far before "Sugartime" ever became a hit. Tommy went on to make a name for himself in the Clovis area as he formed his own popular band called Tommy Haney and the Rainbow Ramblers using Doug Roberts as the drummer before Doug began playing for the Fireballs. Pop Echols once booked Mel Tillis at the Marshall Auditorium in Clovis and Mel's band inadvertently left their sound system at their last gig, so Pop began calling around and secured Tommy Haney's sound system. Tommy struck up a friendship with Tillis from this experience. Tommy and his band were asked on occasions to backup artists like Kris Kristofferson, Wanda Jackson and Loretta Lynn. Other musicians who played with the Rainbow Ramblers include Jim Bowman, Jimmy James, "Smiling" Truman Welch, Bud Hornsby, Humpty and Irene Knuckles, and Pete and Peggy Wallace.

Hanson, Forrest- Hanson worked at the Avalon in Amarillo for years with "Honest" Jess and His Western Cavaliers. After leaving the Avalon, he collaborated with Charlie as a Sugartimer playing lead guitar and singing. He was an excellent singer who sang Ray Price songs, some saying better than Price could do himself. One night Charlie had loaned Forrest his vintage guitar, and as the night progressed, Forrest drank a bit too much alcohol and inadvertently stumbled off the stage. He knew as he fell, Charlie would probably fire him if he harmed Charlie's priceless guitar, so he protected the instrument with his life as he tumbled to the Aviatrix dance floor. Forrest was bruised up, but managed to keep the guitar intact, well *almost* unscathed. A strap connection broke whereby Forrest ultimately fixed it by replacing the guitar strap connection with a screen door eyehook! Charlie was flabbergasted.

Hardcastle, Frank- Frank Hardcastle played lead guitar for the Sugartimers longer than any other. He was one of the finest western swing, country & western and rock 'n' roll guitar players. "An outstanding guitar player," according to Charlie, "he knew so much stuff." Although legally blind, he worked with many, many local bands. Frank took a job at Tolzien Music in Amarillo teaching guitar lessons. He taught hundreds of eager students how to strum the guitar, some of which went on to play in larger bands throughout the country. He worked for years with the Sugartimers at the Aviatrix and would accompany Charlie at the Over-39 Singles Dance Club as well as jobs throughout the Tri-State area. Frank would also work closely with the Texas Panhandle Heritage Foundation assisting the outdoor musical *Texas* and also labored with Charlie and the Sugartimers playing special events for the Texas Panhandle Heritage Foundation.

Harris, Freddy- If you could say one thing about Fred Rayford Harris, he was a punctual man- most of the time. Known as quite the prankster with a great sense of humor, Freddy was a joy to play with when called to be a Sugartimer for the evening. Freddy backed up the group with his guitar playing skills and his vocals. Some of his favorite musicians were Hank Williams and Merle Haggard. He played with the Sugartimers on a limited basis, partially because of his large family. He was known to spontaneously load the family car and take to the open road. Freddy worked many years as a staff musician at another famous Amarillo Boulevard nightclub, the Cattleman's Club. Folks in Amarillo will always remember him for his kindness as well as his musical talents.

Hawkins, Betty- Betty Hawkins would be the first locally professional band the very young Charlie Phillips would play with- at the request of Betty. Of course Betty played primarily for contest events and the local PTA. A good-looking ole' farm gal from around Bovina, she played guitar, piano and was a great singer. Charlie wouldn't forget Betty Hawkins as he began his ascent as he often welcomed her to sit-in when he was in her area.

Holly, Cotton- Cotton Holly is considered one of the best in a long list of Texas steel guitar players. He worked at and retired from Sears & Roebuck. Cotton regularly played as a Sugartimer. Holly was friends and colleagues with Vic Ashmead, another great steel guitarist. Cotton often played with Jimmy Young on the fiddle, Jim Benjamin on the drums, Tiny Duncan playing piano and Chet Calcote on bass and even filled-in on the steel guitar for Merl Lindsay. For many years, he played at the Avalon Ballroom. Cotton performed gigs with the Sugartimer band and was also available for recording sessions. "About the best musician around," Charlie would say about Cotton. He worked with Charlie many years at the Aviatrix Ballroom and gigs throughout the Tri-State area. Cotton and Roger Miller were lifetime, close friends as both were from Sayre, Oklahoma.

Hopkins, Bob- Compared to the average age of Sugartimers as time has marched on, Bob Hopkins might be considered a youngster of the group. But don't let his age fool ya. An accomplished musician, Bob has regularly performed when the Sugartimers call, playing piano and adding his vocal skills. A fixture of the Amarillo music scene since the early 1980's, Bob is most known for his work with the Panhandle-American band, KRAKT. The KRAKT band opened respectively for acts like The Doobie Brothers, David Frizzell, Sammy Davis Jr., Stevie Ray Vaughn, Creedence Clearwater Revival, and Pat Benatar. Hopkins is a graduate of Berklee College of Music in Boston graduating Magna Cum Laude with a M.A. degree. Bob Hopkins was Production Manager at the Amarillo Civic Center and has taught as a full-time teacher at Cal Farley's Boys Ranch. His work with the Sugartimer band has always been appreciated. Bob's company, Robert James Music Company, is active in music production for commercials, videos and recording artists.

Huckert, Donnie- Donnie grew up not too far from Charlie in Hereford, Texas. He was an exquisite drummer who regularly worked with the Sugartimers at the Aviatrix Ballroom. He moved to Amarillo probably to get a little closer to the music scene. Donnie would eventually move to Wellington, Texas where he continued playing throughout his life.

Hughes, Billy- Billy Hughes started playing the drums professionally around 1970. Billy played drums frequently with the Sugartimers when needed. He performed with other bands locally and nationally and is very musically inclined, playing numerous other instruments as well. And it's no wonder he's so musical, his father is the acclaimed Bobby Hughes who also plays steel guitar, fiddle and lead guitar on some of Billy's songs.

Hughes, Bobby- Bobby Hughes was about as skillful of a musician as you could get. Over the years, Bobby would be an instrumental Sugartimer teammate as he could perform anything. Throughout his very long musical career, and oftentimes as a Sugartimer, Bobby would play steel guitar, guitar, fiddle and vocals. "There's nothin' that man couldn't play!" exclaimed Charlie Phillips. He had a great voice. His two claims to fame were his own bands, Bobby Hughes and the Western Heartbeats and The Bobby Hughes Band that would play at the Avalon Ballroom, the Clover Club, the Casa Del, the Panhandle Barn Dance and another Panhandle venue called the Spud & Bud (across the street from the Avalon). However, if Charlie ever needed him and he wasn't busy with his own band, he was there. Jimmy Young supported his multi-talented friend, Hughes, at the Panhandle Barn Dance, a popular Amarillo dance hall. He most often played at the Avalon Ballroom where he was the staff musician and

25-percent owner with "Honest" Jess Williams. He later recorded at Billy Stull's recording studio in Amarillo. Over his career, Bobby performed with notable artists like Leroy Van Dyke, George Jones, Sheb Wooley, Wanda Jackson, Charlie Walker, Vern Gosdin and one of Charlie's all-time favorites, Rose Maddox. Bobby would join Charlie and the Sugartimers on occasion for events they played for the Texas Panhandle Heritage Foundation, who manages the world-renowned play, *Texas*. Bobby performed many summer shows at the popular tourist venue, the Big Texan Steakhouse, where he would call on his friend, Charlie Phillips as his special guest. Years later, Charlie and Bobby worked together at the 45 & Uppers Good Times Dance Club. Also, Hughes worked a stint with Charlie at KZIP radio station. His son is the drummer, Billy Hughes.

Hughes, Dudley- One rarely hears the name Charlie Phillips mentioned without Dudley Hughes' name emerging. Before all the fame of "Sugartime," Dudley Hughes was just one of the guys who had the same dream as Charlie. He was an original Sugartimer, before the Sugartimers even existed, alongside Charlie, Jimmy Schell and James Norton as the guys played in their first band, Hernando's Hideaway. These guys were all peas in the pod so to speak. Dudley graduated a year after Charlie from Farwell High School. He was such a laid back type of person the other guys nicknamed him "Droopy." Dudley would be one of the first guys from Farwell to accompany Charlie playing on the *Louisiana Hayride*. The most common local establishment the boys played at was the Pioneer Club in Kenna, New Mexico. Dudley would usually be the band member stuck riding with Charlie when they traveled from gig to gig. The guys would load all the equipment up in Charlie's big Mercury and tie Dudley's bass to the top of the car. One of their early disaster stories occurred when Dudley purchased a French-made vehicle, a Renault, and decided he would drive Charlie to one of their gigs instead of taking Charlie's gas-guzzling Mercury. The boys loaded up their gear as always and filled the Renault with music equipment, tying Dudley's stand-up bass to the top of the French mobile. No one had considered the southerly-blowing high winds from the plains of New Mexico as the boys took off for their gig. With the bass attached to the top of the vehicle and the excess mass weighing the small auto down, the car would barely drive more than 20 miles per hour. The boys arrived at their gig over an hour late as people were starting to walk out the door. Needless to say, the Renault never made another musical trip with Charlie. Hughes often told the story of one trip the guys took to the *Louisiana Hayride*. The men all loaded their equipment in the car with the bass strapped to the roof and drove straight through from Clovis to the Shreveport Municipal Auditorium. The guys unloaded, entered onto the stage and played two numbers for the audience. When they were finished playing, they reloaded their equipment back into (and onto) the car, and drove the long ten-hour trip back that very night! Dudley would play bass on the first unissued recordings of "One Faded Rose" and "Sugartime" as well as the unissued cuts of "Be My Bride" and "Have I Stayed Away Too Long?" Dudley was multi-talented and could not only play bass, but could also play electric keyboards, a hammer dulcimer, and guitar. One guitar Dudley crafted himself- out of a toilet seat. He regularly played with Tiny Lynn over the years and would appear with the Tiny Lynn Band on KICA-TV in the Clovis area. He would also join the Border Town 4 Band as well as the Stella and the Fellas Band. The last time he would play with his longtime friend, Charlie, would be a guest appearance with the latter Sugartimers at the 45 & Uppers Club in Amarillo. Dudley went on to become a business person owning his own parts store in the Texico, Farwell and Bovina areas, but he continued to play music throughout his life.

Hunter, Ray- Ray Hunter was originally an Okie, who moved to the Amarillo area. He was an accomplished western swing drummer who worked with the Sugartimers on a regular basis, especially at the Aviatrix Ballroom or the Clover Club. He was a board member of the Western Swing Music Society of the Southwest out of Oklahoma City, OK. Over his career, he played with notables like Webb Pierce, George Jones, Ferlin Husky, Merl Lindsay, Wanda Jackson, Wynn Stewart, Stonewall Jackson, Willie Nelson and even Bob Wills, just to name a few. He too was inducted into the Western Swing Music Society of the Southwest Hall of Fame.

Hutcheson, Jerry- Jerry Hutcheson initially began playing with the Clovis rag-tag band, The Flips, but soon regularly performed in the Tiny Lynn Band. Tiny Lynn had a local television show in Clovis,

New Mexico and occasionally featured Charlie Phillips as a guest artist. This is where Charlie would meet Jerry for the first time. He was an excellent fiddler and once played with Spade Cooley. Jerry mainly backed the Sugartimers in the Clovis area. He filled-in at times as Charlie performed at an annual fundraiser show, and dance for the Farwell Convalescent Home held at the Holiday Inn in Clovis, NM.

Jackson, Bob- Bob Jackson worked with Charlie at KZIP radio in Amarillo, in fact, Charlie is quoted as saying he "was one of the best DJ's at KZIP." He was known for creating abundant characters and voices used as on-air personalities and in his commercial productions. "He could produce an ad that'd blow your mind," Charlie describes. While working at KZIP, Jackson played saxophone and sang with the Sugartimers at the Aviatrix and also collaborated with other area bands. Bob had worked at a big radio station in Los Angeles, California, but moved to the Panhandle where Ray Winkler, who had an eye for talent, hired him. He had a booming deep voice. After some time in Amarillo, Jackson moved to Wichita Falls where he recorded gospel music albums.

James, Otis- Otis was a big guy with a bigger heart. He was one heck of a western swing drummer and often worked with Rick Sudduth. Otis occasionally collaborated with the Sugartimers at the 45 & Uppers Club in Amarillo. Otis James was inducted into the Western Swing Society of the Southwest Hall of Fame. He also joined the society's Hall of Fame Band as they headlined regionally.

Kennahand, Johnny- Johnny was just a young man when he started working with the Sugartimers at the Playboy Club in Amarillo. He was principally a rock drummer, but he took to country well and proved himself on the western swing scene. He took Gary Thurlow's place when Gary moved on to greener pastures. Jon Sisco was lighting up the music scene when Johnny began playing country. Rumor has it Johnny eventually moved to Las Vegas and began a business career. No one knows if he continued his drumming.

Lynn, Tiny- Ah, heck, who knows how Lehman Lynn Denison came to be known as Tiny Lynn? Some say one night at the La Vista

Lounge in Clovis, Big Jim Bowman (and his Roadrunner band) couldn't pronounce or remember young Lehman's name when introducing him at the performance, so Jim announced him as Tiny, and the name stuck. "Let's give a big hand here to, to, to, Tiny Lynn!!!" Young Tiny began playing music shortly after his parents bought him a $10 Stella guitar when he was just seven years old. He and his brother, Coy, created and performed their first radio show receiving 15 minutes of airtime each Saturday afternoon on KENM radio in Portales. He would make his television debut at KSWS out of Roswell at 12 years old. By age 15, the young musician formed his first band with his older brother, Hubert, his younger brother, Coy, and Gary Beevers, and eventually started playing at the Red Onion in Clovis. They played all over eastern New Mexico and by 18 years old were getting paid $40 for two nights of playing music at the Pink Pony in Taiban, NM. Tiny is one of Charlie's closest and dearest lifelong friends. He was raised near Clovis in the town of Portales, New Mexico and it was here he'd meet Charlie and play as a Sugartimer in the premature Sugartimer days; however, of the musicians associated with young Charlie Phillips in the early days, Tiny would be one of the few who didn't jump on the "Sugartime" music-train. Tiny always marched to the beat of his own drum, or in his case, strummed to the beat of his own guitar. Lynn often played between Clovis and Portales at an establishment in Midway during the early years. Tiny worked at KZOL (now KIJN) radio from Farwell, TX. He played with Bob Tucker (the man who first recorded Charlie Phillips), with Tucker's Clovis-based Caron Records that produced the Sparkles and Murle Richardson, a man who is now in the Rockabilly Hall of Fame. Lynn would be one of the first to be recorded by Gary Beevers at Maunay George's home in Portales. Tiny Lynn would enjoy a rewarding music career spanning for decades in the West Texas and Eastern New Mexico regions. Over the years, Tiny would play with Odie James on drums and his brother, Coy Lynn on bass. Tiny Lynn's Cattle Capitol Boys was a favorite band to contend with in the day. Friends of Lynn's, Tommy Haney and the Rainbow Ramblers, worked out a deal with Tiny's band in the late 1950's alternating gigs at the La Vista Club in Clovis playing several gigs a week. It's worth mentioning, Tommy and his band would later backup both Wanda Jackson and Loretta Lynn at their musical appearances in Clovis, and their drummer, Doug Roberts, would win a Gold Record for his drumming on the Fireball's song, "Sugar Shack." KVER-TV in Clovis endorsed a local television segment with Lynn hosting and Charlie Phillips guest starring. Tiny is known for *Little Lehman's Half-Fast Songs*, which is a comedy act of sorts, with uncanny renditions of country songs. He had an extremely tight four-piece band that played locally and according to some, "never missed a beat." Tiny's band alternated with Charlie's band playing weekly for the Country Barn. Charlie wrote a song called, "Graveyard Waltz" for a Halloween event and Tiny recorded the song on his album, *Tiny Lynn*, on the Tinymite Records label. According to Phillips, "Tiny was always in high-demand. People loved his music." Tiny eventually worked a day job at the Attorney General's Office in Lubbock for Emil Schattel, a boss who had a long history in country music, especially with the West Texas Express band.

Marchbanks, Dwight- Dwight and his brother, Larry, always had some big shoes to fill when it came to music. Their father, Curtis Marchbanks, was a well-known bandleader of a western swing ensemble in the Panhandle with a huge following, but with that being said, Dwight perhaps learned many of his talents from his father. Curtis Marchbanks spent many years commanding his band at the Casa Del nightclub. Dwight played bass for the Sugartimers on several occasions at the Aviatrix in Amarillo. Dwight and his brother, Larry, played in a band formed by their father called the Kountry Kut-ups, playing nights and weekends across the Panhandle. In addition to many years as a musician, Dwight worked at the Curtis Sales parts business for much of his life.

Marchbanks, Larry- Like his brother Dwight, Larry always played in the shadow of his father's musical career, but he excelled nonetheless even in the aftermath of a tragedy. Larry and his brother Dwight were both in a tragic automobile accident leaving Larry in a wheelchair. This didn't stop Larry from pursuing his dream to be a musician. Larry, was an unbelievable steel guitar player, but after the advent of the accident was unable to continue playing steel guitar. He picked up the guitar instead and mastered it as well as he had the steel. Charlie exclaimed he was "one helluva player" and "he could hit licks like you never heard" as Larry performed with the Sugartimers at the Aviatrix. The Aviatrix had not initially been constructed for wheelchairs, so the guys all chipped in and built a ramp for Larry, who would roll in and out of the location with his guitar and amp piled on his lap, accepting help from no one. He would also accompany his brother in their father's band, the Kountry Kut-ups, in addition to other great local bands.

Marcum, Larry- Larry Marcum played lead guitar with the Sugartimers for quite some period when they performed at the Aviatrix in Amarillo. Marcum often worked for himself or Don Clay as a cement contractor, but let loose in the evenings doing what he loved. Marcum was a musician who started off as a rock 'n' roller but adapted his style to accommodate the western swing and country-feel, almost coming across as Nashville-sounding. Charlie Phillips secretly stated he thought Marcum was less interested in participating with the Sugartimers than he was in playing Charlie's prized Les Paul Gibson- a treat for anyone really.

McClure, Chuck- Chuck played both guitar and bass on a limited basis with the Sugartimers, but boy could the man could play. He often worked with Gary Thurlow in a band they had formed. If Charlie needed, Chuck was continuously willing to join the Sugartimers at the Aviatrix. Perhaps McClure is most known for performing with Buddy Holly in the younger days and for his lead guitar work with the Checkmates, playing with other future Sugartimers like Larry Marcum and Gary Swafford.

McKee, Ron- Ron McKee played bass and sang with the Sugartimer band off and on over the years at the Aviatrix and accompanied the men to various out of town gigs. Ron moved from Oklahoma to Amarillo sometime in the 1970's and would travel the short drive south to Canyon, Texas to study music at West Texas State University (now West Texas A & M University). During the day, he was a heavy equipment operator, but in the evenings and weekends, Ron dazzled audiences with his vocal skills and his bass playing. McKee had the staff band at the local nightspot, the Cattleman's

Club, often working with fellow Sugartimers, Chano Preciado, Benny Couch and Jimmy Young.

Messer, Shorty- According to Charlie Phillips, when it came to steel guitar playing, Shorty was "one of the best." He could play virtually anything. Shorty was a laid back quiet sort of guy. The guys remember it would take a lot to get a rise out of him. Occasionally, Charlie and the Sugartimers would be hired to perform in the neighboring town of Canyon, Texas for one of the fraternity organizations. Before undergoing a name change to West Texas A&M University, West Texas State University housed many of the area's fraternities and sororities. On one occasion, the Sugartimers were to perform a "Cowboy-themed" country & western party and dance at a large building rented by the fraternity house. The frat boys were all dressed up in their cowboy gear, many of whom were either wearing cap guns or in some cases real guns that were to be unloaded of course. As the night marched on and after much alcohol consumption, one big ole' boy dressed in his rancher gear, pulled out his real pistol that happened to be loaded with blanks, but, of course, no one really knew. As he passed in front of the bandstand where Charlie and the boys were unsuspectingly playing, he pulled his six-shooter out of his holster and pointed it at Shorty Messer who was on the far side of the stage playing his steel guitar. Shorty froze when he saw the gun pointed directly at him; suddenly, the weapon fired! The debris from the blanks splattered all over Shorty's shirt and glasses. He was mortified. Bassist, Don Campbell, a man known for having a short fuse, gently sat his bass down on the stage and flew into the audience aiming straight for the gunslinger who was apologizing profusely. A scuffle ensued, and the shooter was ejected from the party. This instance was about the only time any of the guys had ever seen Shorty show any emotion. Shorty Messer played steel guitar for Bob Wills at a time when Wills had assembled an excellent troupe of musicians- even comprising of two steel guitar players at one time (the other being Bob White). Messer was recorded in Dallas on the 1952 MGM record of Bob Wills And His Texas Playboys playing "SNATCHIN' AND GRABBIN" written by Fred Rose and Ray Scrivner and sung by Joe Holley. Shorty appears with Bob White on "A Red Hot Needle And A Burning Thread" and "Steamboat Stomp," both on Wills' album. He appears on the 2001 release of

Bob Wills & His Texas Playboys- Boot Heel Drag: The MGM Years. Shorty performed on the song, "I'm Only a Friend Why Do You Call Me Your Sweetheart" by Wills on MGM with legendary steel guitar player, Bob White. It's possible considering the timeframe when Bob Wills cries out, "AHHH, Shorty" during the steel guitar breaks, he was immortalizing Shorty Messer within his music. Buddy McPeters wrote in a western swing discussion forum, "Shorty Messer is somewhat of a mystery, but he played a style of steel guitar that is talked about in steel guitar quarters in which he is elevated to legendary status by virtue of a handful of sides he cut with Bob Wills in Dallas on MGM. His solos are in the same class as [Billy] Bowman and [Bobby] Koefer both breathtaking and daring." Messer also played on a regular stretch with Lou Walker & The Western Playboys. At the request of Norman Petty, Shorty used his skills as steel guitarist on Jimmy Dean Self's 45 rpm recorded song, "An Old Christmas Card" produced on the NorVaJak label. Some have stated Shorty Messer was a very underappreciated steel guitar aficionado, but obviously Bob Wills, Lou Walker and Charlie Phillips saw something amazing in him. After years of steadfast playing, Shorty would be inducted into the Western Swing Music Hall of Fame. Shorty and Charlie stayed lifelong friends, even opening up an automobile body shop together at one time. Shorty Messer worked with Charlie and the Sugartimers for many years until he eventually moved to Colorado to retire and spend time with his son.

Mitchell, Mike- Mike Mitchell was a drummer who joined Charlie on some gigs around Clovis. He inaugurated his music know-how early and began perfecting his skills by age 15 in high school as he formed and played in the Blues Note Band around 1951 for Clovis High School. When Jack Vaughn left the Norman Petty Trio, Mike joined the trio with a music partnership lasting over 30 years. The three toured states in the Southwest as well as Illinois and Michigan performing for both military and civilian crowds in some of the nation's finest ballrooms. Mike roughly played with the Sugartimers in the late 1950's drumming on some recordings of Charlie's at the Norman Petty Studio. One of the first Sugartimers, Jimmy Schell, was quoted as saying, "I was enthused when Mike played with us. I thought, man, we're in high cotton here!" He would join Charlie,

Jack Smith, Jack Vaughn, Joe B. Mauldin, Norman Petty and Bill Pickering on a recording session of Charlie's in September of 1959 to record "Welcome to the Wedding" and "No More Sugartime." Mitchell worked for quite some time with Charlie Phillips at KCLV radio in Clovis as a disc jockey primarily playing pop music. Years later he would lend his drumming expertise to the Bill Case Country Band who played venues around the Clovis and Amarillo areas and also with the band called Moondance. Mike worked at Clovis Floral Co., his family's business.

Morris, Rooster- Rooster Morris is a larger than life man, as his name implies, and might be considered a Sugartimer only because he played fiddle and sang with the guys at the Aviatrix in Amarillo on a few select occasions. Rooster was a good-looking man with terrific stage presence and the few times he played with the Sugartimers, the crowd cheered after he sang. Mr. Crowd-pleaser was born for much bigger and better things. Throughout his life he became a very successful musician, songwriter and writer. Morris is the author of the much-loved children's book series, *Axle Galench*. Morris played fiddle for the celebrated Western Cowpunchers Association and has been recorded by the Smithsonian Institution playing traditional fiddle music. He also performed for children's author, John R. Erickson, on the wildly popular *Hank the Cowdog* audiobooks playing fiddle, guitar and performing vocal harmonies. It's been told this larger than life man has performed for over two and a half million children since publishing his first book. Morris was featured in *Southern Living Magazine* in January of 2007. Legendary fiddle player, Jimmy Young, affirmed Rooster "was one of my favorite guys to hear play."

Nemire, Terry- Terry Nemire worked with Charlie at KZIP radio in Amarillo. He was one heck of a radio DJ and was very popular on the airwaves. Terry collaborated with the Sugartimers as a drummer primarily at the Rainbow Ballroom when Ray Winkler, Johnny Hathcock and Charlie Phillips owned it.

New, L.E.- Ray Price once called an audition in Amarillo hiring musicians for an upcoming show he would be headlining. L.E. answered the call and put forth one heck of an audition, but the man hiring for Price had a particular problem with New- he couldn't read music. What they could have never known was that New happened to be one of the greatest fiddle players in the world and could play *precisely* by ear. Charlie would brag L.E. didn't know one key from the next, but the moment the Sugartimers began their song, no matter what key it was played in, L.E. would hit the right note every single time. L.E. played with the Sugartimers off and on over the years at the Aviatrix and the 45 & Uppers Club. He would eventually leave Amarillo and become a businessman down south. His biggest claim to fame is developing and owning the very popular and successful secret recipes for the famous Red Creek Mesquite Flavored All-Purpose Marinade, Red Creek Mesquite Flavored Jerky Marinade, and Red Creek Mesquite Flavored Bold & Spicy All-Purpose Marinade. L.E. located his nationwide headquarters in Amarillo, Texas and would steal more than 20 first place awards from his competitors since 1995.

Norton, James- James Norton was a distant cousin of Charlie's who grew up and graduated from Farwell. He was from a farm family in Parmer County with an older brother, Darrell, who was Charlie's best childhood friend. He played with Charlie a lot in the early Clovis days, both before and after "Sugartime" became a success, but he would never record with Charlie. The boys performed together at talent shows around Farwell and the Muleshoe areas and also played on Charlie's live radio show at KCLV. In later years, James and his young son, along with another youngster, all tragically died in a small plane crash on a farm near Farwell, Texas.

Paulk, Steve- Steve was an entertaining rock and country singer who came to Charlie fresh out of high school. Charlie thought he was such an excellent showman that he used Steve in several of his acts at the Aviatrix, which the crowd loved. "That boy had some moves, I'll admit," chuckles Charlie in remembrance. Steve never got paid to perform at any of the local shows, but Charlie took him on the road a few times so he could earn a little money for his talents. Paulk loved rock' n' roll as well as country and moved out to Nashville for a while where it's rumored he even got his own songs recorded.

Pearson, Jimmy- Not much is remembered about Jimmy Pearson other than he worked with Charlie in the early Clovis area days. He accompanied the guys as lead guitarist on many occasions. Jimmy would also work with Tiny Lynn on several of his projects.

Perrin, Rex- Rex Perrin was a suave dresser and always appeared quite dapper. He more enjoyed jazz and pop, but could pull off western swing with ease. Perrin often worked with Carlton Scale's big band at the Aviatrix and was respectably the trumpet player. He worked in radio sales during the day and blew his trumpet nightly. After the era of big band music, he would continue working some at the Aviatrix with Charlie playing country and western swing.

Pettigrew, Joe- Joe was an excellent drummer who moved temporarily from Clovis to Amarillo so he could attend barber school. While in Amarillo, he approached Charlie, who allowed him to begin playing with the Sugartimers. He did so throughout his barber schooling until he eventually moved back to Clovis and opened up a barbershop of his own. He would rejoin Charlie and the guys later in life and would occasionally play some gigs with the fellows.

Phillips, Dean- Dean Phillips was a bass player who worked with the Sugartimers at the Aviatrix. Almost as much as his music, he's remembered for his red hair. In addition to being an outstanding bass player, Dean was a darn good vocalist. Dean worked with both Lou Walker and Curtis Marchbanks.

Preciado, "Chano" Louis- It's rumored Louis "Chano" Preciado was an early drummer for the rocker band, The Checkmates, before he resigned and was replaced by Dick Miller, who had been with The Cinders. Chano may have started off as a rock drummer, but he adapted quite nicely to the country and western swing scene. He worked some nights at the Aviatrix with the Sugartimers, but most conspicuously he worked seven nights a week as the staff drummer for the Cattleman's Club off East Amarillo Boulevard. He collaborated with Benny Couch and Ron McKee too.

Redwine, Buster- Chet Calcote introduced Buster Redwine to Charlie explaining Buster's specialty was western swing. Buster was a firefighter with a passion for music, but alas, was always on call and could only fill-in as a Sugartimer when his job would allow him time away. He played guitar and excited audiences with his vocals when singing his version of George Straight's songs. He regularly joined Chet and Jimmy Young on gigs and played with various other bands like Cowjazz Western Swing. Buster joined the Sugartimers at the 45 & Upper's Club and even helped Charlie work a benefit for the Amarillo Little Theater.

Roberts, Doug- Doug Roberts was a Farwell boy who graduated high school soon after Charlie. Charlie and the Sugartimers gave Doug his first big break as a serious drummer and musician- the rest is history. Folks categorically remember him as a spunky hell raiser who wasn't afraid to speak his mind. Doug's talents as a drummer seemed to come naturally and in 1958, he joined up with Tommy Haney and the Rainbow Ramblers, which included Doug on drums, Bennie Summers on steel guitar, Bill Anson on bass and Tommy Lee Haney on lead guitar and vocals. Soon after that, Roberts would be asked to audition for the then unheard of Fireballs and would be hired. It wouldn't be too long after he joined the band, the mega-hit from the Fireballs, "Sugar Shack," became the No. 1 song in the country. Doug took time from his schedule to work with Charlie and the Sugartimers on a few gigs around the Clovis area. Charlie tells of a day when several of the guys from the area drove out to Buffalo Lake (near Canyon, Texas) in Doug's new Chevy convertible for an afternoon of boating, fishing and of course drinking. Doug inadvertently locked his keys in the car. In true form, Doug wouldn't let this curtail the boys' afternoon of fun, so he took out his pocketknife, sliced a hole in the convertible top, and retrieved his keys. The problem was solved. Doug continued playing in the area with two other Sugartimers, Dudley Hughes and Jimmy Schell.

Rogers, Charlie- Charlie Rogers was a foreperson for a construction company, but in his spare time drummed for a lot of local musicians and bands. He was a dependable player who never let the

Sugartimers down. He worked every Saturday night, most especially at the Aviatrix where he played for a couple of years.

Roundtree, Bobby- Bobby was a fellow DJ at KZIP radio after moving to Amarillo from the south. He was a big cut-up, and that made him perfect as an on-air radio personality. He was an excellent deejay and bass player who primarily worked with the Sugartimers at the Rainbow Ballroom.

Scales, Carlton- Scales is most known in Amarillo as one of the owners of the popular Aviatrix. Before western swing became the genre to dance to, Carlton headed up one of the Big Bands with a full ensemble of musicians. All of the Scales' kids grew up in the Aviatrix, even living in a home just a few steps from the famed ballroom. For many years, Carlton and his band played to packed houses at the Aviatrix starting as early as the 1940's.

Scales, Iweta- Iweta could be considered the mother of the big band era and the western swing age for the Texas Panhandle. She was the gal who got it all started when she opened up the Aviatrix Ballroom. Her wonderful sister was the ballroom's hatcheck girl who continued taking folk's hats for decades. The local radio stations like KZIP always announced the Aviatrix "had the oldest and best hatcheck girl in America" as their advertising ploy. Iweta's sister worked well into her 90's.

Scales, Margaret- Better known as Maggie Scales, this gal had music in her blood with her father Carlton as her educator. Maggie could blow the fiddle away often competing with Texas Playboy and Sugartimer, Jimmy Young, who she performed with on many instances. She recorded on occasion at the Norman Petty Studio and appeared as fiddle player on a Windy Wood album. Scales played with the Amarillo Symphony for over thirty years and helped open up a local music shop in Amarillo called Scales Strings and Things.

Scales, Tommy- The lanky Tommy Scales was a gifted drummer playing many engagements with the Sugartimers at the Aviatrix as well as other gigs in the area. He too was a member of the musically gifted Scales family. He was brilliant with other instruments like the keyboard, but only played drums when working with Charlie. Scales ultimately began working with a rock 'n' roll band and eventually hooked up with other artists in West Texas like the Larry Martin Band and became lead guitarist for Charley Pride and Bill Martin. Tommy's musical talents would transcend to the studio as he worked as a sound engineer for The Cadillac Jack Band and owns the TCS Productions recording studio. Scales married Buddy Holley's niece and sometimes performed events with his wife, honoring the real Buddy Holley. Tommy's siblings, Carlie, Frankie and Sherry Scales all went on to outstanding careers in music.

Scalise, Odie- Not a lot is known about Odie (including the correct spellin' of his name). Odie might have been from Dumas, Texas. He did play with various bands in the Panhandle, this is known. Frank Hardcastle introduced this talented drummer to Charlie. Odie played off and on with the Sugartimers for a couple of years, but the guys lost track of him as time marched on.

Schell, Jimmy- Jimmy Schell grew up on a farm about five miles south of the Phillips' family farm outside Farwell. If anyone knew anything about Charlie's good friend Jimmy, it was that he did not drink alcohol, and he was almost always the designated driver for the group of young partying musicians. Even though Jimmy was always sober, it didn't mean he was the most careful driver. Guys that hung with Jimmy in the early days tell the same story of almost dying once when Jimmy was at the wheel. Schell was driving Charlie's 1954 Oldsmobile 88 with Roy Snodgrass, Carroll "Lash" LaRue, Charlie and maybe three other guys crammed into the car as the group was heading to Grady, NM to pick up some beer, as Clovis was, of course, dry in those days. The guys were flying down the street in that big Oldsmobile, yet no one noticed they were heading down a dead-end road that was ultimately blocked by posts. By the time Jimmy saw they were going to crash into the dead-end, he had moments to slam on the breaks as the car spun briskly around and into a field. Charlie thinks there were seven guys in that car that needed to change their shorts. Nonetheless, Jimmy was a superb guitarist with an excellent voice. Schell played rhythm guitar on Charlie's first 1956 demo recording of "Sugartime" and the unissued demo of "One Faded Rose." He would also record another two songs with Charlie at the Norman Petty Studio. Jimmy decided he just might become a professional guitar player, so he made a trip to Plainview, Texas to retrieve a Gibson ES5 Switchmaster he had purchased on credit at a music store. The price of the guitar in the 50's was around $1000- a whopping amount of money to pay for a musical instrument in those days! Yet, Jimmy learned to master that guitar and performed lots of local gigs around Clovis with Charlie. He could mimic Charlie and Buddy Holly's introduction to "Sugartime" almost exactly as the two had done it. To make a long story short, Jimmy met a gal at an American Legion dance one night and fell in love, they married, and that was about the end of Jimmy's musical career. Jimmy was going to let the Gibson guitar be repossessed by the music company, but Charlie stepped in and purchased the remainder of the note. This was the same guitar many years later was almost destroyed when Forrest Hanson fell off of the bandstand. Schell remained a lifelong friend of Charlie's and has become quite the music historian around Clovis.

Scott, Bill- Bill Scott is remembered as a good bass player. He played on occasion with the Sugartimers at the Aviatrix. Bill also was a regular patron of the club and brought his wife most every week so they could dance.

Scott, Russell- Russell is the bass player, Bill Scott's, son. He was a drummer with movie star good looks who played on occasion at the Aviatrix. Although it's not known, a couple of artists believe Russell moved on to play with some large bands in both rock and country genres.

Sheetz, Hayden- Hayden Sheetz was an airman stationed at the Cannon Air Force Base outside of Clovis. Like Jimmy Schell, he was a teetotaler and refrained from any alcohol, but don't let that fool you, he was a cut-up and funny entertainer. Originally a Yankee from Pennsylvania, he found himself in the middle-of-nowhere, New Mexico, where he occupied his free time playing rhythm guitar and singing. He participated with Charlie at many of the clubs in the surrounding area. Charlie always thought of him as a great showman.

Sherwood, Benny- Benny Sherwood was a friend of Charlie's who was stricken with blindness from childhood, but that never stopped him from using his musical talents. He worked at a bar just west of the Aviatrix and was known throughout town for his successful one-man-band. Benny had a great voice and played rhythm guitar as he filled-in from time to time with the Sugartimers. The talented singer was brilliant as a backup singer. He's always been the easiest to find onstage- donning his dark sunglasses.

Sisco, Jon- Jon was a sure and accomplished bass player with a musical career spanning decades. He was one of the guys who first started the band, The Electras, with Eugene Brown and Bobby Hacker. Sisco later started his own band by the early 1960's called The Jon Sisco Quartet. He would be intimately involved with the music business throughout his life, releasing his own records and eventually producing some top-notch acts. It would be Jon Sisco's prompting leading Charlie to cut the *Full Circle* album. Jon spent years working on and producing this album for Charlie.

Skidmore, Bill- Bill Skidmore was on a regular roster as a Sugartimer during the Aviatrix years. He worked over a year with the band. Charlie is quoted as saying Bill "was one of the smoothest drummers I ever worked with." He was a great country music drummer who also worked with other popular bands throughout the Panhandle.

Smith, "Smitty"- Smitty was a musician who drummed for the Sugartimers intermittently during the Sugartimers' reign at the Aviatrix in the late 1970's and 1980's. He was well liked by the band members and the patrons.

Star, Dennis- Dennis was a tall Native-American artist and an exceptional lead guitarist, saxophone player and vocalist who met Charlie through the Amarillo Air Force Base. He played with the Sugartimers off and on at the Aviatrix in Amarillo and other local venues. Over his career, Dennis put out some of his own recordings and worked with his personal band out of Tulsa, Oklahoma meeting with much success.

Steagall Red (Rusty)- Known as one of the greatest American storytellers of our time, Red or "Rusty" as the guys knew him, met Charlie sometime in the 1960's. If one hears Red's name today, one probably thinks of his involvements and presentations of cowboy poetry and rightfully so- he's one of the best. Although a talented musician, Red wasn't a Sugartimer, but he would bring Charlie some of his early songs to see if Charlie wanted to record them. Steagall became a successful record producer and asked Charlie to join him in California where Red produced a few songs for A&R man, Jimmy Bowen, on the Warner Bros./Reprise label, seeing only mild success. Red saw many accomplishments of his own as a recording artist, songwriter, radio personality, television actor and movie star. He made appearances on *Hee Haw* and *Nashville on the Road* to name a few. He also hosted a syndicated radio program called *Cowboy Corner*, as well as *In the Bunkhouse with Red Steagall* on RFD-TV. Red appeared in motion pictures like *Benji the Hunted*, *Dark Before Dawn* and *Abilene*, as well as produced the motion picture, *Big Bad John*. Red Steagall is credited with discovering the bright and talented Reba McEntire. He released an album entitled *Here We Go Again* featuring duets with Charlie Daniels, Larry Gatlin, Ray Benson, Toby Keith, Neal McCoy, Reba McEntire and Charley Pride. Although Red had charted many songs over his career, two favorites were "Someone Cares for You" and "Lone Star Beer and Bob Wills Music." In 1991, the Texas Legislature named Red The Official Cowboy Poet of Texas, and he is also the official Cowboy Poet Laureate of San Juan Capistrano, California. He was inducted into the Hall of Great Westerners in the National Cowboy and Western Heritage Museum in Oklahoma City and was also inducted into the Texas Cowboy Hall of Fame in Fort Worth, Texas. Steagall has received the "Spirit of Texas" Award and is inducted into the Texas Rodeo Cowboy Hall of Fame. Charlie Phillips is grateful to have been friends with and is appreciative of his hard work on his Warner Bro.'s (Reprise) recordings.

Stephens, Marcus- Marcus was not a Sugartimer but did play at times with Charlie, who recognized Stephens's talents. Attempting to be a mentor, Charlie always encouraged the shy musician to branch out and begin doing his own thing. "He's a remarkable singer and guitar player," Charlie says. Marcus, or Mark as Charlie calls him, headlines a very sought after band in the Amarillo area.

Sudduth, Rick- Rick was a fantastic fiddle player who often played when Jimmy Young wasn't available. Like Jimmy, Rick also worked with the Texas Playboys, resounding the music of Bob Wills from yesteryear. Sudduth collaborated with the Sugartimers at the 45 & Uppers Club and would be seen on occasion rosining his bow and entertaining audiences at the Big Texan Steak Ranch in Amarillo. Rick had lost his middle and ring finger in a cotton gin (feeder machine) accident over fifty years ago, but that never slowed the country music cowboy down. The fiddle was his most prized musical instrument, but he was accomplished with other apparatuses as well, namely the guitar. He and his brother had pooled their money when Sudduth was 14 years old and purchased their first guitar from a Sears catalog. Rick and his family grew up about 45 miles east of Lubbock on a rural farm in Crosby County. Like many farm families of the day, young Sudduth enjoyed the pleasure of listening to the radio where he'd hear the music of the Chuck Wagon Gang and the sounds of the Stamps Quartet. Rick played in two Crosby County bands, the West Texas Express and the very popular Texas band, Blue Denim. After moving to Amarillo, Rick would collaborate with several local western swing bands and would become instrumental to the success of the Sugartimers. Over time, Rick began performing with his wife, Brenda, with Blue Denim II and even asked other talented musicians to join him when he performed with Blue Denim II and Friends. He became friends and colleagues with renowned musicians like Jimmy Young and Dwight Cook. Cook nominated Sudduth for Oklahoma's Swing Music Society of the Southwest Hall of Fame where he was inducted in 2008. Cook was quoted in a *Lubbock Avalanche-Journal* article stating, "Rick does things on that fiddle with two fingers that a lot of people can't do with four," adding, "He's got a lot of talent." Sudduth would begin teaching music lessons from his home showing other folks how to play the music he most undoubtedly cherished.

Swafford, Gary- Gary played drums with Ray Ruff and the Checkmates and with future Sugartimers like Chuck McClure on lead guitar and Larry Marcum on guitar. Gary was a great drum soloist who recorded a lot of sessions at the Norman Petty Studio for various bands over the years. Gary played with notable talented musicians in the area like Earl Whitt, Steve Dodge, Jon Sisco, Chuck Tharp, Tom Beck, Jerry Hodges and Chico Apodacca. He is known for his work with the "electric surfer music" band, the Fayros, who recorded for RCA Victor. Swafford played a few times with the Sugartimers at the Aviatrix.

Terry, Rex- Rex Terry came from a musical family. He regularly worked with Charlie and the Sugartimers in the 1960's, traveling and working at airbase gigs. Rex was a very talented bass player and stayed in close touch with Charlie over the years. He teamed up with Charlie and the Sugartimers in latter years for a few gigs. Rex's brother, Roy, was also a talented musician who worked at the Avalon before "Honest" Jess became the staff musician and bandleader.

Thompson, Wayne- Wayne had his own personal band and played across the street from the Aviatrix at a little nightclub. When his gig ended, he often brought an instrument over and sat-in with the Sugartimers. He became such a fixture at the club, Charlie often allowed him to head the show if Charlie was called out of town for a larger event.

Thurlow, Gary- Gary's first gig was with a couple of friends at a beatnik coffee house on Polk Street in Amarillo, Texas in 1958. His drum set consisted of a snare and a large ashtray stand for his cymbal. The guys didn't get paid for their work, but they could have their pick of free tea. He moved forward that year working a few times with Jimmy Cano and The Bop Kings. Thurlow formed his own group in the late 50's or early 60's called The Chips. Gary played drums, Eugene Brown sang vocals, Tommy Ewton played lead guitar, and Tom Beck performed on bass. The band broke up after six months. Thurlow sat in with Bobby Hacker and The Electras for a few gigs before moving on to Kenneth Trent & The Continentals where he played with Charles McClure, a mean strat player. He then joined The Jon Sisco Quartet. Thurlow played with Jerry & The Sparkletones before drumming with Ray Ruff and the Checkmates. During 1961 and 1962, Gary worked with Red Steagall,

Donnie Lanier and then eventually became a Sugartimer when Charlie was with Columbia Records.

Trider, Larry- It's clear Larry Trider was one of the finest country musicians to play in the Panhandle of Texas and eastern New Mexico. But try as he might, Larry never could get his big break in the music industry, as a big "hit" seemed always a grasp away. Larry grew up in the Panhandle originating from Lazbuddie, Texas. He was a strapping young man standing six-feet-two. By age 16, he had formed his own band, Larry Trider and the Nomads, who began traveling the country from venue to bar. Charlie had met the young artist while Larry was in the Clovis area, inviting him to play with the Sugartimers on many regular gigs. With his musical talent, it wouldn't be long before Trider would venture out and begin a recording career of his own. His first known record would be recorded in April of 1961 and be released on the Roulette Record Label with "Don't Stop" on the A side (co-written by Norman Petty) and "The Ha Ha Song" on the flip side. His next three known records would be registered with Norman Petty on the NorVaJak label prompting Norman Petty to call his contacts at Coral Records. He would also record with Amy Records and Ranwood Records over his career. Larry and his band paid their dues while traveling the circuit incorporating 42 states. While on the road, Trider made a lucrative connection in Las Vegas at the Golden Nugget and began playing as a nightly regular with the *Larry Trider Show*. Many young and budding artists appeared as guests on Larry's show as he continued to make needed connections in the music industry like Tanya Tucker, Glen Campbell and lifelong friend, Waylon Jennings. After Vegas, he constantly made music and traveled the country, even making many appearances back in the Panhandle as he played clubs like the Cotton Club and the large crowd capacity, Red Raider Inn. Larry was known for having a good voice, but most importantly, he surrounded himself with some of the finest musicians. Even though he was wildly popular on the club circuit, had several records released, and played nationally, Larry never could bolster a chart-topping song. He would again play on occasion with the Sugartimers, reliving his younger days, but would never truly be recognized for his country music talents. Charlie took Trider with him on a trip to the annual

Deejay Convention held in Nashville where the boys once again stayed at the Andrew Jackson Hotel. As the night progressed, there came a knock at the door. When they opened up, there was Hank Snow standing in the doorway holding up an inebriated Larry Trider asking, "Does this fellow belong with any of you?" They shuttered to tell the great Hank Snow, "Yes. Bring him on in." It was apparent Larry had visited too many record company's hospitality suites that evening.

Vihil, Johnny- Johnny was referred to Charlie by other local musicians in the field and was always glad to help when the need arose. He played both drums and bass several times when the Sugartimers were in need down through the years. Like many musicians, he too performed with various bands in the area.

Walker, Howard- Howard Walker was a darn good saxophonist with a great voice to boot. Folks enjoyed his sense of humor, as Walker was known to be quite the comedian. Howard worked for some time with Charlie at KZIP radio in Amarillo. Former Sugartimers reminisce, speaking fondly of Howard's excellent voice. Walker moved on and worked for a spell at a radio station out of Dumas, Texas. Charlie talks about Howard Walker's disc jockey career and states he was, "one helluva DJ and sax player."

Walker, Lou- Lou Walker was another Texas Playboy playing and recording with the great Bob Wills on occasion until he branched out fashioning a band of his own. Lou became a famous fixture in the country and western swing scene. He was a "darned good" guitar player and singer who was much loved in the South. Walker recorded a couple of albums on his own seeing great local success, but perhaps not as much on the national level, even though his talents were often unequaled. After Charlie Phillips moved to Amarillo in 1960, Lou would often call Charlie up on stage at the famous dance hall in Amarillo, the Casa Del, announcing, "let's bring Jolly Cholly up onstage!" Since Charlie worked at KZIP radio, Lou would sometimes bring his newly recorded records in for Charlie to play on the radio. Eventually, Lou Walker would begin to retire from his ballroom days and would purchase a pig farm in Arkansas settling into life on his land. His son, Tink, was an amazing drummer who continued playing. A story Charlie always tells about Lou Walker involves a car. Charlie had traded a 60's model light pink Lincoln Premiere at a Clovis dealership. Lou Walker happened to be the next owner of the vehicle. Charlie told Lou what a great car it was and that assertion would prove to be an understatement. Heading back from an event, Lou would unfortunately be involved in a head-on collision with another vehicle while driving the solid steel American-made Lincoln. He survived. Lou would frequently mention had he not been driving that car when he had the accident, he would unlikely have survived.

Walker, Tink- Tink Walker was a talented drummer and worked from time to time with the Sugartimers at the Aviatrix Ballroom. Tink worked with various bands throughout his career and very notably, with his famous father, Lou Walker. The Sugartimers always enjoyed working with the larger than life drummer.

Wallace, Pete- Pete Wallace was another boy who grew up in the Clovis area when all of the musical action began to peak. He learned to master both the fiddle and guitar and became an excellent local musician. Pete was known to be "all business" when it came to music and never partook in alcohol, although he regularly worked in many of the bootleg joints in the area. He was already an accomplished musician before Charlie met him and would be one of the local guys who would show Charlie the ropes in his early days. "Pete was a good musician and I learned a lot from him," Charlie tells of his friend. Perhaps the earliest Sugartimer drummer is Gerald Brown, who happened to be Pete's brother-in-law. Wallace also worked on a limited basis with Tiny Lynn and Hershel Parker. Pete appears on Charlie's first 1956 recording of "One Faded Rose" and the very first demo of "Sugartime." He would also accompany Charlie, Dudley Hughes, Gerald Brown, Buddy Holly and Niki Sullivan to the Norman Petty Studios in April of 1957 to record the first demo version of Charlie's song, "Be My Bride."

Walton, Dee- The West Camp is exactly what its name implies; it was a western camp located within the boundaries of the original XIT Ranch and became a settlement location for several Texas families. Just eight miles southeast of Farwell, Dee Walton, hailed from the West Camp community where he and his family lived and worked. Dee might not be considered a Sugartimer, because "Sugartime" hadn't been written yet; however, Dee Walton was an influential fiddle player Charlie met in his early semi-professional days through Dee's son, Marvin Walton. Charlie would be invited to the Walton's home in West Camp where the family welcomed him to join with singing and playing of instruments as Charlie would take his banjo and do a little picking with the clan. It would be at Dee Walton's home Charlie would hear "Courtin' in the Rain" and "Put Your Arms Around Me," which became the first two songs Charlie would officially record in the early 1950's.

Walton, Marvin- Marvin and Charlie first became friends while attending Farwell High School. The two shared a passion for old jalopies, which they often traded. Marvin Walton first invited Charlie to the Walton home in West Camp, Texas, where Charlie would meet and essentially jam with the musical family. Charlie would take his banjo and attempt to join the festivities and he will readily admit, he couldn't even play three cords on a guitar yet. Marvin had a good deep singing voice.

Webb, Delbert- Delbert drummed for the Sugartimers a few times at the Aviatrix when needed. Tiny Duncan was the man who referred him to Charlie. Delbert would play with other local area bands like Frankie McWhorter, Bobby Koefer, Lee Barlow and Buster Redwine. He was always a joy to be around when he accompanied the Sugartimers. Years down the line, Delbert assisted Charlie by playing with the guys at a bar opening on Polk Street in Amarillo.

Welch, Truman- Truman Welch worked as a musician around the Clovis area for years. He not only worked with Tiny Lynn on some projects, but also he collaborated with Bob Tucker from the Tucker Recording Studio as well as Big Ed Hardage and the Texas Jay Boys. He was a guitarist working at many of the local venues like the La Vista, an area favorite serving Clovis as a motel, bar, and restaurant.

Wheeler, Lloyd- Lloyd was a classic country and western fiddler who also played the violin. He performed a couple of years with the Sugartimers during the Aviatrix era. Lloyd would play with several area bands but most notably, Bob Wills, Lou Walker and his band, in addition to touring with the highly sought after Merl Lindsay. He also knew classical music and would often surprise other band mates, as well as the audience, by switching up his genre midstream by playing a tune from say, Brahms or Beethoven. He was always known as a jokester and might yell at a rowdy spectator from the bandstand, "You better watch out! I might be drinking!" in attempts to lighten the mood of the audience.

Whisenhunt, Jim- Jim was a bassist working with the Sugartimers on occasion at the Aviatrix as a stand-in. He collaborated with other groups in the area. It is rumored Jim went on to play with larger more widely recognized groups, as with the wildly popular band, Cooder Graw, playing pedal steel guitar. (Actor Matthew McConaughey was listed as the executive producer on the first Cooder Graw album). His brother is the drummer, Mike Whisenhunt.

Whisenhunt, Mike- Mike made his home in Amarillo and played with various bands in the area. His wife worked for many years at a Potter County office. Mike performed some in the early years at the Aviatrix but chose a more docile, alcohol-free environment as years progressed. He continued to drum throughout his life and sat-in with the Sugartimers in latter years at the 45 & Uppers dance club. His brother is Jim Whisenhunt.

Whitt, Earl- Earl Whitt played fiddle, guitar and sang with the Sugartimers on a limited basis at the Aviatrix Ballroom in Amarillo. Earl was a local musician, perhaps better known for his work with the "electric surfer music" band, The Fayros, who recorded on RCA Victor Records with Earl playing lead guitar. He was also in a popular local band called The Tiaras, who released a record with Alliance Record Co. Whitt once worked for an Altec-Lansing and J.B. Lansing distributor. Earl was a talented all-around musician who adapted well to both country and western styles of music. In later years, Whitt would perform in his own one-man-band at the V.F.W. in Amarillo where he played for years.

Wilbanks, Glen- Glen was a friend of Charlie's in the early days and played some with the Sugartimers at the Aviatrix. Glen was multi-talented and could play drums, guitar and bass when needed.

Williamson, Kenneth- Kenneth played with the Sugartimers on a regular basis off and on for years. Charlie would marvel at his ability to walk his musical cords, stating, "I'd love to play like him." Williamson played with the Texas Playboys, Frankie McWhorter, Merl Lindsay and a lot of other great bands. "With Vic Ashmead on steel guitar, Jimmy Young on fiddle and Kenneth on lead guitar, they could blow your mind playing three-part harmonies!" Charlie exclaimed. "These three guys were always a big draw for the Sugartimers band." In later years, he played with Chet Calcote in the Over-the-Hill Gang. Williamson proudly worked as a postal clerk for the U.S. Postal Service for 30 years. In 2005, he was inducted into the Western Swing Society of the Southwest Hall of Fame.

Wynn, Bobby- If you could say one thing about Bobby Wynne, it was that he didn't need a microphone when he belted notes from his trumpet. Wynn played with the Sugartimers on a few occasions at the Aviatrix in Amarillo and filled-in when needed. He played steel guitar, but could blow the audience's mind when he performed on the trumpet. He was a good singer and would go on to form his own band. Wynn would cofound the Western Swing Music Society of the Southwest based out of Oklahoma City. Bobby also owned and operated Artist International Music Productions-Artist International Music Co., where he recorded and produced DVD's and CD's. He was also the owner and bandleader of the King of Western Swing Band specializing in classic country, western swing, jazz and Big Band genres of music.

Young, Hattie- Hattie Young was a very talented piano player known throughout the Clovis area. "One helluva musician," would be how Charlie described Hattie, who often invited Charlie onstage to do a few numbers with her. She played at many venues in Eastern New Mexico like the Holiday Inn and the La Vista, sometimes even playing with Tiny Lynn. "She will always be remembered as a good ole' gal," says Charlie. She was much beloved all over Clovis.

Young, Jimmy- Born in Dunbar, Oklahoma, a fledgling Jimmy Young would grow up in Tuskahoma and eventually move with his family to Oklahoma City, Oklahoma, where he started out as a teenager earning $25 a week working 10-hour days at the Humpty Dumpty grocery store. One summer, his brother tracked down Jimmy at a local swimming hole and told him a man was paying musicians $5 to play a few ditties at his beer joint in OKC. With his hair still wet and his damp swimsuit in his pocket, Young played at the bar and was offered the chance to play again the following Sunday afternoon. He performed on his fiddle for four hours and walked away with $20 in tips for only a half-day's work. Jimmy thought, "...boy this is for me." As he continued refining his skills and playing more often, young Jimmy Young's passion for western swing grew, and he honed his skills well enough to be introduced on KBYE radio. As they say, the rest was history. After completing his service in World War II, Jimmy would relocate to Amarillo, Texas somewhere around the early 1950's. Around 1964, Bob Wills was touring the country as a solo artist and came through Amarillo. Jimmy Young was asked to join up with Wills' newly formed band, with whom he played with off and on for many years. The illustrious Jimmy Young would perform with some of the finest musicians throughout his successful career, which spanned more than seven decades. After joining Bob Wills and becoming a member of the Texas Playboy family, Young would play with Hank Thompson, Lefty Frizzell, Ray Price and many other western and country legends including Charlie Phillips and the Sugartimers Classic Country Dance Band, who he played with off and on for more than 30 years. "I think he was one the best fiddle players in the country," adds Charlie. As late as 2012 he played with The Texas Playboys, which was still headed by Leon Rausch and Tommy Allsup. Jimmy was inducted into the Western Swing Society of the Southwest Hall of Fame in 2005 and would perform with the Texas Playboys at the Texas State Society's Black Tie and Boots Inaugural Ball in Washington, D.C. in 2009. It was very unfortunate, but Young was involuntarily pressured into working many years past when a man ought to. The door company Jimmy worked for many years as his day job filed for bankruptcy taking with it Jimmy's hard-earned retirement; however, he played on, doing the one thing he loved- tearing up the fiddle. When Jimmy

Young passed away on October 3, 2014 at age 85, there were no big parades or important write-ups in major country music magazines- just a few newspaper mentions and an eloquent obituary written by Young's grandson, Dustin Young. One of the paramount fiddle players who ever lived, Jimmy Young, silently passed leaving humanity with few recordings from his fiery fiddle and a lifetime of everlasting entertainment. There has been and might always be fiddle playing luminaries, but few may ever surpass the prominence of the late, great Jimmy Young.

Young, Dustin- Dustin Young won't always be remembered as *just* the grandson of the two talented West Texas musicians, Tom Hadaway and Jimmy Young. According to Charlie Phillips, Dustin is a virtuoso who not only picks up music quickly but also can play eloquently after hearing a song only once. Dustin's grandfather, Jimmy, talked Charlie into hearing the young man play and so he brought him onstage one evening. During a Sugartimer break, Charlie invited Dustin up to the 45 & Uppers to entertain for a moment while the other guys rested. Young played a classic piece and according to Phillips, "You could hear a pin drop." The crowd exploded in applause when Young finished! Tiny Duncan looked over at Charlie and said, "Boy, this guy's good." It wouldn't be long before Dustin would be invited to fill-in with the Sugartimers on a more regular basis. One evening the guys wanted to play a Chuck Berry song that Dustin had never heard before, and in moments, he was playing the song like he'd performed it his whole life. The Sugartimers might someday be credited with giving Dustin one of his first paying gigs. Should fate have it, great things will come from Dustin Young.

• It's important to note a lot of care and research went into locating and describing the men and women who played with Charlie over the course of six decades. Charlie has stated on many occasions that he surrounded himself with the best and the brightest musicians. He states he actually kept the Sugartimer band intact years after it should have expired- not only because the crowds were still entertained and danced to the music, but also because he wanted to keep many of his musician friends working.

This is the most inclusive compilation list relying primarily on the memory of those involved. It does *not* include all of the fine men and women who played as a Sugartimer. Both Charlie and the author sincerely apologize should anyone be left off this list. Additionally, some Sugartimers have a larger biography than others, which is not meant to intentionally favor some over others. It simply means more information was readily available on a particular individual via newspaper articles, magazine articles and the memory of folks who participated in the band during specific eras. Every person on this list was a contributing factor to the success of Charlie Phillips and the Sugartimer band.

In the *Amarillo Globe-News* feature article, "Band Entertains Audiences with Variety of Musical Styles- Bandstand," Charlie puts forth his best quotes concerning the Sugartimers, stating:

"Sugartimers come and go, according to who's ready to retire, or who's called away for another gig." When responding to the statement that time has moved on and no band member thinks he or she is more important than any other, he adds, "I can't tell them what to do, and I wouldn't want to…that's probably the reason we sound so good- because I get out of their way and let them play."

"I never claimed to be a hot shot musician," Charlie states, adding, "but I sure know one when I hear one and that's the trick to having a great dance and show band- the talent."

Chapter 13
Finale

Who could have foreseen that a young Texas farm boy who grew up in destitution would write and record a song heard by millions of music lovers throughout the world? "Sugartime" has been covered by hundreds (if not thousands) of artists worldwide and has been performed by churches, commercials, plays, musicals and purely loving individuals recapturing a simpler time in music history. There are currently dozens if not hundreds of renditions of "Sugartime" posted on the World Wide Web (WWW) easily viewed on YouTube or other venues. Some are brilliant and others are comical. Charlie finds many of these versions exciting, as he's happy to see so many people, especially young folks, taking an interest in his song decades after the original was released.

Charlie lost his father, two of his brothers, his sister and ultimately his mother, Ma Kate, who passed away in 1986 at 86 years young. Her tombstone would simply read, "I Am Home Now" as she was laid to rest in the Farwell, Texas cemetery. Charlie had lost his biggest fan and supporter. She watched the "tumor" grow into a fine young man as she supported his radio and music livelihood. From the first time he sat at a piano; to the first time he strummed a guitar; to his first job on Pop's radio station; to his first recording- Ma Kate was there.

Maybe it was Charlie's humble upbringing on the farm that kept him safe and sane throughout his years in the country music business. The boy called Scrooge wasn't one to take too many chances and still repeats the mantra, "A bird in the hand is worth two in the bush." He will tell you his biggest mistake in his career was to turn down the regular position on the *Grand Ole Opry*, but he wasn't about to gamble away a life he'd already built in Texas. Other artists like Waylon Jennings, Merle Haggard and Willie Nelson all bucked the Nashville system like Charlie did, but ultimately became highly successful in country music.

Charlie Phillips will tell anyone his career was plagued with poor management, other than Ray Winkler who worked hard setting him up with a few successful years at Columbia Records. A person can write the best song ever written and can sing it better than anyone, but if he or she can't get the song played before the masses, the song will die a sudden death. He witnessed this many times throughout his career.

It would be Ms. Jobes who would nurture Charlie's early singing voice and it would be Pop Echols who would give Charlie a career in radio as well as provide the initial money launching his recording career. The misunderstood Norman Petty would take Charlie's career to the next level. It's hard to speculate, but would Buddy Holly's music profession ever have become the success it was if not for Norman Petty? Would we have ever even heard of Buddy Knox? This question was asked of Charlie and he stated, "I think Norman Petty would have continued recording the music of many fine musicians, even if he never saw success. That's just the kind of guy he was."

One thing's for sure, had it not been for Buddy Holly's sudden rise in the late 1950's plus the fact he played on Charlie's dub of "Sugartime," Coral Records probably wouldn't have even listened to the song and the world would have never heard "Sugartime" as sung by the McGuire Sisters. It was Norman Petty who helped further the lives of so many musicians, including Charlie Phillips. "No one helped more people than I think Norman Petty did," he continues, "I watched so many times over the years as Norman got screwed over by the record companies." "I think he did more for rock 'n' roll than almost anyone."

Because of Norman Petty, Charlie lived a dream few can fathom. He not only met some of the biggest stars in country music, he became their contemporary and was offered the opportunity to play with them, as many of them performed with him. Norman was instrumental in the lives of so many musicians. If you visit the small town of Clovis, New Mexico there are no big signs commemorating the life of one of their greatest residents. The Norman & Vi Petty Rock & Roll Museum was ultimately created to commemorate the lives of the couple who changed the music world eternally. Charlie's music and photographs are displayed alongside greats like the Fireballs, Buddy Holly and the Crickets, The Roses, and so many other artists who were mentored by the musical genius.

The original Norman Petty Studio still stands right where it did at 1313 W. 7th St. when the hits began pouring out of the sleepy New Mexico town. The studio would have fallen into disrepair had it not been for Vi Petty, Kenneth Broad, John Ingman and so many others who had the forethought to preserve this important piece of music history. Norman and Vi's friend, Ken, dedicated much of his life to keeping the legacy of the Petty's alive for future generations. As of this writing, Ken still administers tours of the facility letting visitors stand and sit where the great Norman Petty and Buddy Holly made music history together. Charlie often wonders if he would have ever seen a musical career had the Petty studio not been so close to his home.

He never forgot his hometown of Farwell and returns as often as he can, witnessing the remnants of the town it once was. Most of the historic buildings have been destroyed and the town seems ghost-like in comparison to its early days. For many years Charlie performed at an annual fundraiser event for the Farwell Convalescent Home, just a small token of gratitude for the town that offered so much to the country farm boy.

Phillips settled in Amarillo when he moved there in 1960 to work for Ray Winkler at KZIP radio. He bought his first home there and has remained in the same house for decades. He still raises Terriers and likes to collect old vehicles. Charlie toured and played to live audiences until November 2013 when a problem with his heart was corrected with a pacemaker. After that, he tries to take it easy. He enjoyed one of the longest clandestine careers in country music history. "I'm grateful that things turned out the way they did. I watched so many of my friends get involved in taking drugs and drinking alcohol just to keep up with all the touring and recording. Maybe I'm still alive today because I refused to get caught up in that world. I've had a wonderful life and I don't have any real regrets."

When asked about his music career he humbly jokes, "Some people call me a one-hit wonder. I always tell them it's a wonder I had a hit at all. Men like Willie Nelson started at the bottom and worked their way to the top. I started at the top and worked my way to the bottom; however, my life has been a dream-come-true."

In Loving Memory of Albert Frank & Katherine Luella Massongill Phillips

Carthon Phillips- Born April 17, 1920
Married Nancy-
One daughter- Mary Catherine
Married Doris (Dee) Wallace
Two sons- Tracy and Todd

Mary Elaine (Sis)- Born September 14, 1921
Married John Tate
One daughter- Mary Charlotte
Married Carter Lawson
Married (Pete) Ralph Peterson

Albert Frank Jr. (Bunk)- Born December 6, 1922
Married Billie Louise Sharpe
Two boys- Albert III (Al) and Tyson (Ty)
Two girls- Linda and Connie

Glenn Darwin- Born November 5, 1927
Married Elizabeth (Liz) Yeary
Three boys- Craig and Thaddeus (Thad) and Frank
Two girls- Cynthia (Cindy) and Penelope (Penny)

Charles Don Phillips- Born July 2, 1934

Also in loving memory of John Ingman, Charlie's music historian friend from Great Britain, who passed away in December of 2015.

Charlie "Sugartime" Phillips Discography

(This is an incomplete compilation of Charlie's songs during his career. These are the most notable examples chronicled by BMI, various record labels, and verified through eyewitness verification. It's possible over time more recordings will surface).

1954 - 1955.

"Put Your Arms Around Me" (Unissued)
"Courtin' In The Rain"(Unissued)
"Almost" (Unissued)
"Too Old To Cut The Mustard" (Unissued)
"Release Me" (Unissued)
"Bully Of The Town"(Unissued)

1956.

"One Faded Rose"(Unissued Demo)
"Sugartime" (Unissued Demo)

1957.

"Be My Bride" (Demo)
"One Faded Rose"(Coral)
"Sugartime"(Coral)

1957 - 1958.

"Be My Bride" (Unissued)
"Have I Stayed Away Too Long?" (Unissued)

1958.

"Be My Bride"(Coral)
"Too Many Tears" (Coral)
"Faker"(Master destroyed)
"I Won't Be Around"(Master destroyed)

1959.

"Welcome to the Wedding"(Columbia)
"No More Sugartime"(Columbia)

1961.

"I Guess I'll Never Learn"(Columbia)
"Now That It's Over"(Columbia)

1962.

"No One To Love"(Columbia)
"'Til Sunday"(Columbia)
"Cancel the Call" (Columbia)
"You're Moving Away" (Columbia)

1963.

"The Street Of Loneliness"(Columbia)
"Later Tonight"(Columbia)
"This Is the House" (Columbia)
"Please Help Me Believe"(Columbia)

1965.

"The Big Ball Is In Cowtown"(Longhorn)
"Rainbow In The Valley"(Longhorn)

1967.

"The Bridge I Can't Burn"(Reprise)
"Souvenirs of Sorrow"(Reprise)
"Be Careful, Walk Easy, Go Slow"(Reprise)
"I'm Trapped"(Reprise)

1968 - 1969.

"Your Going Is Coming"(K-Ark)
"Just Let The Flowers Grow"(K-Ark)
"Twenty Fools Ago"(K-Ark)
"Blue Blue Bottle"(K-Ark)
"Ballad Of Bill Jones"(K-Ark)
"Before The Next Daybreak's Gone"(K-Ark)

1974.

"Bend Me Straight Again"(Artco)
"Who Are You"(Artco)
"I Walk Alone Tomorrow"(Artco)
"The Big Ball Is In Cowtown"(Unissued)
"Sugartime"(Unissued)
"I'm Giving Her Love"(Artco)
"Rainbow In The Valley"(Unissued)

1976 - 1977.

"The Big Ball Is In Cowtown"(Unissued/ K-tel)
"I Guess I'll Never Learn"(Unissued/ K-tel)
"Sugartime"(Unissued/ K-tel)

1977.

"Wild Side Of Houston"(Spirit)
"No Greater Love"(Spirit)

1980.

"Goin' Away"(Oak)
"No Greater Love"(Oak)

1980 - 1983.

"Lonely Women (Make Good Lovers)"(SMG)
"More And More"(SMG)
"Nuevo Laredo"(SMG)
"Back In The Shadows"(SMG)
"Yesterday Passed My Way Again"(SMG)
"Memory Number One"(SMG)
"Now That It's Over"(SMG)
"It's A Heartache"(SMG)
"Going Away"(SMG)
"Brother Jukebox"(SMG)
"Shambles Of My Home"(SMG)
"Woman, Woman"(SMG)
"Souvenirs Of Sorrow"(SMG)
"Bye Bye Love"(SMG)

1987.

"Has Anyone Seen Me Lately?"[Windy Wood]
"Where Do I GO From Here?"[Windy Wood]
Unknown"Faker"
"Hurry Up Sundown"
"I'll Take What's Left Of You"
"Listen (Could It Be Her)"
"Phoney Angel"
"You're My LSD"
"R & R Medley"

Care to Order Charlie's CD, *Charlie Phillips Sugartime?*

Please visit: www.bear-family.com

BOOKS You Might Enjoy Reading

*The King of Clovis Norman Petty: American Music Legend
The Man Behind Rock 'n' Roll's Greatest Artists*
By Frank Blanas
Rollercoaster Books, A Division of Rollercoaster Records

Whatever Happened to Peggy Sue? A Memoir by Buddy Holly's Peggy Sue
By Peggy Sue Gerron and Glenda Cameron
TogiEntertainment

Remembering Buddy
By John Goldrosen and John Beecher
Penguin Books

The Last Rock and Roll Show
By Danny White
White Holdings LLC-Sixteen Ton Press

Tillman Franks: I Was There When It Happened
By Tillman Franks (Robert Gentry as Interviewer)
Sweet Dreams Publishing Company

Those Who Made the Music in Clovis and Outlying Areas
By Don McAlavy
City Printing Inc. Clovis, NM

Buddy Holly Day-by-Day (Books 1-5),
By Bill Griggs
Rockin' 50s

Historic Amarillo- An Illustrated History
By Mike Cox
Historical Publishing Network, a Division of Lammert Publications, Inc.

Amarillo- The Story of a Western Town
By Paul H. Carlson
Lubbock: Texas Tech UP

A.O.K.: Record Labels of West Texas & New Mexico
By John Ingman
Ingman Music Research

Cricket's Fact File
By John Ingman
*Possibly Sold Out

American Wax Facts Vol.1 1950 – 1951
American Wax Facts Vol.2 1952 – 1953
American Wax Facts Vol.3 1954 – 1955
By John Ingman
(Loose Pages)

What a Wonderful World: A Lifetime of Recordings by Thiele
By Bob Thiele and Bob Golden
New York City: Oxford UP, 1995
www.oup.com

Magazines

American Music Magazine
www.americanmusicmagazine.com

Accent West Magazine
Accent West | Facebook

Texas Monthly
www.texasmonthly.com

Grand Ole Opry: WSM Official Opry Picture History Book

Rockin' 50's Magazine
www.rockin50s.com

Just for Fun Websites

www.charliesugartimephillips.com

www.rollercoasterrecords.com
www.thecrickets.com
www.16ton.com
www.buddyhollyandthecrickets.com
www.hillbillyhits.com
www.billboard.com
www.rockhall.com
www.buddyhollycenter.org
www.royorbison.com
www.rockabillyhall.com
www.vh1.com
www.buddyhollylives.info

You've Just Gotta Visit These Places - Bucket List

Texas Country Music Hall of Fame
310 W. Panola Street
Carthage, Texas 75633
(903) 694-9561
www.carthagetexas.us/halloffame/

Norman & Vi Petty Rock & Roll Museum
105 E. Grand Ave.
Clovis, New Mexico 88101
(575) 763-3435
www.pettymuseum.com

The Norman Petty Studio
1313 W. 7th St.
Clovis, New Mexico 88101
(575) 763-3435

The *Grand Ole Opry* at the Ryman Auditorium
116 5th Ave N
Nashville, Tennessee 37219
(800) 733-6779
www.opry.com

The *Grand Ole Opry* House
2804 Opryland Drive
Nashville, Tennessee 37214
(800) 733-6779
www.opry.com

The Shreveport Municipal Auditorium
705 Elvis Presley Avenue
Shreveport, Louisiana 71101
(318) 841-4196
www.shreveportmunicipalauditorium.com

Country Music Hall of Fame
222 5th Ave. South
Nashville, Tennessee 37203
(615) 416-2001
www.countrymusichalloffame.org

Branson Missouri
(417) 334-3345
www.cityofbranson.org

Tootsies Orchid Lounge
422 Broadway
Nashville, Tennessee 37203
www.tootsies.net

Buddy Holly Center *plus*
Jerry Allison's childhood home where Buddy and J.I. wrote "That'll Be the Day"
1801 Crickets Avenue
Lubbock, Texas 79401
(806) 775-3560
www.buddyhollycenter.org

Texas Tech University Southwest Collections/Special Collections Library (On the Texas Tech Campus)
2500 Broadway- Main Campus
Lubbock, Texas 79409
(806) 742-3749
www.swco.ttu.edu

TEXAS Outdoor Musical (*TEXAS* Musical Drama)
Set in Palo Duro Canyon near Amarillo, TX and Canyon, TX
www.texas-show.com

Panhandle-Plains Historical Museum
2503 4th Ave.
Canyon, Texas 79015
(806) 651-2244
www.panhandleplains.org

American Quarter Horse Hall of Fame & Museum
2601 East Interstate 40
Amarillo, Texas 79104
(806) 376-5181
www.aqha.com

Heart of Texas Country Music Museum
1701 South Bridge
Brady, Texas 76825
www.hillbillyhits.com/museum
also www.texasfortstrail.com

Texas Music Museum
1009 East 11th Street
Austin, Texas 78702
(512) 471-0520
www.texasmusicmuseum.org

West Texas Music Hall of Fame
6204 S. Freeway
Fort Worth, Texas 76134
(817) 293-1333
www.westexmusichof.com

National Cowgirl Museum and Hall of Fame
1720 Gendy Street
Fort Worth, Texas 76107
(817) 336-4475
www.cowgirl.net

Springfield, Missouri
(417) 864-1000
www.springfieldmo.gov

Works Cited

Condray-Hancock, Charlene. Personal interview. 13 June 2013. Interview conducted by Curtis L. Peoples in Lubbock, Texas.

"'Gospel Music Man' Honored by Peers." Pampa Daily News 11 Aug. 1972, Pampa, Texas ed. Print.

Hank Snow Home Town Museum. Web. 23 June 2015. <www.hanksnow.com>.

Logansport Pharos- Tribune 2 Mar. 1958, Logansport, Indiana ed.: 13. Web. 10 Jan. 2014. <www.newspapers.com/image/#3916709>.

"'Sugar' Time Promised." *Miami Daily News*-Record 11 May 1958, Miami, Oklahoma ed. Print.

"'Sugartime' Camera Lied, Says McGuire." The Galveston Daily News 1996, Galveston, Texas ed. Print.

"Alan Freed - Wikipedia, the free encyclopedia." N.p., Web. 16 Jul. 2015 <http://en.wikipedia.org/wiki/Alan_Freed>."All About Buddy Holly

"Accident impairs, but doesn't stop, musician's playing..." N.p., Web. 01 Aug. 2015 <http://lubbockonline.com/stories/100709/fea_501863881.shtml>.

Allison, J.I. "Personal Telephone Interview." (Cricket's Drummer). Sep. 2013.

Associated Press. "McGuire Objects to Film Portrayal." News Record 21 Nov. 1995, North Hills, Pennsylvania ed.: 18. Print.

"BTD to Honor 'Sugartime' Charlie Phillips." State Line Tribune 1 July 2001. Print.

Bagel Bites Commercial Jingle. 1990's. Television. Transcript.

Beecher, John. "Various Email Correspondences To and From John Beecher (April 2015 - June 2015)." Rollercoaster Records, Apr. 2015. Web. 2015.

"Best Selling Pop Records in Britain; Best Selling Sheet Music in Britain, Best Selling Pop Records in U.S. (Billboard)." NME Music Charts 12 Mar. 1958. Print.

"Best Selling Sheet Music in the U.S." Billboard 16 June 1958: 37. Print.

"Big D Jamboree." Rockabilly Hall of Fame. Web. 2013. <http://www.rockabillyhall.com/BigD.html>.

"Billy Briggs & X.I.T. Boys: Alarm Clock Boogie." Bopping.org, 13 Oct. 2010. Web. 7 Mar. 2015. <http://www.bopping.org/billy-briggs-x-i-t-boys-alarm-clock-boogie/>.

Blanas, Frank. The King of Clovis Norman Petty: American Music Legend The Man Behind Rock 'n' Roll's Greatest Artists. Stroud: Rollercoaster, 2013. Print.

"Brenda Lee - Wikipedia, the free encyclopedia." N.p., n.d. Web. 22 Jul. 2015 <http://en.wikipedia.org/wiki/I_Wonder_(Brenda_Lee_song)>.

Brigham, Cathy. "Louisiana Hayride." Louisiana Hayride | The Handbook of Texas Online | Texas State Historical Association (TSHA). Texas State Historical Association (TSHA). Web. 10 July 2013. <http://www.tshaonline.org/handbook/online/articles/xfl01>.

Broad, Kenneth. "Personal Interview." 2013

Brown, Robin. "The Amarillo-Canyon Music Scene of the Sixties." 1960s Garage Bands. 60sgaragebands.com. Web. 7 Mar. 2015. <http://www.60sgaragebands.com/scenesthings/amarillorobinbrown.html>.

"Bubba's House Band." *Mama's Family*. N. d. Television. Loose Transcript.

"C & W Artist of the Week- Charlie Phillips' Current Single 'Cancel The Call'" Music Reporter 1 Dec. 1962: Unknown. Print.

"C&W Wax to Watch." Music Reporter 12 May 1962. Print.

Carlson, Paul H. Amarillo- The Story of a Western Town. Lubbock:

Texas Tech UP, 2006. Print.

"Charlie "Sugartime" Phillips Swingin', Writing D.-J." Country Time Review 1 July 1967. Print.

"Charlie Phillips Named "Mr. Disc-Jockey U. S. A."" Clovis News-Journal 1961. Print.

Coffey, Kevin. "Bob Wills and His Texas Playboys - Skeeter Elkin." Skeeter Elkin. The Western Swing Journal. Web. 7 Mar. 2015.
<http://www.texasplayboys.net/Biographies/skeeter.htm>

Cook, Dwight. "Don Bristow." The Steel Guitar Forum, 8 Aug. 2009. Web. 7 Mar. 2015.
<http://bb.steelguitarforum.com/viewtopic.php?t=164431&sid=4fe58c0359f3e67ac686d110f686b3f2>.

Cooper, Alex. "History of Record Labels and the Music Industry." History of Record Labels and the Music Industry. Web. 22 Nov. 2014.
<http://www.playlistresearch.com/recordindustry.htm>.

"Coral Re-Signs McGuire Gals." Billboard 17 Aug. 1959: 3. Print.

"Country Reviews." Cash Box (Chart) 1962. Print.

"Country Show Down-home Fun (but Where's George Jones?)." Colorado Springs Sun 9 July 1978, Review sec. Print.

Cox, Mike. Historic Amarillo- An Illustrated History. Historical Network, 2000. Print.

Crawford, Jim. "Still Swingin' - Song as Sweet as Sugar for Hall of Famer." Still Swingin' Amarillo.com. Amarillo Globe-News, 26 Dec. 2004. Web. 13 Aug. 2013.
<http://amarillo.com/stories/122604/fea_780949.shtml>.

Cyberspace Law & Ethics. Waco: Sentinel- A Publishing and Research, 1999. Print.

"DJ- Artist's Life Not All Gravy." Unknown- Country Music 17 June 1967. Print.

"David "Pappy Dave Stone" Pinkston: Founder of Country Music Radio." Lubbock Avalanche-Journal 21 Feb. 2004. Web. 22 June 2015.
<http://lubbockonline.com/stories/022104/obi_022104086.shtml>.

Dickens, Little Jimmy. "Personal Interview." Nashville., 6 Dec. 2013. Telephone. 2013.

"Echols Funeral Tomorrow." The Corpus Christi Caller 25 Mar. 1974: 28. Web. 11 Jan. 2014. <www.newspapers.com/image/#31230926>.

Echols, Odis. "The Melody Album of Odis Echols and His Melody Boys A Collection of Songs, Poems and Pictures." Melody Album. Print.

Echols Jr., Odis. "Pop Echols Important Cog of Clovis Music." Interview. 4 Sept. 1998.

"Episode 5; Tommy Sands." Edwards, Ralph. This Is Your Life. NBC-Television, . 10 Apr. 1957. Television.

Escott, Colin. ""Billy Walker"" The Encyclopedia of Country Music. Ed. Paul Kingsbury. New York: Oxford UP, 1998. 566-7. Print.

Escott, Colin. The Encyclopedia of Country Music. Ed. Paul Kingsbury. New York City: Oxford UP, 1998. 247-8. Print.

"Ex-Girlfriend Isn't Feeling Sweet About 'Sugartime'" Editorial. *TV Guide* n.d.: n. pag. Deseret News, 20 Nov. 1995. 2014

Folsom, Rebecca. "Give the World a Smile: A Professional Gospel Quartet of All-Stars, 1927-1932." Society for American Music Bulletin, Volume XXV, No. 3, 1999. Web. 2014. <http://www.american-music.org/publications/bullarchive/Folsom.html>.

"For the Love of VI- All Star Tribute to Vi Petty." Memorial Leaflet 30 May 1992. Print.

"Forney Aircraft Co. (Owners Manual)." Flight Manual for Ercoupe Model 415-D; Ercoupes Model E & G; (1959). Print.

"Gospel Told in Bass Clef - Original Stamps Baritone Sings out." Brownwood Bulletin 7 July 1972, Brownwood, Texas ed. Print.

"Gospel Singer to Be Honored." Hope Star 7 July 1973, Hope, Arkansas ed.: 1. Hope Star. Web. 10 Jan. 2014. <www.newspapers.com/image/#4436720>.

"Gospel Told in Bass Clef- Original Stamps Baritone Sings out."

Brownwood Bulletin 7 July 1972, Brownwood, Texas ed.: 9. Brownwood Bulletin. Web. 10 Jan. 2014. <www.newspapers.com/image/#6177277>.

Greene, Howard. "Personal Letter to Charlie Phillips." TV Radio Mirror 30 June 1958: 1. Print.

Griggs, Bill. "Here Is a Short Note From Bill Griggs." The Buddy Holly Memorial Society (Letter to Charlie Phillips from Bill Griggs). Print.

Guertin, Joan B. "Larry Trider Country Soul Man." Lone Starr Music. Pope Publishing Company, 1973. Web. 26 Mar. 2015. <http://www.lonestarrmusic.com/html/larry_trider.html>. Article obtained from Country Song Roundup Annual 1973

Hacker, Bobby. "Bobby Hacker- Music Biography." Garage Bands of the 1960s. bobbyhacker.com, n.d. Web. 5 June 2014. <http://www.bobbyhacker.com/>.

Hacker, Bobby, Dave Penny, and Tony Wilkinson. "Charlie "Sugartime" Phillips." American Music Magazine 1 Mar. 2011: 38-43. Print.

"Hank the Cowdog." The Official Website of Hank the Cowdog. Maverick Books, 10 Feb. 2015. Web. 7 Mar. 2015.

"Hathcock, Alfred Jason [Johnny]." The Handbook of Texas Online. Texas State Historical Association (TSHA). Web. 7 Mar. 2015. <http://www.tshaonline.org/handbook/online/articles/fhagl>.

"Hats Off! to WSM's Annual Country Music Festival from All of Us..." Billboard Music Book 30 Oct. 1961: 17. Print.

Heath, Jennifer. "Musicians to Receive Honors." Amarillo Globe-News 16 July 2005. Web. 7 Mar. 2015. <http://scalesstrings.com/young.htm>.

"Holly's Success Reflected Norman Petty's Influence." Billboard 8 Aug. 1984: 62. Print.

Hughes, Dudley. Chattel Mortgage (Contract) Contract between Dudley Hughes and Murray-Davis Aviation Inc (1959). Print.

Hutchings, David. "The Mcguire Sisters, Those Sugartime Princesses of Pop, Have Reunited After a 17-Year Split." People.com 3 Mar. 1986. Print.

Ingman, John. "Charlie Phillips Sugartime." Personal Research Collected by John Ingman for the Bear Family Records CD (2011). Print.

Ingman, John. "Personal E-mail from John Ingman." Recap (2). 2015. Web. 12 May 2015.

Ingman, John. "Personal E-mail from John Ingman to Cy Cushenberry." Information regarding Charlie Phillips. 25 Apr. 2015. Web. 25 Apr. 2015.

Ingman, John. "Various Email Correspondences To and From John Ingman (April 2015 - June 2015)." Apr. 2015. Web. 2015.

"James "Jim" Benjamin." Amarillo Globe-News 22 May 2011, Obituaries sec. Web. 13 Mar. 2015. <http://amarillo.com/obituaries/2011-05-22/james-jim-benjamin>.

Johnson, Loudilla, Loretta Johnson, and Kay Johnson. "Biggest Little News Sheet In Country Music" Tri-Son News (1980). Print.

Jones, George. "Personal Interview." Nashville. Apr. 2013.

Jones, Keith. "Personal Telephone Interview with Keith Jones." July 2014

Jones, Tamara. "Musician's Ear Becomes a Career After Long Line of Jobs, Man Finds His Calling in Tuning." Amarillo Globe-News 10 June 2008. Web. 7 Mar. 2015. <http://amarillo.com/stories061008/new_10525844.shtml#.VPtHBEuGreg>.

"K-Yall's Country "40" Survey." KYAL 1600 Country Western Station 1965. Print."KRLD Big D Jamboree." Hillbilly-Music.com. Web. 2013. <http://www.hillbilly-music.com/programs/story/index.php?prog=430>.

Kernes, William. "Four Part Series: As Crickets Finally Get Their Due, a Glimpse into past." Four Part Series: As Crickets Finally Get Their Due, a Glimpse into past | Buddy Holly Archives. Buddyhollyarchives.com, 2012. Web. 25 Nov. 2014. <http://www.buddyhollyarchives.com/2012/04/four-

part-series-as-crickets-finally-get-their-due-a-glimpse-into-past/>.

"Kountry KAGT Top 40 Survey." Kountry KAGT 1340 on Your Dial 19 Sept. 1966. Print.

Larkin, Colin, ed. The Encyclopedia of Popular Music. 3rd ed. New York: Muze, 1998. Print.

LaRue, Carroll (Lash). "Personal Interview." 2013

Laufer, Charles. "Personal Letter to Charlie Phillips." 'Teen Magazine 5 Dec. 1958: 1. Print.

"Letter Regarding Charlie and KZIP Radio Station." Charlie Phillips Personal Letterhead: 1. Print.

Lloyd, Jack. "It's 'Sugartime' Again For McGuire Sisters." Knight-Ridder Newspapers 29 May 1986, Show Business sec. Chicago Tribune. Web. 27 Feb. 2014.

"Local Radio Station KZIP Names Two New Officials." Amarillo Globe- News 1973. Print.

Lynn, Tiny. "Personal Interviews." Clovis. 2013

Macy, Robert. "McGuire-Giancana: Romance Was Epitome of Opposites Attract." Indiana Gazette 1996. Print.

Mauldin, Joe B. "Personal Telephone Interview." (Cricket's bassist). 3 Dec. 2014.

McAlavy, Don. "Buddy Holly, Norman Petty at the Heart of 'the Clovis Sound" Clovis News-Journal, Special To The News Journal sec.: 1-2. Print.

McAlavy, Don. "Echoes from the Back Trails." Clovis News-Journal 22 July 1984. Print.

McAlavy, Don. "Echoes from the Back Trails." Clovis News-Journal 26 Aug. 1984. Print.

McAlavy, Don. "Small Town Studio Has National Reputation." Clovis News-Journal 4 May 1986: 56. Print.

McAlavy, Don. "Christmas Tunes Yield Tales of 1950s Studio." (2005). Print.

McAlavy, Don. "The return of the country barn dance." (2003): n. pag. Print.

McAlavy, Don. Those Who Made the Music In Clovis and Outlying

Areas 1907- 2004. Clovis: City Printing, 2005. Print.

"Music Exec Murray Deutch Dies." Billboardbiz. Billboard, 22 Oct. 2010. Web. 12 June 2014. <http://www.billboard.com/biz/articles/news/1198658/music-exec-murray-deutch-dies>.

Nelson, Willie. "Personal Backstage Interview." Amarillo. N.p., 24 Aug. 2013. Web. 2013.

Newman, Brad. "Accident Impairs, but Doesn't Stop, Musician's Playing." Lubbock Avalanche-Journal 7 Oct. 2009. Web. 7 Mar. 2015. <htt://lubbockonline.com/stories/100709/fea_501863881.shtml#.VPtE90uGreg>.

Newman, Jimmy C. "Personal Interview." Nashville. 7 Dec. 2013.

"Norman & Vi Petty Rock & Roll Museum." Norman & Vi Petty Rock & Roll Museum Home. Web. 6 Aug. 2013.

"Norman Petty's Trio on Tour: Makes Big Hit." Clovis News-Journal 31 Aug. 1949: 2. Print.

Oermann, Robert K. "The Story Behind The Show That Made Country Music Famous/ Grand Ole Opry: The Show That Made Country Music Famous." What Is the Opry? - Opry.com. Web. 10 Aug. 2013. <http://www.opry.com/about/WhatisTheOpry.html>.

"Ozark Jubilee - Wikipedia, the free encyclopedia." N.p., n.d. Web. 22 Jul. 2015 <http://en.wikipedia.org/wiki/Ozark_Jubilee>.

"Pappy Stone." ROOTS of Country Music, Internet Encyclopedia of Original Country Music, 2009 6 July 2013. Print.

Peoples, Curtis. "Personal Email from Curtis Peoples." (Odis Echols Information). N.p., 22 Nov. 2013. Web. 2013.

Peoples, Curtis L. "The Lubbock Texas Quartet and Odis "Pop" Echols: Promoting Southern Gospel Music on the High Plains of Texas 2014." (2014): 12-20. Print.

Peterson, Ron. "Personal Interview." Nov. 2014.

"Petty Receives Gold Record." The Curry County Times 9 June 1984. Print.

"Phillips Named "Mr. DJ USA"" The Amarillo Globe-Times 6 July

1962: 17. Print.

"Phillips Signs With K-Ark." Music City News 1 Oct. 1968. Print.

Phillips, Charlie. "Letter from Charlie on KZIP Radio Station Stationary- A Dave Stone Station." 30 Nov. 1977: 1. Print.

Phillips, Charlie, and Norman Petty. "Sugartime Twist." NorVaJak Music, Inc. Music Book: n. pag. Print.

Phillips, Charlie, and Odis Echols. "Sugartime (Sugar in the Morning) Recorded by Jim Dale." Southern Music Publishing Co. Song Book: n. pag. Print.

"Presenting Charlie "Sugartime" Phillips and "Full Circle"" Charlie "Sugartime" Phillips Biography. Lonestarmusic.com. Web. 2 Aug. 2013. <http://lonestarmusic.com/html/charlie_sugartime_phillips_b.html>.

Preston, Frances W. "Dear BMI Million-Air." Personal Letter from BMI (1958). Print.

Price, M. H. "The Complete Circle of Charlie Phillip's Career." Accent West 1 Mar. 1980: 53-8. Print.

Price, Ray. "Personal Telephone Interview." Mt. Pleasant. 6 Oct. 2013.

Qualls, Greg. "Phillips Inducted into Texas Panhandle Broadcasting Hall of Fame." The State Line Tribune "Official Publication of Parmer County" 11 June 1999. Print.

Ragland, Ruth Ann. "Kids Like Gospel Singing." The Corbin Times-Tribune 9 July 1972, Corbin, Kentucky ed., A New Interest sec.: 12. Web. 10 Jan. 2014. <www.newspapers.com/image/#30491201>.

"Ray Price and The Cherokee Cowboys Opening Act…Charlie Phillips and The Sugartimers." Amarillo Globe-News 18 Dec. 1999. Print.

Re: Texas Playboys Steel Guitarists." N.p., Web. 10 Sep. 2015 <http://www.texasplayboys.net/_disc3/00000054.htm>.

"Recording Artist Named KZIP Manager." The Amarillo Globe-Times 24 Sept. 1967, Amarillo, Texas ed.: 5. Print.

"Red Steagall - inthebunkhousetv." N.p., n.d. Web. 01 Aug. 2015 <http://www.inthebunkhousetv.com/About_Red.html>.

"Red Steagall & the Coleman County Cowboys | New Music And Songs." N.p., n.d. Web. 02 Aug. 2015 <http://www.cmt.com/artists/red-steagall-the-coleman-county-cowboys/>.

"Revival of Gospel Music Seen by Long-time Singer." The Anniston Star 17 July 1972, Anniston, Alabama ed.: 12. Web. 10 Jan. 2014. <www.newspapers.com/image/#31716668>.

Rock, Rock, Rock! Dir. Will Price. By Phyllis Coe and Milton Subotski. Perf. Chuck Berry and Alan Freed. Distributors Corporation of America, 1956. Film.

"Rooster Morris." Wikipedia. Wikipedia. Print.

Roughstock. "Roughstock History of Country Music." Outlaw Country | Roughstock's History of Country Music. roughstock.com, 18 Jan. 2009. Web. 11 Jan. 2014.

Roughstock Staff. "Western Swing." Roughstock's History of Country Music. Roughstock.com, 27 Jan. 2009. Web. 11 Jan. 2014. <http://www.roughstock.com/history/western-swing>.

"Sammy Jackson; TV Actor, Disc Jockey." Sammy Jackson; TV Actor, Disc Jockey- Los Angeles Times. L.A. Times, 1 May 1995. Web. 26 Feb. 2015. <http://articles.latimes.com/1995-05-01/news/mn-60941_1_sammy-jackson>.

Schell, Jimmy. "Personal Interviews." 2013- 2015

"Season 10- Episode 26." *The Perry Como Show*. NBC-TV. 15 Mar. 1958. Television. Transcript

"Sees New Surge Of Youthful Interest In Gospel Music." The Kokomo Tribune 9 July 1972, Kokomo, Indiana ed.: 48. Web. 11 Jan. 2014. <www.newspapers.com/image/#45669286>.

"Shreveport Municipal Auditorium (History)." Shreveport Municipal Auditorium. 2013. Web. 10 July 2013. <http://www.shreveportmunicipalauditorium.com/history/>.

Sisco, Jon. "Charlie "Sugartime" Phillips Full Circle." Research Collected by Jon Sisco for the Full Circle CD Insert (2008). Print.

Smith, Karen D. "The Music Man- Musician Develops Love for a

Variety of Music Chet Calcote Was Country When Country Wasn't Exactly Cool." Amarillo Globe- News 10 Nov. 1999. Web. 7 Mar. 2015. <http://amarillo.com/stories/1999/11/10/fri_111099-20.shtml#.VPs6tkuGreg>.

Soloman, Harvey. "Mobster & Singer Made for Strange Love." The Kokomo Tribune 1 Nov. 1995, Kokomo, Indiana ed.: 25. Print.

Stecklein, Janelle. "Coors Cowboy Club Ranch Rodeo: Tunes Underscore Events Band Belts out about 12 Hours of Music." Amarillo Globe-News 5 June 2010. Web. 7 Mar. 2015. <http://amrillo.com/2010/06/05/new_news1.shtml#.VPsz-EuGreg>.

Steve, Rich. "Facebook Correspondences with Steve Rich." [Dallas] Oct. 2014: n. pag. Print.

Stewart, Dick. "Up Close with David Bigham of The Roses - A Member of a Legendary Vocal Group That Backed Buddy Holly in Most of 1958." MusicDish E-Journal - Up Close with David Bigham of The Roses. The Lance Monthly, 14 July 2003. Web. 24 Oct. 2014. <http://www.musicdish.com/mag/index.php3?id=8272>.

Stim, Richard. Getting Permission- How to License & Clear Copyrighted Materials Online & Off. 1st ed. Nolo.com Law For All. Print.

Storm, Rick. "Western Swing's the Thing for Duncan." Amarillo Globe- News 9 Dec. 2000. Web. 6 Mar. 2015. <http://amarillo.com/stories/2000/12/09/new_westswing.shtml>.

"Sugartime." Phonolog Reports- Top Hits 1 Mar. 1958. Print.

"Sugartime" Phillips - K-Ark 874."
   Record World 1 Mar. 1969. Print.

"Tex Ritter's Ranch Party." *Tex Ritter's Ranch Party*. ABC. 1958. Television. Transcript

"The Louisiana Hayride Radio Program Premieres on KWKH-AM Shreveport." The Louisiana Hayride Radio Program

Premieres on KWKH-AM Shreveport - History.com This Day in History- 4/3/1948. History.com. Web. 10 July 2013. <http://www.history.com/this-day-in-history/the-louisiana-hayride-radio-program-premieres-on-kwkh-am-shreveport>.

"The McGuire Sisters - Sugartime Lyrics | MetroLyrics." Insert Name of Site in Italics. N.p., Web. 21 Jul. 2015 <http://www.metrolyrics.com/sugartime-lyrics-the-mcguire-sisters.html>.

"The Norman Petty Recording Studios Announces Something New in the Southwest." Clovis News-Journal 26 Oct. 1947: 17. Print.

The Real Buddy Holly Story. BBC and MPL Productions. 1 Jan. 1987. Television.

"The Sugartime Kid Rides Again - Charlie Phillips With "Be My Bride" And "Too Many Tears"" Cash Box Bullseye 1957. Print.

The Wil-helm Agency A World of Talent for All Occasions: n. pag. Print.

Thiele, Bob, and Bob Golden. What a Wonderful World: A Lifetime of Recordings by Thiele. New York City: Oxford UP, 1995. Print. By permission of Oxford University Press, USA

"Thomas Lee Hadaway." Amarillo Globe-News 24 Aug. 2010, Obituaries sec. Web. 7 Mar. 2015.

"Thursday December 4th Big Autograph Party Country Western Star Charlie Sugartime Phillips." Wrestling, King of Sports Official Program 27 Nov. 1969. Print.

"Tinker Air Force Base." Buddy Holly & The Crickets.com- Tinker Air Force Base (Oklahoma City, OK). Web. 11 July 2014. <http://buddyhollyandthecrickets.com/tinker.html>.

Tippens, Matthew. "Petty, Norman." Norman Petty- The Handbook of Texas Online. Texas State Historical Association (TSHA), 31 Aug. 2010. Web. 12 Mar. 2014. <http://www.tshaonline.org/handbook/online/articles/fpe91>.

"Unknown." *Cash Box Magazine* 1958: n. pag. Print.

Unterberger, Richie. "Norman Petty Biography." Norman Petty Biography Allmusic. Allmusic. Web. 9 June 2014. <http://www.allmusic.com/artist/norman-petty-mn0000460266>.

Weize, Richard, John Ingman, and Praguefrank. "Praguefrank's Country Music Discographies." Praguefrank's Country Music Discographies. N.p., Web. 2014.

Westex. "Tiny Lynn, Lubbock/ Clovis." Lubbock/Clovis | LoneStarStomp. LoneStarStomp, 31 Oct. 2009. Web. 7 Mar. 2015.

Williams, Jack, Billy Roach, and Ray Williams. "Checkmates- An Interview With Jack Williams." Researching the Local & Regional U.S. Rock Groups of the 1960s. 60sgaragebands.com. Web. 7 Mar. 2015. <http://www.60sgaragebands.comcheckmates.html>.

Wolfe, Charles. The Encyclopedia of Country Music. Ed. Paul Kingsbury. New York City: Oxford UP, 1998. 494-5. Print.

Wolfe, Charles. "Stamps Quartet." Encyclopedia of Gospel Music. Ed. W. K. McNeil. New York City: Routledge, 2005. 370. Print.

"Your Going Is Coming (Smokey, SESAC) - Charlie

Bibliography

50th Anniversary Louisiana Hayride Homecoming Apr. 1999: Print.

Condray-Hancock, Charlene. Personal interview. 13 June 2013. Interview conducted by Curtis L. Peoples in Lubbock, Texas.

"'Gospel Music Man' Honored by Peers." Pampa Daily News 11 Aug. 1972, Pampa, Texas ed. Print.

Hank Snow Home Town Museum. Web. 23 June 2015. <www.hanksnow.com>.

Logansport Pharos- Tribune 2 Mar. 1958, Logansport, Indiana ed.: 13. Web. 10 Jan. 2014. <www.newspapers.com/image/#3916709>.

Louisiana Hayride Playbill Published by Radio Station KWKH. Print.

myhighplains.com . KAMR, Amarillo. 23 July 2012. Web. Transcript.

The Shreveport Times 18 Mar. 1945: 19. Print.

The Shreveport Times 10 Apr. 1945: 7. Print.

"'Sugar' Time Promised." *Miami Daily News*-Record 11 May 1958, Miami, Oklahoma ed. Print.

"'Sugartime'" The Ottawa Journal 27 Aug. 1977, Ottawa, Canada ed.: 22. Web. 10 Jan. 2014.

"'Sugartime' Phillips Coming." The State Line Tribune "Official Publication of Parmer County" 7 July 1989. Print.

"'Sugartime' Phillips to Be Honored at BTD." State Line Tribune 26 July 2001. Print.

"'Sugartime' Camera Lied, Says McGuire." The Galveston Daily News 1996, Galveston, Texas ed. Print.

"2010 Inductee…Ray Winkler." Texas Country Music Hall of Fame Excerpt 2010. Print.

"A serving of best wishes country-style to WSM's Country Music Festival." Columbia Records promotional 1961: n. pag. Print.

"Alan Freed - Wikipedia, the free encyclopedia." N.p., Web. 16 Jul. 2015 <http://en.wikipedia.org/wiki/Alan_Freed>."All About Buddy Holly

"Accident impairs, but doesn't stop, musician's playing..." N.p., Web. 01 Aug. 2015 <http://lubbockonline.com/stories/100709/fea_501863881.shtml>.

Allison, J.I. "Personal Telephone Interview." (Cricket's Drummer). Sep. 2013.

Arkin, David. "Charlie Phillips Bringing Classic Tunes to Clovis." Clovis News-Journal 27 July 2000: 2; 6. Print.

Associated Press. "McGuire Objects to Film Portrayal." News Record 21 Nov. 1995, North Hills, Pennsylvania ed.: 18. Print.

"Aubrey L. Caldwell (Obituary)." Amarillo Globe-News 14 July 2004. Web. 7 Mar. 2015. <http://amarillo.com/stories/2004/07/14/obi_caldwell.shtml#.VPs7QkuGreg>.

"Award of the Week- The Street of Loneliness (Tuckahoe, BMI) Please Help Me Believe (Painted Desert, BMI)." Music Vendor 4 Apr. 1964. Print.

"BTD to Honor 'Sugartime' Charlie Phillips." State Line Tribune 1 July 2001. Print.

Bacas, Harry. "Top Teen Tunes." Washington Star 12 Jan. 1958. Print.

Bagel Bites Commercial Jingle. 1990's. Television. Transcript.

"Bands, Singers, Musicians &...of West Texas." West Texas Musicians. Robin Brown Presents. Web. 7 Mar. 2015. <http://sw_index.tripod.com/musician-band.html>.

Bates, Michael. "Jimmy Young RIP." BatesLine Tulsa Straight Ahead. 8 Oct. 2014. Web. 7 Mar. 2015. <http://www.batesline.com/archives/2014/10/jimmy-young-fiddler.html>.

Beasley, Berrin. "Vi Petty Is Dead at 63: Tribute Due." Clovis News

Journal 23 Mar. 1992. Print.

Beecher, John, and John Goldrosen. Remembering Buddy. New York City: Penguin, 1987. Print.

Beecher, John. "Various Email Correspondences To and From John Beecher (April 2015 - June 2015)." Rollercoaster Records, Apr. 2015. Web. 2015.

Bell, Stuart. "Personal Email from Stuart Bell (P. McCartney Publicist)." Marshall Arts., 2 Apr. 2014. Web.

Berry, Norma Jean. "Norman Petty Recordings Put Clovis On Map." Clovis News Journal 20 Nov. 1959, Clovis, New Mexico ed.: 6. Print.

"Best Selling Pop Records in Britain; Best Selling Sheet Music in Britain, Best Selling Pop Records in U.S. (Billboard)." NME Music Charts 12 Mar. 1958. Print.

"Best Selling Sheet Music in the U.S." Billboard 16 June 1958: 37. Print.

Betty, Helen. "Creativity in Clovis." New Mexico Magazine 1 Sept. 1960. Print.

"Big D Jamboree." Rockabilly Hall of Fame. Web. 2013. <http://www.rockabillyhall.com/BigD.html>.

"Billy Briggs & X.I.T. Boys: Alarm Clock Boogie." Bopping.org, 13 Oct. 2010. Web. 7 Mar. 2015. <http://www.bopping.org/billy-briggs-x-i-t-boys-alarm-clock-boogie/>.

"Billy Gene Stull, Jr." Memorial Obituaries Stull, Jr., Billy. Thomason Funeral Home- Wimberly, 2012. Web. 7 Mar. 2015.

Biracree, Tom. The Country Music Almanac. 1st ed. New York City: Macmillan General Reference, 1993. Print.

Black, Shelly. "Border Cities Celebrate This Weekend." The State Line Tribune "Official Publication of Parmer County" Print.

Blanas, Frank. The King of Clovis Norman Petty: American Music Legend The Man Behind Rock 'n' Roll's Greatest Artists. Stroud: Rollercoaster, 2013. Print.

"Bob Hopkins Joins on the Mic at for the Fundraiser." Bob Hopkins Joins on the Mic at for the Fundraiser | Friends of Fogelberg

Connection. Wordpress. Web. 7 Mar. 2015.

"Bob Wills Day 2014." Plains Trail Region. Texas Plains Trail Region, 28 Apr. 2014. Web. 7 Mar. 2015. <http://texasplainstrail.com/events/bob-wills-day2014>.

"Bobby Wynne- Owner, Artist International Music Productions." Bobby Wynne. Linkedin. Web. 8 Mar. 2015. <https://www.linkedin.com/pub/bobby-wynne/35/48a/8>.

Bowen, Jimmy, and Jim Jerome. Rough Mix. New York City, 1997. Print.

Boyett, Ben. "Norman Petty." Accent West 1 Nov. 1982. Print.

"Brady- Petty United in Church Ceremony." Clovis News-Journal 24 June 1948: 2. Print.

"Brenda Lee - Wikipedia, the free encyclopedia." N.p., n.d. Web. 22 Jul. 2015 <http://en.wikipedia.org/wiki/I_Wonder_(Brenda_Lee_song)>.

Brigham, Cathy. "Louisiana Hayride." Louisiana Hayride | The Handbook of Texas Online | Texas State Historical Association (TSHA). Texas State Historical Association (TSHA). Web. 10 July 2013. <http://www.tshaonline.org/handbook/online/articles/xfl01>.

Broad, Kenneth. "Personal Interview." 2013

Brown, Robin. "The Early Rock 'n' Rollers of Amarillo, Texas." Lonestarrmusic.com. Web. 7 Mar. 2015. <http://www.lonestarrmusic.com/html/_stories_c.html>.

Brown, Robin. "Amarillo-Canyon Music #2." Amarillo Music Scene. Robin Brown Presents. Web. 7 Mar. 2015. <http://sw_index.tripod.com/amarillo-music2.html>.

Brown, Robin. "The Amarillo-Canyon Music Scene of the Sixties." 1960s Garage Bands. 60sgaragebands.com. Web. 7 Mar. 2015. <http://www.60sgaragebands.com/scenesthings/amarillorobinbrown.html>.

Brown, Robin. "Early Recording Studios of West Texas." 1960's Texas Music. Web. 7 Mar. 2015.

<http://www.scarletdukes.com/st/tm_wtstudios.html>.

Brown, Robin. "The Amarillo-Canyon Music Scene." The Amarillo-Canyon Music Scene. Robin Brown Presents. Web. 7 Mar. 2015. <http://sw_index.tripod.com/amarillo-canyon1.html>.

Brown, Robin. "1960s Texas Music." 1960s Texas Music. Rockin' Robin Brown. Web. 7 Mar. 2015. <http://www.scarletdukes.com/st/tm_wtbands.html>.

Brown, Robin. "Lubbock's Nightclub Music Scene: 1940's, 1950's, 1960's." Lubbock's Nightclub Music Scene: 1940's, 1950's, 1960's : Lubbock Musicians. Lubbock Musicians, 2014. Web. 7 Mar. 2015. <htt://www.reddit.com/r/LubbockMusicians/comments/26zmws/lubbocks_night_club_music_scene_1940s_50s_60s/>.

"Bubba's House Band." *Mama's Family*. N. d. Television. Loose Transcript.

Buck, Jerry. "Aspiring Singers Invade Television." Del Rio News Herald 28 Aug. 1977, Del Rio, Texas ed.: 15. Print.

"Buddy Holly Center Buddy Holly Gallery Guide." Buddy Holly Center Buddy Holly Gallery Guide. Print.

"Buddy Holly and the Crickets." Buddy Holly. History-of-rock.com. Web. 27 Aug. 2013. <http://www.history-of-rock.com/buddy_holly.htm>.

Butler, Eric. "Clovis Music Festival Honors Petty Studios." Amarillo Globe-News 10 Sept. 2005. Web. 7 Mar. 2015. <http://amrillo.com/stories/091005/new_2754698.shtml#.VPtr6EuGreg>.

"C & W Artist of the Week- Charlie Phillips' Current Single 'Cancel The Call'" Music Reporter 1 Dec. 1962: Unknown. Print.

"C&W Wax to Watch." Music Reporter 12 May 1962. Print.

Campbell, Bob. "Petty Left Stamp On Pupil (Industry)." Lubbock Avalanche-Journal 19 Aug. 1984, sec. E: 1-2. Print.

Carlson, Paul H. Amarillo- The Story of a Western Town. Lubbock: Texas Tech UP, 2006. Print.

"Carlton Scales' Aviatrix Club." N.p., n.d. Web. 30 Jul. 2015 <http://aviatrixclub.com/>.

Chandler, Chip. "Get Down: History Has No Limit for Agave Posse."

Amarillo Globe- News 26 June 2013, Entertainment sec. Web. 17 Mar. 2015. <http://amarillo.com/entertainment/get-out-music/2013-06-26/locals-discover-musical-chemistry>.

Chandler, Chip. "Personal Email from Chip Chandler, Features Editor ." AGN Media/ Amarillo Globe-News. N.p., 23 Oct. 2013. Web. 2013.

"Charlie "Sugartime" Phillips." Clovis Music Festival 2009 Program 2009: 2. Print.

"Charlie "Sugartime" Phillips Swingin', Writing D.-J." Country Time Review 1 July 1967. Print.

"Charlie 'Sugartime' Phillips to Appear." State Line Tribune 28 July 1989: 7. Print.

"Charlie Phillips." Cashbox Country Round Up 1963: 43. Print.

"Charlie Phillips Named "Mr. Disc-Jockey U. S. A."" Clovis News-Journal 1961. Print.

"Charlie Phillips to Entertain." State Line Tribune 30 July 1999: 15. Print.

"Charlie Phillips, Band to Give Benefit in Clovis." The State Line Tribune "Official Publication of Parmer County" 26 July 1991. Print.

"Charlie to Also Play at BTD 'Sugartime' Phillips, the Farwell Legend, to Play Here Again." The State Line Tribune "Official Publication of Parmer County" Print.

"Clovis Senator's Father Marries." The Amarillo Globe-Times 3 Aug. 1973, Amarillo, Texas ed.: 43. The Amarillo Globe-Times. Web. 10 Jan. 2014.
<www.newspapers.com/image/#30028559>.

Coffey, Kevin. "Bob Wills and His Texas Playboys - Skeeter Elkin." Skeeter Elkin. The Western Swing Journal. Web. 7 Mar. 2015.
<http://www.texasplayboys.net/Biographies/skeeter.htm>

Coleman, Betty. "Bob's Holler Echoes in Tribute by WT Professor." Western Swing Of Texas. Lonestarrmusic.com, 19 Dec. 1974. Web. 8 Mar. 2015.
<http://www.lonestarrmusic.com/html/western_swing_of_te

xas.html>.

"Concert Sponsored." State Line Tribune 21 July 1989: 3. Print.

Cook, Dwight. "Don Bristow." The Steel Guitar Forum, 8 Aug. 2009. Web. 7 Mar. 2015. <http://bb.steelguitarforum.com/viewtopic.php?t=164431&sid=4fe58c0359f3e67ac686d110f686b3f2>.

Cooper, Alex. "History of Record Labels and the Music Industry." History of Record Labels and the Music Industry. Web. 22 Nov. 2014. <http://www.playlistresearch.com/recordindustry.htm>.

"Coral Re-Signs McGuire Gals." Billboard 17 Aug. 1959: 3. Print.

"Country Reviews." Cash Box (Chart) 1962. Print.

"Country Show Down-home Fun (but Where's George Jones?)." Colorado Springs Sun 9 July 1978, Review sec. Print.

"Country and Western Show and Dance July 3." Chaparral Convention Center 3 July: Print.

Cowling, Jerry. "Delta Countians Review Past in Fashions, Songs." The Paris News 3 Sept. 1970, Paris, Texas ed.: 1. Web. 11 Jan. 2014. <www.newspapers.com/image/#13651807>.

Cox, Mike. Historic Amarillo- An Illustrated History. Historical Network, 2000. Print.

Crawford, Jim. "Still Swingin' - Song as Sweet as Sugar for Hall of Famer." Still Swingin' Amarillo.com. Amarillo Globe-News, 26 Dec. 2004. Web. 13 Aug. 2013. <http://amarillo.com/stories/122604/fea_780949.shtml>.

Cyberspace Law & Ethics. Waco: Sentinel- A Publishing and Research, 1999. Print.

"DJ- Artist's Life Not All Gravy." Unknown- Country Music 17 June 1967. Print.

"David "Pappy Dave Stone" Pinkston: Founder of Country Music Radio." Lubbock Avalanche-Journal 21 Feb. 2004. Web. 22 June 2015. <http://lubbockonline.com/stories/022104/obi_022104086.shtml>.

Dickens, Little Jimmy. "Personal Interview." Nashville., 6 Dec. 2013. Telephone. 2013.

"DigitalDreamDoor.com." N.p., Web. 16 Jul. 2015<http://www.digitaldreamdoor.com/pages/best_artists-bio/buddyholly.html>.

Diekman, Diane. Live Fast, Love Hard: The Faron Young Story. Chicago: U of Illinois, 2012. Print.

"Dinah Puts More Into Song Than Meets The Ear." The Ottawa Journal 5 May 1971: 4; 65. Web. 10 Jan. 2014. <www.newspapers.com/image/#45751630>.

"Don Guess." Buddy Holly & The Crickets.com- Don Guess. Superoldies.com. Web. 7 Mar. 2015. <http://superoldies.com/buddyholly/related/guess.html>.

"Echols Funeral Tomorrow." The Corpus Christi Caller 25 Mar. 1974: 28. Web. 11 Jan. 2014. <www.newspapers.com/image/#31230926>.

Echols Jr., Odis. "Pop Echols Important Cog of Clovis Music." Interview. 4 Sept. 1998.

Echols, Odis. "The Melody Album of Odis Echols and His Melody Boys A Collection of Songs, Poems and Pictures." Melody Album. Print.

"Episode 5; Tommy Sands." Edwards, Ralph. This Is Your Life. NBC-Television, . 10 Apr. 1957. Television.

Escott, Colin. ""Billy Walker"" The Encyclopedia of Country Music. Ed. Paul Kingsbury. New York: Oxford UP, 1998. 566-7. Print.

Escott, Colin. The Encyclopedia of Country Music. Ed. Paul Kingsbury. New York City: Oxford UP, 1998. 247-8. Print.

"Ex-Girlfriend Isn't Feeling Sweet About 'Sugartime'" Editorial. *TV Guide* n.d.: n. pag. Deseret News, 20 Nov. 1995. 2014

Fink, Stu. "Buddy Holly: Those Who Knew Him." Goldmine Magazine 16 Dec. 1988: 18. Print.

Fiona, Connie. "Personal Email Correspondences with Connie Fiona." N.p., May 2015. Web. June 2015.

Folsom, Rebecca. "Give the World a Smile: A Professional Gospel Quartet of All-Stars, 1927-1932." Society for American Music Bulletin, Volume XXV, No. 3, 1999. Web. 2014.

<http://www.american-music.org/publications/bullarchive/Folsom.html>.

"For the Love of VI- All Star Tribute to Vi Petty." Memorial Leaflet 30 May 1992. Print.

"Former Musician Odis 'Pop' Echols Dies." Las Vegas Optic 25 Mar. 1974, Las Vegas, New Mexico ed.: 2. Web. 10 Jan. 2014. <www.newspapers.com/image/#35601081>.

"Forney Aircraft Co. (Owners Manual)." Flight Manual for Ercoupe Model 415-D; Ercoupes Model E & G; (1959). Print.

Foust-Peeples, Shanna. "Band Entertains Audiences with a Variety of Music Styles." Amarillo Globe-News 28 July 1999, Friends and Neighbors sec.: 2. Print.

"Fred Rayford Harris." Amarillo Globe-News 22 July 2012, Obituaries sec. Web. 7 Mar. 2015.

Gann, Lynne. "Farwell Convalescent Center Chit Chat." Farwell Convalescent Center Newsletter. Print.

"Garland Ray Hunter." Garland Ray Hunter 7 Aug. 2013, Obituaries sec. Amarillo Globe-News. Web. 7 Mar. 2015. <http://amarillo.com/obituaries/2013-08-07/garland-ray-hunter>.

Gentry, Robert. Tillman Franks- I Was There When It Happened. Ed. Patricia Martinez. Many: Sweet Dreams, 2000. Print.

Gerron, Peggy Sue. "Various Emails and Phone Correspondences with Peggy Sue Gerron." N.p., Winter 2013. Web. 2013.

"Gospel Told in Bass Clef - Original Stamps Baritone Sings out." Brownwood Bulletin 7 July 1972, Brownwood, Texas ed. Print.

"Gospel Singer to Be Honored." Hope Star 7 July 1973, Hope, Arkansas ed.: 1. Hope Star. Web. 10 Jan. 2014. <www.newspapers.com/image/#4436720>.

"Gospel Told in Bass Clef- Original Stamps Baritone Sings out." Brownwood Bulletin 7 July 1972, Brownwood, Texas ed.: 9. Brownwood Bulletin. Web. 10 Jan. 2014. <www.newspapers.com/image/#6177277>.

Greene, Howard. "Personal Letter to Charlie Phillips." TV Radio Mirror 30 June 1958: 1. Print.

Griggs, Bill. Buddy Holly Day-by-Day: Book One (January 1936 to December 1956. Lubbock: Rockin' 50s. Print.

Griggs, Bill. Buddy Holly Day-by-Day: Book Two (January 1957 to December 1957). Lubbock: Rockin' 50s. Print.

Griggs, Bill. "Here Is a Short Note From Bill Griggs." The Buddy Holly Memorial Society (Letter to Charlie Phillips from Bill Griggs). Print.

Griggs, Bill. Rockin' 50s Collector's Issue (Dedicated to the TRUE Rock 'n' Roll Era) 1 Feb. 1992. Print.

Guertin, Joan B. "Larry Trider Country Soul Man." Lone Starr Music. Pope Publishing Company, 1973. Web. 26 Mar. 2015. <http://www.lonestarrmusic.com/html/larry_trider.html>. Article obtained from Country Song Roundup Annual 1973

Guertin, Joan B. "Las Vegas Country." Las Vegas Country 1 Mar. 1975. Print.

Hacker, Bobby. "Bobby Hacker- Music Biography." Garage Bands of the 1960s. bobbyhacker.com, n.d. Web. 5 June 2014. <http://www.bobbyhacker.com/>.

Hacker, Bobby, Dave Penny, and Tony Wilkinson. "Charlie "Sugartime" Phillips." American Music Magazine 1 Mar. 2011: 38-43. Print.

Hamilton, Larry. "Vic Ashmead Passed Away." The Steel Guitar Forum, 14 Nov. 2008. Web. 7 Mar. 2015. <http://bb.steelguitarforum.com/viewtopic.php?t=145844>.

"Hank the Cowdog." The Official Website of Hank the Cowdog. Maverick Books, 10 Feb. 2015. Web. 7 Mar. 2015.

Harris, Brandon L. "The Norman Petty Chronicles." Time Barrier Express 1 Apr. 1980. Print.

"Harry Coffman (Obituary)." The Oklahoman-News OK Powered by the Oklahoman 2014, Obituaries sec. Web. 7 Mar. 2015. <http://www.legacy.com/obituaries/oklahoman/obituary.aspx?pid=168848745>.

Hartz, Marlena. "Clovis officials interested in Petty studio." Clovis News-Journal [Clovis] 9 Dec. 2005: Print.

"Hathcock, Alfred Jason [Johnny]." The Handbook of Texas Online. Texas State Historical Association (TSHA). Web. 7 Mar. 2015.
<http://www.tshaonline.org/handbook/online/articles/fhagl>.

"Hats Off! to WSM's Annual Country Music Festival from All of Us..." Billboard Music Book 30 Oct. 1961: 17. Print.

"He Needs 'Em Bad." Music Reporter- Scoopin' the Jocks 28 July 1962. Print.

Heath, Jennifer. "Musicians to Receive Honors." Amarillo Globe-News 16 July 2005. Web. 7 Mar. 2015.
<http://scalesstrings.com/young.htm>.

"History | Ryman Auditorium." N.p., Web. 22 Jul. 2015
<https://rymanauditorium.wordpress.com/category/history/>.

"Holly's Success Reflected Norman Petty's Influence." Billboard 8 Aug. 1984: 62. Print.

"Honky Tonk Texas, USA- Honky Tonk Legends." Honky Tonk Texas, USA- Honky Tonk Legends. Honkytonktx.com. Web. 13 Mar. 2015.
<http://www.honkytonktx.com/legends/>.

"Honor Roll Artists- Buddy Holly." West Texas Music Hall of Fame. Web. 7 Mar. 2015.
<http://www.westexmusichof.com/artists/buddyholly.html>.

Hughes, Bill. "Bill Hughes/ Bio." Bill Hughes- Reverb Nation. Reverb Nation. Web. 7 Mar. 2015.
<http://www.reverbnation.com/artist_2788114/bio>.

Hughes, Dudley. Chattel Mortgage (Contract) Contract between Dudley Hughes and Murray-Davis Aviation Inc (1959). Print.

Hutchings, David. "The Mcguire Sisters, Those Sugartime Princesses of Pop, Have Reunited After a 17-Year Split." People.com 3 Mar. 1986. Print.

Ingman, John. "Charlie Phillips Sugartime." Personal Research Collected by John Ingman for the Bear Family Records CD (2011). Print.

Ingman, John. "Personal E-mail from John Ingman." Recap (2). 2015. Web. 12 May 2015.

Ingman, John. "Personal E-mail from John Ingman to Cy Cushenberry." Information regarding Charlie Phillips. 25 Apr. 2015. Web. 25 Apr. 2015.

Ingman, John. "Various Email Correspondences To and From John Ingman (April 2015 - June 2015)." Apr. 2015. Web. 2015.

"It's 'Sugartime!" State Line Tribune 16 July 1999. Print.

Jacome, David. "Personal Email Correspondences with David Jacome." Peermusic. June 2015. Web. June – Nov 2015.

"James "Jim" Benjamin." Amarillo Globe-News 22 May 2011, Obituaries sec. Web. 13 Mar. 2015. <http://amarillo.com/obituaries/2011-05-22/james-jim-benjamin>.

"John Ritter Tribute Showcase/ Tex Ritter Roundup." 15th Anniversary Country Music Celebration 2012: Texas Country Music Hall of Fame & The Tex Ritter Museum. Web.

Johnson, Loretta. "Remembering When." Country Music Stories 6 July 2013. Print.

Johnson, Loudilla, Loretta Johnson, and Kay Johnson. "Biggest Little News Sheet In Country Music" Tri-Son News (1980). Print.

Johnson, Loudilla. "Personal Telephone Interviews." 2013.

Jones, George. "Personal Interview." Nashville. Apr. 2013.

Jones, Keith. "Personal Telephone Interview with Keith Jones." July 2014

Jones, Tamara. "Musician's Ear Becomes a Career After Long Line of Jobs, Man Finds His Calling in Tuning." Amarillo Globe-News 10 June 2008. Web. 7 Mar. 2015. <http://amarillo.com/stories061008/new_10525844.shtml#.VPtHBEuGreg>.

Jonny, Whiteside. Ramblin' Rose: The Life and Career of Rose Maddox. 1st ed. Vanderbilt UP Co-published with Country Music Foundation, 1997. Print.

Kantrowitz, Dani. "Personal Email from Dani Kantrowitz." Hatch Show Print's Haley Gallery. 7 Dec. 2013. Web. 2013.

"K-Yall's Country "40" Survey." KYAL 1600 Country Western

Station 1965. Print."KRLD Big D Jamboree." Hillbilly-Music.com. Web. 2013. <http://www.hillbilly-music.com/programs/story/index.php?prog=430>.

Keevil, Sabine. Guitars & Cadillacs. Oakville: Thinking Dog, 2002. Print.

"Kenneth Ewell Williamson." Amarillo Globe-News 21 Nov. 2010, Obituaries sec. Print.

Kernes, William. "Four Part Series: As Crickets Finally Get Their Due, a Glimpse into past." Four Part Series: As Crickets Finally Get Their Due, a Glimpse into past | Buddy Holly Archives. Buddyhollyarchives.com, 2012. Web. 25 Nov. 2014. <http://www.buddyhollyarchives.com/2012/04/four-part-series-as-crickets-finally-get-their-due-a-glimpse-into-past/>.

Kerns, William. "Crickets Visit Childhood Home." Amarillo Globe-News 8 Sept. 2013: A3. Print.

Kirkland, Janie. "Personal Letter to Charlie Phillips." KKYN (1984): n. pag. Print.

"Kountry KAGT Top 40 Survey." Kountry KAGT 1340 on Your Dial 19 Sept. 1966. Print.

Larkin, Colin, ed. The Encyclopedia of Popular Music. 3rd ed. New York: Muze, 1998. Print.

LaRue, Carroll (Lash). "Personal Interview." 2013

Laufer, Charles. "Personal Letter to Charlie Phillips." 'Teen Magazine 5 Dec. 1958: 1. Print.

"Letter Regarding Charlie and KZIP Radio Station." Charlie Phillips Personal Letterhead: 1. Print.

Lloyd, Jack. "It's 'Sugartime' Again For McGuire Sisters." Knight-Ridder Newspapers 29 May 1986, Show Business sec. Chicago Tribune. Web. 27 Feb. 2014.

"Local Radio Station KZIP Names Two New Officials." Amarillo Globe-News 1973. Print.

Lynn, Tiny. "Personal Interviews." Clovis. 2013

MacNeish, Jerry. "The Fireballs: Petty Proteges." Goldmine Magazine 16 Dec. 1988. Print.

Macy, Robert. "McGuire-Giancana: Romance Was Epitome of Opposites Attract." Indiana Gazette 1996. Print.

Mauldin , Joe B. "Personal Telephone Interview." (Cricket's bassist). 3 Dec. 2014.

McAlavy, Don. "Buddy Holly, Norman Petty at the Heart of 'the Clovis Sound" Clovis News-Journal, Special To The News Journal sec.: 1-2. Print.

McAlavy, Don. "Echoes from the Back Trails." Clovis News-Journal 22 July 1984. Print.

McAlavy, Don. "Echoes from the Back Trails." Clovis News-Journal 26 Aug. 1984. Print.

McAlavy, Don. "Small Town Studio Has National Reputation." Clovis News-Journal 4 May 1986: 56. Print.

McAlavy, Don. "Christmas Tunes Yield Tales of 1950s Studio." (2005). Print.

McAlavy, Don. "The return of the country barn dance." (2003): n. pag. Print.

McAlavy, Don. Those Who Made the Music In Clovis and Outlying Areas 1907- 2004. Clovis: City Printing, 2005. Print.

"McGuire Sister Testifies Before Federal Grand Jury." Albuquerque Journal 20 May 1965: 7. Print.

"Media Confidential: April 3 In Radio History." N.p., Web. 22 Jul. 2015 <http://mediaconfidential.blogspot.com/2015/04/april-3-in-radio-history.html>.

Melin, Ann. "Tractor-Riding Daydream Basis for a Hit." The Amarillo Globe-Times 9 Oct. 1970, Amarillo, Texas ed., Night People sec. Print.

"Milton DeLugg." Milton DeLugg - Wikipedia, the Free Encyclopedia. Wikipedia. Web. 12 June 2014. <http://en.wikipedia.org/wiki/Milton_DeLugg>.

Mitchell, Gary. "Sugartime to Sweeten Benefit." Clovis News-Journal 22 July 1990: 6A. Print.

Moore, Frazier. "'Sugartime' a Sweet Role for Parker- Barbie-doll Look Suits Her Fine in HBO Film." The Salina Journal 26 Nov. 1995, Salina, Kansas ed. Print.

"MusicDish e-Journal - Up Close with David Bigham of The Roses." N.p., n.d. Web. 16 Jul. 2015 <http://www.musicdish.com/mag/index.php3?id=8272>.

"Music Exec Murray Deutch Dies." Billboardbiz. Billboard, 22 Oct. 2010. Web. 12 June 2014. <http://www.billboard.com/biz/articles/news/1198658/music-exec-murray-deutch-dies>.

"Music Fete Will Honor 'Pop' Echols." The Baytown Sun 7 July 1972, Baytown, Texas ed.: 12. The Baytown Sun. Web. 10 Jan. 2014. <www.newspapers.com/image/#23825879>.

"Music and memories in country's Nashville home by Various..." N.p., Web. 22 Jul. 2015 <http://www.creators.com/lifestylefeatures/travel/travel-and-adventure/music-and->.

Nelson, Willie. "Personal Backstage Interview." Amarillo. N.p., 24 Aug. 2013. Web. 2013.

Newman, Brad. "A Changing Music Scene- Fewer Area Performers Hit Bigtime." Amarillo Globe-News, Scene sec.: 13A. Print.

Newman, Brad. "Accident Impairs, but Doesn't Stop, Musician's Playing." Lubbock Avalanche-Journal 7 Oct. 2009. Web. 7 Mar. 2015. <htt://lubbockonline.com/stories/100709/fea_501863881.shtml#.VPtE90uGreg>.

Newman, Jimmy C. "Personal Interview." Nashville. 7 Dec. 2013.

"Norman & Vi Petty Rock & Roll Museum." Norman & Vi Petty Rock & Roll Museum Home. Web. 6 Aug. 2013.

"Norman Petty's Dream as Lad Turns into Reality and Success." Clovis News-Journal 7 Aug. 1955: 20. Print.

"Norman Petty Studio Recordings." Buddy Holly & The Crickets.com. superoldies.com, Web. 24 Nov. 2014. <http://www.superoldies.com/buddyholly/pettyrec.html>.

"Norman Petty's Trio on Tour: Makes Big Hit." Clovis News-Journal 31 Aug. 1949: 2. Print.

Oermann, Robert K. "The Story Behind The Show That Made Country Music Famous/ Grand Ole Opry: The Show That Made Country Music Famous." What Is the Opry? -

Opry.com. Web. 10 Aug. 2013. <http://www.opry.com/about/WhatisTheOpry.html>.

"Ozark Jubilee - Wikipedia, the free encyclopedia." N.p., n.d. Web. 22 Jul. 2015 <http://en.wikipedia.org/wiki/Ozark_Jubilee>.

"Pappy Stone." ROOTS of Country Music, Internet Encyclopedia of Original Country Music, 2009 6 July 2013. Print.

Pearson, Drew. "Roulette Records." Atchison Daily Globe 27 Mar. 1960: 12. Print.

Penman, Eric W. "Webb Pierce, Pillar of Honkytonk." Web. 6 July 2013. <http://hammer.prohosting.com/~coollz/webb.htm>.

Peoples, Curtis. "Personal Email from Curtis Peoples." (Odis Echols Information). N.p., 22 Nov. 2013. Web. 2013.

Peoples, Curtis L. "The Lubbock Texas Quartet and Odis "Pop" Echols: Promoting Southern Gospel Music on the High Plains of Texas 2014." (2014): 12-20. Print.

Peterson, Richard A. Creating Country Music: Fabricating Authenticity. Chicago: U of Chicago, 1999. Print.

Peterson, Ron. "Personal Interview." Nov. 2014.

"Petty Receives Gold Record." The Curry County Times 9 June 1984. Print.

"Petty Trio 'Tapes' Accepted by USAF for Recruiting Use." Clovis News-Journal 30 Sept. 1955: 2. Print.

"Phillips Named "Mr. DJ USA"" The Amarillo Globe-Times 6 July 1962: 17. Print.

"Phillips Signs With K-Ark." Music City News 1 Oct. 1968. Print.

"Phillips' Band to Entertain." The State Line Tribune "Official Publication of Parmer County" 20 July 1990, 47th ed. Print.

Phillips, Charlie. "Letter from Charlie on KZIP Radio Station Stationary- A Dave Stone Station." 30 Nov. 1977: 1. Print.

Phillips, Charlie, and Norman Petty. "Sugartime Twist." NorVaJak Music, Inc. Music Book: n. pag. Print.

Phillips, Charlie, and Odis Echols. "Sugartime (Sugar in the Morning) Recorded by Jim Dale." Southern Music Publishing Co. Song Book: n. pag. Print.

"Pictures (Musical Groups of the 60's)." Pictures. Lonestarmusic.com. Web. 7 Mar. 2015. <http://lonestarmusic.com/html/pictures.html>.

"Platter Plaudits." Valley News 19 Dec. 1957, Van Nuys, California ed.: 3-C. Web. 11 Jan. 2014. <www.newspapers.com/image/#30352923>.

"Presenting Charlie "Sugartime" Phillips and "Full Circle"" Charlie "Sugartime" Phillips Biography. Lonestarmusic.com. Web. 2 Aug. 2013. <http://lonestarmusic.com/html/charlie_sugartime_phillips_b.html>.

Preston, Frances W. "Dear BMI Million-Air." Personal Letter from BMI (1958). Print.

Price, M. H. "The Complete Circle of Charlie Phillip's Career." Accent West 1 Mar. 1980: 53-8. Print.

Price, Ray. "Personal Telephone Interview." Mt. Pleasant. 6 Oct. 2013.

Qualls, Greg. "Phillips Inducted into Texas Panhandle Broadcasting Hall of Fame." The State Line Tribune "Official Publication of Parmer County" 11 June 1999. Print.

"Raised On Records." N.p., n.d. Web. 31 Jul. 2015 <http://raisedonrecords.blogspot.com/2011/02/charlie-phillips-sugartime-bear-fami>.

"Radio Show Scheduled." Amarillo Globe-News 1 Sept. 2001: 4C. Print.

Ragland, Ruth Ann. "Kids Like Gospel Singing." The Corbin Times-Tribune 9 July 1972, Corbin, Kentucky ed., A New Interest sec.: 12. Web. 10 Jan. 2014. <www.newspapers.com/image/#30491201>.

Ramsey, Jan V. "Maggie Warwick- The First Heroine of Louisiana Music." Offbeat Magazine 11 July 2012. Print.

"Ray Price and The Cherokee Cowboys Opening Act…Charlie Phillips and The Sugartimers." Amarillo Globe-News 18 Dec. 1999. Print.

Re: Texas Playboys Steel Guitarists." N.p., Web. 10 Sep. 2015 <http://www.texasplayboys.net/_disc3/00000054.htm>.

"Recording Artist Named KZIP Manager." The Amarillo Globe-Times 24 Sept. 1967, Amarillo, Texas ed.: 5. Print.

"Recording Artist To Be Club Guest." The Amarillo Globe-Times 3 July 1964, Amarillo, Texas ed. Print.

"Red Steagall - inthebunkhousetv." N.p., n.d. Web. 01 Aug. 2015 <http://www.inthebunkhousetv.com/About_Red.html>.

"Red Steagall & the Coleman County Cowboys | New Music And Songs." N.p., n.d. Web. 02 Aug. 2015 <http://www.cmt.com/artists/red-steagall-the-coleman-county-cowboys/>.

"Revival of Gospel Music Seen by Long-time Singer." The Anniston Star 17 July 1972, Anniston, Alabama ed.: 12. Web. 10 Jan. 2014. <www.newspapers.com/image/#31716668>.

"Robert Kevin DeWeese (Obituary)." Amarillo Globe-News 5 Jan. 2003, Obituaries sec. Web. <http://amarillo.com/stories/2003/01/05/obi_ob010503-13.shtml#.VPtHR0uGreg>.

Roberts, Mark. "Petty's Musical Genius Influenced Today's Tunes." Clovis News-Journal 19 Aug. 1984, 121st ed.: 1-2. Print.

"Rock/Pop Music History." Rock/Pop Music History. inthe00s.com, n.p. Web. 2 Aug. 2013. <http://www.Inthe00s.com/archive/ontherecord/smf/1170519215.shtml>.

Rock, Rock, Rock! Dir. Will Price. By Phyllis Coe and Milton Subotski. Perf. Chuck Berry and Alan Freed. Distributors Corporation of America, 1956. Film.

Romanowski, Patricia. The Rolling Stone Encyclopedia of Rock & Roll. New York: Rolling Stone, 1995. Print.

"Ronnie McKee." Amarillo Globe-News 29 Dec. 2009, Obituaries sec. Web.

"Rooster Morris." Wikipedia. Wikipedia. Print.

Ross, Phil. "Clovis Popular Music Man Gave Stars First Chance." Albuquerque Journal 29 Sept. 1977. Print.

Roughstock. "Roughstock History of Country Music." Outlaw Country | Roughstock's History of Country Music.

roughstock.com, 18 Jan. 2009. Web. 11 Jan. 2014.

Roughstock Staff. "Western Swing." Roughstock's History of Country Music. Roughstock.com, 27 Jan. 2009. Web. 11 Jan. 2014. <http://www.roughstock.com/history/western-swing>.

"Sammy Jackson; TV Actor, Disc Jockey." Sammy Jackson; TV Actor, Disc Jockey- Los Angeles Times. L.A. Times, 1 May 1995. Web. 26 Feb. 2015. <http://articles.latimes.com/1995-05-01/news/mn-60941_1_sammy-jackson>.

Schell, Jimmy. "Personal Interviews." 2013- 2015

Schwarz, George. "Sound of Music Continues Store's New Owner to Carry on Amarillo Tradition." Amarillo Globe-News 16 July 2005. Web. 7 Mar. 2015. <http://scalesstrings.com/Globenews1.htm>.

"Season 10- Episode 26." *The Perry Como Show*. NBC-TV. 15 Mar. 1958. Television. Transcript

"Sees New Surge Of Youthful Interest In Gospel Music." The Kokomo Tribune 9 July 1972, Kokomo, Indiana ed.: 48. Web. 11 Jan. 2014. <www.newspapers.com/image/#45669286>.

Shelton, Gene. "Southwest's Only Major Recording Studio Operated by Clovis Musician." Amarillo Sunday News-Globe 20 Dec. 1959: 4C. Print.

"Shreveport Municipal Auditorium (History)." Shreveport Municipal Auditorium. 2013. Web. 10 July 2013. <http://www.shreveportmunicipalauditorium.com/history/>.

Sisco, Jon. "Charlie "Sugartime" Phillips Full Circle." Research Collected by Jon Sisco for the Full Circle CD Insert (2008). Print.

Smith, Karen D. "The Music Man- Musician Develops Love for a Variety of Music Chet Calcote Was Country When Country Wasn't Exactly Cool." Amarillo Globe- News 10 Nov. 1999. Web. 7 Mar. 2015. <http://amarillo.com/stories/1999/11/10/fri_111099-20.shtml#.VPs6tkuGreg>.

Soloman, Harvey. "Mobster & Singer Made for Strange Love." The

Kokomo Tribune 1 Nov. 1995, Kokomo, Indiana ed.: 25. Print.

Spurrier, Jeff. "The Return of Roy Orbison." Music & Sound Output 1 Apr. 1988. Print.

Stecklein, Janelle. "Coors Cowboy Club Ranch Rodeo: Tunes Underscore Events Band Belts out about 12 Hours of Music." Amarillo Globe-News 5 June 2010. Web. 7 Mar. 2015. <http://amrillo.com/2010/06/05/new_news1.shtml#.VPsz-EuGreg>.

Stevens, Daryll. "Personal Email from Daryll Stevens, Music Librarian." Colorado College. N.p., 11 Dec. 2014. Web. 2014.

Steve, Rich. "Facebook Correspondences with Steve Rich." [Dallas] Oct. 2014: n. pag. Print.

Stewart, Dick. "Up Close with David Bigham of The Roses - A Member of a Legendary Vocal Group That Backed Buddy Holly in Most of 1958." MusicDish E-Journal - Up Close with David Bigham of The Roses. The Lance Monthly, 14 July 2003. Web. 24 Oct. 2014. <http://www.musicdish.com/mag/index.php3?id=8272>.

Stim, Richard. Getting Permission- How to License & Clear Copyrighted Materials Online & Off. 1st ed. Nolo.com Law For All. Print.

Storm, Rick. "Western Swing's the Thing for Duncan." Amarillo Globe- News 9 Dec. 2000. Web. 6 Mar. 2015. <http://amarillo.com/stories/2000/12/09/new_westswing.shtml>.

Stringer, Lou. "From The Editor." Countrypolitan 1 Aug. 1967: 3. Print.

Submissions Dept. "Personal Letter from CAA." Creative Artist Agency (2013): n. pag. Print.

"Sugartime." Phonolog Reports- Top Hits 1 Mar. 1958. Print.

"Sugartime" Phillips - K-Ark 874."
    Record World 1 Mar. 1969. Print.

"Sugartimers to Play Benefit Dance." Clovis News-Journal 23 July 1999: 5. Print.

"Sugartimers to Stage Benefit Concert in Farwell." Clovis News-Journal, Around Corner sec.: 2A. Print.

Sullivan, Phil. Nashville Report. Print.

"Tex Ritter's Ranch Party." *Tex Ritter's Ranch Party*. ABC. 1958. Television. Transcript

"Texas Panhandle Association of Broadcasters 2000- 2002 Banquet Program." 11 Mar. 2000. Print.

"The Fireballs." Web. 7 Mar. 2015. <http://www.fireballs-original.com/>.

"The First Annual Southern American Music Conference." Southern American Music Jam! 2 May 2002: n. pag. Print.

"The Louisiana Hayride Radio Program Premieres on KWKH-AM Shreveport." The Louisiana Hayride Radio Program Premieres on KWKH-AM Shreveport - History.com This Day in History- 4/3/1948. History.com. Web. 10 July 2013. <http://www.history.com/this-day-in-history/the-louisiana-hayride-radio-program-premieres-on-kwkh-am-shreveport>.

"The McGuire Sisters - Sugartime Lyrics | MetroLyrics." Insert Name of Site in Italics. N.p., Web. 21 Jul. 2015 <http://www.metrolyrics.com/sugartime-lyrics-the-mcguire-sisters.html>.

"The Norman Petty Recording Studios Announces Something New in the Southwest." Clovis News-Journal 26 Oct. 1947: 17. Print.

The Real Buddy Holly Story. BBC and MPL Productions. 1 Jan. 1987. Television.

"The Story of the Louisiana Hayride." TV Guide- Close Up 26 May 1985. Print.

"The Sugartime Kid Rides Again - Charlie Phillips With "Be My Bride" And "Too Many Tears"" Cash Box Bullseye 1957. Print.

The Wil-helm Agency A World of Talent for All Occasions: n. pag. Print.

Thiele, Bob, and Bob Golden. What a Wonderful World: A Lifetime of Recordings by Thiele. New York City: Oxford UP, 1995. Print. By permission of Oxford University Press, USA

"Thomas Lee Hadaway." Amarillo Globe-News 24 Aug. 2010, Obituaries sec. Web. 7 Mar. 2015.

"Thursday December 4th Big Autograph Party Country Western Star Charlie Sugartime Phillips." Wrestling, King of Sports Official Program 27 Nov. 1969. Print.

"Tinker Air Force Base." Buddy Holly & The Crickets.com- Tinker Air Force Base (Oklahoma City, OK). Web. 11 July 2014. <http://buddyhollyandthecrickets.com/tinker.html>.

Tippens, Matthew. "Petty, Norman." Norman Petty- The Handbook of Texas Online. Texas State Historical Association (TSHA), 31 Aug. 2010. Web. 12 Mar. 2014. <http://www.tshaonline.org/handbook/online/articles/fpe91.

"Tommy Tomlinson A Great Rockabilly Guitar Picker." A Rockabilly Hall of Fame Presentation. A Rockabilly Hall of Fame Presentation, 1 Oct. 2007. Web. 6 July 2013. <http://www.rockabillyhall.com/TommyTomlinson.html>.

Trinajstick, Blanche. "Charlie Phillips." K-T Country Roundup July: 19-20. Print.

"Unknown." *Cash Box Magazine* 1958: n. pag. Print.

Unterberger, Richie. "Norman Petty Biography." Norman Petty Biography Allmusic. Allmusic. Web. 9 June 2014. <http://www.allmusic.com/artist/norman-petty-mn0000460266>.

"Vi Petty's All Star Tribune." Nor-Vi Music Scholarship Foundation 30 May 1992. Print.

Walker, Scott. "Personality Parade." Parade 27 Jan. 1963: 2. Print.

Warwick, Alton and Maggie. "Personal Interview." 2013

"We Built This City on Rock & Roll." Clovis Music Festival Rocks Sep. 2010: n. pag. Print.

Weize, Richard, John Ingman, and Praguefrank. "Praguefrank's Country Music Discographies." Praguefrank's Country Music Discographies. N.p., Web. 2014.

Wertman, Nelson. "Nelson Wertman Recalls The Barons." 1960's

Garage Bands. 1960's Garage Bands, 1 June 2013. Web. 7 Mar. 2015. <http://www.60sgaragebands.com/barons.html>.

Westex. "Tiny Lynn, Lubbock/ Clovis." Lubbock/Clovis | LoneStarStomp. LoneStarStomp, 31 Oct. 2009. Web. 7 Mar. 2015. <http://lonestarstomp.blogspot.com/2009/10/graveyard-waltz.html>.

Whitfield, Liz. "Personal email from Liz Whitfield." N.p., 23 Jan. 2014. Web. 8 Mar. 2015.

Williams, Jack, Billy Roach, and Ray Williams. "Checkmates- An Interview With Jack Williams." Researching the Local & Regional U.S. Rock Groups of the 1960s. 60sgaragebands.com. Web. 7 Mar. 2015. <http://www.60sgaragebands.comcheckmates.html>.

Wolfe, Charles. The Encyclopedia of Country Music. Ed. Paul Kingsbury. New York City: Oxford UP, 1998. 494-5. Print.

Wolfe, Charles. "Stamps Quartet." Encyclopedia of Gospel Music. Ed. W. K. McNeil. New York City: Routledge, 2005. 370. Print.

"WSM Picture- History Book." Grand Ole Opry 1984: 2-152. Print.

"WT Club Competes In Tri-State Rodeo." The Canyon News [Canyon] 3 Mar. 1974: 7. Print.

"Your Going Is Coming (Smokey, SESAC) - Charlie

Index

'Til Sunday", 214, 296
23 Club, 253
45 & Uppers Good Times Dance Club
   Country, x, 169, 235, 237, 240, 246, 247, 248, 250, 251, 252, 253, 257, 261, 262, 263, 270, 278, 284, 287
4th Creation Graphic Studio, 230
4th Creation Recording Studio, 230
A Christmas Carol, 49
A Rebel Without a Cause, 169
A Red Hot Needle And A Burning Thread", 267
A.O.K.: Record Labels of West Texas & New Mexico, 302
ABC- Paramount Records, 41
Abilene, 277
Academy Awards, 112, 169
Accent West Magazine, x, 252, 303
Acciaioli, Carmen, 237
Ace of Clubs Bar, 253
Acuff
   Roy, 24, 129, 130
Adams, Dustin, 238
Addams Family, The, 169
Adventures of Ozzie and Harriet, The, 99
Agnew, Spiro, 142
Albert Talley Band, 249
Aldean, Jason, 170
Aldean, Wynonna, 170
Allard, Weldon, 145, 238, 239
Alldred, Dave, 47
Alliance Record Co., 284
Allison, Jerry (J.I.), ix, 53, 57, 65, 67, 68, 70, 230, 255, 256, 306
Allm, Harold, 238
All-Star Quartet, 106
Allsup, Tommy, 286
Almost Paradise", 50, 59, 60
Almost", 295
Altec-Lansing, 45, 284
Amarillo Advertising Association, 252
Amarillo Air Force Base, 35, 154, 161, 166, 252, 276
Amarillo Army Airfield, 154
Amarillo Boulevard, 140, 164, 166, 211, 250, 259, 271

Amarillo Civic Center, 155, 165, 167, 217, 260
Amarillo College, x, 247
Amarillo Globe-News, 163, 237, 253, 288, 331
Amarillo High School, 153, 170
Amarillo Little Theater, 246, 272
Amarillo Municipal Auditorium, 154
Amarillo Public Library, x
Amarillo Slim, 171
Amarillo Symphony, 273
Amarillo- The Story of a Western Town, 302
America's Best-Lighted Main Street, 152
American Bandstand, 207
American Civil War, 1
American Idol, 170
American Music Magazine, x, 303
American Theater Hall of Fame, 98
Ammen, Drexal, 238, 239
Amy Records, 280
An Empty Cup", 70
An Old Christmas Card", 268
Anderson, "Whisperin, 128, 130, 132, 146, 216
Anderson, Dub, 239
Anderson, Helen, 239
Anderson, Larry, 239
Anderson, Maurice, 249
Anderson, Senator Clinton, 37
Andrew Jackson Hotel (Nashville), 98, 129, 136, 281
Animal Crackers", 86
Anson, Bill, 272
Anthony, Buck, 239
Apache, the tribe, 152
Apodacca, Chico, 279
April Love", 78
Archer, Jennifer, 169
Arizona Wranglers, 39
Arkansas, Hot Springs, 108
Arkansas, Lake Ouachita, 2
Arkansas, Montgomery County, 2
Arkansas, Mt. Ida, 2
Arkansas, Ouachita National Forest, 2

Arkansas, Pencil Bluff, 2, 4, 108
Armed Forces Radio, 116
Armstrong, Louis, 19, 164
Army Air Corps, 4, 40
Army Technical School, 154
Arnold, Clyde (and the Blew Boys), 253
Arnold, Eddy, 39, 112, 127, 148, 163, 214, 222
Artco Record Label, 225, 226, 297
Arthur Godfrey, 73, 111, 112
Arthur Godfrey's Talent Scouts, 111
Artist International Music Co., 285
Artist International Music Productions, 285
Ashmead, Vic, 160, 236, 240, 249, 253, 259, 285
Ashmead, Victoria (Vicki), 240
At the Hop", 78
Atchison, Topeka and Santa Fe Railroad, the, 19
Atkins, Chet, 128
Atlanta Falcons, 170
Attaway, Buddy, 215
Atwood, George, 67, 68, 230
Audio Refinery Recording Studio, 248
Audiodisc, 56
Australian Silky Terrier, 17
Autry, Gene, 39, 249
Avalon Ballroom, 155, 160, 164, 240, 253, 258, 259, 260, 279
Aviatrix Ballroom, 149, 155, 163, 164, 165, 166, 225, 238, 239, 241, 242, 245, 246, 247, 248, 250, 251, 258, 259, 260, 262, 263, 265, 266, 269, 270, 271, 273, 275, 276, 279, 282, 283, 284, 285
Axle Galench, 269
B-17 Flying Fortress Aircraft, 154
B-29 Aircraft, 154
Baby I Don't Care", 78
Baby Won't You Come Out Tonight", 256
Back In The Shadows", 298
Bagel Bites (Commercial), 101
Bailes Brothers, 116
Bailey, Bob, 241
Bailey, Jack, 241
Baker Brothers Orchestra, 39
Balin' Wire Bob, 215
Ballad of Bill Jones", 224

Ballad of Jed Clampett, The", 56
Banana Split", 77
Barlow, Lee, 236, 242, 283
Barnes, Benny, 121
Barnes, Mr., 89
Barris, Glen (and the Blue Jackets), 39
Basden, Jerry, 159
Baylor County, 4
BBC (British Broadcasting Corporation), 233
Be Careful, Go Easy, Walk Slow", 223
Be My Bride", 62, 63, 64, 66, 93, 95, 96, 205, 206, 207, 235, 262, 295, 296
Be My Little Honey", 99
Beach Boys, the, 222, 223
Bear Family Records, viii, x, 234
Beard, Dean, 57
Beatles, the, xvi, 97, 99, 110, 202
Beatty, Freddy, 244
Beck, Tom, 279
Beecher, John (Rollercoaster Records), viii, x, 231, 232, 233, 234, 301
Beevers, Gary, 242, 255, 264
Before The Next Daybreak's Gone", 297
Bell Sound Studio, 96, 208
Bell, Art, 169
Benatar, Pat, 259
Bend Me Straight Again", 297
Benjamin, Jimmy, 242, 243, 253
Benji the Hunted, 277
Benny Martin Band, 241
Benson, Ray, 277
Benton, Barbi, 101
Berghofer, Chuck, 223
Berle, Milton, 84
Berry, Chuck, 70
Berry, Norma Jean, 62
Beverly Hillbillies, The, 5
Beverly, James, 170
Big "D" Jamboree, the, xxi, 58, 121, 125, 126, 127, 156, 209, 211, 215
Big and Rich, 170
Big Bad John, 277
Big Ball in Cowtown", 221
Big Ball in Texas", 221
Big Ball Is In Cowtown" The, 220, 221, 222, 225, 226, 296, 297
Big Balls in Cowtown", 36, 221
Big Texan Steak House, 241, 261, 278
Biggest Show of Stars of 1957 tour, 70

Bill Case Country Band, 269
Bill Cullen Show, The, 96
Bill Haley (and the Comets), 41, 139, 204
Bill Wimberly's Band, 249
Billboard Magazine, x, 58, 77, 78, 204, 205, 207, 212, 217
Billingsley, Brad, 255
Billy Bayou", 157
Billy Briggs Night Club, 155
Bimbo", 157
Bingham, David, 58, 59
Bivins, Teel, 170
Black Tuesday, 5
Black, Marianne, 101
Blackburn, John, 243
Blackie Foster and his Blackhawks, 254
Blaine, Hal, 223
Blair, Teddy, 243
Blakely, Jimmy, 67, 68, 230
Blanas, Frank, ix, x, 301
Blanton, Governor Ray, 226
Blue Blue Bottle", 224, 297
Blue Christmas", 129
Blue Collar Comedy Tour, 171
Blue Days- Black Nights", 53
Blue Denim I, II, III, 247, 278
Blues Note Band, 268
BMI, 59, 79, 80, 82, 86, 102, 144, 170, 219, 221, 295
Bob "Pappy" Watson Memorial Scholarship Fund, 138
Bob Tucker and His Sky Riders, 43
Bob Wills & His Texas Playboys- Boot Heel Drag: The MGM Years, 268
Bob Wills Day (Turkey, TX), 221, 241
Bobby Hughes Band, The, 260
Bone Crushers, the, 100
Boner, D. William, 41
Boone, Pat, 78
Border Town 4 Band, 262
Border Town Days, 248
Borge, Victor, 142, 143
Boulter, Beau, 170
Bowen, Jimmy, 47, 48, 54, 61, 80, 222, 223, 224, 244, 277
Bowerman, Bruce, 243, 244
Bowman, Big Jim (and his Roadrunner Band), 242, 257, 264
Bowman, Billy, 268
Boys Come Marching Home, The", 109

Bradley Film & Recording Studio, 212, 234
Bradley, Owen, 208
Bradshaw, Carolyn, 215
Breakfast Club, the, 37, 134
Brewer, Teresa, 65
Bridge I Can't Burn, The", 223, 297
Briggs, Billy (and the Chew Tobacco Rag Boys), 155, 156, 157, 160, 238, 244, 249
Brill Building, the, 60, 95
Bringing in the Sheaves", 106
Bristow, Don, 230, 244, 245
Broad, Kenneth, viii, xvi, 291
Broad, Shirley, viii
Broadway Open House, 96
Brock, Dwight, 106
Broken Promises", 203
Broomhead, Charlie, 138
Brother Jukebox", 298
Brown, Eugene, 245, 276, 279
Brown, Gerald, 56, 62, 63, 94, 202, 206, 209, 245, 282
Brown, Jerry, 146
Brown, Lacey, 169
Brown, Les, 164
Brown, Maxine, 215
Brown, Milton (Musical Brownies), 244
Brown-Eyed Handsome Man", 61
Browning, James Nathan, 170
Browns, The, 123
Brunswick Record Label, 60, 65, 71, 74
Bryant, Brad, 170
Bubba's House Band, 100
Buddy Holly Center, the, x, 306
Buddy Holly Day-by-Day (Books 1 -5), 301
Buddy Holly Music Festival, 233
Buentello, Paul, 170
Bugbee, Harold (artist), 153
Bully Of The Town", 45, 295
Bummin' Around", 108
Burke, Martyn, 85
Burnette, Smiley, 39
Burton, Tim, 169
Bush, George Herbert Walker, 84
Bush, George W., 218
Bye Bye Love", 298
Byrds, the, 223
Cadillac Jack Band, The, 274
Cal Farley's Boys Ranch, 260

Calcote, Chet, 236, 241, 245, 246, 247, 249, 253, 259, 272, 285
Caldwell, Aubrey, 246
Caldwell, Gail, 169
Caldwell, Goerge, 116
California, Hollywood, 124, 222, 242
Calloway Family (Farwell, TX), 16, 17
Cameron, Glenda, 301
Camp, Blair, 230
Campbell, Archie, 253
Campbell, Don, 246, 267
Campbell, Glen, xvii, 142, 222, 223, 253, 280
Can't Get Enough of Texas, 246
Canadian Country Music Hall of Fame, 122
Canadian River, the, 151
Cancel the Call", 128, 214, 296
Cannon Air Force Base, 43, 82, 275
Cannon, Henry, 142
Cano, Jimmy (and The Bop Kings), 279
Cañon City College, 216
Capitol Records, 59, 163, 165, 222, 224
Capps, John, 224
Capranica, Larry, 247
Caravan Nightclub, the, 253
Carlson, Paul (author), x, 302
Carpenter, Don, 245
Carpenter, Harold, 247
Carr, Didi, 101
Carter, June, 126
Carter, Marion, 247
Carter, President Jimmy, 84
Cartrite, Richard, 247
Casa Del Nightclub, 155, 158, 159, 164, 239, 260, 265, 281
Casa Mañana Theater (Ft. Worth), 108
Cash, Johnny, 97, 101, 111, 119, 126, 128, 131, 155, 212, 215, 222
Cashbox Magazine, 41, 77, 78, 97, 214
Cassidy Family (Farwell, TX), 11, 12, 13
Casso, Carlos, x, 247, 248
Catch a Falling Star", 78
Cattle Capitol Boys, the. *See* Leaman Denison
Celebrity Apprentice, 170
Chalker, Curley, 249
Chandler, Chip, x, 237
Chandler, Fred, 248

Charles, Ray, 222
Charlie Phillips Sugartime, 234, 299
Chatwell, J.R., 244
Checkmates, the, 266, 271, 278, 279
Chew Tobacco Rag Boys, 156, 244, 249
Chew Tobacco Rag", 156, 244, 249
Cheyenne tribe, 152
Chicago Bears, 170
Chips, The, 245, 279
Chirping Crickets, The, 65
Chubby Checker ("The Twist"), 205
Cincinnati Bengals, the, 170
Circle 13 Dude Ranch Show, 110
City Auditorium (Albuquerque), 215
City Printing Inc. (Clovis, NM), x, 301
Clampet, Jed (fictional character), 5
Clapton, Eric, 99, 222
Clark, Bob, 139
Clark, Royce (Bentley), 226, 227
Clarke, Bo, 58
Classics, The, 246
Clay, Don, 248, 266
Cliff, Earl, 169, 248
Cline, Patsy, 92, 128, 208, 214, 235, 253
Clooney, Rosemary, 96, 222
Clover Club, the, 35, 155, 158, 162, 164, 219, 253, 260, 262
Clovis Cowboy Band, 39
Clovis Floral Co., 269
Clovis Municipal Airport, 89
Clovis Sound, 43
Coal Miner's Daughter, 227
Cochran, Eddie, 70
Coffman, Harry, 239, 248
Cogan, Alma, 96, 205
Cohen, Paul, 208
Cold Country Band, 242
Collingsworth, Bob, 158
Collins, Doug, 227, 244
Collins, Larry, 98, 99
Collins, Lorrie, 98, 99
Colorado Corral, The, 246
Columbia Record's Showcase, 145
Columbia Recording Studio, 148, 213
Columbia Records, 47, 58, 59, 127, 128, 141, 145, 148, 210, 211, 224, 231, 280, 290
Comanche tribe, 152
Comedy in Music, 142

Commodores, the, 111
Como, Perry, 78, 83, 84
Condray, Charlene, 110, 309, 323
Coney Island (Clovis, NM), 20
Congressional Space Medal of Honor, 171
Cooder Graw, 161, 284
Cook, Curley, 242
Cook, Dwight, 236, 249
Cooley, Spade, 244, 263
Cooper, Joe, 146
Coors Cowboy Club Ranch Rodeo, 241
Coral Records, xvii, 60, 65, 71, 72, 73, 74, 77, 78, 83, 86, 93, 94, 95, 96, 115, 127, 141, 201, 202, 203, 204, 205, 206, 208, 280, 290, 295, 296
Cornelius, Corky, 249
Cornelius, David, 250
Corsage, 50
Cotton Club, the, 280
Couch, Benny, 250, 267
Couch, Judy, 250
Country Barn Supper Club, 155
Country Music Hall of Fame Bob Wills Compilation, 238
Country Music Hall of Fame, the, ix, x, xii, 125, 165, 214, 238, 305, 306
Country Music Holiday, 165
Courtin' in the Rain", 44, 56, 202, 283, 295
Cowboy Corner, 277
Cowboy Poet Laureate of San Juan Capistrano, 277
Cowjazz Western Swing band, 272
Cox, Mike (author), 301
Cracker Barrel Show, 227, 247
Cradle of the Stars, the. *See* Louisiana Hayride
Cramer, Floyd, 213, 214
Craven, Bill, 216
Crawford, Jim (reporter), 27
Crawford, Walter T., 146, 147
Crazy Otto's Club, 253
Creedence Clearwater Revival, 259
Cricket's Fact File, 302
Crickets, the, viii, xvi, xvii, 41, 53, 54, 55, 57, 58, 60, 61, 64, 65, 66, 70, 78, 80, 107, 201, 203, 204, 205, 206, 228, 231, 256, 291, 306
Crosby, Bing, 222
Crosby, Bob, 110

Crowder Family, 111
Cry! Cry! Cry!", 97
Crying", 47
Curtis, Sonny, 53, 72, 256
Cushenberry, Cy, 236
Cutlip, Marisa Madge, vii
Czechchowski, Ted, x, 236, 251, 252, 253
Dale, Jim, 97, 98
Dallas Sportatorium, 126
Dang Me", 137
Daniels, Charlie, 277
Dannhelm, William "Willie", 16
Danny & The Juniors, 212
Darby, Marc, 251
Dark Before Dawn, 277
Darnell, Mildred "Millie", x, 214, 215
Davenport, Mike, 138
Davis, Don, 215
Davis, Sammy Jr., 259
Davis, Sherry, 203
Davis. Governor Jimmy, 37
Day, Doris, 222
Day, Jimmy, 155
Dean, Dizzy, 134
Dean, George, 107
Dean, James, 53, 169
Dean, Jimmy, 107, 145
Deaton, Betty, 48
Decca Records, 41, 53, 54, 57, 59, 71, 139, 141, 202, 203, 208, 209, 210, 222, 242
Deejay Convention, 144, 213, 281
Delmar Brothers, 221
Delta Dawn", 99
Delugg, Milton, 96
Denison, Coy, 264
Denison, Hubert, 264
Denison, Leaman "Tiny Lynn", ix, x, 224, 231, 242, 262, 263, 264, 265, 271, 282, 283, 285
Deutch, Murray, 60, 65, 70, 71, 72, 73, 74, 206, 207
Devil Doll", 58
Deweese, Robert Kevin "Doc", 146, 252
Diamond Rio, 167, 168
Dick Bivins Stadium, 167
Dickens, Charles, 49
Dickens, Little Jimmy, x, xvii, 127, 209, 241, 249
Dixie Chicks, 161, 170

Dixon, Billy Edd, 138
Dodd, Bobby, 252
Dodge, Steve, 279
Dolman, Andy, 252
Domino, Fats, 70
Don't Stop", 280
Donaldson place, the old, 1, 7, 23, 26
Doobie Brothers, 259
Doran, Ann, 169
Dorsey Brothers, 161
Dorsey, Jimmy, 164
Dorsey, Tommy, 164
Double Dip Drive-in (Amarillo, TX), 153
Douglas, Glen, 97
Down Yonder on the Piano", 129
Drake, Eddie, 223
Draper, Rusty, 112
Duncan, "Hi Pockets", 111
Duncan, Rupert M "Tiny", 111, 160, 236, 240, 249, 250, 252, 253, 259, 283, 287
Dunn, Bob, 244
Durham, Marc, 254
Dust Bowl of 1935, the, 14
Dylan, Bob, 222
Earhart, Amelia, 163
Eastridge Bowling Alley, 164
Echols' All-Star Texans Quartet, 108
Echols, Coy, 107, 110
Echols, Horace, 107
Echols, Mr. and Mrs. W.L., 105
Echols, Odis "Pop", 37, 38, 49, 61, 62, 66, 67, 69, 73, 74, 79, 81, 82, 83, 86, 87, 88, 92, 94, 105, 106, 107, 108, 109, 110, 111, 112, 113, 117, 118, 119, 121, 133, 134, 137, 140, 141, 146, 202, 203, 204, 207, 210, 241, 257, 289, 290
Echols, Odis and his Faultless Melody Boys, 109
Echols, Odis Jr., 81, 82, 86, 93, 94, 95, 111, 113, 146
Ed Sullivan Show, 61, 84
Ed's Place, 82
Eddy, Duane, 205
Edenton, Raymond Q "Ray", 212
Edwards Twins, the, 205, 211
Edwards, Ralph, 112
Electra's, the, 245

Elfman, Danny, 169
Elizabeth II, Queen, 84
Elkins Bar, 243
Ellington, Duke, 41, 161, 164
Elmore, Leroy, 139
Elvis, Hank and Me: Making Musical History on the 'Hayride', 117
Ely, Joe, 161, 169
Ely, Ron, 169
Empire Room, the (Waldorf-Astoria), 95
English Airfield, 163
English, Todd, 169
Engvall, Bill, 171
Epic Records, 219
Ercoupe, 88, 89
Erickson, John R., 269
Euton, Tommy, 245
Fair Park Coliseum (Lubbock), 54
Faker", 208, 256, 296, 298
Fallon, Jimmy, 101
Farmall Tractor, 27
Farwell brothers, 8
Farwell Convalescent Home, 263, 291
Farwell High School, 261, 283
Farwell Junior High School, 27
Farwell, Charles, 8
Farwell, John, 8
Fayros, the, 279, 284
FCC (Federal Communications Commission), 138, 139
Felty, Gregg, 254
Ferris, Bob, 146
Fireballs, the, 209, 228, 232, 233, 242, 254, 257, 272, 291
Fireman's Benefit in Houston, 207
First Church of God, the (Miamisburg, OH), 73
Flatt and Scruggs, 56
Flips, The, 262
Flower Of My Heart", 256
Foley, Red, xvii, xxi, 58, 123, 124, 125, 208, 212, 217, 241, 243
Fool's Paradise", 66
Ford, Doyle, 118
Ford, Jack, 215
Ford, President Gerald, 84
Ford, Tennessee Ernie, 39, 44, 142
Foster, Blackie, 239, 254
Four Deacons, 116

Four Square Gospel Church, 110
Fowler, Kevin, 169
Fox Drug Store (Clovis, NM), 107
Fox, Mike, 146, 147
Foxworthy, Jeff, 171
Foxx, Redd, 222
Franks, Tillman, 58, 121, 162, 219, 220, 224, 230, 301
Freckle-Face Snaggle-Tooth Gal", 244
Freed, Alan, 54
Frizzell, David, 253, 259
Frizzell, Lefty, 39, 127, 241, 253, 286
Full Circle Album- The Last Norman Petty Sessions, 230
Fun Brothers Band, 255
Funderburk, Janet, 240
Funk, Dory, 170
Funk, Dory Jr, 144, 170
Funk, Terry, 170
Gabroy, Calder, vii
Garner, Blair, 169
Gary Dale Singers, 220, 230
Gatlin, Larry, 277
Gentry, Robert, 301
George, Maunay, 264
Gerron, Peggy Sue, ix, xi, 301
Giancana, Sam, 84, 85
Gibbs, Georgia, 96
Gibson ES5 Switchmaster, 275
Gibson, Don, 97
Gibson, Susan, 161, 170
Gill, Kent, viii
Gill, Vince, 39
Girl On My Mind", 256
Gisele MacKenzie Show, The, 84
Give the World a Smile", 106
Goad, Paul, 254, 255
Godfrey, Arthur, 73, 111
Goin' Away", 228, 298
Going Away", 298
Gold Record, xix, xxi, 79, 81, 83, 84, 86, 134, 144, 265
Golden Spread, the, 152, 170
Goldrosen, John, 301
Good Night, Irene", 238
Goodman, Benny, 161
Goodnight, Charles, 152
Goodnite, Sweetheart, Goodnite", 73
Gordon Fitzhugh and the Hotel Clovis Orchestra, 39
Gosdin, Vern, 261

Grammy Award, 98, 125, 169, 223
Grand Old Opry, the (band), 256
Grand Ole Opry, the, viii, ix, xi, xvii, xx, xxi, 23, 39, 53, 56, 58, 87, 116, 117, 121, 122, 127, 128, 129, 130, 131, 132, 144, 146, 155, 209, 211, 213, 215, 289, 303, 305
Grant Turner Radio Show, 144
Grant, Jack, 146
Graveyard Waltz", 231, 265
Great Depression, the, 14, 107, 108
Green Bay Packers, the, 170
Green, George, 96
Griffin, Jim, 255
Griggs, Bill, 301
Groom, Dewey, 220
Guess Family Gospel Show, 255
Guess Sisters, 255
Guess, Don, 53, 141, 208, 209, 255, 256, 330
Guinness Book of World Records, 142
Ha Ha Song, The", 280
Hacker, Bobby, 245, 276, 279
Hadaway, Dorothy, 256
Hadaway, Tom, 256, 257, 287
Haggard, Merle, xi, 142, 167, 224, 258, 290
Hal Roach Studios, 108
Haley, Bill. *See* Bill Haley (and the Comets)
Hall Music Store (Abilene, TX), 108
Hall of Great Westerners, 277
Ham, Earl, 257
Hamilton, Larry, 257
Hamlin Memorial Methodist Church, 26, 29
Hamlin, Judge, 26
Hancock, Tommy, 110
Haney, Tommy Lee (and the Rainbow Ramblers), 242, 257, 264, 272
Hank the Cowdog, 248, 269
Hanson, Forrest, 258, 275
Hardcastle, Frank, 258, 274
Harley Sadler Tent Show, 39, 108
Harman Jr, Murray "Buddy", 212
Harper, Jo "Josie", 71
Harper, Thelma (fictional character), 100
Harris, Freddy, 258, 259
Harry Potter, 98
Hart, Freddy, 253
Hartford Music Company, 109

Hartman, Tom, 225, 226
Has Anyone Seen Me Lately?", 298
Hatch Show Print's Haley Gallery, xi
Hathcock, Johnny, 140, 145, 146, 148, 158, 161, 162, 163, 165, 212, 213, 219, 238, 269, 313, 333
Have I Stayed Away Too Long?", 262, 295
Hawkins, Betty, 36, 259
HBO (Home Box Office), 85
He'll Have to Go", 158
Hearne, Michael, 237
Hearst, William Randolph, 94
Heatherly, Hubert, 245
Hee Haw, xx, 87, 169, 277
Hefner, Hugh, 102
Hefti, Neil, 72
Henderson, William Kennon W.K., 118
Here We Go Again, 277
Herman, Woody, 164
Herring Hotel (Amarillo, TX), 153
Hey Porter", 97
Hicks, Jeanette, 215
Hi-Flyers, the, 244
Hill, Faith, 170
Hillhouse, Betty, 48
Hillsboro Theatre (Nashville, TN), 127
Hit Parade, 78, 125
Hodges, Jerry, 279
Hodges, John, 247
Holley, Charles Hardin "Buddy", 51, 53, 111, 139, 255, 256, 274
Holley, Joe, 267
Holly, Buddy, viii, ix, x, xv, xvi, xvii, 41, 53, 54, 55, 57, 58, 59, 61, 64, 65, 66, 67, 68, 70, 80, 92, 96, 99, 100, 107, 111, 121, 161, 201, 202, 203, 204, 205, 206, 208, 209, 228, 230, 231, 232, 233, 235, 244, 246, 255, 256, 266, 275, 282, 290, 291, 301, 306
Holly, Cotton, 259
Holston, Johnny 'Reverb', 254
Holt, Kimberly Willis, 169
Home Cookin' Band, 255
Home of the Blues", 97
Honest" Jess Williams and His Western Cavaliers, 253, 258
Hooper, Earl, 163
Hoot & Curley, 215
Hopalong Cassidy, 18
Hopkins, Bob, 259, 260
Hornando's Hideaway, 32, 33
Hornsby, Bud, 257
Horton, Johnny, 120, 121, 209, 215, 219, 235, 253
Hotel Clovis, the, 19
Houston Oilers, the, 170
Houston, David, viii, 162, 215, 219
Howard Theater (Washington, D.C.), 70
Hub City of the Land of Modern Pioneers (Amarillo, TX), 154
Huckert, Donnie, 260
Hughes, Billy, 260, 261
Hughes, Bobby (and the Western Heartbeats), 146, 160, 260
Hughes, Dudley, 28, 38, 49, 56, 62, 88, 91, 94, 202, 206, 209, 230, 261, 272, 282
Hughes, Howard, 89
Humble Heart", 203
Hume, Virgil, 43
Hunter, Ray, 262
Hurry Up Sundown", 298
Husband, Rick, 171
Husky, Ferlin, 128, 158, 162, 165, 262
Hutcheson, Jerry, 262
Hypnotized", 74
I Am Giving Her Love", 225
I Can Help", 147
I Couldn't Keep From Crying", 97
I Guess I'll Never Learn", 128, 167, 212, 213, 226, 238, 296, 297
I Walk Alone Tomorrow", 225, 297
I Won't Be Around", 208, 256, 296
I'll Take What's Left Of You", 298
I'm Giving Her Love", 225, 297
I'm Gonna Love You", 66
I'm Looking for Someone to Love", 61
I'm Only a Friend Why Do You Call Me Your Sweetheart", 268
I'm Sticking With You", 48, 222
I'm Trapped", 223, 297
Impulse!, 222
In the Bunkhouse with Red Steagall, 277
Ingman, John, viii, xi, 211, 231, 233, 234, 235, 291, 293, 302
Inman, Jerry, 223
Interstate-40, 151, 153, 166
It's A Heartache", 298
It's So Easy", 66

Izzard, Bob, 138
Jack, Wolfman, 138
Jackson, Bob, 146, 263
Jackson, Jack, 158
Jackson, Stonewall, 262
Jackson, Wanda, 264
James, Harry, 161
James, Jimmy, 257
James, Odie, 264
James, Otis, 263
James, Sonny the "Southern Gentleman", 123, 165, 256
Jennings, Waylon, 33, 39, 111, 139, 146, 215, 218, 253, 280, 290
Jerry & The Sparkletones, 279
Jimmy Dean Sausage Company, 108
Jimmy Dean Show, The, 145
Jobes, Mrs., 27, 33, 290
John, Elton, 222
Johnson, Lyndon Baines, 157
Jolly Cholly (Charlie Phillips' radio handle), 140, 142, 146, 158, 281
Jones, Bruce, 120
Jones, Carolyn, 169
Jones, George, xvii, 119, 121, 126, 127, 131, 142, 158, 162, 215, 217, 218, 224, 253, 256, 261, 262
Jones, Grandpa, 127
Jones, John Marvin, 170
Jones, Rufus R. "The King", 144
Jones, Spike, 164
Just Let the Flowers Grow", 224
KAMQ radio station, 137, 238
Kane, Harnett Thomas, 115
K-Ark Record Label, 224, 225, 226, 297
KBYE radio station, 286
KCLV radio station, 37, 38, 62, 81, 87, 110, 111, 112, 133, 134, 135, 137, 146, 269, 270
KDUB television, 110
Keith, Toby, 277
Kelly, Dean, 138, 146, 148, 155, 213
KENM radio station, 42, 264
Kennedy, President John F., 85, 89, 157
Kenton, Stan, 164
Key, Woody, 230
Khiva Shrine Temple Western Swing Band, 249
KICA radio station, 40, 42, 45, 58, 202, 255, 262

KIJN radio station, 264
Kiker, Bob, 18
King of Rock, 155
King of the Road", 137
King of Western Bop, 155
King of Western Swing Band, 285
King, Pee Wee, 241
Kinsey, Curley, 116
Kiowa tribe, 152
Kirkland, Janie, 146, 147
KLLL radio station, 111
KLMR radio station, 246
Knox, Buddy, 47, 48, 50, 54, 59, 61, 67, 80, 206, 210, 222, 244, 256, 290
Knox, Mike, 170
Knuckles, Humpty, 257
Knuckles, Irene, 257
Koefer, Bobby, 268, 283
KOKO radio station, 246
KOMA radio station, 147, 241
Kommer Du I Aften" (Sugartime, Netherlands), 100
Korean War, the, 4, 49, 109, 154, 256
Kountry Kut-ups, 265, 266
KPAR radio station, 147
KPEP radio station, 139
KRAKT band, 259
Kristofferson, Kris, 257
KSL radio station (Salt Lake City, UT), 41
KSWS television, 264
K-tel International, 226
KTHS radio station, 108, 109
KTQM radio station (Clovis, NM), 42, 225
KTRB radio station, 35
KVER television, 265
KWKA radio station (Clovis, NM), 42, 225
KWKH radio station, 109, 115, 117, 118, 120, 157, 235, 241, 323
KWTO radio station, 123
KZIP radio station (Amarillo, TX), 128, 130, 136, 137, 138, 139, 140, 141, 142, 143, 144, 145, 146, 147, 148, 149, 156, 157, 158, 159, 161, 165, 210, 211, 212, 218, 219, 221, 225, 227, 242, 252, 261, 263, 269, 273, 281, 291
KZOL radio station (Farwell, TX), 42, 264

La Fonda drive-in, 133
La Vista, the, 39, 263, 264, 283, 285
Lakeside Club, the, 155, 159, 239
Langley Army Air Field, 40
Lanier, Don "Donnie", 47, 280
Lareau, Sébastien, 170
Larry Martin Band, the, 274
Larry the Cable Guy, 171
Larry Trider Show, the, 242, 280
LaRue, Carroll "Lash", ix, 31, 274
Last Night", 61
Last Rock and Roll Show, The, 301
Late Night With Jimmy Fallon, 101
Later Tonight", 217, 296
Law, Don, 148, 210, 213
Lawrence, Vicki, 100
Leach, Colonel Bill, 40, 41
Ledbetter, Huddie, 119, 238
Lee, Brenda, xi, 123, 124, 207, 208, 214
Lehman Denison Band, the, 242
Lennon, Cynthia, 97
Lennon, John, 97, 223
Les Paul Gibson guitar, 266
Lewis, Jerry Lee, 165
Lewis, Ruby "Lady Cool Breeze", xi, 137, 138
Lifetime Achievement Grammy Award, 125
Linville, Robert, 58
Listen (Could It Be Her)", 298
Listen to Me", 66
Little Lehman's Half-Fast Songs, 265
Little Miss Dynamite
  see Brenda Lee, 124, 125
Little Rascals, the, 12
Little Richard, 70, 161, 204
Lockhart, Paul, 171
Logan, Horace Lee "Hoss", 115, 116, 117, 118, 119, 120, 201, 204, 215
Lombardo, Guy, 161
Lone Star Beer and Bob Wills Music", 277
Lonesome Tears", 66
Longhorn Ballroom, the, 215, 220
Lord, Bobby, 155
Los Angeles' Club 15, 109
Louisiana Hayride, the, ix, xi, xvii, xxi, 39, 56, 58, 87, 115, 116, 117, 118, 119, 120, 121, 122, 124, 125, 126, 132, 156, 201, 203, 204, 211, 214, 215, 219, 252, 256, 261, 262
Louisiana Music Hall of Fame, the, 214
Louvin Bros., the, 126
Love Queen", 228
Lubbock Avalanche-Journal, the, xi, 278
Lyceum Theater, the, 242
Lynn, Loretta, xx, 128, 224, 257, 264
MacKenzie, Gisele, 84
MacLaine, Shirley, 29
MacNesh, Jerry, 233
Maddox Brothers and Rose, the, 35, 219, 238
Magnus, Ted, 12
Maheu, Robert, 89
Mailman Bring Me No More Blues", 58, 61
Mama's Family, 100
Marchbanks, Curtis, 265
Marchbanks, Dwight, 265
Marchbanks, Larry, 265, 266
Marcum, Larry, 266, 279
Marshall Auditorium, the (Clovis, NM), 257
Marson, Herschell, 244
Martin, Bill, 274
Martin, Dean, 84, 148, 163
Martin, Thomas Grady, 208, 212
Marx, Chico, 86, 87
Massongill, Mary, 2, 9, 10
Massongill, Thad, 2, 3, 4, 5, 7
Massongill, the family, 3, 108
Masterpiece Mastering, 230
Mauldin, Joe B., xi, xvii, 210, 269
Maybe Baby", 61, 70, 205
MCA/Universal Studio, 208
McAlpin, Vic, 97
McAuliff, Leon (Western Swing Band), 246
McCall, Darrell, 167, 212
McCartney, Linda, 99, 101
McCartney, Sir Paul, x, 99, 100, 233
McClure, Charles Chuck, 266, 278, 279
McConaughey, Matthew, 284
McCoy, Neal, 277
McDonald, Skeets, 249
McDuff, Eddie, 157
McGuire Sisters, the, viii, xix, 65, 72, 73, 74, 77, 79, 80, 83, 84, 85, 86, 95, 96,

97, 100, 101, 102, 111, 117, 122, 126, 145, 204, 205, 206, 290
McGuire, Christine, 73, 79, 83, 95
McGuire, Dorothy, 73, 79, 83, 95
McGuire, Phyllis, xi, 73, 79, 83, 84, 85, 86, 95
McIntyre, Reba, 39
McKee, Ron, 266, 271
McKenna, Maureen, 246
McKenzie, Big Tex, 144
McLemore, Ed, 126
McNeil, Don, 37
McPeters, Buddy, 268
McWhorter, Frankie, 241, 253, 283, 285
Meatloaf (singer), 101
Melody Boys Quartet, the, 107, 109, 110
Melody Lane Publications, 60
Melvoin, Michael, 223
Memory Number One", 298
Mercury Record label, 59
Mercy Brothers, the, 116
Mesa Theater, the (Clovis, NM), 19, 20, 39, 92, 227, 232, 242
Messer, Shorty, 247, 267, 268
Mexican Joe", 157
MGM Records, 222
Miami Daily News, xi, 102
Miami Dolphins, the, 170
Michael Martin Murphey Band, 237
Middleton, Velma, 164
Midgie (the dog), 16
Miller, Clyde, 39
Miller, Glenn, 19
Miller, Mitch, 47
Miller, Roger, 39, 111, 112, 136, 137, 138, 140, 211, 224, 259
Millinder, Lucky, 244
Minneapolis Moline tractor, 27
Minnesota, Moorhead, 209
Miskovsky, Senator George, 102
Mission Garden Cemetery, 30
Missouri, Springfield, 123, 124, 217
Mitchell, Loren, 244
Mitchell, Mike, 146, 210, 268
Modern Don Juan", 256
Montgomery, Bob, 255, 256
Mood Indigo", 41, 42, 50
Moondance band, 269
Moore, Chris, 168
More And More", 298

Morell, Louis, 222
Morgan, George, 127, 216, 217
Morrell, Tommy, 249
Morris, Rooster, 269
Morton, Professor "Prof", 28
Mountain of Love", 219
Mr. DJ, USA, xxi, 145, 213
Mr. Rock & Roll, 165
Mulhair Studios, the, 255
Mulhair, Jill, 255
Mulhair, Johnny, 242, 255
Murray-Davis Aviation Inc., 89
Muscle Shoals Sound Studio, 202
Music City Recordings, 242
Music Reporter, the, 145
Musical Grays, the, 39
Musicians Hall of Fame, 223
N.B.C. or Neighborhood Boys Cut-up Quartet, the, 108
Nashville Area Chamber of Commerce, xi
Nashville on the Road, 277
Nashville Star, 170
Nat Ballroom, the, 155, 161
National Academy of Recording Arts and Sciences Award, 223
National Cowboy and Western Heritage Museum, 277
National Life & Accident Insurance Company, 127
Neal, Bob, 149, 213
Neilrae Music, 149
Nelson, Ricky, 99, 148
Nelson, Willie, xx, 111, 140, 142, 158, 162, 163, 166, 167, 215, 238, 254, 262, 290, 292
Nemire, Terry, 269
Nesman Studio, the, 53
New Mexico, Albuquerque, 19, 151, 212, 215
New Mexico, Blacktower, 105
New Mexico, Carlsbad Caverns, 20
New Mexico, Clovis, viii, x, xvi, 8, 9, 18, 19, 20, 21, 29, 30, 35, 36, 37, 38, 39, 40, 41, 42, 43, 45, 46, 47, 48, 50, 54, 57, 58, 59, 60, 61, 64, 65, 66, 71, 72, 80, 81, 82, 86, 87, 88, 89, 90, 91, 92, 93, 94, 105, 107, 110, 111, 112, 113, 118, 122, 125, 126, 133, 134, 137, 159, 166, 201, 202, 206, 210, 220, 225, 227, 228, 229, 231, 232,

233, 235, 242, 243, 245, 248, 254,
255, 257, 262, 263, 264, 265, 268,
269, 270, 271, 272, 274, 275, 280,
282, 283, 285, 291, 301, 305, 324
New Mexico, Farmington, 50
New Mexico, Grady, 30, 82, 91, 93, 274
New Mexico, Kenna, 81, 243, 245, 261
New Mexico, Portales, 42, 81, 88, 264
New Mexico, Taiban, 82, 264
New Mexico, Texico, 8, 18, 26, 262
New Orleans Saints, the, 170
New York, New York City, xvii, 20, 39,
43, 44, 60, 65, 71, 72, 77, 79, 81, 82,
86, 93, 94, 95, 111, 124, 135, 206,
208, 251, 252, 302
New, L.E., 269, 270
Newman, Jimmy C., xvii, 128, 130, 155,
215
Newton, Ralph, 146
Niemire, Terry, 146
*Night the Lights Went Out in Georgia,
The"*, 227
Nix, Hoyle, 221
Nix, Jody, 221
Nixon, President Richard, 84
NME reader's poll, 97
No Greater Love", 227, 297, 298
No More Sugartime", 128, 210, 211,
269, 296
No One To Love", 149, 214, 296
No Show Jones (George Jones), 217
Noland, Terry, 74, 256
Norman & Vi Petty Rock & Roll
Museum, xi, 291, 305
Norman Petty Agency, the (NYC), 71
Norman Petty Ensemble, the, 40
Norman Petty Show, The, 40
Norman Petty Studio, the, viii, ix, xi, xvi,
42, 43, 44, 47, 53, 55, 57, 59, 60, 66,
80, 94, 95, 105, 112, 121, 137, 202,
205, 208, 211, 226, 227, 233, 242,
255, 256, 268, 273, 275, 279, 291,
305
Norman Petty Trio, the, 40, 41, 42, 43,
59, 67, 70, 73, 268
North Pole Boogie", 244
Norton, James, 28, 38, 91, 92, 261, 270
NorVaJak label, 40, 42, 50, 60, 71, 79,
81, 86, 99, 228, 268, 280
Now Here's Johnny Cash, 97

Now That It's Over", 128, 212, 296,
298
Nudie Suit, a, 98
Nuevo Laredo", 298
Nutt, Grady, 169
O'Brien, Alex, 170
Oak Records, 228
Oakland Raiders, the, 170
Ode to Bagel Bites", 101
Odessa Junior College (Texas), 58
Official Cowboy Poet of Texas, The,
277
Oh Boy!", 66, 205
Oh, Pretty Woman", 47
Ol' Man River", 106
Old Southern Jamboree, 122
Old Tascosa Room, 153
On My Mind Again", 57, 58
One Faded Rose", 56, 61, 62, 66, 67, 68,
72, 120, 121, 141, 202, 204, 235,
245, 262, 275, 282, 295
One-Take Charlie (Phillips), 96, 208,
229
Only the Lonely", 47
Ooby Dooby", 47
Opry Star Spotlight, 146
Orbison, Roy, 47, 54, 58, 66, 67, 111,
112, 161, 206, 244, 256
Orton, Barry, 170
Over-39 Singles Dance Club (Country),
168, 240, 247, 257, 258
Over-the-Hill Gang, the, 285
Owens, Buck, 146, 224
Ozark Jubilee Band, the, 241, 253
Ozark Jubilee, Red Foley's, xvii, xxi, 58,
123, 124, 125, 156, 212, 217, 241,
243, 253
Ozark Mountaineers, the, 116
Page, Frank, 120
Paint (the horse), 16, 17
Palmer, Ryan, 170
Palo Duro High School (Amarillo), 240
Panhandle Barn Dance, the, 155, 260
Paramount Theater, the (Amarillo), 152
Parker, Colonel Tom, 112
Parker, Hershel, 282
Parker, Lana, 127
Parker, Mary-Louise, xi, 85, 86
Parton, Dolly, xx, 128, 224
Party Doll", 50, 59, 61, 80, 210, 222

Paulk, Steve, 270
Pearl, Minnie, xx, 24, 112, 127, 142, 209, 241
Pearson, Jimmy, 271
Pedigrew, Ed, 82
Peer Publishing, 86
Peer, Ralph, 60, 106, 107
Peer-International, 60
Peer-Southern Music, 60
Peggy Sue", ix, xi, 61, 66, 78, 80, 100, 205, 301
People Magazine, xi, 85
Percussive Arts Society Hall of Fame, 223
Perrin, Rex, 271
Perry Como Show, The, 83
Perryman, Tom, 215
Peterson, Roger, 209
Peterson, Ron, 142, 146, 147, 218
Pettigrew, Joe, 271
Petty, Norman, viii, ix, xi, xvi, 27, 40, 41, 42, 43, 44, 45, 46, 47, 50, 53, 54, 55, 56, 57, 58, 59, 60, 61, 62, 63, 64, 65, 66, 67, 68, 69, 70, 71, 72, 73, 74, 79, 80, 81, 86, 87, 92, 93, 94, 95, 96, 100, 105, 112, 121, 137, 201, 202, 203, 205, 206, 208, 209, 210, 211, 220, 222, 225, 226, 227, 228, 229, 230, 231, 232, 233, 234, 242, 244, 255, 256, 268, 269, 273, 275, 279, 280, 282, 290, 291, 301, 305
Petty, Vi, viii, xi, 53, 54, 67, 68, 232, 233, 291, 305
Philadelphia Eagles, the, 170
Phillips, Albert Frank Jr.. *See* Bunk Phillips
Phillips, Bill, 122, 123
Phillips, Bum, 170
Phillips, Bunk, 5, 13, 20, 28, 29, 30, 293
Phillips, Carthon, xi, 4, 9, 10, 13, 15, 16, 20, 26, 30, 78, 79, 293
Phillips, Charles Don Charlie, vii, viii, ix, xi, xv, xvi, xvii, xviii, xix, xx, xxi, 9, 10, 12, 13, 14, 15, 16, 17, 18, 19, 20, 21, 24, 25, 26, 27, 28, 30, 31, 32, 33, 35, 36, 37, 38, 39, 44, 45, 48, 49, 55, 56, 61, 62, 63, 64, 66, 67, 68, 69, 72, 73, 74, 75, 77, 78, 79, 80, 81, 82, 83, 86, 87, 88, 89, 90, 91, 92, 93, 94, 95, 96, 97, 98, 101, 102, 105, 107, 108, 110, 112, 113, 115, 117, 118, 119, 120, 121, 122, 123, 124, 125, 126, 127, 128, 129, 130, 131, 132, 133, 134, 135, 136, 137, 138, 140, 141, 142, 143, 144, 145, 146, 147, 148, 149, 155, 156, 157, 158, 159, 160, 161, 162, 163, 164, 165, 166, 167, 168, 169, 171, 201, 202, 203, 204, 205, 206, 207, 208, 209, 210, 211, 212, 213, 214, 215, 216, 217, 218, 219, 220, 221, 222, 223, 224, 225, 226, 227, 228, 229, 230, 231, 232, 233, 234, 235, 236, 237, 238, 239, 240, 241, 242, 243, 244, 245, 246, 247, 248, 250, 251, 252, 253, 256, 257, 258, 259, 260, 261, 262, 263, 264, 265, 266, 267, 268, 269, 270, 271, 272, 274, 275, 276, 277, 278, 279, 280, 281, 282, 283, 285, 286, 287, 288, 289, 290, 291, 295, 299
Phillips, Dean, 271
Phillips, Frank "A.F.", 3, 4, 5, 13, 15, 16, 17, 23, 24, 25, 26, 28, 29, 30, 289
Phillips, Glenn, 8, 13, 29, 30, 48, 293
Phillips, Katherine Luella "Ma Kate", 1, 2, 3, 4, 5, 9, 10, 15, 16, 17, 19, 23, 25, 29, 30, 31, 32, 45, 48, 78, 90, 92, 122, 134, 289
Phillips, Mary Elaine, 5, 293
Phillips, Sam, 47, 58, 97
Phillips, Stu, 122, 123, 128
Phoney Angel", 298
Pickens, T Boone, 170
Pickering, Bill, 211, 269
Picks, The, 70
Pierce, Webb, 53, 109, 117, 123, 127, 158, 162, 208, 216, 226, 262
Pink Floyd's Dark Side of the Moon, 255
Pink Pony, the (Taiban, NM), 264
Pinkston, "Pappy" Dave Stone, 111, 136, 139, 140, 142, 146, 149, 156, 165, 210, 227
Pioneer Bar and Lounge, the (Kenna, NM), 81, 82
Pioneers of Western Swing Hall of Fame and Honor Roll, 231
Pioneers of Western Swing Music (Everett, WA), 249
Pipkin, Donald Joe, 161
Plainsman Motel, the (Amarillo, TX), 140, 157

Plantation Records, 227
Playboy Club, the (Amarillo, TX), 155, 159, 239, 263
PLAYBOY Magazine, 102
Please Help Me Believe", 217, 296
Polk Street (Amarillo, TX), 138, 152, 153, 247, 279, 283
Poor Man's Riches", 121
Pop Echols Reunion Show, 111
Preciado, "Chano" Louis, 267, 271
Presley, Elvis, xvi, 39, 41, 54, 58, 64, 78, 94, 111, 112, 116, 117, 119, 131, 139, 148, 155, 163, 201, 209, 214, 215, 222, 231, 256, 306
Preston, Frances W., 79, 80, 220
Price, Ray, xvii, 39, 128, 137, 148, 159, 162, 166, 207, 241, 253, 258, 269, 286
Pride, Charley, xi, 143, 144, 274, 277
Printer's Alley (Nashville), 129
Pueblo tribe, 152
Pulitzer Prize, 169
Purcell, William Whitley "Bill", 208, 212
Put Your Arms Around Me", 44, 56, 81, 202, 283, 295
Queen Of The Ballroom", 256
Qwick, Ben, 220, 230
R & R Medley", 298
Rainbow Ballroom, the (Amarillo, TX), 155, 162, 165, 219, 245, 269, 273
Rainbow Ballroom, the (Clovis, NM), 39
Rainbow in the Valley", 220, 225, 296, 297
Ramsey, Buck, 243
Randy's Music Mart (Amarillo, TX), 167
Ranwood Records, 280
Rausch, Leon, 286
Rave On!, 96
Ray, Elmer, 57
RCA- Victor, 42, 50, 59, 112, 143, 279, 284
Reagan, President Ronald, 84
Real Buddy Holly Story, The, 100, 233
Real Country, 147
Record Stockman, 163
Red Creek Mesquite Flavored All-Purpose Marinade, 270
Red Creek Mesquite Flavored Bold & Spicy All-Purpose Marinade, 270
Red Creek Mesquite Flavored Jerky Marinade, 270
Red Onion, the (Clovis, NM), 264
Red Raider Inn, the (Lubbock, TX), 280
Redwine, Buster, 272, 283
Reece, Jimmy Band, the, 249
Reeves, Jim (and the Blue Boys), 92, 109, 112, 128, 139, 146, 148, 156, 157, 158, 162, 163, 213, 214, 215, 235
Release Me", 44, 295
Remembering Buddy, 301
Rescue the Perishing", 106
Rex Baxter Building, the (Amarillo, TX), 166
Reynolds, Debbie, 65
Rhodes, Dusty, 144
Rhythm Playboys, The, 256
Rich, John, 170
Rich, Steve (Lewis), 146, 147
Richards, Governor Ann, 218
Richardson, Big Bopper, the J.P., 209
Richardson, Jim, 138, 227
Richardson, Murle, 264
Richey, George, 249
Rick Husband International Airport, the, 171
Riels, Johnny (and Sisters), 127
Rime, LeAnn, 242
Rimstone label, the, 231
Ringside Club, the (Ft. Worth, TX), 108
Ritter, Tex, 98, 119, 146
Rivers, Jimmy Band, the, 253
Robbins, Hargus "Pig", 224
Robbins, Marty, 27, 53, 97, 128, 136, 137, 207, 210, 256
Robert James Music Company, the, 260
Roberts, Doug, 209, 257, 265, 272
Roberts, Jim, 146
Robin Hood Brians studio, the (Tyler, TX), 219, 234
Rock 'n' roll, ix, x, 36, 41, 47, 48, 50, 54, 55, 57, 60, 79, 100, 116, 131, 137, 153, 161, 201, 204, 207, 234, 256, 258, 274, 290
Rock and Roll Hall of Fame, the, 125, 214
Rock Me Baby", 70

Rock, Rock, Rock, 54
Rockabilly, xviii, 64, 69, 72, 99, 204, 207, 208, 210
Rockabilly Hall of Fame, the, 125, 264
Rockin' 50's Magazine, 303
Rock-Ola Ruby", 50
Rodgers, Jimmy, 39, 84
Rogers, Charlie, 272
Rogers, Kenny, 224
Rogers, Roy, 39
Rolling Stone magazine, 99
Rolling Stones, the, 202, 222
Romero, Chris, 170
Romero, Mark, 170
Romero, Ricky, 170
Romero, Steven, 170
Rose, Fred, 267
Roses, The, 58, 59, 66, 291
Roulette Record Label, 280
Roundtree, Bobby, 146, 273
Route 66, 35, 140, 153, 154, 161, 164, 166, 211
Rubin, Allonah E.A., vii
Rush, Ray, 59, 228, 244
Russell, Leon, 222
Ryman Auditorium, the, ix, xi, 127, 128, 129, 131, 144, 145, 305
Sands, Tommy, xi, 109, 112
Santa Fe Band, the, 242
Sargent, Ben, 169
Saturday Night All Gospel Show, 109
Save a Horse (Ride a Cowboy)", 170
Scales Strings and Things, 273
Scales, Carlie, 274
Scales, Carlton, 163, 164, 166, 271, 273
Scales, Frankie, 274
Scales, Hurles, 170
Scales, Iweta, 163, 164, 166, 273
Scales, Margaret "Maggie", 273
Scales, Odie, 264, 274
Scales, Sherry, 274
Scales, Tommy, 273, 274
Schattel, Emil, 265
Schell, Jimmy, ix, xi, 28, 38, 56, 62, 92, 93, 202, 206, 209, 245, 261, 268, 272, 274, 275
Schettler, Katie, vii
Scott, Bill, 275
Scott, Russell, 222, 275
Scrivner, Ray, 267

Scrooge (Charlie Phillips), 10, 49, 94, 162, 289
Searchers, The, 57
Self, Jimmy Dean, 42, 45, 56, 61, 202, 268
Seliger, Senator Kel, 170
Seth Ward Baptist Church, 107
Shambles of My Home", 228, 298
sharecroppers, 1, 26
Sheetz, Hayden, 275
Sheppard, Jean, 123, 128
Sherwood, Benny, 276
Shore, Dinah, 96
Shreveport Chamber of Commerce, xi
Shreveport Tourist Bureau, xi
Silver Grill, the (Clovis, NM), 37, 134
Sinatra, Frank, 112, 222
Sinatra, Nancy, 112, 222
Sincerely", 73, 80, 83
Siners, Anita Kerr, 213
Singing All Day and Better on the Ground, 25
Sir Walter Raleigh Tobacco Company, the, 216
Sisco, Jon, ix, xi, 227, 229, 230, 231, 245, 263, 276, 279
Sissy Song, The", 244
Skelton, Red, 84
Skidmore, Bill, 276
Slay, Bob, 146
Smith, "Smitty", 276
Smith, Garland "Cotton John", 152
Smith, Harmie, 116
Smith, Jack, 269
Smith, James Monroe, 115
SNATCHIN' AND GRABBIN, 267
Snodgrass, Roy, 274
Snow, Hank, 27, 35, 43, 67, 128, 129, 216, 281
Someone Cares for You", 277
Soundcraft recording disc, 56
Souther, J.D., 169
Southern Living Magazine, 269
Southern Maid Donuts, 120
Southern Music Publishing, 71, 107
Souvenirs of Sorrow", 223, 228, 297, 298
Sparkles, the, 264
Spirit (Of The 21st Century) label, 227
Spirit of Texas Award, 277
Spud & Bud bar (Amarillo, TX), 260

St. Louis Cardinals, the, 170
Stamps Melody Boys, The, 109
Stamps Quartet, 106, 111, 278
Stamps-Baxter Music Company, the, 107
Stamps-Baxter School of Music, the, 107
Star Night Club, the, 253
Star, Dennis, 276
Steagall, Red "Rusty", 221, 222, 223, 277, 279
Steamboat Stomp", 267
Stein, Lou, 42
Stella and the Fellas Band, 262
Stephens, Marcus, 277, 278
Stewart, Wynn, 262
Straight, George, 272
Strategic Air Command B-52 operations, 154
Strayhorn, Billy, 164
Street of Loneliness, The", 217, 296
Streisand, Barbra, 222
String Technicians, The, 246
Stull, Billy, 228, 229, 230, 231, 261
Sudduth, Brenda, 278
Sudduth, Rick, 236, 247, 249, 263, 278
Sugartime (HBO movie), 85
Sugartime Music Group, 230
Sugartime television show, 101
Sugartime Twist", 205
Sugartime", xv, xvi, xix, xx, 27, 39, 56, 61, 62, 64, 66, 68, 69, 70, 72, 73, 74, 75, 77, 78, 79, 80, 81, 82, 83, 84, 85, 86, 87, 92, 96, 97, 98, 99, 100, 101, 102, 112, 115, 117, 120, 121, 122, 123, 125, 126, 128, 131, 132, 133, 134, 136, 140, 141, 145, 149, 156, 164, 167, 201, 202, 203, 204, 205, 206, 207, 211, 214, 225, 226, 228, 235, 236, 237, 242, 245, 248, 257, 261, 262, 264, 270, 274, 275, 282, 283, 289, 290, 295, 297
Sugartimer band, the (or Sugartimers), 82, 244, 259, 260, 266, 287, 288
Sugartimers, the, 82, 158, 159, 160, 162, 166, 167, 168, 169, 209, 216, 237, 238, 239, 240, 241, 242, 243, 245, 246, 247, 248, 249, 250, 251, 252, 253, 254, 255, 257, 258, 259, 260, 261, 262, 263, 265, 266, 267,
268, 269, 270, 271, 272, 273, 274, 275, 276, 278, 279, 280, 281, 282, 283, 284, 285, 286, 287, 288
Sullivan, Niki, 64, 230, 282
Summers, Bennie, 272
Sun Greatest Hits album, 97
Sun Records, 47, 97, 201, 202
Swafford, Gary, 266, 278, 279
Swan, Billy, 147
Sweet & Sour (poetry), 163
Sweet and Easy to Love", 58
Sweet Rockin' Baby", 50
Swindell, Patrick, 249, 251
Swinging Steel band, 244
Tanner, Evan, 170
Tanner, Gid, 221
Tarzan, 169
TCS Productions recording studio, 274
Tears Are Only Rain", 238
Telefunken microphone (German-made), 63
Tennessee Mountain Boys, the, 116
Tennessee Ridge Runners, the, 116
Tennessee, Memphis, 47, 58
Tennessee, Nashville, ix, xi, 23, 39, 41, 43, 44, 49, 53, 57, 58, 98, 109, 122, 123, 127, 128, 129, 130, 131, 132, 136, 144, 146, 148, 149, 158, 163, 170, 208, 210, 212, 213, 216, 217, 218, 224, 227, 245, 252, 255, 256, 266, 270, 277, 281, 290, 305, 306
Terry, Rex, 216, 279
Terry, Roy, 279
Tex Ritter's Ranch Party, 98
Texas Blues Rangers, The, 254
Texas Country Music Hall of Fame, the, 305
Texas Monthly, 303
Texas Music For Life, 254
Texas Musical Drama, 152
TEXAS Outdoor Musical. *See* TEXAS Musical Drama
Texas Panhandle Association of Broadcasters Hall of Fame, the, xxi, 138, 149, 245, 248
Texas Panhandle Heritage Foundation, the. See Texas Musical Drama, See Texas Musical Drama, See Texas Musical Drama, See Texas Musical Drama

Texas Rhythm and Starjazz band, the, 246
Texas Rodeo Cowboy Hall of Fame, the, 277
Texas State Society's Black Tie and Boots Inaugural Ball, 286
Texas Tech University, xii, 4, 113, 306
Texas Technical College. See Texas Tech University
Texas, Amarillo, x, xvi, 8, 28, 31, 35, 39, 42, 45, 49, 91, 94, 128, 130, 132, 136, 137, 138, 139, 140, 141, 142, 143, 144, 145, 146, 149, 151, 152, 153, 154, 155, 156, 157, 158, 159, 160, 161, 162, 163, 164, 165, 166, 167, 168, 169, 170, 171, 210, 211, 216, 217, 218, 219, 225, 227, 228, 237, 238, 239, 240, 241, 242, 244, 245, 246, 247, 248, 249, 250, 251, 252, 253, 254, 256, 257, 258, 259, 260, 261, 262, 263, 265, 266, 269, 270, 271, 272, 273, 276, 278, 279, 281, 283, 284, 285, 286, 288, 291, 301, 302, 307, 323, 331
Texas, Bovina, 36, 37, 82, 105, 259, 262
Texas, Canyon, 47, 151, 152, 240, 266, 267, 272, 307
Texas, Crosby County, 278
Texas, Dallas, 19, 58, 89, 121, 123, 126, 127, 139, 149, 151, 157, 164, 215, 220, 267, 268
Texas, El Paso, 210
Texas, Enloe, 105
Texas, Farwell, 1, 5, 7, 8, 14, 17, 18, 20, 25, 26, 27, 31, 38, 42, 48, 50, 72, 78, 82, 89, 92, 94, 122, 130, 141, 145, 156, 161, 171, 248, 250, 261, 262, 263, 264, 270, 272, 274, 282, 283, 289, 291
Texas, Friona, 28, 82
Texas, Happy, 47
Texas, Hereford, 31, 82, 260
Texas, Lazbuddie, 159, 280
Texas, Lubbock, xi, 4, 39, 41, 45, 53, 54, 74, 91, 94, 105, 107, 110, 111, 113, 139, 209, 210, 233, 252, 256, 265, 278, 302, 306
Texas, Muleshoe, 17, 33, 82, 111, 226, 270
Texas, Palo Duro Canyon, 151

Texas, Parmer County, 8, 16, 17, 270
Texas, Seymour, 4
Texas, the Panhandle, 53, 145, 153, 155, 156, 159, 170, 238, 243, 252, 254, 259, 260, 263, 265, 274, 276, 280
Texas, Vera, 4, 5
Texico Hotel, the (Texico, NM), 18
Tharp, Chuck, 279
That'll Be the Day", 57, 60, 65, 70, 71, 80, 306
That's All Right Mama", 117
These Boots Are Made For Walking", 222
They Call Me Renegade, 227
Thiele, Bob, 65, 70, 71, 72, 73, 74, 93, 96, 206, 207, 302
Think It Over", 66
This Is the House", 217, 296
Thomas, Jodi (Koumalatz), 169
Thomas, William, 170
Thomas, Zach, 170
Thompson, Hank, 39, 42, 163, 238, 242, 246, 249, 256, 286
Thompson, Uncle Jimmy, 127
Thompson, Wayne, 279
Thompson's Brazos Valley Boys, 42
Those Who Made the Music in Clovis and Outlying Areas, 301
Thrasher, Ernie, 146
Three Tunes, The, 256
Thurlow, Gary, xii, 216, 230, 263, 266, 279
Tiaras, The, 284
Tillis, Mel, 257
Tillman Franks: I Was There When It Happened, 301
Tinker Air Force Base, 70
Tinymite LP, 231
Tinymite Records, 265
Toast of the Town, 142
TogiEntertainment, 301
Tolzien Music, 165, 251, 258
Tomlinson, "Tommy" Gerald Delmar, 120, 121, 219, 220, 230, 344
Tonight Show with Johnny Carson, The, 96
Tony Award, the, 98
Too Many Tears", 96, 141, 206, 207, 296
Too Old To Cut The Mustard", 44, 295

Tootsie's World Famous Orchid Lounge, 131
Torchy Swingsters, the, 40
Traweek, Grace, 105, 117
Trent, Kenneth (& The Continentals), 279
Trider, Larry (and the Nomads), 159, 242, 280, 281
Triple D recording label, 47
Tri-State Fairgrounds, the (Amarillo, TX), 144
Trump, Donald, 170
Tubb, Ernest, 24, 39, 126, 127, 129, 208, 241
Tucker, Bob, 42, 43, 44, 56, 215, 264, 283
Tumor (Charlie Phillips), 9, 289
Turner, Al, 126
Turner, Jack, 224
Turturro, John, 85
TV Guide, xii, 85
TV Radio Mirror, 135
Twenty Fools Ago", 224, 225, 297
Twist, The", 205
Twistin' & Twangin' album, 205
U.S. Ration's Board, 26
Union Gospel Tabernacle, the, 127
Universal Pictures, 108
University of New Mexico, the, 71
University of Texas, the, xii, 41
Utsman, Jerry Don, 12, 14, 19, 202
Utsman, Ollie, 19
V.F.W. Ballroom (Amarillo, TX), 155, 284
Valens, Ritchie, 209
Van Dyke, Leroy, 261
Vaughn, Doyle, 89, 118
Vaughn, Jack, 40, 43, 67, 68, 210, 230, 268, 269
Vaughn, Stevie Ray, 259
Vee, Bobby, 223
Veit, Georgiana, 40
Vietnam War, the, 5
Vihil, Johnny, 281
Vineyard, Mrs. (piano instructor), 25
Vinyard, Ken, 170
Wagoner, Porter, 123, 128, 155
Wake Up Irene", 145, 163, 238
Waldorf-Astoria, the (NYC, NY), 79, 82, 95

Walker, Billy, 57, 58
Walker, Charlie, 261
Walker, Cindy, 44
Walker, Howard, 146, 281
Walker, Jerry Jeff, 254
Walker, Lou, 158, 159, 239, 268, 271, 281, 282, 284
Walker, Tink, 282
Wallace, Peggy, 257
Wallace, Pete, 56, 62, 92, 202, 206, 209, 230, 245, 257, 282
Walton, Dee, 282, 283
Walton, Marvin, 283
Waltz Across Texas", 130
Wanda Jackson Rockabilly Party Girls, 205
War Memorial Auditorium, the, 127
Warner Bros. (Reprise) Records, xvii, 224, 277
Warwick Hotel (NYC, NY), 94, 95
Watts, Erik, 170
Wayne, John, 57
WDAG radio station, 137, 152
Weaver, Cowboy, 127
Webb, Delbert, 283
Weeks, Jay, 254
Weir, Rusty, 254
Weize, Richard, 234
Welborn, Larry, 209
Welch, "Smiling" Truman, 257, 283
Welcome To My World", 148
Welcome to the Wedding", 126, 128, 210, 211, 269, 296
Welk, Lawrence, 65
Wells, Kitty, 97, 116, 117, 122, 127, 207, 208, 209, 216, 243
West Texas Express band, the, 265
West Texas Music Hall of Fame, 170, 307
West Texas State College, 47
West, Carl, 222
West, Dottie, 128
West, Sonny, 50
Western Cowpunchers Association, the, 269
Western Horseman Club, the, 257
Western Rainbows, the, 242
Western Swing Music Hall of Fame, the, xii, xxi, 236, 239, 240, 246, 268
Western Swing Showcase, a, 247

Western Swing Society of the Southwest, the, 246, 263, 285, 286
WGAU radio station, 132
WHAS radio station, 109
What a Wonderful World, 65, 302
What Will I Do Next Monday", 238
What's My Line, 96
Whatever Happened to Peggy Sue? A Memoir by Buddy Holly's Peggy Sue, 301
Wheeler, Lloyd, 283
Wheels", 228
When the Battles are Over", 109
When Your Love Burns Low", 238
Where Do I Go From Here?", 231
Whisenhunt, Jim, 284
Whisenhunt, Mike, 284
White, Bob, 267, 268
White, Danny, 301
White, Ron, 171
White, Shea, 171
Whitson, Wayne, 146
Whitt, Earl, 279, 284
Whitworth, Ray, 146
Who Are You", 225, 297
Wide Open Spaces", 161, 170
Wide Prairie, 100
Wienstroer, Norman, 71
Wilbanks, Glen, 285
Wilburn Brothers, the, 100, 241
Wild Side of Houston, the, 227, 297
Wil-Helm Talent Management, 213
Will Rogers Memorial Highway. *See* Route 66
Willett, Slim, 57
Williams Jr., Hank, 121
Williams, Andy, 163
Williams, Hank, xx, 19, 39, 67, 117, 119, 121, 127, 258
Williams, \Honest" Jess, 240, 244, 253, 258, 261, 279
Williams, Jack, 28
Williams, Roger, 42
Williamson, Kenneth, 249, 285
Willmon, Trent, 169
Wills, Bob, xx, 39, 43, 55, 116, 158, 162, 221, 238, 241, 242, 246, 262, 267, 268, 277, 278, 281, 284, 286
Wilson, Gretchen, 170
Wilson, Woodrow, 3
Winchell and Mahoney Show, the, 96

Windy Wood & New Sons of the West, 231
Windy Wood LP, the, 231
Windy Wood- The Classic Sound of Western Swing, 246
Wings (band), 99
Winkler, Ray, 127, 128, 130, 136, 137, 139, 140, 142, 143, 145, 146, 148, 149, 155, 156, 157, 158, 161, 163, 165, 210, 211, 212, 213, 219, 220, 263, 269, 290, 291
Winter Dance Party, The, 209
Wise, Brenda, 230
Wise, Carey, 230
WJJC radio station, 132
WJW radio station (Cleveland), 54
WLAC radio station (Nashville, TN), 109
Woman, Woman", 298
Wood, Windy, 231, 240, 246, 253, 273, 298
Woods, Dale, 129, 130
Wooly, Sheb, 39, 136, 261
Words of Love", 58, 61
Works Progress Administration, 154
World War I, 3, 5, 119
World War II, 4, 26, 55, 92, 127, 140, 154, 241, 256, 286
Wright, Johnnie, 122
WSM Barn Dance, The, 127
WSM Breakfast Show (Grant Turner's), 213
WSM radio station (Nashville, TN), 23, 24, 127, 128, 129, 144, 145, 146, 213, 303
Wynette, Tammy, 218
Wynne, Bobby, 249, 285
XIT Boys, the, 238, 244
XIT Ranch, the, 8, 9, 282
Yesterday Passed My Way Again", 298
You Are My One Desire", 256
You're Moving Away", 214, 296
You're My LSD", 298
You're the Reason God Made Oklahoma", 99
You've Got Love", 70
Young, Dustin, 257, 287
Young, Faron, 109, 112, 117, 128, 148, 256
Young, Hattie, 285

Young, Jimmy, xvii, 168, 235, 240, 241, 249, 252, 254, 257, 259, 260, 267, 269, 272, 273, 278, 285, 286, 287, 324

Your Going Is Coming", 225, 297
Yucca drive-in, the, 133
Zach's Club 54, 170
Zinkan, Joseph S., 212